DK

LONDON, NEW YORK, MUNICH, MELBOURNE, DELHI

Senior Designer   Mabel Chan
Senior Editor   Paula Regan
Production Controller   Elizabeth Warman
DTP   John Goldsmid
Managing Editor   Debra Wolter
Managing Art Editor   Louise Dick
Art Director   Bryn Walls
Publisher   Jonathan Metcalf
US Editor   Jenny Siklos
3D Illustrations   Adam Howard of Invisiblecities
3D Models   Andy Kay

Produced for Dorling Kindersley by
cobaltid

The Stables, Wood Farm, Deopham Road,
Attleborough, Norfolk NR17 1AJ
www.cobaltid.co.uk

EDITORS	ART EDITORS
Marek Walisiewicz,	Paul Reid, Lloyd Tilbury,
Maddy King, Kati Dye,	Darren Bland, Claire Oldman,
Jamie Dickson	Rebecca Johns

Published in the United States by
DK Publishing, Inc.
375 Hudson Street, New York, New York 10014

09 10   10 9 8 7 6

Copyright © 2006 Dorling Kindersley Limited
Text copyright © 2006 Jonathan Glancey

Library of Congress Cataloging-in-Publication Data

Glancey, Jonathan.
Architecture / Jonathan Glancey.-- 1st American ed.
p. cm. -- (Eyewitness companions)
Previously published as: Story of architecture.
Includes index.
ISBN 0-7566-1732-4 (flexi binding with flaps)
1. Architecture--History. I. Title. II. Series.
NA200.G527 2006
720.9--dc22

2005036013
ISBN-13: 978-0-7566-1732-5
ISBN-10: 0-7566-1732-4
Color reproduction by GRB, Italy.
Printed in China by Leo.

Discover more at
www.dk.com

CONTENTS

INTRODUCTION

Architecture is an enormous subject, plumbing the depths of ancient history while embracing the world. How could we ever have thought of squeezing its sky-piercing towers, mighty domes, and flying buttresses into a book designed to fit neatly into handbag, briefcase, or backpack? Well, we did, and we have done what we hope is our best to please as many readers as possible. Of course, there will be those of you who will ask why we have left out the temple of X or the cathedral of Y. There are very many thousands of buildings worth

celebrating in a guide to world architecture, but even the world itself could not contain the books that should be written if they were all to have their rightful place.

There is, though, a simple logic to this book. We have tried to include, as far as possible, buildings that I have visited. This amounts to nine in ten. Those we have included that I have not seen are there because it would be impolite and improper to exclude them: these are often pivotal buildings in the story of architecture. Equally, there are those that I long to see. Some

I am more than grateful to have seen, such as the ziggurats of ancient Iraq, because it may be a long while yet before it is safe to travel there again. We have also included buildings that I could not possibly have visited because they were destroyed long ago; these are designs of such importance to the story of architecture that it would have been wrong to ignore them.

As to dates, we have tried our best to give those that correspond to the known completion of a particular building. These cannot always be wholly accurate, not only because historical sources disagree with one another, but also because there are times when we simply do not know.

Divine detail
Visiting a site enables an appreciation not just of its context, but of details such as this dragon's head at the Platform of Venus, Chichén Itzá, Mexico.

Names of architects become apparent, and then clear, from around 1450 at the start of the Renaissance, when the works of individual artists were celebrated. It is not that there are no earlier records of architects, but that these are few and far between. We do know, though, the name of one of the very early architects: Imhotep. He designed pyramids and became a god. The words modesty and architect have rarely gone together since.

We have tried to include as much of the world as possible. Even so, the buildings of many countries are missing from this guide. This is, again, for the obvious reason that the book would have to be as big as a building to squeeze them all in, but also because there are a number of other countries, or regions, of the world that have produced a disproportionate amount of the world's best and most significant architecture. There is very little "vernacular" architecture here. I think this is a subject for a separate guide, or a much bigger one. This guide concentrates on buildings that are self-conscious works of art.

Buildings in this book are listed and illustrated mostly as if they stand proudly alone. This is so that they can be readily identified, described, and understood. Many, of course, are in streets and avenues among crowds and rows of other buildings. I remember first looking for Gaudí's Casa Batlló—a dragonlike apartment block in Barcelona. On a cloudy day, it seemed to fit all too comfortably into the flow of the tall buildings lining the city's

Potala Palace, Tibet
Great buildings may completely dominate the landscape or rub shoulders with others in crowded city streets.

Masters of the modern age
Le Corbusier bestrode the built landscape of
the 20th century with his inventive and poetic
interpretations of the Machine Age.

Shock of the new
Were exemplars of Classical
architecture, in their time, as
provocative as modern masterpieces,
such as Gaudí's Casa Batlló *(below)?*

Paseo de Gracia, despite its colorful
and unusual design. This, though,
made me think more of the building,
not less; it has, despite its eccentricities,
good urban manners, unlike the Post-
Modern architecture of the 1980s
found in Barcelona, as elsewhere.

Post-Modernism reminds me that
I should mention that there are a few
episodes in the history of architecture
where I find myself totally out of tune
with a particular style. Architecture
might be a continuum and its history
a book to treasure and borrow from,
yet "Po-Mo" design, virulent worldwide
in the 1980s, was a case of ripping
up the pages of history books and
plastering the torn fragments childishly
across the steel and concrete frames of
otherwise nondescript buildings in the
hope of eliciting a laugh from passers-
by. A few of these buildings have been
included in these pages in order to
present a continuous record of
architectural development, even
though I personally do not like them.

I hope this book will be just
the beginning of an adventure for
those setting out to discover the
world through its buildings and its
architectural history. It is a unending
journey and might just be the start of
a lifetime's pleasure.

Introducing architecture

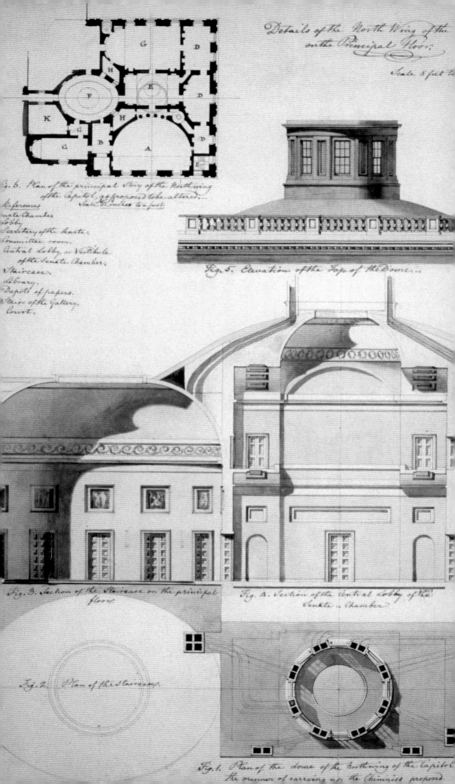

Details of the North Wing of the
on the Principal Floor.

Scale 8 feet to

Fig. 6. Plan of the principal Story of the North wing
of the Capitol, as proposed to be altered.
Scale 12 inches to a foot

References
Senate Chamber
Lobby
Secretary of the Senate.
Committee room.
Central Lobby, or Vestibule
of the Senate Chamber.
Staircase.
Library.
Depots of papers.
Stairs of the Gallery.
Court.

Fig. 5. Elevation of the Top of the Dome in

Fig. 3. Section of the Staircase on the principal
floor.

Fig. 4. Section of the Central Lobby of the
Senate Chamber

Fig. 2. Plan of the Staircase.

Fig. 1. Plan of the dome of the North wing of the Capitol
the manner of carrying up the Chimnies proposed

WHAT IS ARCHITECTURE?

Architecture began, said the German architect Ludwig Mies van der Rohe, "when two bricks were put together well." This might sound too easy to be true, yet Mies was right. What he meant was that architecture is the self-conscious act of building: of building not just with common sense, but with artistry.

One day, travelers will be able to return to Iraq and see for themselves the great ziggurat at Ur. This daunting ancient monument is, on one level, no more and no less than an immense pile of sun-baked bricks, piled in stepped layers high into the desert sky. But what fine bricks!—and what a spirited design.

The ziggurat at Ur was not just a building. It was not made for shelter or to store grain. It was built as an artwork, as the greatest artefact humans could shape at the time to honor their gods and to invite those divinities down the great brick steps of their monument to their city of Ur. The ziggurat was a giant stairway to Heaven and back down to earth, connecting humankind to the gods and, hopefully, making the earth, and the city of Ur, fruitful. The ziggurat of Ur is also important in our story because it shows us how architecture was always more than a functional

tool: it was a form of celebration of human artistry and of the imagination, and a way of formalizing, by shaping in brick (and, later and elsewhere, in stone, marble, concrete, iron, steel, zinc, and titanium), the rituals of urban life.

IN THE BEGINNING

People first came together to create cities some seven thousand years ago, and possibly even earlier, in the Fertile Crescent—the crescent-shaped region that extends from the eastern shore of the Mediterranean Sea to the Persian Gulf. The oldest monumental cities we know of, although there will always be other claims and perhaps new discoveries, are in what is southern Iraq today. Here, people settled, and by that simple act they were able to create surpluses of food and to store these over the winter months—thus, they had time to create rituals and festivals. They created gods, too, and

◁ BLUEPRINT FOR THE NORTH WING OF THE US CAPITOL, WASHINGTON, D.C., DESIGNED IN THE EARLY 19TH CENTURY BY BENJAMIN HENRY LATROBE.

Ziggurat at Ur
Ancient monuments reaching skyward were built to honor, please, and appease gods who lived, literally, on a higher plane. These buildings were therefore fundamentally necessary and "functional" in a way we may find hard to understand today.

put kings in power to protect them. And so there was a need for public places, for temples, palaces, and lookout towers. Mud huts would never do for gods, priests, soldiers, and kings—and so two, and then many millions, of bricks were put together on their behalf, and architecture emerged. Civilization, cities, and architecture rose together.

Mies van der Rohe (1886–1969), a Modern architect with a passion for—and knowledge of—ancient culture,

also defined architecture as "the will of the epoch translated into space." Anyone looking at a Greek temple, Gothic cathedral, New York skyscraper, or Nazi stadium will know exactly what Mies meant. His was one way of saying that people get the architecture they deserve, or the architecture they will into being, in brick and stone. An architectural interpretation of history is, in fact, as good as any other. By understanding architecture from across the ages and around the world, the

stories of different peoples and regimes can be read and, to a greater or lesser degree, understood. We understand not just their culture, as in the arts, but something of their politics and their political economy, too.

FORM AND FUNCTION
From two bricks put together well to monuments that tracked the stars and aligned humanity with the heavens, architecture had great and even other-worldly ambitions from the very start. One of its purposes, from the smallest well-put-together building to the highest skyscraper, is to lift the human spirit. In architecture we find a way of celebrating our humanity and of raising ourselves above the concerns of the matter-of-fact, the here and now. Not exclusively, of course. Architecture might be the self-conscious act of building artistically, and hopefully well, but it is also about

shelter. One of the marked differences between architecture and the fine arts is that buildings have very particular functions to perform. Few artworks, with the exception of Marcel Duchamp's *Fountain* (1917), need lavatories. Or, for that matter, gutters, drainpipes, wiring, gas, electricity, heating, lighting, ventilation, windows, and air-conditioning. On this level, architecture is a machine.

LET THERE BE LIGHT
Another great modern architect, Le Corbusier (1887–1965), defined architecture as "the masterly, correct, and magnificent play of masses brought together in light." Here is a new dimension: to Mies's well-put-together bricks and "will of the

Ancient architecture of Mesopotamia
From the lonely desert ruins we see today, we attempt to extrapolate and interpret the color, vibrancy, and daily life of ancient societies.

epoch," we add the play of light. All great architects have been masters of light. Stand in front of a Greek temple and watch how its moods change and its space is animated by different plays of light as the sun moves around it over the course of a day. Sit quietly in Le Corbusier's pilgrimage chapel at Ronchamp *(see above, right)* and feel the light directed so knowingly, and carefully, through slits and chutes, windows and shafts: the ever-changing light not only animates and celebrates the architecture, but sends gentle shivers down the spine of the observer.

The moon and the stars played equally important roles in the artistry and planning of ancient temples and of Gothic cathedrals. Imagine the play of moonlight, or of the stars, on the sheer and polished surfaces of the Great Pyramid of Khufu. Their light would have set up a celestial dance in tune with the rhythms of the architecture they played upon. As for their planning, the design of Egyptian pyramids and Gothic cathedrals was aligned with stars and constellations.

RISE OF THE MACHINE

Immediately after the senseless slaughter of World War I, which killed more than 8.5 million soldiers and millions of civilians, an increasing number of European architects began to think of how they could express their desire to get away from the old regimes and what they saw as the overly complex, messy, and decadent way of life that had led to the war.

Architecture, so they decided, should be as clean, white, and efficient as the very best new sanatorium, as beautifully functional as the white ocean liners that took people on health-giving voyages away from the grime of European cities. This was the birth of the Modernist Movement, a time when many of the brightest architects believed they could create an architecture that was free of the weight of history and as smoothly working as a well-oiled machine. A house, in the famous words of Le Corbusier, might be a *machine à habiter* —a machine for living in.

And, yet, Le Corbusier, Mies van der Rohe, and the other brave new moderns were never free of history. In fact, these two particular architects rooted their work in ancient history even as they thought as far ahead as they were able. As for architects who really did think they could turn buildings into pure machines for living, designing gigantic concrete housing

Harnessing light
Compare the play of light inside a traditional cathedral, such as Morelia, Mexico *(far left)*, and the chapel at Ronchamp *(left)* by Le Corbusier. In the first, the eye is drawn inexorably upward; in the second, it is the human context of the act of worship that is illuminated.

1856), gave us the skylines of New York and Chicago. Now buildings could rise almost impossibly high into the sky, and, certainly, from the invention of the first electric elevators (Werner von Siemens, 1880), it was consummately easy to get to the top of them and back down to the ground.

THE MODERN FREE-FOR-ALL

At the end of the 20th century, computers and new materials allowed architects to play with forms more than ever before. Computers could tell architects exactly how much an extra curve here, or fashionable projection there, would cost their clients. Computers in the design studio could communicate with their peers in machine shops where building materials could be cut to measure to fit exactly into place on building sites.

The computer has proved to be a liberating tool for some architects, one toy too many for others.

Architecture is not just about architects. It is also about those who commission them. The story of architecture is the story of, among others, priests, kings, queens, emperors, captains of industry, queens of commerce, housebuilders, enlightened patrons, and wrong-headed and even demonic politicians.

This is partly what Mies meant when he defined architecture as "the will

estates, for example, they were to make all too many heartbreaking mistakes with other people's lives. Architecture matters. Architecture needs a soul. Architecture is a continuum connecting us back through skyscrapers and cathedrals to pedimented temples and ziggurats made of well-put-together bricks.

There have been, of course, many new inventions and discoveries that have at various junctures through history allowed and encouraged architecture to move in sudden leaps and bounds. The pointed arch led to the high vaulting of Gothic cathedrals and to a generation of magical buildings that, for all their great scale and mass, seemed like weightless caskets of colored glass. The elevator or lift (Elisha Otis, 1853), combined with the invention of steel (Henry Bessemer,

Breaking new ground
With the coming of the industrial age, architecture once again reached for the sky, as nations and cities competed to build the tallest structures ever seen. The Empire State Building, New York *(right)*, took the record in 1931.

of the epoch translated into space."
Many of the buildings we have
learned to admire, or even adore
intuitively, have been the playthings of
monstrous tyrants, most of whom
have been forgotten. They are lucky,
in a way: the great art they
commissioned has outgunned their
murderous intent. Where once there
was savagery and pain, now we see
beauty and repose.

Equally, many of the finest works
of architecture are modest creations.
Sir Christopher Wren (1632–1723)
might be remembered first and
foremost by those looking around
St. Paul's Cathedral, yet—although
the dome of this great church is one
of the world's finest—it is the lovely
necklace of small parish churches
Wren rebuilt around St. Paul's in
the aftermath of the Great Fire
of London (1666) that shows him
at his sensitive best.

Architecture is about proportion,
too. Inside his church of St. Stephen
Walbrook, Wren created a scaled-
down model of the dome he wanted
to build for his rejected Greek cross

Evolution and revolution
Both organic in form and futuristic in aspect,
the Guggenheim Museum in New York *(below)*
redefined space and the way we use it.

Relic of history
The Lutine bell sits in the cathedral-like atrium
in the Lloyds of London building *(right)*, cradled
(or, it could be said, dwarfed) by this modern
temple of commerce.

design for St. Paul's; to find this
miniature magnificence behind the
door of what appears to be, from the
street, a tiny ragstone parish church
is not just a delight, but one of the
reasons why anyone might learn to
love architecture.

BACK TO THE FUTURE
The story of architecture is one of
remarkable human endeavor, one
of the means through which we try
to create order and make sense of our
endlessly intriguing, yet messy world.
We all live and work in buildings.
From the humblest to the most
sublime, there is no reason why any
of these should be less than inspiring
even in small ways: the turn of a stair;
the way sunlight falls through
windows in mesmerizing patterns on
floors; materials cool to the touch in
the heat of summer; the rhythm of
an arcade; the pregnant quality of a
dome. At its best, architecture should
lift our spirits, while serving as guide
to our ambitions, vanities, our needs,
our gods, and our dreams.

THE BUILDING BLOCKS OF ARCHITECTURE

The beginning of brickmaking and the birth of architecture belong together. The first great works of architecture we know of—the first attempts at building beyond necessity, of building to express desires, beliefs, goals, and cultures—were made of brick. In fact, the very first structures of any kind that we have evidence of today were brick-built.

In 2002, I was privileged to be able to travel the length and breadth of Iraq. This was at the tail end of the dictatorship of Saddam Hussein—a brutal ruler who saw himself as a successor to the very kings of ancient Mesopotamia who raised those first monuments in brick and, in so doing, created architecture and cities. The development of walled villages and fortified towns was taking place elsewhere in the world at much the same time—Jericho is one of the world's earliest settlements with any pretensions to architecture—yet in what was once Mesopotamia, we can be sure that architecture existed, because we can see it with our eyes, touch it with our hands. And what we touch is brick—enduring, sun-baked brick.

ON THE TRAIL OF THE FIRST CITY
I spent several hours one extremely hot morning on my trip to Iraq in the office of the Governor of Nasiriyah.

What I wanted was permission to travel to Eridu, which might well be the world's first city. The Governor's press attaché suggested that I might instead like to see the great ziggurat of Ur just a few miles away. Of course, I was tempted. This is one of the greatest examples of ancient architecture, even though heavily restored by Saddam. But still, Eridu it had to be. The very thought of it was haunting. Could this really be the world's first city? Since 1991, it had been cut off from the rest of Iraq, the rest of the world, because it was at the heart of local military operations. The shell-holed tracks leading to it were strewn with Gulf War detritus: unexploded bombs, rockets, hundreds of tons of depleted uranium US munitions left lying in the desert. Nevertheless, I wanted to go there.

With an armed escort, I finally got to Eridu. The temperature was exactly 122°F (50°C). All around us was

◁ GLASS-AND-STEEL ROOF OF THE QUEEN ELIZABETH II GREAT COURT AT THE BRITISH MUSEUM, LONDON, 2000, DESIGNED BY FOSTER AND PARTNERS.

shimmering sand. Here, though, I was able to brush away some of the burning sand and touch the bricks of what was once the ziggurat of Eridu, even though it now looks like a mound of earth and sand. Between these topmost bricks and the base of the ziggurat were at least 16 different layers of temple, the first dating back to around 5,000BCE. This is where architecture was born, when this land was rich in date palms and fresh water, when human settlement was a new venture. At the heart of this ziggurat, its structural core, were bricks, carefully put together.

The history of Eridu was only pieced together by Iraqi archaeologists and experts from the British Museum between 1946 and 1949. There may well be other ancient cities and temples to be discovered elsewhere, but this is as good a beginning for civilization as any. There were other building materials at the time elsewhere in the world that might have shaped architecture, but not here between the Tigris and Euphrates rivers, where the only possible way to build on a large scale was with brick. Happily, this building block of the earliest architecture was not just immediately available, but it was strong and enduring. Where timber rots, steel corrodes, and concrete cracks, brick seems to endure as if forever. It is also a warm material, and because it was shaped and laid by human hands, it helped raise buildings that were essentially human, too.

Brick has never really gone out of date or fashion, and it has been used

Mud-brick city, Shibam, Yemen
This astonishing 16th-century city of mud-brick blocks—the "Manhattan of the desert"—is still inhabited today.

Unchanging scene
In many parts of the world, mud bricks are still very much in use: here in modern-day Tunisia, a brickmaker shapes them from clay and water and lays them out to dry. Afterward they will be baked in the kilns in the background.

to shape some of the most beautiful buildings in the world. And some of the most influential and radical, too: even Le Corbusier, the great proponent of concrete architecture in the 1920s, turned to brick again in the 1950s. Brick has moved with the times and, from the 19th century, was made increasingly through industrial processes. Today, it is used by architects mostly for cladding new buildings, not as a structural material. Yet there are few greater pleasures, if you love buildings, than coming across one crafted in warm, handmade brick. The first building block of architecture may yet be the last.

BUILDING WITH TIMBER

Elsewhere in the world, where there were woods and forests, timber was a key building material. Timber is strong, warm, and beautiful, but ultimately it rots or dries out and cracks. Or catches fire. It is hard to find a timber building, an original timber building, much over 750 or, at the most, 1,000 years old. One can argue that, on the whole, there is no reason for most buildings to last so long. Or, equally, one can fall into the Japanese way

of thinking and reason that a building ought to be ritually reconstructed every so many years, so that it is always perfect and not allowed to show signs of decay. Throughout this book you will find timber buildings of extraordinary daring and refinement and examples of timber construction that are quite breathtaking. I still look up at the great lantern of Ely Cathedral in Cambridgeshire with awe. Supported by the sawn trunks of eight mighty oak trees, each weighing 10 tons, the timber lantern itself weighs 200 tons and yet seems to be floating effortlessly above the crossing of the medieval cathedral. For the record, it is the work of William Hurley, Edward III's royal carpenter. It took 14 years to craft and dates from *ca.* 1342.

The very last building shown in this book, the Jean Marie Tjibaou Cultural Center, Noumea, in the French colony of New Caledonia, is made

Timber triumph
In thickly forested Norway and Sweden, "stave churches" built entirely of wood—as at Heddal, Norway *(left)*—made a very distinctive contribution to medieval architecture.

New ways with wood
The J. M. Tjibaou Cultural Center, the work of Renzo Piano, evokes the traditional huts of the indigenous people of the island of New Caledonia.

of wood, too. Timber remains a fine material to build with, although the fear of fire is always present.

THE USE OF STONE

Stone was readily available in other parts of the world. From Egypt, through Greece and Rome, we see how it was used in increasingly adventurous ways. The Egyptians tended to use stone in great blocks that could be brought to building sites on rollers. The Greeks shaped their stones more subtly but still treated them as a stiffly noble material lacking in flexibility. Greek temples are the apotheosis of trabeated—or post-and-lintel—construction, whereby posts (or, in the case of Greek temples, columns) are set into the ground and then set over with beams (in their case entablatures). The Greeks made a great art of this simple form of construction, which, it has been argued by theorists and historians from the 18th century, was developed from timber buildings. Perhaps it was.

It was the Romans, though, who demonstrated the plastic properties of stone. This is not to suggest that stone can be squeezed like dough or shaped like putty, but it does possess a dynamic quality if one knows how

to lay stones in a particular order to achieve unexpected and, as seen in this book, spectacular results. Although the arch was known to the Greeks, it was the Romans who made it their trademark. Without the arch, there would be no Colosseum, no bridges across high rivers, no aqueducts. By extension, an arch could become a barrel vault to cover a room. Where two barrel vaults intersected they formed a groin vault, as seen in many Roman basilicas. If an arch is stretched and rotated, it becomes the base of a dome.

But it was the European Gothic masters who made stone one of the most exciting of all building materials. Generation by generation, ambitious clients, imaginative architects, and superbly talented craftsmen used the support gained by adding flying buttresses to stretch their arches higher and their vaults into ever more

BUILDING THE ACROPOLIS

The key buildings of the Acropolis date from Pericles' "Golden Age" of Athens, from 460 to 430 BCE. It is said that, in a popular move, Pericles used not slaves but unemployed Athenians as workers, thus ensuring all Athenian families had food on their tables. Complex scaffolds and pulleys aided the work of lifting the huge stone blocks into place.

Roman arches
The Roman aqueduct at Segovia, in Spain *(below)*, brings water 2,950 ft (899 m) from the Frío River to the city. Built in the reign of the emperor Trajan, it is one of the best-preserved examples of Roman "provincial" architecture.

complex patterns of mutually supporting groins—so much so that the later medieval churches were little more than caskets of glass framed by what appeared to be slivers of stone.

Ambition did, however, prove the limitation of stone technology. In 1284, the vaulting of the choir of Beauvais cathedral, in France, collapsed. The aim of its founder, Bishop Guillaume de Grez, had been to build the tallest cathedral in Europe. To do so required the vault to be raised by 16 ft (5 m).

Gothic stonework
Even after its rebuilding with sturdier supports, the vaulting of Beauvais cathedral still powerfully communicates the soaring ambition of its creators.

This was six feet too far, and the vault caved in. In 1573, the even more ambitious central tower of the cathedral, still under construction, collapsed. Only the choir and transepts of this stratospherically ambitious building were finally completed. They tell a tale of hubris, and yet the sky-high vaults of the choir are, it has to be said, breathtaking. Would the ancient

Greeks have thought such construction possible? Probably not, although it should be said that they were content with what they wanted to achieve. They let their mountainous landscape climb toward Heaven, while on the flat plains of Europe, ambitious clerics built holy mountains in sensational leaps and bounds of adventurous stone.

ADDING CONCRETE TO THE MIX
Roman builders had another trick up their togas: concrete. By mixing lime and clay, or *pozzolana* (a volcanic dust), with water they produced a cement that when mixed with aggregate—stones, pebbles, sand, gravel, rubble—formed concrete, a strong, plastic, easily worked, fireproof material that could be used to span previously inconceivable spaces, such as that over the voluminous drum of the Pantheon in Rome.

The cores of very many other Roman engineering structures and buildings were also concrete; but, by and large, this truly empire-building material vanished with the Romans. Modern concrete was invented by John Smeaton in England in *ca.* 1756, although it was to be some while before concrete was seen as a thing of beauty. Only in the 20th century was it truly admired. Even then, architects did their best to make concrete as smooth as possible, so that, especially when polished, it resembled stone. Raw concrete was made fashionable by Le Corbusier in the 1950s and today remains the choice core material of many of the world's buildings, whether artistic or not.

In the meantime, reinforced concrete had been invented by a French gardener, Joseph Monier, in the mid-19th century. His first experiments had been with flower pots, but once he showed his revolutionary material—concrete

Concrete concealed
The dome of the Pantheon, Rome, is built of concrete, although it is clad in what were considered more decorative materials.

made many times stronger with the addition of reinforcing bars—at the Paris Exposition of 1867, engineers, then contractors, and finally architects began to beat a path to his door.

Architects, especially in the 19th century when there was so much technological change going on around them, often found it hard to accept or to adapt to new materials. Equally, they often refused to see how a new material might be beautiful. They fought an increasingly rear guard action against new materials but finally gave into them and, in the case of concrete, did so with a vengeance.

THE STEEL REVOLUTION

In modern construction, there is one major rival to concrete: steel. In fact, far more steel is used in building

Harsh reality
The J. Edgar Hoover Building, Washington, D.C. —headquarters of the FBI—takes a tough line with its Brutalist boxiness and raw concrete.

construction today than concrete. Steel took over from iron, which, although it had been forged since 1600BCE, was essentially a soft material. By the 19th century, it was still much used in architectural decoration and for small-span structures, but it would never have been strong enough to allow the construction of skyscrapers. This, of course, is exactly what steel allowed.

WHAT IS STEEL?

Steel took over from iron in 1856, when the Englishman Henry Bessemer (1813–98) first proved that pig iron could be decarbonized, via his "Bessemer converter," to produce an immensely strong alloy that would revolutionize architecture. The lightness of steel and concrete compared to masonry allowed towering structures to be built.

Within a few decades of its invention, the New York skyline had become a wonder of the modern world.

Today, of the approximately one billion tons of steel manufactured worldwide, 60 percent is recycled. For this reason alone, steel is, beyond the manufacturing process, an environmentally sound material. It loses nothing in terms of strength or reliability through recycling. It allows for buildings that climb into the sky seemingly forever. No one is quite sure how tall a steel-framed building could be, although in 1956 Frank Lloyd Wright published sensational sketches of a 1 mile (1,600 m) high, 528-story office tower he would have liked to have built. His tower, The Illinois, never happened because of the costs involved and because no one (then or now) could quite see how to get around the problem of providing sufficient elevators traveling at a comfortable speed. What was not questioned was the ability of engineers and contractors to build so high.

INTO THE FUTURE

Today, there are many new materials available for architects to toy with, from plastic reinforced with glass to neoprene (a synthetic rubber), artificial stone, glass-reinforced concrete, titanium, and even "sea-cretion"— the curious coral-like invention of the German architect Wolf Hilbertz. Yet many of these materials are used only decoratively, for cladding, or for modest structures. The "living houses" that adapt their structures to human emotions as described so thrillingly and darkly in a short story in J. G. Ballard's *Vermilion Sands* (1971) have yet to come. The basic building blocks of architecture remain brick,

Modern use of steel
In architect Santiago Calatrava's City of Arts and Sciences, in Valencia, Spain, steel is used not as a concealed, reinforcing armature but celebrates its contribution to these sweeping structures.

A new Eden
The domes of Britain's Eden Project are clad in transparent foil "pillows," fixed to a framework that is designed to allow the substitution of even newer "breathable" materials as they become available.

stone, timber, concrete, and steel. These are the materials still used to create monumental buildings, not simply the ordinary dwellings shaped with no eye for posterity.

Throughout the world and across history, shelters of one sort or another have been built from hides, bones, wooden poles, bamboo, leaves, bark, fur, branches, reeds, ice, vegetable fibers, rocks, and mud. Occasionally these have been used to create architecture, as in the extraordinary mud mosques of Mali. For the most part, though, these are the materials of temporary structures: igloos and tepees, yurts, and clay-and-wattle huts. These are beautiful structures, but gone, in terms of the stretch of architectural history, with the wind, while the ziggurats of Mesopotamia carry on from ancient history to

infinity. The natural world, however, may well have provided humans with ideas for both materials and structures that would evolve into complex and thrilling architectural forms. Have birds' eggs, spiders' webs, the hexagons of beehives, or the brilliant ventilation systems of termites' nests affected the way we have built as the flight of birds has to the development aircraft? Perhaps. Yet what seems remarkable after so many centuries is that the basic building blocks have changed so little. As toddlers, our first act of building is to set one brick on another. When we learn to do it well, we are on the way to architecture.

FROM CONCEPTS TO COMPLETION

30 ST. MARY AXE

Dramatic new buildings such as the 590 ft (180 m) high 30 St. Mary Axe office building in the City of London, designed by Foster and Partners, are a test of the strength of the relationship between architect, contractor, and client.

A key first step in the creation of any major new building is the decision as to whether its construction is necessary or justified. Popularly known as the Gherkin (Pickle) due to its unusual shape, 30 St. Mary Axe—the headquarters of the insurance firm Swiss Re—came about through particularly dramatic circumstances. The Edwardian building it replaced, the Baltic Exchange, was severely damaged by an IRA bomb blast in 1992. The decision was made for it to be demolished, and to replace it with an entirely new building.

Once the decision to build has been made, the role of the architect is to fathom the needs of the new building's clients, and then consider how these needs can be met within the constraints of local planning guidelines and laws, while also satisfying the wider cultural concerns of bodies charged by the government with protecting, and even enhancing, local and national heritage.

STUDY MODELS

Study models of particular sections of the design of a building help the architect to consider how light and shadow will fall during the course of the day. They can also be used to demonstrate the flow of air through the building, and to get a feel of what it might be like to work or live in specific areas.

Model of rotations
This model of 30 St. Mary Axe shows how each floor plan rotates 5 degrees from the floor below, creating spiraling lightwells and "sky gardens."

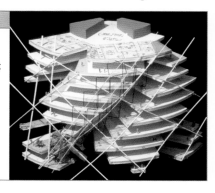

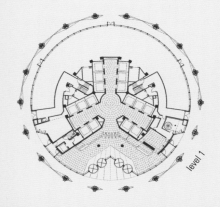

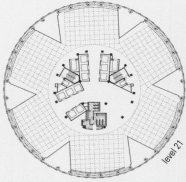

level 1

level 21

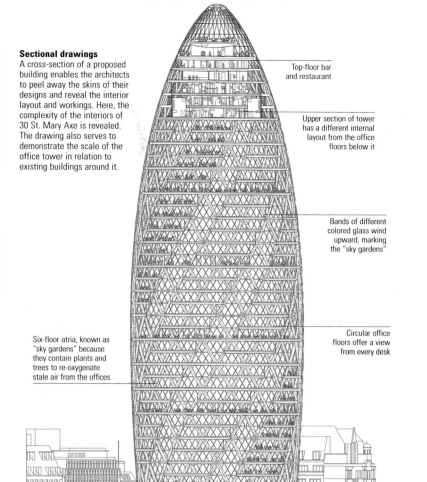

Sectional drawings

A cross-section of a proposed building enables the architects to peel away the skins of their designs and reveal the interior layout and workings. Here, the complexity of the interiors of 30 St. Mary Axe is revealed. The drawing also serves to demonstrate the scale of the office tower in relation to existing buildings around it.

Top-floor bar and restaurant

Upper section of tower has a different internal layout from the office floors below it

Bands of different colored glass wind upward, marking the "sky gardens"

Circular office floors offer a view from every desk

Six-floor atria, known as "sky gardens" because they contain plants and trees to re-oxygenate stale air from the offices

level 39

level 40

Floor plans

Individual floor plans help to visualize the interior spaces of a building, and can inform its overall design. These circular floor plans from 30 St. Mary Axe are, from left to right: entrance lobby, typical office floor, 70-seat restaurant below bar, 40th-floor bar.

The architects commissioned to deliver 30 St. Mary Axe, Foster and Partners, are known for their uncompromising exploration of technological innovation and forms, and made environmental considerations an important concern in their design for the building.

The design of a building may move through many stages, with the architects making sketches, computer drawings, and 3-D models of the proposed building, working closely with structural engineers and, gradually, as the form and detailed design of the project become clear, with a wide range of specialist engineers concerned with heating, ventilation, elevators, and lighting. Before construction of a building can begin, drawings and models must be approved by planners in many stages.

Once all parties are satisfied and in agreement, the final working drawings are signed off, and the contractors begin their work. Few changes are made to the design at this stage, and certainly not to the essential structure of the building. Office towers like 30 St. Mary Axe rise from the ground with astonishing

3-D models
Despite great advances made in computer drawings, cutaway models remain one of the most effective ways of explaining the design of a building.

speed, their builders locked into tight and demanding contracts. Once completed and hopefully well received by clients, public, and critics, a building like this remains a concern of the architects who shaped it. It serves as their most effective calling card, determines their reputation, and is a key part of their historical legacy.

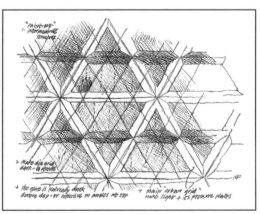

Window design
An architect's early sketch shows how the visual effect and structural design will combine. Note that people are included to give a sense of scale, and as a reminder of the purpose of the building.

Window construction
Only when the skin of a building begins to cover its skeleton does it start to look like the drawings.

The finished building
With its eye-catching design and unique shape, 30 St. Mary Axe, completed in 2004, is an unmistakable feature of the London skyline.

From village
to city

THE CITY IS ALMOST the defining characteristic of civilization. It is a place where people live and work cooperatively, producing food to sustain not only themselves, but "specialists"—artisans, artists, architects, scribes, administrators, and priests—who shape a unique culture. The story of architecture therefore begins with the first cities.

There are many theories about how and when civilization—and architecture with it—began. All need to be prefaced with the word "perhaps" because we are unlikely to ever be sure why people first settled and began to build on a heroic scale, with artistry beyond craft. However, most archaeologists agree that urban life evolved in the Middle East long before the first cities of Central America and China, and that the location of this giant leap forward was Mesopotamia—an area roughly equivalent to modern Iraq. Mesopotamia—the land bounded by the Tigris and Euphrates rivers (the name means "between the rivers" in Greek)—was essentially a dry land; its position between the two mighty rivers, however, allowed for easy irrigation of the desert, where reliable native grasses—barley and wheat— could be grown as crops. Fish and wildfowl were also plentiful, allowing settlers to build up the surpluses of food on which the beginnings of urban civilization depended.

BUILDING COMMUNITIES

Urban settlement was driven on by agricultural success and technological development. From around 3500BCE, bronze-age technology spread through the Middle East, replacing stone tools with metal. The ox-drawn plow appeared in Mesopotamia around 3000BCE, providing the first motive force beyond human muscle.

Ancient Mesopotamia hosted a procession of great civilizations: the Sumerians (3300–1900BCE) were succeeded by the Akkadians, then the Babylonians, Assyrians, and Persians. The first Sumerian cities differed from earlier village settlements because their surrounding lands were thought to be "owned" by a local god (rather than by families of clans).

Cuneiform script
The Sumerians developed the first writing in the 4th millenium BCE. Marks in clay tablets were made using wedge-shaped (cuneiform) ends of cut reeds.

KEY DATES

ca. **5300**BCE Possible construction of first temple at Eridu; beginnings of cities and architecture in Mesopotamia

ca. **3300**BCE Invention of writing, with cuneiform script developed at Uruk

ca. **2700**BCE Egyptians begin writing on papyrus scrolls, which can be stored in libraries

ca. **1755**BCE First known legal system codified by Babylonian king, Hammurabi

5000BCE   **3000**BCE   **2000**BCE

ca. **3500**BCE Sumerians invent the wheel, revolutionizing the means and speed of exchanging goods and ideas

ca. **3150**BCE Rise of Egyptian civilization along banks of the Nile River

ca. **2650**BCE Imhotep, high priest of Ptah at Memphis, erects a pyramid made of stone at Sakkara

1492BCE Tuthmosis I is the first pharaoh buried in a tomb cut into the rock in Egypt's Valley of the Kings

THE CITY AS TEMPLE

Mesopotamian people – from Babylonians to Persians – saw their cities as sacred places. Babylon, the greatest of all Mesopotamian cities, was known as Babi-ilani, or "the Gate of the Gods" – the place where the gods were thought to have descended to earth. In its time, Babylon was also an important center for trade, linking the Persian Gulf with the Mediterranean.

Ancient city
Around 570BCE, Babylon was the largest city in the known world, covering more than 2,500 acres (1,000 ha).

Looking to the skies
The brilliant light and ever-changing positions of sun, moon, stars, and planets overhead in the first cities encouraged those who founded them to design their monumental buildings in tune with the geometry of the heavens.

ca. **1200**BCE The first chapters of the Bible are written, in Hebrew; the birth of monotheism

ca. **600**BCE Zarathustra forms a new religion called Zoroastrianism in Persia

ca. **30**BCE Defeat, by Augustus, and suicide of Cleopatra, last of Greco-Egyptian monarchs

ca. **150**CE The astronomer Ptolemy of Alexandria proves the world is round

1000BCE

1CE

ca. **1450**BCE Egyptians begin telling the time with sundials

1020BCE The Hebrew king David conquers the Philistines and unifies Israel

332BCE Alexander the Great conquers Egypt and the Hellenization of the country begins

ca. **50** Christianity emerges from Palestine, and is spread by Paul to Rome after death of Christ

Priests organized work on the land, which in turn provided food for the whole community. A temple dedicated to the local god was typically the center of the settlement, surrounded by public buildings and marketplaces, and built up on a stepped pyramid, or ziggurat—a kind of cosmic mountain. The priests were at the hub of society because, on behalf of the gods, they controlled much of a city's lands and irrigation systems, as well as distributing the all-important agricultural surplus. The Sumerians created the very notion of the state, of law and kingship, while inventing the calendar, the wheel, abstract mathematics, timekeeping (with the 60-minute hour), literature (exemplified by the *Epic of Gilgamesh, see opposite*), and the zodiac.

MOVING IDEAS

Were the early Mesopotamian city states, complete with their sacred temple mountains, the blueprint for later cities beyond the Middle East— from Egypt to China, India, and the Americas? Certainly, the stepped pyramid form appears in Egypt soon after its development in Sumeria, and

Gods of ancient Egypt
The Egyptians had as many as 2,000 gods, often represented as part human, part animal. This mural, picturing the gods Anubis and Horus, was discovered on tomb walls in the Valley of the Kings.

Fertile floods
As in Mesopotamia, Egyptian civilization depended on water. Regular flooding of the Nile made the strips of land on either side of the river extremely fertile.

it is likely that Sumerian masons and craftsmen did travel to Egypt. But although Egypt produced its own great cities, they never assumed the independent identity and dynamism of those in Mesopotamia—partly because the activity in Egyptian cities focused more on serving the royal court than on building civic identity. Accordingly, the most famous monumental architecture of Egypt is dedicated to dead pharaohs, rather than living communities.

The Bronze Age (which lasted until around 1200BCE in the Middle East) was a time when people traveled freely over surprisingly large distances, spreading trade, myths, and ideas. Some commentators suggest that links between the Old and New Worlds were well established during this time, explaining the appearance of the stepped pyramid form in Central America. These notions are highly controversial, but what is certain is that something profound occurred around 3000BCE, changing peoples who subsisted by hunting and gathering, and lived in makeshift homes, into

builders of great cities girdled with walls and adorned with temples and palaces. Some claim that this change gives credence to the destruction-and-renewal myth of the Great Flood enshrined in so many cultures; for others it simply marks a shift—no less remarkable—in human consciousness.

SUMERIAN LITERATURE

The world's first known work of literature—the *Epic of Gilgamesh*—began life in southern Sumeria between 2700 and 2500 BCE. Gilgamesh was a real Sumerian ruler who reigned around 2700BCE, and the epic drew together poems and legends surrounding his reign into a complete, mythologized story, inscribed in cuneiform, on 12 clay tablets. It includes an account of a cataclysmic flood, similar in detail to that in the Bible, promoting great interest from scholars.

Epic of Gilgamesh
Elements of the epic have been woven into later biblical and classical literature; this illustration is from Zabelle C. Boyajian's 1924 book *Gilgamesh*.

ANCIENT MIDDLE EAST
ca. 5300–350BCE

Gods and kings: the architecture of the ancient Middle East is the story, as far as we can see, of these two forces—one divine, one would-be divine. This is largely because the everyday buildings of this period, in which people lived and worked, have long since vanished. What we are left with are the ruins, in various states of decay, of ambitious palaces and temples—the architecture of religion and power.

The surviving monuments of ancient Iraq, from *ca.* 3000BCE, are all built of brick. Stone was largely unavailable, as were the lengths of unyielding timber necessary to span large spaces. The most impressive of the early works of architecture in the ancient Middle East is the Ziggurat of Ur *(see p.47)*; but the one we would all like to see, if only we could, is the "Tower of Babel"—the great ziggurat at Babylon. The base of this temple, measuring 295 ft (90 m) square, does indeed suggest a daringly ambitious structure. Faced with blue-glazed bricks and rising in seven stages, it would have towered over King Nebuchadnezzar's legendary palace beside the Euphrates, famous for the Hanging Gardens that cascaded in great perfumed terraces from the top of the building. It is vital to remember that what today are ruins in a war-torn desert were once the raiments of powerful civilizations.

A NEW ARCHITECTURAL PROCESS

Eventually, the region was swallowed up by the world's first great empire, founded by Persia's Cyrus the Great (*ca.* 600–530BCE). From this time on, building styles were not only transferred from one city, or kingdom, to another, but they also began to be mingled to produce fusions of styles that pushed architecture down new pathways and into creative risk-taking. Craftsmen from across the Persian empire—Assyria, Babylon, Egypt, and Ionia—joined forces to shape a new architecture that was far more fluid and sensual than that of the Sumerians, Akkadians, Babylonians, and Assyrians before them. Lavishly decorated and brightly colored, the Palace of Persepolis *(see p.51)*, founded in 518BCE, shows just how far architecture had moved from the elementary ziggurats that had introduced humanity to architecture some 2,500 years earlier.

◁ STAIRCASE TO THE PALACE OF DARIUS I AT PERSEPOLIS, WITH RELIEF SHOWING A LION AND A BULL IN COMBAT, AND SERVANTS CLIMBING STEPS TO SERVE AT THE KING'S TABLE.

ELEMENTS

The basic building materials of ancient Middle Eastern architecture were brick and stone. Increasingly, surfaces were adorned, and then covered, in tiles and relief sculpture. Much of this symbolic sculpture was brightly colored and supported by inscriptions. The Palace of Persepolis, begun by Darius I in 518BCE, is the most impressive example of this era.

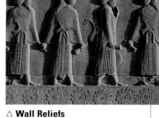

△ **Wall Reliefs**
Stairs and terraces in Persepolis are lined with layers of relief carvings, separated from one another by bands of rosettes. The figures depict stately processions of Persian and foreign nobles, chieftains, courtiers, guardsmen, and tribute bearers from across the ancient empire.

Monumental script ▷
Babylonian buildings can be read like books. The palace at Nimrud, for example, features reliefs of kings and courtiers superimposed with detailed and lengthy inscriptions listing their achievements.

Inscriptions run
across the reliefs

Design intended
to instil fear

Winged bulls used
in place of columns

◁ **Animal statuary**
Powerfully sculpted heads, wings, beaks, and claws of real and mythical beasts symbolized the power of kings across the region.

Gateway guardians ▷
Enormous winged bulls with bearded human heads were used to flank the entrances to Assyrian and Persian cities and palaces.

Carving at the height of
the Persian Empire was
highly accomplished

▽ **Hunting scenes**
Realistic scenes of lion hunts and of lions attacking weaker animals can be found in Assyrian, Babylonian, and Persian palaces. Here—at Persepolis—visitors were left in no doubt as to the characters of the kings they were to meet at the top of the stairs.

Stepped
castellations

Carved stone panels
attached to the side
of the stairway

ZIGGURAT OF URNAMMU, UR

🖳 *ca.* 2125BCE   📍 MUQAIYIR, IRAQ   ⚒ URNAMMU   🏛 PLACE OF WORSHIP/CEREMONIAL BUILDING

In the flat, sun-baked desert of southern Iraq, in what was once ancient Sumeria, lies the biblical city of Ur, home of Abraham and the site of one of the most significant early architectural monuments—the Ziggurat of Urnammu. This imposing structure commanded what was then a great walled city.

The Ziggurat stands alone and apart from the extensive remains of the excavated streets and tombs of the city of Ur. Originally it was walled around, at the heart a religious complex, and reached through a grand courtyard. This artificial sacred mountain was once topped by a temple dedicated to the Moon god Nanna, gained by daunting flights of stairs that still survive.

When the Ziggurat was remodeled and expanded by Urnammu *(see below)* and his successors in the 21st century BCE, it was already an extremely old building. It is constructed from mud bricks, the ubiquitous building material of ancient Mesopotamia; each layer is bonded with bitumen, and some with matting to improve stability. The outer layer of bricks is baked for sharpness of profile and durability.

Urnammu's monument has survived over the centuries, not least because of the ingenuity of its construction: "weeper holes" in the vast mass of brickwork allow the

CEREMONIAL STAIRWAY

evaporation of water from the mud core, while drainage channels built into the structure carry away rainwater. It remains a tantalizing feature of a landscape fought over almost as long as it has been inhabited.

URNAMMU

The powerful third dynasty of Ur was founded by Urnammu, an ancient Sumerian king who reigned between *ca.* 2113BCE and *ca.* 2096BCE and who built and restored many public buildings in Ur, including the great Ziggurat. In a bid for immortality, it must be said that Urnammu has done rather well— each of the many individual bricks used to build this amazing structure, the best preserved of all Mesopotamian ziggurats, is stamped with his name.

Mighty construction
Only the base remains today, but this mountainous building once had three tiers, and some suggest that each level was planted with trees.

PALACE OF SARGON

706BCE KHORSABAD, NORTHERN IRAQ SARGON II PALACE

The palaces of the Assyrian Empire are some of the largest and most imposing ancient buildings in Mesopotamia, demonstrating the affluence, aspirations, and determination of the fierce military regime that shaped them. Though dramatic, the empire was short-lived, and its kings were

clearly in a hurry to build on a heroic scale; the Palace of Sargon in the city of Khorsabad was almost shoddily built in parts, making use of soft bricks laid on top of one another without mortar. And yet, the overall effect of the architecture would have been overwhelming. Raised on a stone platform at a height level with the top of the city walls, the palace covered almost 23 acres (9 ha). At its heart was a throne room measuring 162 x 35 ft (49 x 10.7 m), crowned with a flat, decorated timber ceiling —luxury in a land where wood was scarce.

Valued materials
The palace was decorated with reliefs showing the transport of precious wood to Khorsabad.

ISHTAR GATE

575BCE BABYLON, CENTRAL IRAQ NEBUCHADNEZZAR II ENTRANCE GATEWAY

One of the eight main entries to the city of Babylon *(see opposite)*, the Ishtar gate today stands inside the Pergamon Museum, Berlin. The structure was moved from Iraq soon after its discovery in the early 20th century, and a two-thirds scale replica was built at its original location, commissioned by Saddam Hussein as part of a controversial reconstruction of Babylon. The original

battlemented gate guarded the way to the city's main processional avenue, impressing visitors to Nebuchadnezzar's court. It is magnificently patterned with dragons and lions, worked in low-relief kiln-fired bricks glazed with liquid asphalt. The dragons symbolize Marduk, god of the city and giver of eternal life, while the lions are a symbol of the goddess Ishtar.

New gate
Today's replica hints at the craftsmanship of the original gate.

BABYLON

562BCE CENTRAL IRAQ
NEBUCHADNEZZAR II CITY

At its peak, Babylon covered an area of at least 3.9 sq miles (10 km²), making it by far the biggest city of its time. Set along the Euphrates River, its walls enclosed a densely packed mix of temples, shrines, markets, and houses, divided by grand avenues set at right angles to one another. The city's legendary Tower of Babel was a seven-tiered ziggurat rising from a base 297 ft (90 m) square. The Hanging Gardens—one of the seven wonders of the ancient world—were built for Nebuchadnezzar's wife, Amytis.

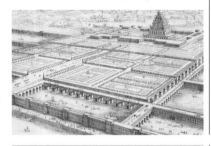

NINEVEH

ca. 700BCE MOSUL, NORTHERN IRAQ
SENNACHERIB CITY

The city of Nineveh, on the eastern bank of the Tigris River, was the final and greatest capital of the Assyrian Empire. It was founded by Nimrod and laid out by Sennacherib, son of Sargon II, but like many ancient cities, its heyday was brief: it was overrun and humbled by the Medes and the Babylonians in 612BCE. Containing several palaces and girdled with 7.5 miles (12 km) of walls, it would have been an imposing sight. Impressive stretches of wall survive to this day, some rebuilt by Saddam Hussein. There are also remains of King Sennacherib's "Palace without a rival"—still decorated with aggressive carved stone reliefs. Many of the best reliefs—including those from King Ashurbanipal's palace—are now in the British Museum, London. They depict vivid scenes of royal lion hunting and gruesome executions of enemies in the bloody campaigns fought by the Assyrians against the Elamites: Nineveh, like all Assyrian cities, was primarily a machine for making war.

NIMRUD

859BCE NEAR MOSUL, NORTHERN IRAQ
ASHURNASIRPAL II CITY

Nimrud is the site of the biblical city of Calah. For its day it was an enormous settlement: its walls extended 4.7 miles (7.5 km), and its peak population is said to have been 100,000. The city was founded by the Assyrian king Shalmaneser I in the 13th century BCE and was enlarged around 880BCE during the reign of Ashurnasirpal II. Nimrud continued to be a major center until it fell to the invading Babylonians and Medes between 614 and 612BCE.

Typically, this Assyrian city boasted a palace set in generous courtyards, complete with a ziggurat and stone relief carvings depicting bloody battles and lion hunting. It was also home to the fascinating Temple of Ezida, built in the 9th century BCE; here was the sanctuary of Nabu, the god of writing. A well in front of Nabu's sanctuary provided the water that, when mixed with fine clay, produced the writing tablets that were such an important part of life for all Mesopotamian cultures.

TEMPLE OF SOLOMON

ca. 1000BCE JERUSALEM, ISRAEL
SOLOMON PLACE OF WORSHIP

According to the Old Testament, the temple was built by David's son, Solomon, to house the Ark of the Covenant—the container of the Ten Commandments. Nothing of the original temple has survived: it was most likely destroyed by the Babylonians in the 6th century BCE. Descriptions in the Bible and archaeological digs suggest a building with an inner sanctum fronted by a courtyard, with both structures surrounded by open courtyards, as seen in the model below.

CITADEL OF VAN

⏳ *ca.* 800BCE   📍 VAN, EASTERN TURKEY
🪶 SARDURI I   🏛 FORTRESS

The remains of the Citadel of Van rise from a rocky outcrop more than 260 ft (80 m) high, offering panoramic views of the surrounding countryside. From around 3,000 years ago, Van was the capital of the kingdom of Urartu, a civilization of which we know little, except that it was an enemy of the Assyrians (as was every other civilization within reach of their chariots). The base of the citadel was constructed from massive stone blocks, many of which are still firmly in place; the superstructure would have been made of mud bricks, while roofs were either thatched or of timber. The one surviving architectural feature is a powerful stone-built barbican, or fortified gateway, that once protected the entrance to the citadel and its water supply. The internal layout of the citadel was probably along the lines of a densely inhabited castle. There are no remains of a temple, though rock tombs, with niches for lamps, have been found in the walls of the south side of the citadel.

TOMB OF DARIUS I

⏳ 485BCE   📍 NAQSH-I-RUSTAM, SOUTHERN IRAN
🪶 DARIUS I   🏛 TOMB

Carved into a solid cliff face, the tomb of Darius I *(see above, right)* is inscribed with the achievements, reflections, and beliefs of the great Persian ruler. The finely executed facade of the tomb is 60 ft (18.3 m) wide; high above the ground and facing the rising sun, the entrance is flanked by four columns supporting an Egyptian-style cornice. The capitals are of the double-bull type—carved bull heads facing away from one another—characteristic of Persian buildings of this period. The design of the facade seems to be adapted from the south front of Darius's palace at Persepolis nearby.

PALACE OF CTESIPHON

⏳ *ca.* 350   📍 CTESIPHON, CENTRAL IRAQ   🪶 CHOSROES I   🏛 PALACE

The Palace of Ctesiphon is one of the late-flowering wonders of Mesopotamian culture. Although built by the Persian kings of the Sassanid dynasty, it is in many ways a summary of the vigor and grand architectural ambitions of the many civilizations of this region. Its most obvious feature—a vast, single-span brick barrel vault—is part of what must have been a truly magnificent open-fronted banqueting hall. This arch (technically a pointed ovoid, a shape typical of Mesopotamia) is an astonishing 121 ft (36.7 m) high and spans 83 ft (25.3 m), rivaling anything built by the Romans. The influence of Rome is very much in evidence throughout the design of the palace: massive walls flanking the central banqueting hall were animated with Roman-style arcading set between pairs of attached columns. The actual building type, however, is very un-Roman: the stupendous banqueting hall was open-ended, forming, in effect, a hugely stylized tent. The east wall of the palace remains; the west and rear walls have collapsed, and, tragically, engineers now fear for the integrity of the arch itself.

Arch construction
The largest vault in the ancient world, the impressive arch at Ctesiphon is made of unfired mud bricks.

PALACE COMPLEX OF PERSEPOLIS

480BCE PERSEPOLIS, SOUTHERN IRAN DARIUS I PALACE

With its imaginatively carved ceremonial stairways and its fabulous Hall of a Hundred Columns, this complex must have been among the most thrilling buildings of its time. Its architecture and decoration reflect the design and craftsmanship of the many civilizations and cultures brought—mostly by force—into the orbit of the Persian Empire, and even its remaining ruins retain real visual power.

Most ancient buildings represent the culture of one specific civilization; at Persepolis, we begin to see how architectural styles could be fused across civilizations, producing hybrid designs. The palace complex stands on a stone platform measuring 1,518 x 907 ft (460 x 275 m), raised 50 ft (15 m) above ground. Its courtyards and halls, built over decades, were reached by a magnificent stairway that can still be seen today; kings would have ascended the stairway on horseback.

The highpoint of the complex was its Hall of a Hundred Columns—an imposing throne room with brick walls 11 ft (3.4 m) thick and 100 double-bull columns supporting an expansive cedar ceiling.

Walls of the principal buildings were lined with stone, those of lesser structures with baked and glazed mud brick. The palace complex was decorated throughout

with stone reliefs and wall paintings of nobles, courtiers, tribute-bearers, foreign dignitaries, soldiers, and others, creating a vivid and lasting picture of life at the court of one of the ancient world's most powerful dynasties. When visiting the bleached ruins of Persepolis today, it is easy to forget that the original decorations were incredibly brightly colored—probably lurid to modern observers—and that the palace would have dazzled the eyes of awed ancient visitors.

THE KING OF KINGS—DARIUS I

DARIUS I

By the time of his death in 486BCE, Darius I had extended the Persian Empire as far as India and Thrace. He built Persepolis as the showcase of his great empire, dedicating it to Ahuramazda, the supreme god of the Persians. Work on the complex's giant platform began around 518BCE, but the task was not completed until many years later by Artaxerxes I.

The fall of Persepolis

The splendor of Persepolis lasted until 330BCE, when it was looted by Alexander the Great. The site was rediscovered in the 17th century.

ANCIENT EGYPT
ca. 3000BCE–300CE

The civilization of the ancient Egyptians will never cease to fascinate us. The complexity of its myths, its highly involved burial rituals, its mummified cats and pet snakes, and the sheer tenacity of a culture that lasted essentially unchanged over thousands of years are utterly compelling. So, too, is its haunting, powerful architecture: the geometric brilliance of the pyramids, and the eeriness of the temples and tombs.

Mysterious, consistent, and, once established, a law unto itself, the architecture of ancient Egypt developed slowly over a period of some 3,000 years, at a time when the country was mostly free of invaders, wealthy, and well organized. The country's fortune and culture were based around the seasonal cycle and flow of the Nile River. Each year, as the waters of the river rose and the valley bloomed, agriculture became the main focus of activity, producing the food that would have to last through the next dry season. There was little farmers and their laborers could do when the river fell, however, and so ancient Egypt was blessed for five months of the year with a surplus of skilled and unskilled workers who could be set to work on monumental architectural projects. And so the pyramids arose, designed to house the mummified bodies of pharaohs and

their treasures. The first, the Step Pyramid of Zoser at Sakkara *(see p.55)*, was designed by Imhotep—also the first architect whom we know by name.

ENDURING LEGACY
Although it eventually ossified, Egyptian culture has continued to fascinate visitors and explorers over the centuries. The ancient Romans were entranced by it. And in 1922, when the English archaeologist Howard Carter discovered the underground tomb of the young king Tutankhamun—an 18th-Dynasty pharaoh (1334–1323BCE) of only moderate significance in Egyptian history—he triggered a craze for all things Egyptian that has yet to die down. It encouraged the Art-Deco movement in the late 1920s and early 1930s, nurtured countless books and films, and enticed millions of tourists down the Nile from Cairo to Luxor.

◁ THE OLDEST OF THE ANCIENT WONDERS OF THE WORLD, THE GREAT PYRAMID OF KHUFU AT GIZA, EGYPT, IS THE ONLY WONDER THAT SURVIVES TODAY.

ELEMENTS

Egyptian architecture is characterized by massive stone elements—huge sloping walls, mountainous pyramids, colossal statuary, and imposing colonnades. Woven into this mix were stone representations of gods, some with human characteristics, others in the guise of animals, while plant forms were used extensively for capitals.

△ **Papyrus capitals**
The design of the capitals of Egyptian columns was rooted in stylized plant forms, such as the papyrus, common to the banks of the Nile River.

◁ **Sphinxes**
Processional avenues leading to temple entrances were often lined with rows of statues of sphinxes—mythical creatures with the body of a lion but the head of a ram or human.

△ **Monumental entrance statuary**
Huge statues of pharaohs were erected in front of temples to impress the divine might of kings on mere mortals. Here, in front of the Great Temple, Abu-Simbel, sit four identical massive statues of Rameses.

△**Relief sculptures**
Ancient Egyptian buildings were designed to be read as well as seen: reliefs on the walls of temples and palaces told stories with pictograms and pictures.

△ **Lotus bud capitals**
These highly abstract capitals, based on closed lotus flowers, sit atop elongated columns that form a hypostyle hall at the heart of the temple of Luxor.

The simple doorway gives little clue to the architectural drama within the temple

◁ **Entrance pylons**
The doorways of many temples are set between massive pylons, such as these at the Temple of Isis, Philae. Pylons conceal either light-filled courtyards or hypostyle halls.

Sloping walls are immensely strong

STEP PYRAMID OF ZOSER

🗿 *ca.* 2650BCE   📍 SAKKARA, EGYPT   ✎ IMHOTEP   🏛 FUNERARY MONUMENT

The tomb of the pharaoh Zoser is the world's first large-scale stone monument and the first of the Egyptian pyramids. Its revolutionary design was the work of the first architect we know by name, Imhotep. Originally simply another "mastaba," or single-story stone funerary monument, the stepped form of the 197 ft (60 m) high limestone pyramid developed over many years.

To create this magnificent stepped pyramid, six traditional, single-story monuments, each smaller than the one below it, are effectively piled on top of one another. The base of the resulting great pyramid measures 410 × 358 ft (125 × 109 m).

The pyramid was only one part of a vast religious complex set within a limestone-walled enclosure measuring 1,795 × 912 ft (547 × 278 m). A single true entrance among many false ones led into a huge courtyard full of dummy buildings, reproduced from those at Zoser's palace; when the pharaoh went to the heavens, he intended to take the architecture he had commissioned with him. Beyond the entrance are avenues, columned halls, shrines, chapels, and store rooms.

In this great monument, stone was used for the first time to roof over spaces, proving that it was a far more flexible material than

IMHOTEP

King Zoser of Egypt, a ruler in the 3rd Dynasty (2675–2625BCE), commissioned his chief vizier, Imhotep, to build his eternal resting place. The monument took many years to complete. Imhotep *(right)*, who has been titled architect, engineer, sage, doctor, astronomer, and high priest, was later worshiped as the god of wisdom.

earlier builders had realized. Five rectangular layers of brilliant white limestone were constructed on top of one another in decreasing dimensions to a height of 204 ft (62 m). The burial chamber is 90 ft (27 m) below the surface and lined with granite. The use of stone instead of mud brick is thought to represent the pharaoh's desire for eternal life.

BRONZE STATUE OF IMHOTEP

The first pyramid
Underground mastabas were usually given an overground presence, but layered mastabas created an astonishing pyramidal monument.

GREAT PYRAMID OF KHUFU

🗓 *ca.* 2566BCE   📍 GIZA, EGYPT   ✍ UNKNOWN   🏛 BURIAL SITE

THE PYRAMIDS AT GIZA

Egyptian pharaoh Khufu ruled 2589–66BCE, and his tomb is the largest of three pyramids at Giza, standing further north and east than the other two. His tomb was robbed thousands of years ago, and the internal layout of the pyramid has changed, so we know little about him. However, we know that the pharaoh was buried alone in this massive, man-made mountain, which probably took 20 years to build with slave labor. The largest pyramid ever built, it originally stood 481 ft (147 m) high and consists of some 2.3 million blocks of stone weighing an average of 2.5 tons. Its four equal sides each measure 791 ft (241 m). The pyramid was originally covered with polished limestone, which has long since eroded or been removed. There are three chambers inside, though only one person was buried here.

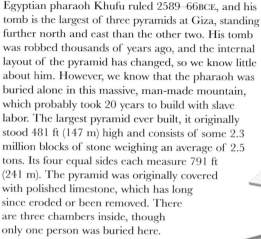

The King's Chamber contained a huge granite sarcophagus without a lid

◁ **Ivory statuette**
This tiny figure, 3.5 in (9 cm) tall, dates from *ca.* 1590BCE. It is the only depiction ever found of Khufu.

◁ **The Grand Gallery**
The high-roofed passageway leading to the entrance to the King's Chamber has slits that allow in the light. The gallery may have been used as an observatory, or possibly to store the huge blocks of granite that ultimately closed off the burial chamber.

The descending passage ends in a natural stone pit and a blank wall

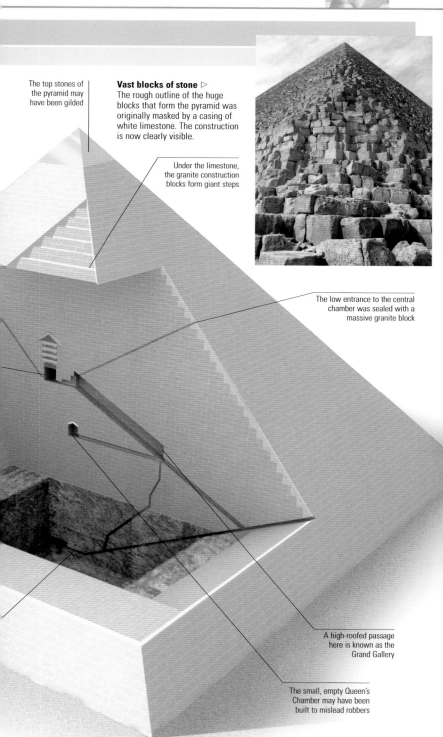

The top stones of the pyramid may have been gilded

Vast blocks of stone ▷
The rough outline of the huge blocks that form the pyramid was originally masked by a casing of white limestone. The construction is now clearly visible.

Under the limestone, the granite construction blocks form giant steps

The low entrance to the central chamber was sealed with a massive granite block

A high-roofed passage here is known as the Grand Gallery

The small, empty Queen's Chamber may have been built to mislead robbers

TOMBS OF THE KINGS, THEBES

🖾 1500BCE   ⚑ VALLEY OF THE KINGS, LUXOR, EGYPT   ✍ IMHOTEP   🏛 TOMB

After the heroic era of pyramid building, later pharaohs of the New Kingdom chose to be buried very differently, in sarcophagi buried deep underground, largely to protect their remains and treasures from tomb robbers. The earliest of these tombs are in the parched mountains on the west side of the Nile near Thebes (now Luxor). Here, the mummies of pharaohs of the 18th, 19th, and 20th Dynasties were hidden in richly decorated rock chambers, some supported by rows of columns. These chambers can be as deep as 315 ft (96 m) below ground and as far as 690 ft (210 m) into the rock face, reached by long, sloping corridors, stairs, and labyrinthine antechambers.

Earthly treasures
Hidden below ground, the walls and ceilings of the many Tombs of the Kings are adorned with colorful paintings and elaborate inscriptions.

TEMPLE OF KHONS, KARNAK

🖾 1198BCE   ⚑ KARNAK, EGYPT   ✍ UNKNOWN   🏛 PLACE OF WORSHIP

While pyramids and mortuary chapels were for the worship of kings, temples were for the worship of gods. There were many of these in the Egyptian pantheon, so there were very many temples. The archetype is the Temple of Khons, within the great religious complex of Karnak, near modern Luxor. An avenue of sphinxes led to an obelisk and then the massive entrance pylon to the temple itself. Within was a cloisterlike courtyard, bordered by a mighty double colonnade. Ordinary people could venture only this far. Beyond, a hypostyle (many-columned) hall lit by a clerestory announced the sanctuary, with its attendant chapels and a further hypostyle hall in the depths of the building. This was the realm of the temple's god and his, her, or its priests. Unlike ziggurats and pyramids, these buildings were not sacred mountains but were entered and used in ways that, despite the exotic and often obscure nature of Egyptian gods, seem familiar to us today.

Dramatic entrance
A narrow gateway in the center of a towering pylon inspires awe in the uninitiated visitor.

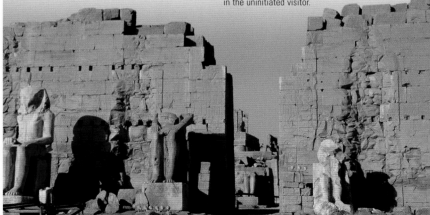

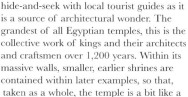

GREAT TEMPLE OF AMUN, KARNAK

🏺 1530BCE   📍 KARNAK, EGYPT   ✎ THOTMES I   🏛 PLACE OF WORSHIP

Enormous, dramatic, and—pyramids aside—one of the most enduring images of ancient Egypt, the Temple of Amun is a truly mesmerizing structure: the hypostyle hall at its core boasts no fewer than 134 immense freestanding columns marching in 16 rows, all exuberantly decorated; those at the center are 69 ft (21 m) high and 12 ft (3.6 m) in diameter. Today, the temple is as much a place to play

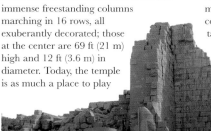

hide-and-seek with local tourist guides as it is a source of architectural wonder. The grandest of all Egyptian temples, this is the collective work of kings and their architects and craftsmen over 1,200 years. Within its massive walls, smaller, earlier shrines are contained within later examples, so that, taken as a whole, the temple is a bit like a Russian doll. The temple site, by a sacred lake, measures a breathtaking 1,200 × 360 ft (366 × 110 m)—daunting for visitors on hot days—and is still connected, more or less, to the Temple at Luxor by an avenue of sphinxes. Once, no fewer than six pylons led into the temple's various and vast courtyards, flanking temples, hypostyle courtyard, and numinous sanctuaries.

Temple guard
A small statue of the Egyptian god Amun Ra stands sentinel by the remains of a massive pylon.

TEMPLE OF QUEEN HATSHEPSUT

🏺 323BCE   📍 DÊR EL-BAHARI, EGYPT   ✎ SENMUT   🏛 PLACE OF WORSHIP

Queen Hatshepsut's burial chamber lies in the mountains far away from this, her magnificent mortuary chapel. Stretched against and dug into an imposing rock face, the chapel looks remarkably modern to contemporary eyes, resembling a 19th-century Neo-Classical museum or gallery.

The temple was designed by the queen's architect, Senmut, who arranged the approach to the chapel in the form of three horizontal terraces, each fronted by shady double colonnades gained by giant ramps. The topmost terrace contains a colonnaded walled court housing the queen's mortuary

chapel and a giant altar to the sun god, Ra. Dug into the cliff face, a sanctuary for priests to go about their ineffable duties is set behind this court. Hatshepsut attained unprecedented power for a queen, and the temple is a work of true adoration: statues and sphinxes of the queen line the upper terraces, while reliefs carved into the structure of the hypostyle hall depict animated stories of her life.

Enduring legacy
The highly decorated walls of the temple include a depiction of Hatshepsut's allegedly divine lineage, detailing the claim that the god Amun Ra is her father.

The temples at Karnak
The complex of ancient temples is awe-inspiring in its size and grandeur. In the great columnar hall of the Temple of Amun, shown here, gloriously colored reliefs and inscriptions honored the kings and gods to whom they were dedicated.

GREAT TEMPLE, ABU-SIMBEL

ca. 1257BCE   ABU-SIMBEL, EGYPT   RAMESES II   PLACE OF WORSHIP

Utterly magnificent, this great rock-cut temple, one of two commissioned by Rameses II to honor his own memory, is lucky to survive. The original setting of the temples on the banks of the Nile is today deep under the waters contained by the Aswan High Dam, itself a fine and memorable structure built to Russian design in the 1960s, some 3,200 years later.

INNER SANCTUARY

The two temples were removed, piece by piece, by craftsmen who sawed painstakingly through the ancient stones, reassembling them in a similar setting not so very far away. Originally approached through a courtyard, the imposing rock-face facade of the Great Temple, shaped in the guise of a giant pylon, is famous for its four gigantic statues of the seated Rameses II: here, quite clearly, was a king not prepared to do things by halves, much less by quarters. At his feet are small statues of his wife, Nefartari, his mother, Mut-tuy, and his children; above, a carved row of smiling baboons greets the sunrise. The haunting facade of the temple is 118 ft (36 m) wide and 105 ft (32 m) high, while the statues reach over 66 ft (20 m) high. Behind them is a 30 ft (9 m) high hall supported by eight finely decorated columns. Beyond this is a smaller, columned hall, flanked by asymmetrically placed shrines, leading into a complex sanctuary, its holiest sanctum presided over by statues of gods sitting with the deified Pharaoh *(see above)*. Rameses II is entombed far away in the mountains, but here, and at the Ramesseum, Thebes, is where he was worshiped.

ASWAN AND UNESCO

During the four years from the start of construction of the Aswan High Dam to when the reservoir began filling, 24 ancient monuments were either moved to safer locations, like the Great Temple and the Temple of Isis, or given to countries that had aided the UNESCO-coordinated work; the Debod Temple, for example, now sits on a hill in Madrid, Spain.

Flawed facade
Earthquake damage to the second of the four statues was retained in the UNESCO reconstruction.

TEMPLE OF ISIS, PHILAE

🗿 247BCE 📍 AGILIKA, EGYPT ⚒ UNKNOWN 🏛 PLACE OF WORSHIP

Originally built on the island of Philae, now completely submerged after the building of the Aswan High Dam, the Temple of Isis was relocated to its present home on the island of Agilika in the late 20th century.

Although the Egyptian era was drawing to a close when the temple was first built on Philae, the temple builders continued in much the same heroic vein as their inspired predecessors had done. By the high standards set a millennium earlier, however, the temple was a little crude in both detail and execution. To the unschooled eye, a temple of 1300BCE can be hard to tell apart from one, like this, from the 3rd century BCE; yet despite the pylons, hypostyle courtyards, clerestory halls, and inner sanctuaries, there are differences. Capitals of the columns, for example, are more ornate than

Perfect backdrop
The Temple of Isis owes its quality as much to its picturesque setting, in its beautiful Nile-island location, as to its architecture.

earlier designs, although more roughly carved. Intriguingly, in the temple complex there is a screen-walled kiosk known as the Pharaoh's Bed, which was built by the Romans in the year 96. The Romans took up Egyptian design enthusiastically from the time of the affair between Cleopatra and Julius Caesar, and the influence of the architecture that graced the island of Philae can be seen far away in the ambitious grounds of Hadrian's Villa, Tivoli *(see p.117)*.

TEMPLE OF HORUS

🗿 57BCE 📍 EDFU, EGYPT ⚒ PTOLEMY III 🏛 PLACE OF WORSHIP

This late Egyptian temple dedicated to the falcon god Horus is famous mostly for its fine state of preservation: it was effectively embalmed for centuries under the desert sands, with only the tops of its pylons visible. When eventually excavated, it revealed itself in all its 2,000-year-old glory. If it lacks the drama and outstanding artistic qualities of the temples at Karnak, for example, then this is not to belittle it: it is like comparing a great medieval parish church with a cathedral.

FORTRESS OF BUHEN

🗿 2130BCE 📍 BUHEN, EGYPT ⚒ SESOSTRIS III 🏛 FORTIFICATION

The fortress at Buhen, capital of Egyptian Nubia, must have been a daunting sight for Egypt's southerly neighbors. Its muscular brick and stone walls, nearly 16 ft (5 m) thick, covered an area of 3.2 acres (1.3 ha). The fortress was surrounded by a dry moat, strengthened by bastions, defended by catapults mounted in purpose-built artillery emplacements, and isolated by drawbridges. Buhen was, in fact, only one of a chain of forts designed not only for war but also to protect trade routes to Egypt from the south. Nevertheless, the memory of Fort Buhen is a powerful reminder that the ancient Egyptians, for all their exquisite culture and religious architecture, were warriors with an impressive record established over thousands of years of crushing their foes. The construction of the Aswan High Dam in 1964 means that Fort Buhen and other warlike monuments along this stretch of the Nile are now submerged under the peaceful waters of Lake Nasser.

The Americas

T HE ANCIENT AMERICAN CIVILIZATIONS seem so very curious to modern eyes that their monuments have been taken as relics of the lost city of Atlantis. The Spanish Conquest of Mexico and Peru in the 16th century witnessed the destruction of native artefacts on a scale that hinders our understanding of these fascinating peoples and cultures.

Thousands of years before Europeans claimed the "New World," the lands of Central and South America were home to civilizations of great size, wealth, and sophistication. The largest and best known were the Maya, Aztecs, and Incas, but others, including the Olmec, Zapotec, Teotihuacáns, Toltec, Moche, and Nazca,

Offerings to the gods
Aztec art was often an expression of religion—this detail from an Aztec manuscript, or codex, depicts human sacrifice on temple steps.

established their own highly distinctive cultures, developing new technologies and building styles. The Olmecs, for example, who rose to prominence on the coast of southern Mexico from 1500BCE to 800BCE, introduced

KEY DATES

ca. **100**BCE Teotihuacán, a monumental city, rises and thrives in the Valley of Mexico

ca. **50** Nazca culture flourishes in Peru, and creates the Nazca lines—vast and mysterious patterns on the ground that can only be interpreted from the air

ca. **250** Classic period of Mayan civilization begins in Guatemala, Honduras, and southern Mexico

ca. **500** Hopewell culture in northern US builds burial mounds, pottery, and iron weapons

ca. **750** Collapse of Teotihuacán civilization in Mexico

1CE   **250**   **500**   **750**

ca. **1** El Mirador, Guatemala, the greatest early Mayan city, is at its height

ca. **150** Mogollon culture develops in southwestern US; interesting painted pottery is produced

ca. **378** Rivalry between leading Mayan cities Tikal and Uaxactún ends in victory for Tikal

ca. **700** In eastern Arizona, Pueblo people live in houses above ground for the first time

the first calendar and the first hieroglyphic writing in the Western hemisphere; and the Teotihuacán civilization, which flourished from *ca.* 300BCE to 500CE, taking in most of Mesoamerica, created the sensationally impressive city of Teotihuacán *(see p.71)* near Mexico City. Mayan history begins around 1500BCE reaching its zenith from 300 to 900CE, evidenced by the huge stone pyramids and temples of the Mayan heartlands and by their achievements in mathematics and astronomy, which were recorded in hieroglyphs.

Historians know more of the Aztec civilization of Mexico and the Inca Empire centered in Peru. Yet, both of these, with their magnificent irrigated cities, were undermined and all but destroyed by the Spanish. Hernán

Cortés (1485–1547), the Spanish conqueror of the Aztec Empire, brought not just firearms, cannons, and armor with him, but also the Inquisition, an insatiable greed for gold and silver, and diseases unknown to Mesoamerica. Within 70 years of his taking of Tenochtitlan, the Aztec capital, in 1521, the Aztec population had fallen from 15 million to three million; a similar fate befell the Incas.

AZTEC ACHIEVEMENTS

At its height, between about 1430 and its conquest by the Spaniards in 1521, the Aztec Empire extended over much of what is now Mexico. Aztec society had a rigid structure, guided by an all-pervasive religion that influenced styles of building; the great city of Tenochtitlan (the site of Mexico City today) included a vast temple complex, a royal palace, and numerous canals.

Aztec Sun Calendar
Originally placed on the temple in Tenochtitlan, the Sun Calendar is evidence of Aztec knowledge of astronomy and mathematics.

Andes mountains
Even today, Quechua (Inca) speakers in Peru make ritual offerings to the sacred mountains, the inspiration of so much in their architecture.

ca. **1000** Leif Ericson, the Viking explorer, reaches North America; European eyes turn to America

ca. **1250** Mayan revival; following collapse of Chichén Itzá, a new capital is built at Mayapán

ca. **1440** In a display of power and skill, Incas build a great fortress at Cuzco

ca. **15th C.** Incas expand their empire throughout the central Andes

1521 Hernando Cortez, Spanish soldier-explorer, brings down the Aztec empire in Mexico

1000 **1250** **1500**

ca. **900** Mayan civilization in southern Mexico collapses; many cities abandoned

ca. **1100** Rise of Incas, farmers led by warrior chiefs, in Peru

ca. **1325** Aztecs found Tenochtitlan, today's Mexico City, on two small islands in Lake Texcoco

ca. **1468** Death of Aztec emperor Moctezuma I

1531 Francisco Pizarro, Spanish soldier of fortune, invades and destroys Inca empire in Peru

CENTRAL AND NORTH AMERICA
ca. 300BCE–1550CE

The sheer scale of the architecture of the Aztecs, Maya, and other civilizations of what is now Mexico and Central America is impressive, even by today's standards. The conquering Spaniards were astonished by the gleaming cities they found, which made their own seem like grubby villages. Indeed, of all the world's cities at the time, only Istanbul had a population greater than that of Tenochtitlan, the Aztec capital.

The greatest builders among the old American civilizations were the Teotihuacáns. Their capital was Teotihuacán, 37 miles (60 km) north-east of present-day Mexico City. Founded around 300BCE, it reached its peak between 200 and 400CE, when its population has been estimated at up to 200,000. Teotihuacán was vast for its day: the main street, the "Avenue of the Dead", runs for at least 1.2 miles (2 km) right through the heart of the city. Measuring 148–295 ft (45–90 m) wide, the avenue was overlooked by houses raised on stone terraces, and two huge pyramids dedicated to the sun and moon *(see p.71)*. Aztec visitors called Teotihuacán "The City of the Gods." Standing among the remains today, one can almost believe that it was indeed built by giants or gods. The city was abandoned during the Toltec invasion in *ca.* 900CE. Sadly, no one has yet found inscriptions, much less clay tablets or scrolls, written in the Teotihuacán language.

MOUNTAINOUS MONUMENTS
The lasting monuments of the civilizations of Central America are stepped pyramids that rise from jungle clearings like mountain peaks. The best of these, such as the Temple of the Warriors at Chichén Itzá or the Palace of the Governors at Uxmal *(see p.73)*, are large, genuinely impressive designs and structures. And yet, we still know far too little about them. North of what today is the Mexican border, there was very little in the way of permanent architecture. With the exception of a small number of rock-face pueblos, the development of architecture in what is now the United States had to wait for the arrival of the Pilgrim Fathers and other settlers from Europe.

◁ A 145 FT (44 M) TALL TEMPLE IN THE MAYAN CITY OF TIKAL, GUATEMALA, TYPICAL OF THE STEPPED PYRAMID STRUCTURES BUILT BY THE CIVILIZATIONS OF CENTRAL AMERICA.

ELEMENTS

Stepped pyramids were the predominant form
of monumental architecture in pre-Colonial
America. These had few rooms, as interiors
mattered less than the ritual presence of these
imposing structures and the public ceremonies they
hosted; so, platforms, altars,
processional stairs, statuary, and
carving were all important.

△ **Serpent columns**
The heads of serpents
and other monsters,
often with bright eyes
and savage teeth,
project from the walls
and columns of many
temples. This particular
guardian can be found
at the Temple of the
Warriors at Chichén Itzá.

△ **Stone masks**
Grimacing stone masks
designed to inspire fear
stare from the walls of
temples and palaces.
This one at Codz-Poop,
Kabah, is of a rain god
clearly in need of
appeasement.

△ **Geometric spiral wall decoration**
Rich carved mosaics dance their way vividly across
the upper sections of the principal facades of the
Governor's Palace, Uxmal. These are based on reliefs
in the form of geometric spirals.

△ **Colonnaded halls**
Few many-columned,
or hypostyle, halls
appear to survive: here,
though, is a spectacular
example at the Temple
of the Warriors, Chichén
Itzá—a Mayan design
rivaling anything in
ancient Egypt.

Simple geometric
openings

Distinctive carved
stone roof-comb

△ **Rectilinear windows**
Rooms at the top of
ancient-American stepped
pyramids were often lit
solely by large doorways
serving as windows. Many
of these rooms appear to
have been very simple
spaces; only a very few
are vaulted.

◁ **Stepped pyramid form**
The many-tiered and immensely
steep stepped pyramid of the
temple at Tikal is one of the
best preserved, and restored,
examples of this typical
Mayan form of religious
architecture.

Steep narrow stairs
heighten drama

THE PYRAMID OF THE SUN

🪦 *ca.* 50CE 📍 TEOTIHUACÁN , MEXICO ⚒ UNKNOWN 🏛 PLACE OF WORSHIP

The Pyramid of the Sun dominates the landscape of Teotihuacán, the earliest city of Mesoamerica. It lies to the left of the "Avenue of the Dead"—a 1.2 mile (2 km) thoroughfare named by 12th-century Aztecs when they inherited the city. They thought the pyramids were burial places; in fact, they were temples.

The great pyramid at Teotihuacán, like other buildings in the region, was built using local adobe, or mud, mixed with rubble, and then faced in stone. It was adorned with plaster, reliefs, and color. There are no chambers inside the pyramid, but it is topped by a temple reached by a series of ramps and steps. Built over an earlier structure, the pyramid measures 711 x 711 ft (217 x 217 m) at its base, and it rises to a height of 187 ft (57 m).

This type of temple was part of a range of sacred pyramid mountains built across a huge area. In Teotihuacán, the pyramid is

STONE RELIEF FROM TEOTIHUACÁN

part of a complex that also includes the Pyramid of the Moon, the Temple of Quetzalcoatl, the Temple of Agriculture, and a palace. The temples would have been finished in burnished white stone or blood-red plaster. In the pre-Aztec cultures, they were centers of religious ritual, requiring daily human sacrifice; their sun-drenched steps must have run with blood.

QUETZALCOATL

This Aztec name, meaning "feathered serpent," relates to an ancient god of much earlier cultures. It is also a name given to the great warrior king who conquered many neighboring peoples in *ca.* 950–1000. The two have become confused in myth. It was believed that, after his death, the god Quetzalcoatl became the Morning Star; and it was prophesied that he would return to earth to reclaim his kingdom.

A sequence of temple-mountains
The Pyramid of the Sun (shown here) and of the Moon, along with lesser temple buildings (in foreground), all echoed the shapes of the coastal mountains.

TEMPLE OF THE GIANT JAGUAR

730 | TIKAL, NORTHERN GUATEMALA | UNKNOWN | PLACE OF WORSHIP

The Temple of the Giant Jaguar, located in the depths of the Petén rainforest, is perhaps the finest surviving Mayan temple. The pyramid marks the tomb of a long-dead ruler and rises in nine steep tiers of finely carved stone, signifying the nine lords of the Mayan underworld. The tiers climb toward a vaulted temple chamber, which is crowned with a roof-comb. This decorative cap, typical of Mayan religious buildings, resembles an upright hair comb, or that of a cockerel.

The temple is tall and narrow, unlike Mesopotamian and Egyptian pyramids. It measures 112 x 98 ft (34 x 29.8 m) at the base and rises to a height of 100 ft (30.5 m). Each tier is characterized by near-vertical walls, which further emphasize

the lofty character of the building. The temple chamber consists of a main sanctuary housing three roofed and vaulted chambers, one of which depicts the feathered serpent god, Kukulcan. The temple is reached by climbing a single monolithic flight of steep ceremonial steps, though secondary stairways are present up to the sixth level of the pyramid.

Mayan grandeur
The Temple of the Giant Jaguar, seen here in the top left of the picture, sits in the magnificent Great Plaza.

TEMPLE OF THE INSCRIPTIONS

ca. 700–800 | PALENQUE, SOUTHERN MEXICO | HUNAB PACAL | PLACE OF WORSHIP

Hidden in an area of heavy jungle in Mexico, the Temple of the Inscriptions was first discovered in 1773. The site was then lost again until its rediscovery in 1841 by the American explorers Stephens and Catherwood. The temple, although extensively restored, is one of the finest ruins uncovered at Palenque, which was a large Mayan settlement. It is 115 ft (35 m)

high, with a base measuring 184 x 131 ft (56 x 40 m). In the 1950s, while excavating the vaulted chamber that crowns the temple, Mexican Archaeologist Alberto Ruz Lhuillier discovered a secret tunnel leading to a triangular slab door. Behind this door, Ruz discovered a crypt housing the sarcophagus of Hunab Pacal, the ruler who commissioned the temple. Inscriptions and friezes relating to the rain god, Chac, also adorn one of the rooms. The stonework is very fine and may once have been rendered in red ocher, which would have made the building's original appearance even more dramatic than it is today.

Extensive remodeling
Originally built as a hefty stone rectangle, terraces and stairs were added later to evoke the familiar pyramid design of ancient Mayan temples.

PALACE OF THE GOVERNORS

⬚ 900 📍 UXMAL, MEXICO ✍ UNKNOWN 🏛 PALACE

This fine palace stands on a massive earth, rubble, and stone base, measuring 591 × 492 ft (180 × 150 m), which once supported a number of smaller buildings, too. The peak of the structure supports a trio of wide, low buildings connected by triangular stone arches. These contain a large number of vaulted rooms but are most notable for the intricate stone carvings that cover their exterior from one end to the other. The carvings bear the characteristic Mayan squared-off spiral patterns—perhaps symbolizing eternity—and other more delicate motifs, set under projecting cornices.

With its rhythmic arrangement of doorways, cornices, and consistent decoration, this is very much a

Site development
The palace is believed to be one of the latest structures to be built at Uxmal, a Mayan city whose name translates as "built three times," reflecting its extensive modifications.

classical building in Mayan terms, quite different in spirit from the same culture's stepped pyramid temples. Like all ancient American buildings, its rooms are dark and seemingly forbidding spaces; here was a culture that placed maximum emphasis on the exterior of buildings, where the sun and moon shone. Nonetheless, in terms of its use of mass and decoration, the Governor's Palace was a significant influence on the work of architect Frank Lloyd Wright during the early 20th century.

TEMPLE OF THE WARRIORS, CHICHÉN ITZÁ

⬚ ca. 1100 📍 YUCATÁN, MEXICO ✍ UNKNOWN 🏛 PLACE OF WORSHIP

The ruins of this temple, flanked on two sides by dozens of columns, are deeply impressive. Less impressive, perhaps, was the weak stone-over-timber design of the two great colonnaded halls that led to their collapse centuries ago. Still, it must have been a remarkable place when first built: it is rare to see even the skeleton of such imposing colonnaded rooms in ancient America. The

temple, crowning the stepped masonry base, contained two vaulted rooms of stone, but is best known for the serpent columns supporting its west-facing doorway. For all its architectural charms, however, the temple was a center for bloody sacrifices during the Mayan era, when the beating hearts carved from the bodies of young victims were offered daily to the gods in exchange for sunrise.

Solitary splendor
Despite its monolithic appearance, the temple was part of a thriving Mayan settlement.

CODZ-POOP

ca. 850 | **KABAH, MEXICO** | **UNKNOWN** | **PALACE**

Found on the Yucatán peninsula of Guatemala, the Codz-Poop, or Palace of Masks, is one of the finest examples of architecture from the Mayan Puuc era. The Puuc style is known for its careful balance between restrained and ornate structure, which manifests itself at Kabah in 200 or so heavy stone wall reliefs depicting the rain god Chac. These so-called "masks" cover the exterior of this fascinating and exotic palace, projecting 1.64 ft (0.5 m) or so from the surface of the walls. They increase in density and intricacy as they rise up the building, which stands on an 262 ft (80 m) square base. Judging from its size and decorative complexity, Codz-Poop was clearly an important structure, but quite what its purpose was, no one knows for sure. Archaeologists refer to it as a palace, but the dense sacred imagery of the entrance hall, which takes the form of stone reliefs, suggests that it might well have served a religious purpose. Religion was an intimate part of Mayan life, and it is not easy to separate the civic from the spiritual in their architecture, as they formed part of a ritualistic whole. However, few Mayan buildings, regardless of their role, were so dramatically decorated from base to roof-comb as this unique and mysterious piece of architecture at Kabah.

Faces of the divine
Some experts believe that the decorative masks at Kabah each represent a day of the Mayan calendar.

TEMPLE OF TLAHUIZCALPANTECUHTLI

ca. 1100 | **TULA, CENTRAL MEXICO** | **UNKNOWN** | **PLACE OF WORSHIP**

This handsomely symmetrical building from the Toltec empire has everything a visitor today might hope to see. The stepped pyramid, 141 ft (43 m) square, is topped with a temple. The walls of its five terraces are carved with friezes depicting a fierce gamut of jaguars, coyotes, and eagles devouring human hearts, and also symbols of the planet Venus. Associated with the goddess of love in European culture, Venus is here identified with Tlahuizcalpantecuhtli, Lord of the Dawn—an altogether colder and more demanding deity. The temple sanctuary, 30 ft (9 m) high, was a single large room, roofed with wooden beams resting on stone columns that represented Toltec warriors, while the temple's windows are believed to have corresponded to the alignments of Venus. Like many early Central American sites, Tula served as a kind of observatory, mapping the movements of the constellations, the transit of the planets, the waxing and waning of the moon, and the rising and setting of the sun.

Map of the heavens
The temple's design reflects the Toltec preoccupation with astronomical events.

STEP PYRAMID, CAHOKIA

🪦 *ca.* 1100 📍 CAHOKIA, ILLINOIS ⚒ UNKNOWN 🏛 PLACE OF WORSHIP

Architecture was a rare commodity in North America before the arrival of European settlers, as Native American tribes lived a seminomadic existence on the plains and rarely constructed fixed buildings. This makes the complex of temple-pyramids at Cahokia all the more fascinating.

Constructed from earth, the mounds take a variety of forms, including flat-topped and conical examples. The largest—Monks Mound—is 98 ft (30 m) high and was probably capped with a structure of some sort, perhaps of thatched timber. Cahokia cannot accurately be called a city, but it was certainly an important religious center until its abandonment around the 15th century.

Focus for worship
The pyramids at Cahokia are arranged around flat areas that were probably plazas and assembly areas.

MESA VERDE PUEBLO, COLORADO

🪦 *ca.* 1000BCE 📍 COLORADO, USA ⚒ UNKNOWN 🏛 CITY

Some of the most impressive ruins in North America are those hewn from the rock faces of canyons at a number of sites scattered through the south west. Here, local people built large clusters of buildings into the protective flanks of canyon walls, which sheltered them from the weather, wild animals, and other tribes. Quite how the different buildings were used is not known, though, as with all ancient cultures, many buildings were given over to the practice of cults and the celebration of rituals. There

are no grand temples, but the pueblo buildings are nonetheless quite impressive: some rise several floors, and others feature round walls. The way in which the buildings are a part of the natural landscape imbues them with a special quality—the antithesis of architecture that has so often sought to transcend and challenge nature.

Stone haven
Though the pueblos of ancient America have long been abandoned, rock dwellings are still in use in other parts of the world, such as Spain and Tunisia.

SOUTH AMERICA
ca. 600BCE–1550CE

The vast Inca Empire stretched 2,500 miles (4,000 km) from Peru down through Chile and across to the Amazon rainforests. It was a short-lived phenomenon, at its height between 1438 and 1532. Despite the terrible destruction wrought by the Spanish conquistadores, the Incas handed down to us some of the most impressive of all medieval civil engineering, in terms of roads, terracing, and hydraulic systems.

The Incas were not the simple, bloodthirsty savage people depicted by those who conquered and demeaned them. Unlike their contemporaries in Europe, they were clean and kept their cities clear of garbage and sewage. But in truth, we know comparatively little about these people, whose civilization was at its peak just over 500 years ago. The reason is writing—or the lack of it. The Incas did not write, although they did have *quipu*, a form of record-keeping using sequences of knots tied in fabric cords, which has yet to be decoded. Because there is no body of Inca literature, or even matter-of-fact accounts of their history and way of life, the Incas can seem as distant as the mythical Bronze-Age "druids" who built Stonehenge, or the long-forgotten Teotihuacáns *(see pp.69, 71).* Lacking a written legacy, our insights into Inca culture must be drawn from artefacts and the haunting remains of their magnificent cities, stone buildings, roads, and landscape art.

INCAN ARCHITECTURE

Inca cities were not the dry places we trek through today; rather, they were alive with the sounds of water pouring from stone spouts into basins and chuckling down the sides of stairways. Sadly, the Incas were only just getting into their architectural stride when they were destroyed by disease and other forces beyond their control. Even so, they left us such unfinished gems as the red porphyry temple at Ollantaytambo near Machu Picchu *(see p.81),* whose massive walls were assembled like vertical jigsaw puzzles without mortar to hold them together. They also left us the foundations on which the modern city of Cuzco stands today, and the hillside terraces that Peruvian farmers still depend on for their living.

◁ **THE INCA MOUNTAIN STRONGHOLD OF MACHU PICCHU, 7,875 FT (2,400 M) ABOVE SEA LEVEL, WAS NEVER FOUND BY THE SPANIARDS, YET IT WAS ABANDONED AROUND THE TIME OF THE CONQUEST.**

ELEMENTS

The great strength of Inca architecture is its heroic masonry construction. This supported terraces, gardens, fountains, and a way of life far more colorful than surviving stones suggest. One of the great tragedies of Inca architecture is that so much of it was destroyed or built over by Spanish invaders. While the conquistadores failed to discover Machu Picchu, it, too, fell into ruin after it was eventually abandoned.

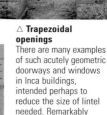

△ **Trapezoidal openings**
There are many examples of such acutely geometric doorways and windows in Inca buildings, intended perhaps to reduce the size of lintel needed. Remarkably robust, many have stood the test of time.

▽ **Wall masks**
This lively use of sculpture adorns the stone-built Gate of the Sun at Tiahuanaco. Many stone gateways originally stood between adobe (mud) walls that have long disappeared.

△ **Wall reliefs**
The long adobe walls of Chan Chan, capital of the kingdom of Chimor, are decorated with precise parallel grooves and bands of repeated, stylized and abstract designs, carefully carved to be virtually identical.

△ **Terracing**
Stepped walls defined mountainside settlements and provided ledges for terraces. Well irrigated, these were used for agriculture, so that city and countryside were one.

Individual stones become smaller as the walls rise to reduce load

▽ **Mortarless stonework**
Inca stonework, seen here at Machu Picchu, was immensely skilful. Walls were built without mortar. Stones cut with great precision were locked into one another to shape earthquake-resistant walls of great strength and durability.

Stones shaped at angles for strength when interlocked

TEMPLE OF THE SUN

📷 ca. 200–600   📍 MOCHE, PERU   ✍ UNKNOWN   🏛 PLACE OF WORSHIP

The architecture of pre-Incan civilization in South America is hard to find because, built of adobe, rubble, and largely unworked materials, it has eroded and vanished. A large number of ancient monuments seem little more than natural outcrops of raised earth—hard to read as architecture—and still wait to be discovered.

What remains of the Temple of the Sun at Moche, on the Pacific coast of Peru, is a highly eroded, yet massive, stepped pyramid measuring 748 × 446 ft (228 × 136 m) at the base and 134 ft (41 m) high. The ancient superstructure comprised five terraces with an offset, seven-stepped pyramid on top. Whatever its original appearance, finish, and decoration may have been, this was clearly a major religious monument of its day.

Eroded monument
This great, terraced mound of earth in coastal Peru was discovered to be an ancient pyramid temple, similar in design to the ziggurats of Mesopotamia.

CHAN CHAN

📷 ca. 1200–1470   📍 CHAN CHAN, PERU   ✍ UNKNOWN   🏛 CITY

Chan Chan is the capital of the pre-Incan kingdom of Chimor. It covered an area of 8 sq miles (21 km²), its ceremonial center alone occupying 2.3 sq miles (6 km²). The city appears to have been made up of nine vast quadrangles, or citadels, each enclosed by 29 ft (9 m) adobe walls designed as protection from coastal winds.

Each of the nine quadrangles was occupied by hundreds of more or less identical buildings made of mud bricks, coated with adobe, and inscribed with decorative patterns. The city seems to have been well supplied with water: not only is there evidence of an irrigation system, but the center of the city also boasts reservoirs complete with walk-in wells containing what would have been purified water.

Palaces and temples in the symmetrical, ceremonial center of the city were decorated with brick mosaics and reliefs. The formal, angular plan of the city, sometimes described as a pattern of broken triangles, is highly characteristic of South American empire builders, right through to the fall of the Incas in the 16th century.

Pre-Incan precision
Symmetry and detailed decoration were very important to this civilization, exemplified here at Chan Chan.

SAQSAYWAMAN

📷 *ca.* 1520 📍 CUZCO, PERU ✍ UNKNOWN 🏛 FORTIFICATION

Cuzco was once the Inca capital. Outside the modern city of the same name stand the extensive remains of what is commonly referred to as the fortress of Saqsaywaman, although no one is really sure what the building was and what it was used for. The ruins could well be the base of a religious complex or ceremonial center of one kind or another. All we know for certain is that the surviving base of this ambitious Inca design is constructed from well-cut stones, slotted together with great precision and without need for mortar. The huge stones suggest the scale of architecture that once rose above them. The base of the building measures 1,312 x 820 ft (400 x 250 m). It is located on a natural ridge with a low range of mountains behind and what appears to be a flat, open space, presumably man-made, in front. This would have made it a good setting for a military as well as a civic or religious building. Sadly, a devastating earthquake in the 19th century put paid to Saqsaywaman, so its purpose may well remain a mystery for as long as we find the Inca civilization a source of fascination.

Master masons
Dry-stone walling on a titanic scale forms the lower ramparts of this building. Its precise function remains unknown.

GATE OF THE SUN, TIAHUANACO

📷 *ca.* 600–1000 📍 TIAHUANACO, NORTHWEST BOLIVIA ✍ UNKNOWN 🏛 GATEWAY

One of the most important monuments of the great ceremonial site in the Titicaca Basin on the northwest border of modern-day Bolivia, the ceremonial city gateway at Tiahuanaco is, effectively, an enormous stone sculpture cut from a single block of stone. Measuring approximately 10 x 12½ ft (3 x 3.8 m), its weight is estimated at 10 tons: a huge stone to maneuver into place some 1,000–1,500 years ago. Above a rectangular opening, emphasized by a plain recess, there is a deep and slightly projecting frieze, in the center of which is carved a formalized representation of the local god Viracocha, from whose head the sun's rays appear to flame out. In his hands, stylized staffs may represent thunderbolts. Flanking this well-cut central figure are 48 small rectangular reliefs depicting figures, some with human heads and some with condors' heads, running toward the god.

The Gate of the Sun is a fine piece of masonry and an excellent example of skilled local stone carving, and yet this isolated gateway is a terrible tease: we walk through, either way, into nothingness. The once-important city it led into, built most probably of adobe, has long since disappeared as civilizations rose and fell and wars and weather took their toll.

MACHU PICCHU

🗓 *ca.* 1500   🏴 PERU   ⚔ UNKNOWN   🏛 CITY

Set high in the Peruvian Andes, the ruins of the Inca city of Machu Picchu are among the world's most magnetic tourist sights. Until recently reaching this mountain aerie meant a long, heart-pounding trek led by local guides. Today, globetrotting tourists arrive with nonchalant ease in air-conditioned comfort.

Spanish colonialists, the collapse of high Incan culture, the elements, and natural calamities have done their best to wipe the historic architecture of Peru off the map. The remote and haunting remains of Machu Picchu, however, allow us to see the great, rigid power of Inca architecture at its best and most daunting. The site of this powerful walled city, lying between two mountain peaks some 3,000 ft (900 m) above the Urubamba River, was a revered place long before the Incas began to build here with real purpose in about 1400. Inside the

TEMPLE OF THE SUN, MACHU PICCHU

well-cut gray granite walls are the remains of a wide range of public buildings including palaces, baths, temples, storehouses, and burial grounds. There are about 150 houses, gathered in groups around communal courtyards and aligned in terraces. The various parts of the city, on their complex series of terraces, were connected by grand stone stairs. One of the important remains found at Machu Picchu is the Intihuatana stone, used in an astronomical ritual for "tying" the sun to the earth at the midday equinox, in the perpetually vain hope of slowing its movement across the sky.

INCA INFRASTRUCTURE

The city of Machu Picchu was a near-perfect model of self-sufficiency. The construction of the various buildings was entirely from local materials, whether stone or rubble. Maize was grown in an area given over to agriculture, while elsewhere there were livestock enclosures. Water from natural springs poured through stone channels built around the perimeter walls so that all parts of the city were irrigated. Masonry terraces throughout the city would have contained gardens.

Magical city
As evening falls, tourist vehicles leave Machu Picchu to the winds, walkers, soaring condors, and the spirit of the Incas.

The Classical
world

T HE CLASSICAL ERA is the point at which those living in the Western
world begin to feel comfortable with ancient history and familiar
with the story of architecture. With the rise of Greece, and then of
Rome, we are in a world of gods, heroes, legends, buildings, cities, and
a language and history that we can readily relate to and comprehend.

Ancient Rome—an enormous city
with, by the year 200, a population of
very possibly 1.25 million drawn from
across its empire—is, for all its faults,
utterly compelling. This is partly
because we know a great deal about
it first-hand, from the Romans
themselves; not just from monumental
inscriptions, nor from laws, literature,
and poetry, but from the intimacy of
private letters, jokes, and graffiti. We
know, for instance, that Julius Caesar
was kept awake by the noise of traffic
bringing goods into the center of the
city before dawn. We know that
Roman mothers sent gifts of socks to
sons stationed on Hadrian's Wall. And
we know, in precise detail, how
Romans dressed, what they ate, and
the rituals of their day. We are even
a little jealous of their great civic
buildings, especially the public baths
that truly must have been wonders
of their, and any other, age.

And, because Classical culture
has been valued through the ages
by Goths, Ostrogoths, and Visigoths,

by Holy Roman Emperors and Anglo-
Saxon kings, the Romans, especially,
and through them the Greeks, have
been part and parcel of Western
civilization, from the founding of
Athens to the Fall of Rome and right
through to the present day. Just look
around you and see how many
modern buildings owe so much to

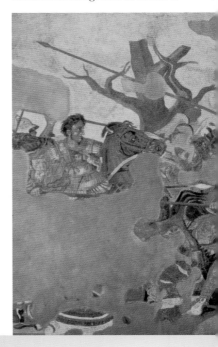

The Battle of Issus
One Classical culture pays tribute to another in this
detail from a Roman mosaic showing Alexander
the Great's victory as Persia fell to the Greeks.

KEY DATES

753BCE Rome
is founded, in
mythological history,
by Romulus and Remus
on the Seven Hills

509BCE The last
king of Rome is
expelled, and the
city-state becomes
a republic

347BCE Death of Plato,
the hugely influential
Greek philosopher and
author of *The Republic*

146BCE Rome
conquers Greece at
the battle of Corinth,
and destroys Corinth
in the process

750 BCE   **500BCE**   **250BCE**

776BCE First Olympic
Games held by Greeks,
a week of competitive
events and religious
ceremonies

600BCE The first
Roman forum is
built and some of
the first Latin
inscriptions made

447BCE Work
begins on the
construction of
the Acropolis
in Athens

ca. **332BCE**
Alexander the
Great, king of
Macedonia,
conquers Persia

213BCE War machines
designed by Greek
mathematician
Archimedes save
Syracuse from
Roman attack

ANCIENT ATHENS

Our sense of what an ideal city might be is derived to a great extent from Athens in around 450BCE, a time when the city was at the height of its power, influence, and artistry. Long-accepted around the world as the apotheosis of the successful democratic city state, Athens was compact and bustling, a mix of magnificent formal buildings, thriving market places, august seats of learning, and tightly clustered housing, all founded on the city's military might under the leadership of Pericles (495–429BCE).

The Acropolis of Athens
Controversially, Pericles spent revenues collected to fund wars against Persia on building peerless architecture on Athens' fortified hill, the Acropolis.

ca. **50BCE** The Gauls are defeated by Roman legions under the command of Julius Caesar

79 Vesuvius erupts, and the town of Pompeii is buried under volcanic ash

395 Roman Empire divided into western and eastern halves

476 Fall of Rome and overthrow of last emperor, Romulus Augustulus

1071 Normans, led by Robert Guiscard, conquer southern Italy from the eastern Roman empire

1CE | **500** | **1000** | **1500**

44BCE Assassination of Julius Caesar, leading to end of Roman Republic and birth of Empire

216 The luxurious Baths of Caracalla are built in Rome

393 Theodosius forbids the pagan Olympic Games and closes the temple of Zeus at Olympia

812 The eastern Roman emperor recognizes Charlemagne as emperor of Rome

1453 The Ottoman Turks under Mehmet II capture Constantinople, signaling the end of the Byzantine empire

Raphael's *The School of Athens*
The highly influential Greek philospher Plato founded his famous school in the Athenian suburb of Academy in 387BCE; it was closed by Justinian in 529CE.

the architecture of Greece and Rome. Look at the typefaces in this book: they are essentially Roman in design.

AN UNBROKEN LINE

The Renaissance is still presented in many history books as a kind of fault line between the medieval and the modern world, but this is not true. Throughout the encircling gloom of what are known as the Dark Ages, the light of Rome shone through. In any case, Roman architecture, Greek philosophy, and Classical learning

thrived and metamorphosed in Constantinople and Byzantium long after the Fall of Rome. Theodoric, Ostrogoth King of Ravenna (493–526), whose own city was nourished by the architecture of Byzantium, sent masons to Rome to restore the ancient monuments. Anglo-Saxon architects studied in Rome, then returned to England to build in a "Roman" style in the 10th and 11th centuries, before this became *de rigueur* under the rule of William the Conqueror (r.1066–87)—whose style, from his armies' uniforms to the arches of his cathedrals, was clearly based on Rome. As for the early Christian church, it not only took over Roman

misfortune, perhaps, to have fallen under Ottoman rule for so many centuries, its architecture falling into ruin and becoming ever more remote from developments in Western Europe. It seems hard to believe that the Parthenon once sprouted the onion dome of a mosque through its roof, or that it was used as a gunpowder store by the Turks. It blew up, of course, which is why the Parthenon was a ruin when rediscovered by Western European travelers.

Again, though, these 18th-century adventurers were hardly exploring unknown historical depths. The learning of ancient Greece had been handed down through Rome and the Church. Plato and Aristotle were never forgotten, nor were the great playwrights. They still speak to us powerfully today—as does the Parthenon, for all its overfamiliarity.

ROMAN COINS

The proliferation of Roman coinage went hand-in-hand with the meteoric growth of Rome from a city state to a republic dominating Italy, and eventually to one of the world's most extensive, powerful, and long-lived empires. By the time of the first emperor of Rome, Augustus (27BCE–14CE), coins had developed to the point where they set the look for those we use today throughout the world. The Romans also gave us the word "money," after a temple dedicated to the goddess Juno Moneta became associated with the mint of Rome.

Roman coins
Early Roman coins featured the heads of ancient gods, but from the late 1st century BCE, these were replaced with portraits of emperors.

temples but also adopted the Roman basilica as the model for its ever more lavish places of worship. You can find Catholic churches in the guise of brick Diocletian basilicas built in London suburbs as late as the 1930s.

GREEK CLASSICISM

The architecture of Greece, however, seems more ascetic, chaste, and perfect than that of Rome. In fact, it was long idealized. The Parthenon was, perhaps from the day it was finished, the Holy Grail of Western architecture, a design so balanced that nothing could be added or taken away from it without destroying it. It was Greece's

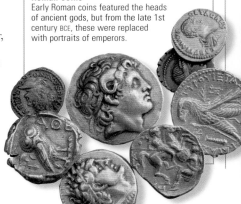

ANCIENT GREECE
ca. 1500BCE–350BCE

From the mid-18th century, Greek temples, statuary, and literature became admired as examples of the highest possible art. The Athens of Pericles, or the Golden Age, lasted from approximately 460 to 370 BCE. It was during this time that political democracy and the rule of law were established, and the hugely charismatic monuments of the Acropolis, including the Parthenon *(see pp.94–5)*, were built.

We know Pericles (*ca.* 495–429BCE) largely through the writings of Plutarch, who lived 500 years later. As a result, this key Athenian figure is as much the stuff of legend as of fact. Nevertheless, it does appear that he was both a popular and enduring leader who, over 40 years, rebuilt the center of Athens with peerless style and precision. He also built up the navy, upon which the imperial city state depended.

FULL-BLOODED ARCHITECTURE
The Greek architecture of this period, although perfectly proportioned, has often been portrayed as cold. This is not true. It was 18th-century Prussian scholars who promoted the notion that Classical Athens was a kind of ideal German military state, with sunshine and olives. Their writings influenced European and American scholars and generations of teachers, who insisted that Pericles' Athens was an upright, scholarly place. It certainly produced great minds and was a formidable fighting machine, yet it was never dull. Athenian buildings may have encouraged this view of ideal purity; they mostly followed the simple principles of trabeated (post-and-lintel) construction, resulting in an architecture of apparent regimented horizontality. It was also an architecture rooted in timber construction (it has been called "carpentry in marble.") But forget the chilly fragments of Greek temples and statuary you see in museums, and imagine these buildings in a world of rich color, song, sex, and spirited conversation; of brutal war, bustling markets, and arcane religious ceremonies. Imagine them, too, in a glorious mountain landscape. Then you will see them for what they were: highly refined frames for a distinct and very much warm-blooded culture.

◁ THE GREEK TEMPLE OF ATHENA AT PRIENE, IN MODERN TURKEY, WAS BUILT IN THE 4TH CENTURY BCE BY PYTHIUS, ARCHITECT OF THE MAUSOLEUM OF HALICARNASSUS. ONLY FIVE OF ITS 66 FLUTED IONIAN COLUMNS STILL STAND.

ELEMENTS

Ancient Greece is truly the cradle of Western architecture. The elements of Greek architecture shown here are the building blocks for generations of designs across the Western world. Although highly familiar, Greek architecture retains its power, presence, and noble beauty, as well as its inherent simplicity, more than 2,500 years on from its zenith.

◁ **Column entasis**
Entasis is the way in which columns are swollen so that, with perspective, they appear to be perfectly straight.

△ **Friezes**
These comprised metopes, or sculpted panels, and triglyphs: vertical panels divided into three by two v-shaped channels.

Sculpted panels featured battle scenes

Sculpture depicts fallen horse and warrior

◁ **Sculpted frieze in pediment**
Pediments were platforms for superb displays of sculpture, often glorifying war. This example is from the Parthenon.

▽ **Caryatids**
These sacred maidens stand in for columns. They are best known for their supporting, or perhaps starring, role at the Erechtheion, Athens.

Doric capital (top of column) is composed of two simple elements

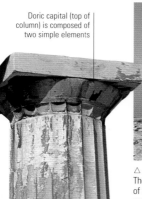

△ **Doric order**
The Doric order, shown here at the Parthenon in Athens, was the oldest of the three Greek orders that ruled the design of columns and their entablature, the area above the capitals. Early columns were slender, but the design developed into a strong, plain, resolutely masculine element.

△ **Ionic order**
The Ionic order, shown here at the Erechtheion, Athens, is characterized by a capital decorated with pairs of volutes, or spirals, on either side of the columns. The columns were normally carved with 24 flutes—concave grooves that run along the shaft of the column.

Scroll-like volutes on either side of capital

Shaft of columns is decorated with flutes

Stylized acanthus leaves curve up and out from the pronounced capital

△ **Corinthian order**
The Corinthian (here at the Temple of Zeus) first appeared as a decorative version of the Ionic order in the 5th century BCE. Initially, it was used only in internal colonnades. The capital is said to be based on a basket of acanthus leaves.

PALACE OF KING MINOS

⚰ DESTROYED 1375BCE   📍 KNOSSOS, CRETE, GREECE   ⚒ DAEDALUS (IN MYTH)   🏛 PALACE

The Palace of King Minos has been immortalized in Greek mythology as the Labyrinth, home to the Minotaur—a terrifying, man-eating, half-man half-bull. The Greek hero, Theseus, finally killed the Minotaur with the help of King Minos's daughter, Ariadne, and the inventor and craftsman, Daedalus, who had been forced to design the Labyrinth for the powerful king.

Two stories high and based around a large open courtyard, the palace comprises a bewildering range of rooms, some colonnaded and ceremonial, others designed for storage and manufacturing of various kinds. What has been called the Throne Room is a windowless chamber.

The *piano nobile*—a floor raised one story above ground level and containing the principal social apartments—has many well-lit and well-ventilated chambers. Far from being the grim place of Greek mythology, Minos's palace boasted good sanitation and drainage, shelter from the sun, gardens, and

THE LEGEND OF THE LABYRINTH

The complex plan of the immense palace at Knossos goes a long way toward explaining the roots of this enduring myth. The palace itself may well be the labyrinth around which the ancient Greeks wove their tales; King Minos, who adorned his power base with statues of bulls, was possibly the Minotaur. Daedalus, who was the legendary architect of the Cretan palace, finally flew away on wings from Crete to Sicily with his son, Icarus.

grand rooms offering fine views. Some of these were reconstructed by the British archaeologist, Sir Arthur Evans, in the 1920s. The rambling and decidedly unclassical plan of the palace has been put down to the organic growth of the building over generations, rather than to the scheming mind of King Minos.

Earthquake survivor
The remains of the ancient palace at Knossos are all that survive of several important Cretan palaces destroyed by major earthquakes in *ca.* 1625BCE and *ca.* 1375BCE.

THE GREEK CITY

The ancient Greeks were loyal to their cities (which could also be states) rather than to their country, as modern peoples might be. During the classical years of ancient Greece, when Hippodamus was at work and Athens was being adorned with its most famous temples, the Greek city reached its peak—a home to democracy, humanism, the arts, and the beginnings of town planning.

The term "ancient Greece" is used to refer to the whole Greek-speaking world in ancient times: not just to the Greek peninsula, but also to settlements in Cyprus, the Aegean coast of Turkey, Sicily, southern Italy, across further stretches of eastern Europe, and north Africa. Athens was the chief city, fortified by the Acropolis, the home of the Parthenon (see pp.94–5). It was also the home of many of the great teachers and philosophers, such as Socrates, Plato, Aeschylus, Sophocles, and Euripides.

Hippodamus of Miletus (498–408BCE) was the first historical figure associated with urban planning. He laid out the cities of

Slaughter in art
Warfare was a major preoccupation in both art and city planning.

Miletus, Priene, and Olynthus along rational, gridiron plans: straight, parallel streets with right-angled intersections. This type of plan optimized wind flow to keep living spaces warm in winter and cool in summer.

Hippodamus's concern was to build cities for trade and peace. However, Aristotle (384–22BCE)— who was born in Stagira, Greece— was worried about the orthogonal, or right-angled, layouts of cities planned by Hippodamus. He could see how easily these could be attacked by invading armies. Aristotle therefore recommended town plans following a more natural growth pattern, as these could baffle enemy soldiers.

The Acropolis of ancient Athens
The original Acropolis was an early fortification, probably with a palace. It took the shape we now recognize around the 5th century BCE, with the building of many temples and the great Parthenon.

THE PARTHENON

🖵 438BCE 📍 ATHENS, GREECE ✏ ICTINUS & CALLICRATES 🏛 PLACE OF WORSHIP

PARTHENON—EXTERIOR VIEW

Commissioned by Pericles at the height of ancient Greek power, from architects Ictinus and Callicrates with the sculptor Phidias, the Parthenon has long been considered the perfect Greek temple. Exquisitely proportioned, it rises from the heart of the Acropolis. Inside, under a painted and gilded roof, the main space housed a magnificent statue of the goddess Athena Parthenos. The only light source was through the great bronze doors of the temple. The fluted Doric columns that surround two interior chambers are 34 ft (10.4 m) high. These curve to give the illusion of perfect straight lines from a distance. Known as "entasis," this subtle distortion is a feature

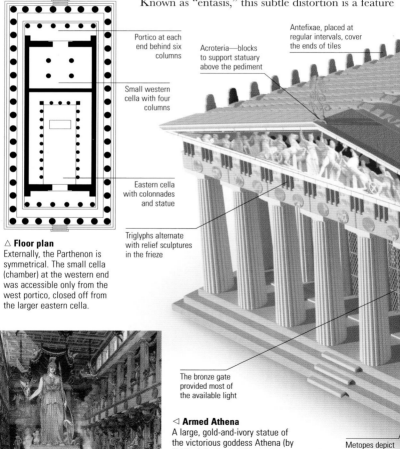

Portico at each end behind six columns

Small western cella with four columns

Eastern cella with colonnades and statue

Triglyphs alternate with relief sculptures in the frieze

Acroteria—blocks to support statuary above the pediment

Antefixae, placed at regular intervals, cover the ends of tiles

The bronze gate provided most of the available light

Metopes depict real and mythical wars

△ **Floor plan**
Externally, the Parthenon is symmetrical. The small cella (chamber) at the western end was accessible only from the west portico, closed off from the larger eastern cella.

◁ **Armed Athena**
A large, gold-and-ivory statue of the victorious goddess Athena (by Phidias) dominated the eastern chamber of the temple.

of the entire building, to ensure visually perfect lines. Above the columns, the temple was once surrounded by a marble frieze of fine relief sculptures. In the late 6th century, the Parthenon was converted into a Christian church, then in 1458 it became a mosque. In 1687, under attack from Venice, gunpowder that was stored there exploded and ruined the revered temple.

△ **Elgin Marbles**
Sculptures removed from the site in the 19th century by Lord Elgin are now held in the British Museum.

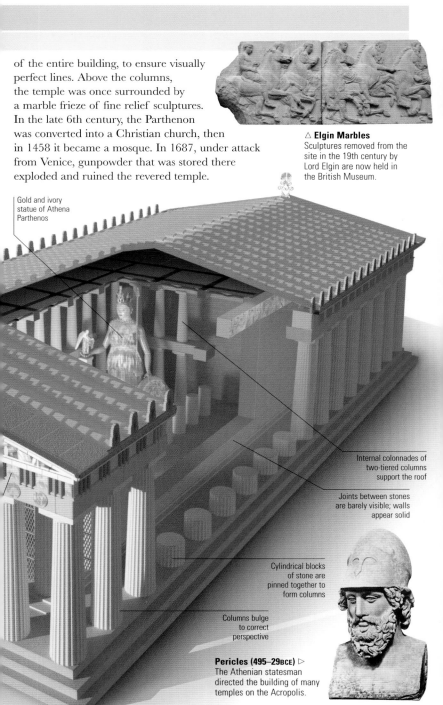

Gold and ivory statue of Athena Parthenos

Internal colonnades of two-tiered columns support the roof

Joints between stones are barely visible; walls appear solid

Cylindrical blocks of stone are pinned together to form columns

Columns bulge to correct perspective

Pericles (495–29BCE) ▷
The Athenian statesman directed the building of many temples on the Acropolis.

TEMPLE OF APHAIA

🏺 *ca.* 490BCE   🏴 AEGINA, GREECE   ✍ UNKNOWN   🏛 PLACE OF WORSHIP

On the island of Aegina near Athens stands the Temple of Aphaia. Dedicated at first to the goddess of hunting, it was later given over to the worship of Athena, goddess of wisdom. This was a fine example of a Doric temple at the outset of the golden age of ancient Greek architecture. Half as wide as it is long, the temple is fronted on its pedimented ends by six fluted Doric columns, and along its sides by twelve. Inside, the temple featured superimposed Doric colonnades along the length of its central hall, or cella. This is where the monumental statue of a temple's divinity stood. Simple and geometrically satisfying, the structure was built of local limestone, marble, and terracotta. Its most important feature, from a 19th-century museum curator's point of view, was the west pediment, animated with scenes of warriors fighting to the death during the battles of Troy while a serenely detached Athena stands between them like some divine referee. This pediment is now in the Neo-Classical halls of the Glyptothek Museum, Munich.

Monumental work
All but three of the outer columns were carved from a single stone.

TEMPLE OF NEPTUNE, PAESTUM

🏺 *ca.* 460BCE   🏴 CAMPANIA, ITALY   ✍ UNKNOWN   🏛 PLACE OF WORSHIP

Popularly known as the Temple of Neptune, this handsome Doric temple was actually dedicated to the goddess Hera. Although one of the best preserved of all Greek temples, it is actually south of Naples on the Italian mainland; Paestum was a Greek colony. The setting is beautiful, and the temple is often occupied today by tourists striking Byronic attitudes. The temple is faced front and rear by pediments supported by six Doric columns; their entasis is marked, giving them a slightly elephantine form, but the temple is no less impressive for this. The sides feature 14 columns, and the interior is characterized by long rows of superimposed columns. Many history books suggest that the Romans took up their own version of Greek architecture after their conquest of Greece, but the temples at Paestum demonstrate that the Romans were quite familiar with the glories of Doric temples some hundreds of years before the birth of the Roman Empire. The Doric order, given powerful expression at Paestum, was the first of the three Greek orders and dates back to the 7th century BCE, when timber temples gave way to stone successors like this one.

Pillars of support
Six fluted and broad-beamed Doric columns support massive pediments at either end of the temple.

THESEION (TEMPLE OF HEPHAESTUS)

ca. 449BCE ATHENS, GREECE UNKNOWN PLACE OF WORSHIP

Standing at the foot of the Acropolis hill, this apparently well preserved Doric temple was completed shortly before construction began on the Parthenon *(see pp.94–5)*. It was converted into a Greek Orthodox church in the 13th century, which explains why it has survived so well on the outside. Inside, however, it was reconstructed with an apse to adapt it to Orthodox ritual. Originally the temple was dedicated to Hephaestus, the Greek god of fire and the forge: it was once surrounded by foundries and workshops. The temple is known as the Theseion because surviving metopes depict scenes from the life of Theseus, who killed the Minotaur in the labyrinth at Knossos. Pediments and cornices are supported by Doric columns that are much slimmer than those at Paestum and demonstrate how the Doric order continued to develop into the golden age of 5th-century BCE Greek architecture. The earliest Doric temples, at Delphi and Corfu, date from *ca.* 600BCE; their development had very nearly been perfected in the elegant design of the Theseion.

Changed perspective
These elegant columns are a far cry from earlier, wooden temples yet are in essence stylized tree trunks.

ERECHTHEION

ca. 406BCE ATHENS, GREECE UNKNOWN PLACE OF WORSHIP

Best known for its porch of caryatids— the sculpted stone maidens that form the columns on its north portico—the Erechtheion is one of the most unusual and elegant of the buildings on the Acropolis. Its irregular plan—extremely rare in largely symmetrical and mathematically perfect Greek architecture—was arrived at so that the building could perform three roles, an early example of an intentionally multipurpose building: it covered the site where Poseidon was said to have left his trident marks in the rocks of the Acropolis; it housed the shrine of the legendary Greek king, Erechtheus, after whom the temple was named; and it enshrined an antique and much revered wooden statue of Athena, protectress of the city, that had earlier been sent away from Athens at the time of the Persian invasion.

Reconstructed at least twice since the early 19th century, the Erechtheion is today far from its original self. All six of the caryatids that support the porch are replicas. Of the originals, Lord Elgin took one to London for

Supporting role
Caryatids had both a practical function (as supporting columns) and a symbolic one. Their male counterparts are known as atlantes (the plural of Atlas).

"safekeeping" in the early 19th century, while the other five are housed in the Acropolis Museum, Athens. Another set of replicas graces Euston Road, London, supporting the northeast porch of the early 19th-century Neo-Classical St. Pancras Church *(see p.356)*.

TEMPLE OF ATHENA NIKE

🏛 *ca.* 421 BCE   📍 ATHENS, GREECE   ✍ UNKNOWN   🏛 PLACE OF WORSHIP

This fine example of an Acropolis temple was built for Nike—the winged goddess of victory—during the Peloponnesian War between Athens and Sparta, at a time when the glory days of Athens as a great city state were over. The theme of victory is evident in the relief sculpture on the entablature frieze, which depicts the Athenians' victories in battle. (Parts of the frieze are now housed in the British Museum in London.)

The temple is surprisingly small, at just over 13 ft (4 m) in height, with a base measuring 27 x 18 ft (8.2 x 5.4 m). It has a portico of four short and sturdy Ionic columns in the front and back of the cella—the principal room in a Greek temple in which the statue depicting the

temple's patron deity stood. The Ionic order was adopted by the Athenians in the 5th century BCE, and the style is defined by the scroll-like volutes of the capitals that top the columns. These were inspired by a number of natural sources, including rams' horns, nautilus shells, and Egyptian lotus flowers.

Two faces
One grand entrance of this tiny temple overlooked Athens, while another welcomed those approaching from the Acropolis.

CHORAGIC MONUMENT OF LYSICRATES

🏛 334 BCE   📍 ATHENS, GREECE   ✍ UNKNOWN   🏛 MONUMENT

The Choragic Monument, also known as the "Lantern of Diogenes," is a small marble rotunda built to commemorate the victory of the Chorus of Lysicrates in a Dionysiac music contest in 335 BCE; it originally displayed the bronze tripod that was awarded as their prize. The graceful composition demonstrates one of the earliest known uses of the elaborate Corinthian order in Greece, said to be the invention of the Athenian sculptor Callimachus, who was inspired by the way in which an acanthus plant had grown from a basket on the grave of a Corinthian maiden.

Choral appreciation
The Choragic monument was built as a celebration of culture rather than of the more usual gods and wars.

The monument is decorated with six half Corinthian columns and stands on a round base of three steps. The colonnade supports three bands of decorated friezes that represent images from the life of the Greek god Dionysos. The monument is fully preserved thanks to French Capuchin monks, who bought it in 1669 and incorporated it into their monastery.

In the 19th century, the Choragic monument became something of a standard-bearer for the Greek revival in Europe, especially in Britain and France. Several imitations of the monument can be found in English landscape gardens, perhaps most convincingly on Calton Hill, in Edinburgh, Scotland—the would-be "Athens of the North."

TEMPLE OF ARTEMIS

📷 ca. 356BCE 📍 EPHESUS, WESTERN TURKEY ✍ DEMETRIUS & PAEONIUS OF EPHESUS 🏛 PLACE OF WORSHIP

The Temple of Artemis at Ephesus was one of the original Seven Wonders of the World, although it owed this accolade perhaps as much to its sheer scale as to its artistic merits. However, famous sculptors, such as Scopas, were employed in its rich decoration, and according to legend, the lavish interior of the temple was filled with silver statuary and magnificent paintings.

Adorned with sculpture, boasting perhaps as many as 117 Ionic columns, and reached by steps set between bronze statues of Amazonian warriors, the flamboyant Temple of Artemis was very different in spirit and execution from the Parthenon *(see pp.94–5)*, completed over 80 years earlier. While the Parthenon and other 5th-century Greek temples were more colorful than many sober-minded 19th-century European scholars wanted them to be, they were far more restrained than this showy, even garish temple. Although perhaps a little unfair, it could be said that the Temple of Artemis is symbolic of the fall in artistic and imaginative powers that mirrored the decline in the Greek ascendancy in general, and Athenian power in particular.

Reconstructions of this "wonderous" building—the fifth temple to have been built on the site—have been based on very little real evidence and generous helpings of wishful thinking and invention. What does seem certain, however, is that the temple

ARTEMIS OF EPHESUS

Artemis of Ephesus, the mother goddess of fertility and protectress of women in childbirth, was quite different from the Greek Artemis, virgin goddess of hunting. The Ephesians' deity, also known as Diana, was often pictured adorned with overt symbols of fertility, such as multiple breasts or the upper body adorned with eggs. Early Ephesian entrepreneurs made a roaring trade in Artemis figurines, which they sold to worshipers visiting the temple.

was fronted by an impressive portico composed of eight Ionic columns, more widely spaced toward the center. The central span of the building may have been more than 260 ft (80 m), which is expansive for a Greek temple. We also know that the bases of many of the columns were richly carved and that the whole building was raised on a prominent base. Indeed, in many ways the Temple of Artemis was the prototype, in spirit if not in fact, of the grandiose Roman temples that were to rise some two or three hundred years later.

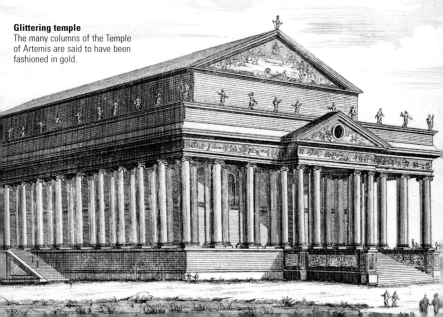

Glittering temple
The many columns of the Temple of Artemis are said to have been fashioned in gold.

THEATER OF EPIDAURUS

🏛 350BCE   📍 ARGOLIS, GREECE   ✍ POLYKLEITOS THE YOUNGER   🏛 THEATRE

Greatly lauded in its time for its beauty, symmetry, acoustics, and location, the magnificent theater at the Sanctuary of Asklepios, Epidaurus, hosted theatrical performances by such famous, and still very much performed, dramatists as Aeschylus, Sophocles, and Aristophanes. Massive in scale, it measures 387 ft (118 m) in diameter and can seat up to 13,000 spectators.

Although exposed to the elements, which, it has to be said, are rather benign in this part of the world, its design has been hard to improve upon. Indeed, the theater at Epidaurus has been the model for many fine theaters in modern times. It was one of the first all-stone Greek theaters. Its design is made up of three parts: auditorium, or seating area; orchestra (meaning the "dancing floor," or stage); and skene (stage building, from which, of course, we get the word "scene.") The semicircular auditorium wraps around three-quarters of the 67 ft (20.4 m) circular orchestra. Its seats, or limestone benches, are arranged in two tiers of 21 and 34 rows, separated by a walkway and divided by 11 stairs. Many of the benches carry inscriptions of the names of donors. The design has not really aged at all: it remains a near-perfect venue to watch plays or listen to music, and it lacks only its stage building to make it complete.

Originally, two ramps would have led up to the stage building, which would have been fronted by an Ionic colonnade of 14 half-columns set against square pillars, with

Emphasizing human insignificance
Raised tiers of seating and a mountainous backdrop would have dwarfed the actors.

ANCIENT GREEK THEATER

A coin dropped on the stage can be heard from the highest seats at Epidaurus. The acoustics had to be superb, since plays were narrated by up to 50 people simultaneously—the Chorus. A single actor portrayed the main character, until the great tragedian Aeschylus introduced a second, and Sophocles a third.

AESCHYLUS

wings projecting on either side of this theatrical facade. The skene would have housed a principal room supported by four columns along its central axis, with a square room on either side. For centuries, this theater remained covered by thick layers of earth. Systematic excavations started in 1881 under the direction of P. Kavvadias, and today, as well as attracting architects of all styles and persuasions, it remains one of the world's most magnificent and superbly sited performance spaces.

TOWER OF THE WINDS

🕰 48BCE   📍 ATHENS, GREECE   ✒ ANDRONIKOS
🏛 OBSERVATORY

This octagonal marble tower, found in the Roman Forum, Athens, was an observatory designed by the Syrian astronomer Andronikos to measure time. It also served as a sundial, weathervane, water clock, and compass. In antiquity, the 40 ft (12 m) high structure supported a rooftop weathervane in the form of a bronze Triton. Sundials were carved or etched into the facades. The relief sculptures on each facade represented eight images of the Greek wind gods; they also indicated the points of the compass. Entry to the observatory was gained through two Corinthian porticos of unequal measure.

STOA OF ATTALOS

🕰 150BCE   📍 ATHENS, GREECE
✒ UNKNOWN   🏛 PUBLIC BUILDING

The Stoa of Attalos is a long, two-story, colonnaded building that, like many stoas, was used to create one side of a square around the central agora, or market place, the heart of public life in ancient Greek cities. The stoa measures 380 x 66 ft (116 x 20 m), with double colonnades on both floors. The external columns on the ground floor are Doric, paired with Ionic columns inside; those of the upper floor are Ionic. The colonnades front 21 rooms on each floor. These would have been used for stores, offices, and public services.

PANATHENAIC STADIUM

🏆 329BCE 📍 ATHENS, GREECE ✍ LYKOURGOS 🏛 STADIUM

Originally a natural hollow in the ground, used for athletic games from 566BCE, this stadium was built in stone by Lykourgos in 330–329BCE for the Panathenaic Games. Between 140 and 144, Herod Atticus rebuilt it in marble, endowing it with the horseshoe form revealed during the excavation of 1870. He also added a Doric propylaeum, or pedimented gateway. The 670 ft (204 m) track was marked out, in terms of distance, by square columns sporting busts of Apollo and Dionysus. Seating capacity was approximately 50,000. Tiers of seats were divided by stairs. During the Roman era, the stadium was used as an arena, with scenes of great violence as well as sporting prowess.

Still in use
During the 2004 Olympics, held in Athens, the stadium was used for archery contests and as the finishing post for the marathon.

TERRACE OF LIONS

🏆 150BCE 📍 DELOS, GREECE ✍ UNKNOWN 🏛 STATUARY

The island of Delos is said to be the birthplace of Apollo and Artemis. The name Delos means "that which appeared," and the island was so named because it suddenly emerged from the waves, doubtless due to underwater volcanic activity.

Delos's guardians are the roaring, if rather emaciated, marble lions that stand in a row facing east at the Sanctuary of Apollo, challenging all comers. Five lions survive, although they would originally have been part of a pride of at least nine, and possibly as many as sixteen. Sculptures of animals played a prominent and inherent

part in Greek architecture: bulls' heads in friezes, rams' heads in the scrolled volutes of Ionic columns, and rearing horses in the famous friezes of the Parthenon. Animals were used in ritual sacrifices to the gods, but they were also worshiped for their strength, grace, and beauty. In mythology, many Greek gods would reveal themselves in the guise of wild animals, so sculptures like the lions at Delos are more than mere decorative appendages to the sanctuary they adorn: they are an inherent part of its symbolism as well as its architectural design. Delos also boasts a Sanctuary of Bulls.

Animal sanctuary
These lions are in fact replicas, as the originals (now in a museum on Delos) were being badly eroded by sea winds.

MAUSOLEUM OF HALICARNASSUS

🏛 350BCE   📍 MILETUS, TURKEY   ✍ PYTHEOS   🏛 TOMB

The term "mausoleum" was derived from this famous and influential tomb erected to the memory of King Mausolus, ruler of Caria, by his widow Artemisia. It was one of the Seven Wonders of the ancient world. The 1st-century Roman architect Vitruvius records that the architect responsible for the Mausoleum was Pytheos, designer of

the Temple of Athena at Priene. The tomb stood proudly on a slope in full view of Halicarnassus, the city that Mausolus made his capital and rebuilt in Greek style. It comprised a lofty podium and a templelike upper part surrounded by Ionic columns. Above this rose an imposing stepped pyramid commanding a third of the 131 ft (40 m) high structure. A chariot drawn by four horses was perched on top, in which images of Mausolus and Artemisia rode high above their favored city. The mausoleum was embellished with reliefs and sculptures by the celebrated sculptors Bryaxis, Leochares, Scopas, and Timotheus. The mausoleum stood, much admired, until, by the 15th century, earthquakes had ruined it. In the early 19th century, European explorers and archaeologists located and excavated the site of this ancient wonder.

Original statue
Although the tomb is ruined, the superb 10 ft (3 m) marble statue of Mausolus found at the site can now be seen in the British Museum, London.

PRIENE

🏛 350BCE   📍 CENTRAL ANATOLIA, TURKEY   ✍ UNKNOWN   🏛 CITY

Priene, now in modern Turkey, may have been founded by either Mausolus or Alexander the Great in the 4th century BCE. Whatever its origins, this is one of the most thoroughly excavated ancient Greek cities: its plan, architecture, and way of life are well documented. Built, with some terracing, as levelly as possible on a sloping coastal shelf with a mountainous backdrop, the city is tucked into a neat, tight site. Its plan, as you would expect, is essentially regular, with a grid pattern of wide streets dividing it into some 80 blocks, or insulae. At its heart is an agora, or marketplace, which by the mid-2nd century BCE would have been surrounded by detached colonnades known as stoas *(see also p.101)*: those on three sides formed one continuous building. The agora, however, was cut through by the city's main streets, so this would have been a lively place, busy with traffic, and far from today's boring pedestrian precincts that rob cities of life and energy. Temples, a theater, and other public buildings were allowed to break

the grid. In many ways, Greek cities were standardized: their architecture was similar, and each was pretty much like the others in its rhythms and rituals: what made them, like Priene, so special was the way in which a recognized pattern and order was tailored to a variety of often very different, and beautiful, landscapes.

Temple of Athena Polias
This temple at Priene was built by Pytheos, architect of the Mausoleum of Halicarnassus; almost twice as long as it was wide, each side featured 11 columns.

ROMAN ARCHITECTURE
753BCE–476CE

Roman architecture is characterized by its relentless energy. From the mythical founding of Rome in 753BCE by Romulus and Remus—the twins in legend suckled by a wolf—to as late as 300CE, Rome grew and grew in power and influence. Its architecture and engineering spread with its legions and the "Pax Romana" as the expanding Roman empire engulfed the Mediterranean region, as well as lands far beyond.

When Rome annexed Greece in 146BCE, it embraced Greek culture. Even as Rome struggled with the transition from republic to empire under Augustus's rule (27BCE–14CE), it produced much of its greatest Greek-inspired culture, including the writings of Horace, the poetry of Virgil and Ovid, the histories of Livy, and the stirrings of great architecture. It was during Augustus's reign (later called the Golden Age) that Rome itself was transformed, as the Emperor boasted, from a city of brick to one of marble. While this was not quite true, Roman architecture did become more grand during this period. The city, though, was always an odd mix of organization and chaos, abounding in both architecture of the highest quality, such as the Pantheon *(see p.110)*, and cheapjack buildings that would often collapse. Grand avenues led into mazes of alleys. Nothing was quite as ordered as it might have been.

RISE AND FALL

Rome's boundless energy was both a blessing and a curse. As the empire grew, resources and soldiery were increasingly stretched. Immigrants poured into Rome, kept under civic control only through a policy of providing free benefits and entertainment ("bread and circuses.") Architects, too, were pushed to the limit: they had to design and build at a punishing pace as the imperial juggernaut rolled on, bringing new lands and peoples under the Roman yoke. Using imagination, arches, and a great deal of concrete, Roman architects produced a wealth of temples, arenas, theaters, baths, and aqueducts. And when Rome finally fell, in 476CE, those architects working at Constantinople (now Istanbul), in the predominantly Greek-speaking eastern empire, were just getting into their own, astonishing stride.

◁ **THE COLOSSEUM IN ROME WAS A VAST, LARGELY CONCRETE AMPHITHEATER WITH TIERS OF SEATING FOR 50,000 SPECTATORS AROUND A CENTRAL ELLIPTICAL ARENA.**

ELEMENTS

Roman architecture was the outward face of a republic that became one
of the world's most powerful empires and stamped its image across its
conquests in eastern and western Europe, North Africa, and the Middle
East. It took its distinctive, highly adaptable
architecture wherever its legions went.

△ **Medallions**
Coinlike carved medallions depicting
mythological interpretations of recent histo
events were popular imperial propaganda.

△ **Triumphal arches**
Roman emperors were proud of their conquests.
Triumphal arches, like Constantine's in Rome,
set their stories in massive marble arches.

▽ **Arches**
The Romans employed arches to great practical
and aesthetic effect. The arcaded Colosseum in
Rome was one of their largest buildings.

Aqueducts ▷
The spectacular triple-
arcaded aqueduct that
brought water to Nîmes
in France reveals the
sheer scale and
ambition of Roman
design. Water flows
across the top arcade.

Arched bridges ▷
Arches enabled
Roman architects and
engineers to span
rivers. The 2nd-
century bridge at
Alcantara, Spain, is
perhaps the most
impressive example.

Arches divided
by columns
form an
arcade

Decorative Roman carving corrupts Classical Greek lines

Composite capital combining Ionic and Corinthian elements

◁ **Composite order**
To the three Greek orders—Doric, Ionic, and Corinthian—the Romans added the Composite, a blend that superimposed the scroll-like volutes of the Ionic capital over Corinthian acanthus leaves, shown here at the Library of Celsus, Ephesus.

△ **Circular plans**
Roman emperors were much taken by circular and oval plans, and others that made dramatic use of curves rather than Classical straight lines. This is the 2nd-century Mausoleum of Hadrian, Rome.

△ **Round-topped pediment**
This highly decorated round-headed pediment from the 2nd-century Library of Celsus, Ephesus, is the Roman equivalent of Baroque design, a style impossible to imagine in Greece.

Style of lettering influenced modern typography

Monumental lettering ▷
Few monumental buildings were without dignified inscriptions incised into their facades. This fine lettering adorns the Pantheon, Rome.

M·AGRIPPA·L·F·COS·TERTIVM·FECIT

△ **Mosaic floors**
Mosaic floors were used throughout many Roman buildings. This marine equestrian is a detail from the 3rd-century Baths of Caracalla, Rome.

△ **Hypocausts**
Central heating in which hot air from furnaces circulated through an underfloor system of ducts (hypocaust) served both civic and domestic buildings.

TEMPLE OF JUPITER

🗿 509BCE   📍 ROME, ITALY   ✎ UNKNOWN
🏛 PLACE OF WORSHIP

The first Temple of Jupiter stood on the Capitoline, the lowest and rockiest of Rome's seven hills. Commissioned by King Lucius Tarquinius Superbus, it was inaugurated at the very beginning of the republican era in the 6th century BCE. This was the greatest of the Etruscan temples, in a style that preceded Roman architecture proper. Though cruder stylistically than contemporary Greek temples and built largely of wood, it was designed on Classical principles and as such, was commented upon by Vitruvius in the first known work of western architectural commentary, theory, and practice. The stone podium of the temple, part of which still stands, measured 203 ft (62 m) long, 174 ft (53 m) wide, and 13 ft (4 m) high. Burned down in 83BCE, the temple was rebuilt using marble columns brought, secondhand, from Greece and covered in gold and mosaic very probably looted from existing temples in the east of what, after the death of Julius Caesar, had become an empire.

TEMPLE OF VESTA

🗿 c.100 BCE   📍 ROME, ITALY
✎ MARCUS OCTAVIUS HERRENUS   🏛 PLACE OF WORSHIP

Built by the prosperous merchant Marcus Octavius Herrenus, the Temple of Vesta is a pretty, circular temple located in the Piazza Bocca della Verità, close to the Tiber River. It is the oldest surviving marble building in Rome; of its 20 finely modeled Corinthian columns, all but one are original. Despite its name, the Corinthian building was probably dedicated to Hercules Olivarius, patron of olive oil merchants. In the 12th century, the temple was transformed into the church of Santo Stefano delle Carrozze, known from the 15th century also as Santa Maria della Sole. It has long been closed to the public.

MAISON CARRÉE

🗿 ca. 19BCE   📍 NÎMES, FRANCE   ✎ MARCUS VIPSANIUS AGRIPPA   🏛 PLACE OF WORSHIP

Maison Carrée, a French name meaning "square house," was commissioned during the reign of Augustus by Marcus Vipsanius Agrippa (63–12BCE), who dedicated the temple to his sons Caius and Lucius. It is, by far, the best preserved of all Roman temples. Raised high on a podium of nearly 10 ft (3 m), its single, west-facing entrance is reached by a flight of stairs leading up to a portico of six 33 ft (10 m) high Corinthian columns. The architrave over the columns has a rich entablature of fine relief carvings of rosettes and acanthus leaves. Built of local limestone by architects and craftsmen from Rome itself, the Maison Carrée is now a museum and sits adjacent to Norman Foster's Mediathèque, or Carrée d'Art, a refined temple to modern muses dating from 1993. The temple was reproduced many times during the Classical Revival of the 19th century, in the guise of town halls and civic art galleries, across Europe and the US.

Square chamber
Externally, the cella is studded with Corinthian half-columns that are chiefly decorative, rather than structural, elements.

TEMPLE OF MARS ULTOR

🗓 2CE 📍 ROME, ITALY ⚒ AUGUSTUS 🏛 PLACE OF WORSHIP

Dedicated to the Roman god of war, this temple was commissioned by Rome's first emperor, Augustus (63BCE–14CE, as part of his vow to avenge the death of his uncle, Julius Caesar. The bombastic focal point of the new, colonnaded Forum of Augustus, its exterior was clad in gleaming white marble from the quarries of Carrara.

Standing among the scattered ruins of the Roman fora today, it is hard to picture the contribution Augustus made here to urban planning with the planning and execution of the Temple of Mars Ultor. Working on an irregular site facing the older Forum of Caesar, the emperor's architects nevertheless created a setting that would have appeared to be wholly symmetrical. The great Corinthian temple closed the long vista of the colonnaded forum laid out in front of it. These colonnades were Corinthian at sidewalk level, but along their second floors, the long roofs of the forum buildings were supported by dozens of caryatids. The temple itself was fronted by 56 ft (17 m)

THE EMPEROR AUGUSTUS

Imperious and luxurious, the Temple of Mars was striking evidence of Augustus's famous claim to have found Rome a city of brick and left it a city of marble. The first emperor's enthusiasm for major building projects was legendary: he claimed to have restored 82 temples in one year alone, in addition to commissioning magnificent new edifices such as the Theater of Apollo and, indeed, his own mausoleum.

EMPEROR AUGUSTUS

high Corinthian columns. Its vast, marble-lined interior contained a single space, a cella broken into nave and aisles by two rows of columns and terminating in an apsidal wall. This was one of the earliest known uses of an apse, which was to become a defining feature of many early Christian churches. It was approached by five full-width steps and enshrined the figures of Mars Ultor in full armor, Venus with Cupid, and Julius Caesar. Today, only ruins remain of this once grandiose temple.

Site of splendor
The temple stood on a podium, approached by marble stairs that are still reasonably well preserved. The site of the central altar to Mars can be discerned among the stumps of ruined columns.

THE PANTHEON

🗓 *ca.* 128 📍 ROME, ITALY ✍ UNKNOWN 🏛 PLACE OF WORSHIP / CIVIC BUILDING

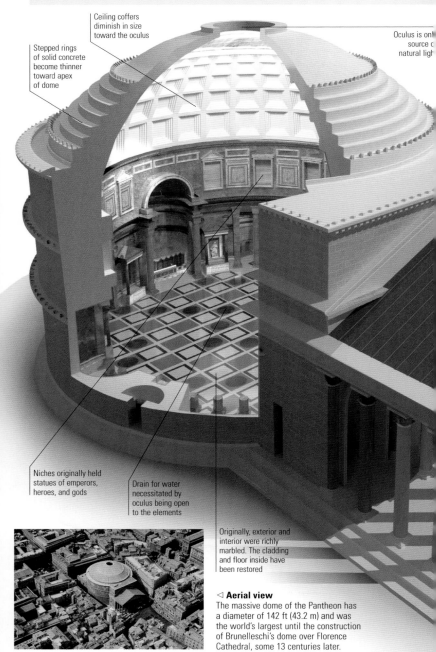

Ceiling coffers diminish in size toward the oculus

Oculus is only source of natural light

Stepped rings of solid concrete become thinner toward apex of dome

Niches originally held statues of emperors, heroes, and gods

Drain for water necessitated by oculus being open to the elements

Originally, exterior and interior were richly marbled. The cladding and floor inside have been restored

◁ **Aerial view**
The massive dome of the Pantheon has a diameter of 142 ft (43.2 m) and was the world's largest until the construction of Brunelleschi's dome over Florence Cathedral, some 13 centuries later.

The Pantheon is one of the world's greatest religious and civic buildings. It was built, and rebuilt, as a Roman temple and later consecrated as a Catholic Church. Its monumental porch with three rows of eight Corinthian columns originally faced a rectangular colonnaded temple courtyard. The great drum-shaped room inside, lined with semiprecious purple porphyry, granite, and marble and covered with a magnificent coffered dome, describes a perfect half-sphere. The only light, when the bronze doors are closed, shines through an opening in the center of the dome called an oculus. Sun and Moon peer through this, their rays moving around the temple like the hands of some celestial clock. Rain is free to fall through the oculus, a beautiful sight.

MAIN FAÇADE, PIAZZA DELLA ROTONDA

△ **Emperor Hadrian (r.117–38)**
Hadrian may have had a hand in the Pantheon's design, and his reign was also marked by other impressive structures, such as his country villa at Tivoli *(see p.117)*.

Superimposed pediment acts as a Classically correct entrance

Distinctive Corinthian capitals feature acanthus leaves

The 24 columns of Egyptian granite are 46 ft (14 m) high

▽ **Floor plan**
The circular cella (chamber) behind the massive portico is an uncharacteristic departure; earlier cellas were usually rectangular.

Circular plan represents the sphere of the world

Each element adds to perfect symmetry

△ **Interior**
The richness of the original decoration of the Pantheon's interior has survived to the present day, whereas all external decoration was stripped long ago.

THE ROMAN TOWN

Wherever the Roman legions conquered, they established
the ideals and the physical characteristics of the Roman
Empire. These included the idea of logical and orderly
towns. In Roman Greece, or Roman Britain, or anywhere
in the empire, the towns might have been built from local
materials, and yet their layouts, and the type of buildings
found in each, would have been almost identical.

The Roman town was laid out on a gridiron
plan centered on the crossing of two main
roads, one heading north–south, the other
east–west. Where they met, the principal
civic buildings and spaces were erected.
These were the basilica, forum, market,
amphitheater, baths, and temple. Apartment
buildings and private courtyard houses were
stretched out along straight streets leading
off the main roads. The town would also
include an army barracks, and would often
be walled around. Where possible, towns
were provided with aqueducts and some
form of sewage-disposal system.

Ruined cities
These ruins in Libya give a clear impression of the
symmetry, and grandeur of Roman architecture, but
little sense of the vitality of the imperial cities.

The reality was
rarely quite as
rational as the
theory. Rome,
with its huge
population drawn from all over the empire,
would have been a particularly lively city;
and, although well-planned in parts, much
of it was "urban sprawl." Noisy and dirty,
the city would have been filled with delivery
carts drawn by oxen, the shouts of
tradesmen, and the bustle of citizens and
soldiers at work or leisure. Roman remains
that we see today are the well-bleached
ruins of towns and cities abandoned long
ago and bereft of the teeming life that often
threatened to choke these busy and ever-
changing imperial settlements.

Trojan's column
This huge stone column (see
p.116) teems with warlike
depictions of Roman life.

POMPEII

🏛 200BCE 🏴 SOUTHERN ITALY ⚒ UNKNOWN 🏛 CITY

In 79CE Mount Vesuvius erupted, burying the Roman city of Pompeii and its population (*ca.* 20,000) in a blanket of molten rock and ash. It was not until 1860, when the archaeologist Giuseppe Fiorelli took charge of the excavations, that ancient Pompeii was fully revealed. Citizens, and even their pet dogs, were found mummified in the places and positions in which they took their last breaths.

Pompeii was not planned on a Roman grid, but twisted and turned on the mountainous terrain. It was a gloriously, and often humorously, decadent city; its houses were richly and sensuously decorated. A number of its more costly houses were outward-looking, with projecting balconies from where residents could enjoy views denied to those living in traditional, if often elegant and well-planned, courtyard villas.

The courtyard houses of Pompeii are fascinating structures, with richly finished residential quarters hidden behind rows of

AMPHITHEATER IN POMPEII

THE DESTRUCTION OF POMPEII

An account of events surrounding the eruption of Mount Vesuvius survives among the letters of Pliny the Younger (61–112). When the eruption began, his uncle, Pliny the Elder (23–79), was in command of a Roman fleet stationed on the Bay of Naples. The commander launched warships to take a closer look and to help with evacuation, but the fierce heat prevented any rescue of the fleeing citizens. The death toll was huge, and the city was never rebuilt.

shops and high walls. The House of Pansa (2nd century BCE) has a narrow entrance, flanked by three shops on either side, opening into a house that is as much office and workshop as home; then a colonnaded peristyle—a domestic cloister—full of flowers, running water, and statuary, leads into a private house adorned with mosaics and frescoes, and out into an extensive walled garden. These houses lacked glass windows and so would have been very chilly in winter, as many Roman writers attest.

Guardians destroyed
Remains found at Pompeii include a large forum, a theater, and this temple —Sacrarium of the Lares—where Pompeii's guardian deities were housed.

INSULAE, OSTIA

🏛 79BCE   📍 OSTIA, ITALY   ✍ UNKNOWN   🏛 RESIDENCE

Ostia lies on the mouth of the Tiber River. It was the principal port of ancient Rome and a vital commercial and military base. Abandoned shortly after the fall of Rome, Ostia has been well preserved by layers of silt and sand. Among the most interesting examples of Roman architecture uncovered here are the blocks of workers' apartments: brick and concrete buildings that might well have stood up to eight stories high. They provide a glimpse of everyday Roman life outside that led to the better-known villas and mansions. These "insulae" (islands), as they were known, would have looked a great deal like many 20th-century apartment blocks, with their common stairwells, rhythmic windows, and large internal courts. Few, if any, had glass windows: openings were

Roman safety laws
These humble dwellings are partially preserved because, after fire destroyed large areas of Rome, city blocks had to be made with fireproof concrete.

covered by shutters and curtains. The blocks were not particularly sanitary, especially when inhabited by families occupying single rooms. Water had to be brought from wells, and so first-floor apartments were at a premium, with top floors getting the lowest rents, the reverse of the situation 2,000 years later.

BATHS OF HADRIAN

🏛 127   📍 NEAR TRIPOLI, LIBYA   ✍ UNKNOWN   🏛 BATHS

Leptis Magna, in modern-day Libya, was once the greatest city in North Africa, an affluent trading post of the Roman Empire. Its ruins are among the most impressive of all ancient Roman remains. The Baths of Hadrian is a complex of buildings constructed, it would appear, almost entirely from marble:

green, pink, black, and white. It was certainly a grand building, every bit as complex and as voluptuous as its counterparts in Rome itself, and was lavishly equipped with all the usual refinements and adorned with mosaics and statues. Hadrian commissioned the baths soon after water was brought to Leptis Magna, via channels rather than an aqueduct. Enlarged between 200 and 216 by the emperor Lucius Septimius Severus, who was born in Leptis Magna, the baths were finally abandoned, along with the city, in 523, when Berber tribes made one final assault on Leptis Magna.

Civic amenity
The baths were not just for sanitation but were a major part of civic life and a place to discuss politics and trade, hence the lavish design.

BATHS OF CARACALLA

🏛 216　📍 ROME, ITALY　✍ UNKNOWN　🏛 BATHS

These magnificent baths, built in the reign of the emperor Marcus Aurelius Antoninus—better known as Caracalla—were for the amusement of all Roman citizens, not just the wealthy. The complex was a vast, symmetrical arrangement of swimming pools, steam rooms, and gyms, within the walls of a colossal compound containing a garden, reservoirs, dining rooms, libraries, lecture halls, art galleries, and public meeting rooms. Two levels of underground stores, furnaces, and hot air ducts heated the baths, while complex plumbing ensured a constant flow of water from the Aqua Marcia aqueduct. Marble seats, fountains, and statues abounded, along with mosaic walls and floors (much of which was later given to the Farnese family's Palazzo, *see p.284–5*). The Baths of Caracalla were later recreated as a New York train station *(see p.453)*.

Ancient leisure center
Entry was cheap, to keep the "plebs" (common people) happy and docile.

BATHS OF DIOCLETIAN

🏛 306　📍 ROME, ITALY
✍ UNKNOWN　🏛 BATHS

The grandest and most extensive of all ancient Roman baths, accommodating over 3,000 bathers and covering over 32 acres (13 ha), the Baths of Diocletian was similar in plan, and in the many services it offered to users, to the earlier Baths of Caracalla: it was impossible in imperial Rome to have too much of a good thing. The luxurious decor and sheer scale of the baths make today's health spas pale in comparison. The building was largely abandoned in the early Christian era because bathing for pleasure was considered somehow sinful. The baths, however, remained in use until the aqueducts that fed them were cut by the Goths in 537. They were later plundered by medieval and Renaissance builders, until finally, in 1563, some fragments of the massive complex were converted by Michelangelo into the Church of Santa Maria degli Angeli. The three soaring vaults of the church transept give a hint of the original splendor of the Roman building.

ROMAN BATHS, AQUAE SULIS

🏛 217　📍 BATH, ENGLAND
✍ UNKNOWN　🏛 BATHS

The city of Bath, or Roman Aquae Sulis, was named in honor of the goddess Sulis Minerva. Its baths were fed by natural hot springs, which retain their legendary healing properties today. The biggest of what were five—the Great Bath—with its lead pipes and stone statuary, is still steaming away. The baths were heavily restored in the 1860s in an attempt to slow down the decline in the levels of tourism Bath had enjoyed in its highly fashionable 18th-century heyday.

TRAJAN'S COLUMN

🗓 112   📍 ROME, ITALY   ✍ UNKNOWN   🏛 MONUMENT

This magnificent and hugely influential 115 ft (35 m) column was erected to celebrate the Emperor Trajan's victories in the Dacian Wars. Scenes of the action against fierce Germanic tribes are carved in a spiraling frieze around the 12 ft (3.7 m) girth of this stylized Doric column. Around two-thirds life-size, the carvings number more than 2,000.

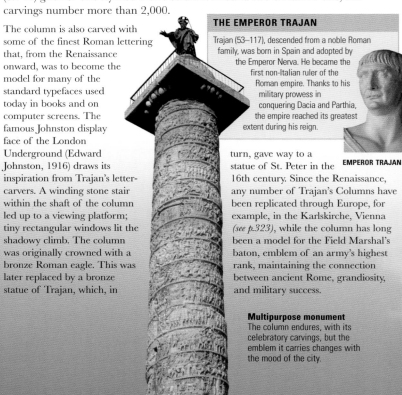

The column is also carved with some of the finest Roman lettering that, from the Renaissance onward, was to become the model for many of the standard typefaces used today in books and on computer screens. The famous Johnston display face of the London Underground (Edward Johnston, 1916) draws its inspiration from Trajan's letter-carvers. A winding stone stair within the shaft of the column led up to a viewing platform; tiny rectangular windows lit the shadowy climb. The column was originally crowned with a bronze Roman eagle. This was later replaced by a bronze statue of Trajan, which, in turn, gave way to a statue of St. Peter in the 16th century. Since the Renaissance, any number of Trajan's Columns have been replicated through Europe, for example, in the Karlskirche, Vienna (*see p.323*), while the column has long been a model for the Field Marshal's baton, emblem of an army's highest rank, maintaining the connection between ancient Rome, grandiosity, and military success.

THE EMPEROR TRAJAN

Trajan (53–117), descended from a noble Roman family, was born in Spain and adopted by the Emperor Nerva. He became the first non-Italian ruler of the Roman empire. Thanks to his military prowess in conquering Dacia and Parthia, the empire reached its greatest extent during his reign.

EMPEROR TRAJAN

Multipurpose monument
The column endures, with its celebratory carvings, but the emblem it carries changes with the mood of the city.

HADRIAN'S VILLA

👤 134 📍 TIVOLI, ITALY ✎ UNKNOWN 🏛 PALACE

This vast and often puzzling imperial country retreat comprises more than 30 buildings set in a sloping landscape of seemingly boundless gardens at Tivoli, reached from Rome along the ancient Roman road, the Via Appia. Here myriad pleasure domes are arranged picturesquely around pools, lakes, and a colonnaded artificial island. The Emperor Hadrian was more than enthusiastic about architecture:

he played a large role in the development of a new architectural language, expressed most impressively in the design of the Pantheon *(see pp.110–1)*, based on domes and curves. Utterly different from the severe formality of ancient Roman temples, Hadrian's Villa twists and turns across its setting, offering any number of unexpected vistas: a kind of gloriously pleasurable architectural walk in tamed landscape.

Most importantly to architecture, the villa features a number of buildings that show off new plans and layouts: apses sprouting from octagons, adventurous vaulting, and a number of rooms that are almost Baroque in their complex theatricality.

The Canopus
Although plundered and largely demolished, the ruins of the Villa still offer visual delights such as this colonnaded pool.

HADRIAN'S MAUSOLEUM

👤 139 📍 ROME, ITALY ✎ UNKNOWN 🏛 TOMB

The Mausoleum of Hadrian was the nearest thing to a Roman version of an ancient Egyptian pyramid. Inside this majestic circular funerary monument on the banks of the Tiber, the mortal remains of the divine emperor were laid in a magnificent porphyry sarcophagus. Standing on a mighty rectangular base, the main colonnaded drum of the monument, 203 ft (62 m) in diameter, 68 ft (21 m) high, was constructed entirely from concrete and faced with gleaming Parian marble. The

drum was bordered by a ring of statues. On top of this a second colonnaded drum was topped by a bronze quadriga.

In the 6th century, the mausoleum became a fortification and was renamed Castel Sant'Angelo after the huge bronze archangel placed on its peak. In 1277, it was incorporated into the Vatican, to which it was connected by a secret passage.

Protecting the city
As Castel Sant'Angelo, the mausoleum was well placed to guard access to the city from the river.

LIBRARY OF CELSUS

🏺 120 📍 EPHESUS, TURKEY ✍ UNKNOWN 🏛 LIBRARY

This handsome library provided three galleried floors of manuscripts fronted by a grandiose facade, which, at 57 ft (17 m) wide, was much more ambitious than the actual library, 36 ft (11 m) deep, behind it. This library is particularly interesting because the walls housing the manuscripts are separate from those of the exterior. A cavity between them not only gave access to the three levels of stacks, but ensured a flow of air through the building that would have kept the manuscripts at, more or less, the temperature and humidity needed for their long-term conservation. In fact, this is one of the earliest known examples of a cavity-walled building. Manuscripts were stored along shelves built into the internal walls. The interior would have been decorated with pilasters and statues at regular intervals. A vaulted chamber can be found beneath an apse where a marble sarcophagus lies, presumed to be of the founder of the library; sadly, there is no manuscript surviving to tell us who he, or she, was.

Show of learning
This showy facade is as the Romans would have wanted it; they laid great emphasis on learning and were proud of their richly stocked libraries.

PONT DU GARD

🏺 19BCE 📍 NÎMES, FRANCE
✍ UNKNOWN 🏛 AQUEDUCT

The highest aqueduct ever built by the Romans, the Pont du Gard, fetching water from near Uzès to Nîmes over the Gard River on three tiers of arches, is wonderfully undamaged and deeply impressive and moving. Built of unadorned, precut stone blocks, the sheer scale and beauty of its construction, along with its noble purpose—to provide free, clean, fresh water to all citizens—remains an impressive symbol of the Pax Romana, the civilization the Romans brought in their military wake.

TRAJAN'S BRIDGE, ALCÁNTARA

🏺 105 📍 ALCÁNTARA, SPAIN
✍ CAIUS JULIUS LACER 🏛 BRIDGE

After the murder of the emperor Domitian in 96, dynastic rule came to an end and Roman emperors were instead nominated by their predecessors and endorsed by the Senate. Successive non-Italian emperors, including Trajan (see p.116), ensured that the provinces enjoyed some splendid new building projects. Still in use, this fine stone bridge marches confidently across the deep valley of the Tagus River on six wide arches. The two central arches, rising on reinforced piers from the riverbed, span approximately 92 ft (28 m) and carry the roadway 157 ft (48 m) above the river. The center of the bridge is marked by a kind of austere triumphal arch, on which the name of the architect is inscribed; it was, indeed, nothing less than a triumph of engineering and architecture to have spanned a great river in such grand, yet unpretentious and lasting style. It was to be many centuries after the fall of Rome before bridges on such an epic scale, and of such innate beauty, were attempted again.

THE TREASURY AT PETRA

📺 *ca.* 25 📍 PETRA, JORDAN ✍ UNKNOWN 🏛 TOMB

The Siq, a 1.25 mile (2 km) chasm winding through rose-red rock faces in southern Jordan, leads visitors to what remains one of the most spine-tingling sights architecture of any age has to offer: the enchanting gateway to Petra, the magical Nabataean city hidden from the outside world for hundreds of years.

Petra was not always so secret. At its height, and during Roman occupation from 106, Petra was a wealthy trading city. Yet, in the long desert sleep of its decline, many myths grew around it. This was where the pharaoh pursuing Moses is said to have left the great treasure his army was carrying. It was deposited, so local tribesmen believed, in the sandstone urn in the center of the great split pediment of the facade of the magnificent tomb known as the Treasury ever since. This still bears the pockmarks of bullets fired by tribesmen hoping to crack it open and so gain the ancient Egyptian booty. In fact, the 131 ft (40 m) high facade conceals nothing at all as far as anyone knows.

THE REDISCOVERY OF PETRA

Although known to travelers in the Middle Ages, and even marked on 18th-century maps, Petra and its fabulous Treasury only came to popular attention when it was "discovered" by the Swiss explorer Johann Ludwig Burckhardt in 1812. Burckhardt, also the first Christian to reach Medina, disguised himself as a tribesman and was guided through the Siq.

Rose-red city
It is thought that the Treasury was hewn from the cliff face by craftsmen working for the energetic builder, King Aretas IV, whose successor Rabbel Soter saw the Nabataean kingdom annexed by the Roman emperor Trajan.

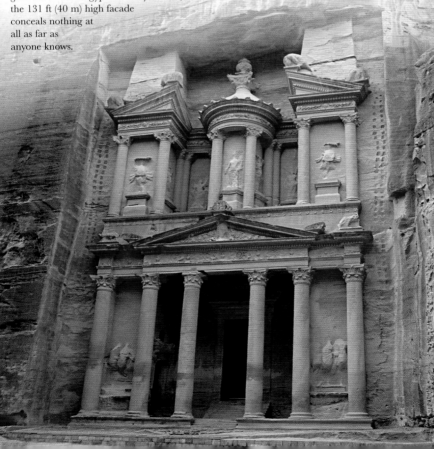

PALACE OF DIOCLETIAN

🏛 300   📍 SPLIT, CROATIA   ⚒ DIOCLETIAN   🏛 PALACE

Fortresslike and more imposing than majestic, the Palace of Diocletian, with glorious views over the Adriatic Sea on what is now the coast of Croatia, was constructed as a retirement home for the Emperor Diocletian. However, quite what Diocletian actually did in his retirement here is anyone's guess.

Diocletian was able to call on the resources of what, until then, was the world's greatest empire. Here, the very architecture of the gigantic palace seems not just exotic, but detached, mannered, and a very long way from the aesthetic values of republican and early imperial Rome. This huge walled and towered palace is pretty much a city in its own right, though modeled not on civic but on military traditions. Its plan is essentially that of a major Roman army camp, with a palace attached at one end. The emperor's south-facing quarters, well inside the walls, were reached along a grand internal street known as the "peristyle" and through a dramatic gateway, its pediment split by an

THE PERISTYLE

arch—characteristic of a building in which arcades played a major role. From here, a domed central vestibule led on either side to grand imperial apartments. Walking the other way along the peristyle, visitors would have discovered a temple, a mausoleum, and other rotundas on either side of it, then a pair of huge courtyards beyond, flanked by what must have been military quarters. The whole of this ambitious undertaking could be gained through three mighty gateways flanked by octagonal towers.

Ancient and modern
Originally standing in its own detached grounds, the stone and concrete palace is now entangled with the buildings of modern-day Split (Roman Spalatum).

EMPEROR DIOCLETIAN

Diocletian (r.284–305) had a passion for building that was not only extravagant but extremely exacting. As Lactantius, a professor of literature appointed by Diocletian at Nicomedia, wrote: "When [his] buildings had been completed and the provinces ruined in the process, he would say: 'They have not been built rightly; they must be done in another way.' They then had to be pulled down and altered—perhaps only to come down a second time."

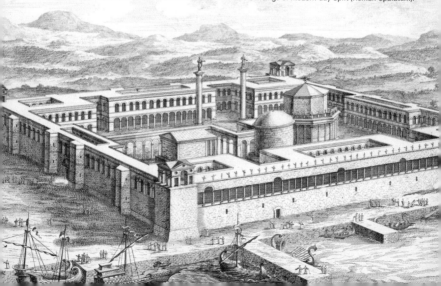

ARCH OF CONSTANTINE

🖥 312   📍 ROME, ITALY   ✎ UNKNOWN   🏛 MONUMENT

This was the last of many triumphal arches erected over the centuries in Rome. Almost in the shadow of the Colosseum, the Arch of Constantine is one of the most influential examples of this type of structure, used not only to celebrate victories but to bring order to the crowded thoroughfares of ancient Rome—which at this time had a population in the region of 1.25 million. The Arch of Constantine was erected to commemorate the Emperor Constantine's victory over Maxentius at the Battle of Milvian Bridge, in 312. The following year, Constantine converted to Christianity. Scenes of the battle are depicted on a rather coarsely sculpted band over the right-hand side arch. Other decorative panels were simply lifted from earlier monuments: although striking and memorable, the Arch of Constantine is also emblematic of the slow decline, if not yet fall, of imperial Roman culture.

Majestic form
The Arch of Constantine is 69 ft (21 m) high, 84 ft (25.7 m) wide, and 24 ft (7.4 m) deep, and was the model for several 19th-century Neo-Classical triumphal arches.

BASILICA OF CONSTANTINE

🖥 307   📍 ROME, ITALY   ✎ UNKNOWN   🏛 PLACE OF WORSHIP

This magnificent public meeting place was every bit as big as the impact it was to have on architecture in the ensuing 1,500 years. Only a few heroic ruins remain today, yet here was a bravura structure that was to influence the design of Hagia Sophia in Constantinople (now Istanbul) as well as much later Romanesque and Gothic cathedrals. Comprising a voluminous central nave, 262 ft (80 m) long by 82 ft (25 m) wide, roofed with groined concrete vaults reaching no less than 115 ft (35 m), and six coffered barrel-vaulted bays, the basilica would have been breathtaking. The interior would have been lavishly decked out in rich marbles, enormous Corinthian columns, statues in recesses, and glass windows. The way in which the vaults spring from the columns on either side of the nave is reminiscent of the structure of medieval cathedrals. The plan and general design of the basilica were derived from those of the great central halls of imperial public baths. Odd, then, perhaps, that so many early Christians were so against this form of bathing: their finest places of worship were, in one sense, ancient public baths revisited.

Epic scale
Three of these magnificent bays flanked the nave on each side.

EARLY CHRISTIAN AND BYZANTINE ARCHITECTURE
ca. 400–1500

The earliest Christians were not especially interested in architecture. They believed that the Kingdom of God was imminent, and so, while it seemed a good idea to worship in houses, there was little point in building churches, or indeed anything else. But when the Roman emperor Constantine founded Constantinople, the "New Rome," in 330, having converted to Christianity in 312, all this was to change dramatically.

The first major Christian churches in Rome and the Italian peninsula were based on basilicas. The most notable example would have been the church of St. Peter, founded by Constantine himself in 330. This was later demolished to build the current Basilica. Fortunately, many basilica churches survive, such as Rome's 5th-century Santa Sabina and Santa Maria Maggiore. However, a new architecture was slow to evolve in Constantinople. It was not until the reign of the emperor Justinian (527–565) that something truly radical occurred: his commission for the church of Hagia Sophia *(see pp.126–7)*.

THE INFLUENCE OF HAGIA SOPHIA
Hagia Sophia married Eastern and Western influences, and in the process produced one of the world's greatest buildings. The church is so special because it broke away completely from an architecture of columns. Its interior space, covered by the highest possible saucer dome, was as large and uninterrupted as it was possible for it to be within the constraints of the building technology of the time. The dome collapsed after the church was dedicated in 537, but it was rebuilt by 563. The architects, Isidorus of Miletus and Anthemius of Tralles, had created a magnificent new building type. As Justinian entered the finished church, he allegedly cried "Solomon, I have surpassed you!"—referring to the Temple of Solomon in Jerusalem, destroyed by the Romans in 70CE. The influence of Hagia Sophia spread back to Italy, across Greece and Turkey, and up through Russia. It was also the basis of the superb 16th-century mosques designed by Sinan, long after Constantinople had fallen to the Turks and Hagia Sophia had been turned into a mosque surrounded by minarets.

◁ **A FUSION OF BYZANTINE AND GOTHIC STYLES, ST. MARK'S CATHEDRAL IN VENICE, ITALY, IS IN PART BASED ON HAGIA SOPHIA AND THE BASILICA OF THE APOSTLES, BOTH IN CONSTANTINOPLE.**

ELEMENTS

When the Roman Empire went east (and also Christian) with its new capital at Constantinople, its architecture became more sensuous and, if anything, more ambitious than ever before. This Byzantine style, with increasingly exotic domes and ever-richer mosaics, traveled west to Ravenna and Venice and as far north as Moscow.

△ **Multiple domes**
Domes began to proliferate, reaching a peak here on the rooftop of St. Mark's, Venice, where there is a dome over each arm of the Greek-cross plan (a cross with four equal arms) as well as the central crossing.

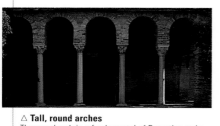

△ **Tall, round arches**
The round arch is a fundamental of Byzantine style. These round-topped arches, from the octagonal portico of Santa Fosca at Torcello, Italy, are bridges between contemporary Islamic and Christian design.

◁ **Mosaic-filled apses**
Magnificent golden mosaics with their graphic simplicity and immense power brought light, warmth, and mystery into the heart of Byzantine churches.

Ubiquitous Virgin and Child motif

Swirling leaf forms appear blown by imaginary winds

△ **Decorated dome ceilings**
High-riding Byzantine domes, like these at St. Mark's, Venice, created vast open spaces at the centers of churches, heightening the sense of grace and light.

Highly colored brickwork decoration

Faceting enhances light and shadows

△ **Naturalistic decoration on column capitals**
Byzantine capitals break away from the Classical conventions of Greece and Rome. Sinuous lines and naturalistic forms are precursors to the Gothic style.

◁ **Onion domes**
The onion dome, seen here at St. Basil's, Moscow, is highly characteristic of Russian Byzantine design. Its influence was to spread in later centuries through Baroque Europe.

SANTO STEFANO ROTONDO

🕰 483   📍 ROME, ITALY
✎ UNKNOWN   🏛 PLACE OF WORSHIP

This is a circular church, modeled on the Church of the Holy Sepulchre, Jerusalem, and dedicated to St. Stephen the Martyr. Built during the reign of Pope St. Simplicius, it is best known for gruesome Renaissance frescoes depicting unspeakably vile tortures.

The church consists of two circular colonnades—an outer ring comprising 34 Ionic columns and an inner ring of 22 Corinthian columns—supporting a timber roof and lit by windows high in the brick drum. There was a third colonnade; this was demolished by Nicholas V in 1450, when the original plan of the church—a Greek cross within a circle—was remodeled.

ST. GEORGE'S CHURCH, SALONIKA

🕰 c.390   📍 SALONIKA, GREECE
✎ UNKNOWN   🏛 PLACE OF WORSHIP

Originally intended as a mausoleum, and first built in the 3rd century to a design modeled on the Pantheon, Rome, the church of St. George was rebuilt in the reign of the emperor Theodosius (d.395). An apse, walkway, and long, arcaded entrance porch were added, and the underside of the 80 ft (24.5 m) diameter dome was adorned with Byzantine mosaics (*ca.* 450) depicting the lives and deaths of early Christian martyrs.

The church was Salonika's cathedral until it was converted into a mosque during the Ottoman empire, then back into a church after 1912. Damaged by an earthquake in 1978, St George's was renovated in 2005.

SANT'APOLLINARE IN CLASSE

🕰 549   📍 RAVENNA, ITALY   ✎ UNKNOWN   🏛 PLACE OF WORSHIP

This handsome basilica is set 5 miles (8 km) outside Ravenna. Beautifully proportioned, its simple Roman-style brick structure was originally adorned with marble walls and mosaic floors. These were stripped out for reuse elsewhere by wealthy local medieval and Renaissance landowners.

Constant change
The handsome, circular bell-tower was added in the 10th or 11th centuries—one of many dramatic changes the church has undergone.

Even so, the apse is adorned with superb, highly colorful mosaics, including such delights as the Apostles in the guise of 12 happy sheep gamboling toward their master's feet from the cities of Bethlehem and Jerusalem. The 183 ft (56 m) nave is twice as high as the aisles on either side; these light-filled spaces are divided from one another by two magnificent colonnades of Greek marble columns crowned with delicate acanthus leaves.

HAGIA SOPHIA, ISTANBUL

🪦 537 📍 ISTANBUL, TURKEY ⚒ ISIDORUS & ANTHEMIUS 🏛 PLACE OF WORSHIP

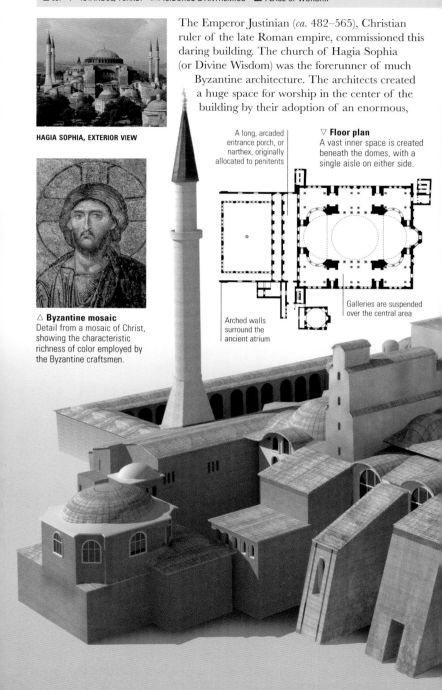

The Emperor Justinian (*ca.* 482–565), Christian ruler of the late Roman empire, commissioned this daring building. The church of Hagia Sophia (or Divine Wisdom) was the forerunner of much Byzantine architecture. The architects created a huge space for worship in the center of the building by their adoption of an enormous,

HAGIA SOPHIA, EXTERIOR VIEW

△ **Byzantine mosaic**
Detail from a mosaic of Christ, showing the characteristic richness of color employed by the Byzantine craftsmen.

A long, arcaded entrance porch, or narthex, originally allocated to penitents

▽ **Floor plan**
A vast inner space is created beneath the domes, with a single aisle on either side.

Galleries are suspended over the central area

Arched walls surround the ancient atrium

light-filled saucer dome. It is supported by four pendentive vaults, which spring from four lofty arches that define the space beneath the dome. Lavishly decorated, the Hagia Sophia showed a number of breaks with the Classicism of Rome: for example, columns topped with capitals decorated with serpentine foliage. Hagia Sophia was built in five years; its first dome was replaced in 563 after earthquakes. The church became a mosque in 1453 and is now a museum.

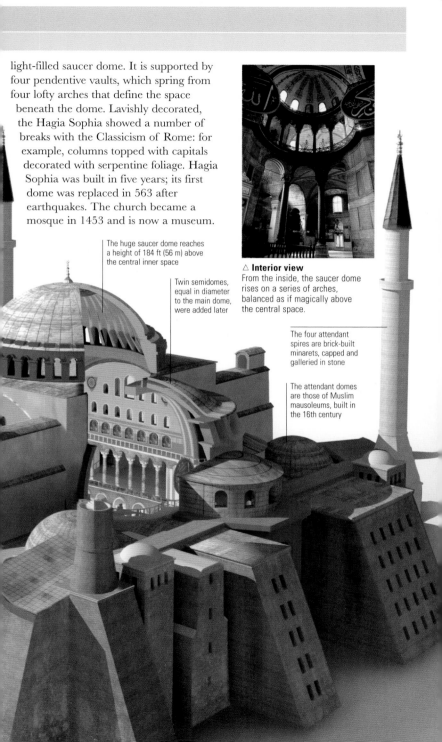

The huge saucer dome reaches a height of 184 ft (56 m) above the central inner space

Twin semidomes, equal in diameter to the main dome, were added later

△ **Interior view**
From the inside, the saucer dome rises on a series of arches, balanced as if magically above the central space.

The four attendant spires are brick-built minarets, capped and galleried in stone

The attendant domes are those of Muslim mausoleums, built in the 16th century

GREAT LAVRA KATHOLIKON

🏛 ca. 963   📍 MOUNT ATHOS, GREECE
✎ UNKNOWN   🏛 MONASTERY

The spectacular Monastery of Great Lavra, home to some 300 Greek Orthodox monks today, is the biggest and earliest of the many religious foundations on Mount Athos, of which about 20 still retain, and celebrate, their original function. Inside its great towered walls are no fewer than 37 chapels dancing quietly in attendance around the handsome red Katholikon, or main church, at the heart of the complex. This domed building, made increasingly cross-shaped over the centuries, is the tomb of St. Athanasius, its founder, and with its apses and domed chapels is the prototype of all the many *katholikon* on Mount Athos.

THEOTOKOS, HOSIOS LUKAS

🏛 ca. 960   📍 PHOCIDE, CENTRAL GREECE
✎ UNKNOWN   🏛 MONASTERY

Hosios Lukas (896–953) was a seer and miracle worker who, after many years of contemplation, established his own monastery—now a World Heritage Site— on the western slope of Mount Helikon. The smaller of its two adjoining churches was built shortly after its founder's death. This is the Theotokos, or church dedicated to the Mother of God, and it is the first of the many characteristic Byzantine churches rising from a cross-in-square plan. The church is built of massive stone blocks with brick ornamentation; its interior is decorated with marble, mosaics, and lively wall paintings dating from the 11th and 12th centuries.

TORCELLO CATHEDRAL

🏛 1008   📍 VENICE, ITALY   ✎ UNKNOWN   🏛 PLACE OF WORSHIP

This gloriously simple church dominates every view of Torcello, once the most important island in the Venetian lagoon. This was where the Venetians settled, after one attack too many on the mainland. In the 6th century, Torcello's population rose to around 30,000, which is why, despite its population of barely 20 today, it boasts such a magnificent cathedral, dedicated to Santa Maria Assunta. The structure dates from 639, but what you see today is a mighty nave built from around 824 and a detached campanile, or bell-tower, completed in 1008. These bare facts, and the sheer bare walls of the church, conceal a powerful and deeply moving interior dominated by awe-inspiring 12th- and 13th-century mosaics. The apse is filled with one of the very finest Byzantine gold mosaics of the Virgin Mary,

an artwork of numinous beauty, while the western wall is graced and disgraced by a depiction of the Last Judgment and imaginatively realized scenes from Heaven and Hell. Often described in guidebooks from the time of John Ruskin's *The Stones of Venice* (1851) as "desolate," Torcello is, in fact, a poignant place made beautiful by this impressive yet unpretentious church.

Vantage point
Although the stairs are steep, the Torcello bell-tower can be climbed for magnificent views of the lagoon.

SANTA FOSCA, TORCELLO

🗓 *ca.* 1100 📍 VENICE, ITALY ✍ UNKNOWN 🏛 PLACE OF WORSHIP

All but surrounded by an octagonal portico of horseshoelike arches, this exquisite, if much reordered Byzantine church can at first sight almost be mistaken for a mosque. Perhaps this is appropriate: for centuries Venice was the great junction connecting eastern and occidental empires, and Christianity and

Islam—or conducting the fight between them. The church was originally designed as a shrine to house the remains of Santa Fosca (235–250), a Roman teenager turned over to the authorities by her own father because of her conversion to Christianity. Many miracles have been attributed to Santa Fosca, and this church is surely one of them. The church was to have been covered with a dome, but this was never built. Even so, the truncated church, directly connected to Torcello Cathedral by a colonnaded portico, has a powerful presence. This is brought home inside, where the centralized plan, based on a short-armed Greek cross, has a real intensity of purpose and feeling.

Divine design
Stripped long ago of rich decoration, the church relies on its beautifully composed architecture to engender a sense of spirituality in its visitors.

ST. THEODORE, ATHENS

🗓 1065 📍 ATHENS, GREECE ✍ UNKNOWN 🏛 PLACE OF WORSHIP

Set slightly below street level in Klafthomonos Square near the Athens stock exchange and surrounded by fast-food outlets and expansive apartment blocks, the tiny domed church of St. Theodore, or Aghioi Theodoroi, is one of the very many small Byzantine churches built during the 11th and 12th centuries that still pepper the city with their domes and delightful brickwork. At this time, Athens was very unlike the 5th-century BCE city of Pericles's time: these churches stood in narrow lanes giving onto tiny squares flanked by densely packed courtyard houses. This church was rebuilt in 1065 by Nicolaos Kalamaos, a court official, on 9th-century foundations. Built largely of brick, it is a classic example of a minor Greek Orthodox church of the time. Curiously, it is decorated on three sides with imitation Arabic script. The church was damaged during the Greek Uprising of 1821

and restored from 1840, when artists got to work on a series of wall paintings inside. The church is dedicated to St. Theodore, who is normally taken to be Theodore of Heraclea, a general in the Roman imperial army who converted to Christianity and was tortured, as a result, by his own troops. He was later burned to death.

Captured in time
An early photograph shows the church minus its hectic modern surroundings.

ST. MARK'S CATHEDRAL

🗺 *ca.* 1096   📍 VENICE, ITALY   ✍ DOMENICO CONTARINI   🏛 PLACE OF WORSHIP

A glorious wave of fairytale architecture seemingly magically washed up from the Venetian lagoon and deposited in front of St. Mark's Square to dazzle generations of worshipers and visitors to the "most serene city," the many-domed St. Mark's cathedral in Venice is a wonderful fusion of Byzantine and early Gothic design and, justifiably, one of the world's most popular buildings.

This spectacular cathedral has been rebuilt and added to over many centuries as Venice's wealth, ambition, and reach grew. It was first built to house the remains of St. Mark, one of the four Evangelists. Tradition has it that the body of St. Mark was brought to Venice after it was taken from its first resting place in Alexandria, Egypt, by Venetian Christians in 828.

The cathedral is laid out on a Greek cross plan and stands on many thousands of wooden piles sunk into the ooze of the lagoon. Over hundreds of years, these have risen and fallen, and the lustrous marble floors they support now undulate as if as much a part of the sea as of the land. The center of the cross and each of its four arms are crowned with

MOSAIC-COVERED DOME INTERIOR

domes. The original saucer-shaped domes seen from inside the basilica are topped by tall timber and lead superstructures, each capped with an onion dome, which were added in the mid-13th century. The exterior walls are lavishly adorned with marble, with the columns surrounding doors carved from different colored marbles, some plundered from older churches and Classical temples from across the Byzantine empire.

Inside, decorative mosaics laid on gold backdrops were added over the generations. Lit by candles and oil lamps and suffused by daylight filtering through high windows, the mosaics conspire to create a spine-tingling and numinous atmosphere.

DOGE DOMENICO CONTARINI

The remains of St. Mark were first housed in Venice in a 9th-century Romanesque basilica, but this was destroyed by fire in 976. Domenico Contarini became doge (or chief magistrate) of Venice in 1043, and he felt strongly that the city needed a more impressive basilica than the previous design. He commissioned the new building in 1063, in the 20th year of his reign, but died in 1071, 25 years before his spectacular cathedral was completed.

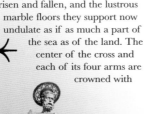

Crowning glory
Atop the highest pinnacle of the facade, a statue of St. Mark surrounded by angels rests on an intricate base supported by two lions.

CATHEDRAL OF SANTA SOPHIA, NOVGOROD

🏛 *ca.* 1052 📍 NOVGOROD, NORTHWESTERN RUSSIA ✍ VLADIMIR II 🏛 PLACE OF WORSHIP

With its sheer white walls and cluster of onion domes, the cathedral of Santa Sophia, or Hagia Sophia (Divine Wisdom), is the quintessential Russian Orthodox church. Somehow both fortresslike and filigree, this mighty church was built by Prince Vladimir II (1020–52) as a sister church to the slightly grander Hagia Sophia in Kiev. The Kiev church was built by his father, Yaroslav, who was the son of Vladimir the Great—a one-time builder of shrines to Thor and Odin, who had converted to Christianity. Unlike the older Kiev church, Novgorod's was never extensively added to or overlaid with Baroque decoration in later centuries and has remained much as it always was.

Santa Sophia is built to a Greek cross-in-square plan, rounded off with three apses and topped with five domes, and is made of stone with brick detailing. Russian architecture has been greatly influenced by external political events, wars, and religious movements, and Santa Sophia incorporates a number of

Russian relic
The cathedral of Santa Sophia, one of the oldest surviving stone churches in Russia, is topped with five domes, the tallest decorated with gold leaf.

foreign elements: inscriptions in the frescoes inside the basilica, for example, are in Greek rather than Russian; carved dog-tooth decoration around the cornices of the drums that support the domes are Romanesque in style; and the church's great 12th-century bronze doors are from Uppsala in Sweden.

CHURCH OF THE TRANSFIGURATION, KIZHI

🏛 1714 📍 KIZHI, NORTHERN RUSSIA ✍ UNKNOWN 🏛 PLACE OF WORSHIP

This eye-boggling church on the island of Kizhi in Lake Onega, a hangover from much earlier Byzantine design traditions, is a tour de force of 18th-century Russian craftsmanship. Built entirely of wood, it was

Wooden wonder
The remarkable timber structure of the church is made up of close-fitting timbers and wooden pegs and does not use a single metal nail.

constructed using only the most basic tools, such as axes and chisels. Legend has it that when construction of the church was completed, the master carpenter, Nestor, hurled his ax into Lake Onega, declaring that no one, not even he, would ever again be able to realize such a building.

The Karelian domain of northern Russia boasts a rich history of building in wood, especially on the many islands—all 1,650 of them—of Lake Onega. Kizhi (meaning "playground") is the most famous of the islands and was traditionally a place of pagan festivals; it was only in the 18th century, after Peter the Great's defeat of the Swedes, that the island was made over as a place of Christian worship. Although there are older churches on the island, the Church of the Transfiguration is undoubtedly the most spectacular: it is crowned with no fewer than 22 domes. Since 1960, the church has been the star of a state-run open-air museum of Russian timber architecture on Kizhi and has been a World Heritage Site since 1990.

St. Basil the Blessed
The iconic Russian church is named after Basil the Blessed (1468–1552), a popular "Holy Fool" who is buried here.

ST. BASIL'S CATHEDRAL

⚰ 1561   📍 MOSCOW, RUSSIA
✍ BARMA & POSNIK YAKOVLEV   🏛 PLACE OF WORSHIP

A polychrome representation, in vegetable-like domes, of the City of God as revealed to St. John the Divine in the Book of Revelation, St. Basil's

INTERIOR VIEW OF ST BASIL'S CATHEDRAL

was ordered by Ivan the Terrible after the defeat of the Mongols at the battle of Kazan in 1552. The church takes the form of eight chapels surrounding a central ninth chapel in a starlike pattern. The whole unlikely confection rises from a stepped pedestal set above Red Square, in the center of Moscow.

Much loved, as much for its eccentricities as for its key place in Russian history, St. Basil's was threatened with demolition by Napoleon in 1812, and again in the 1930s, when Joseph Stalin—trainee Orthodox priest turned atheist Communist dictator—asked his architects to draw up sketches of Red Square, minus St. Basil's.

Each chapel is topped by a whimsical tower, in turn capped with onion domes. Each of the domes has its own special character, some featuring zigzag patterns, others prickling with deeply facetted brickwork. The almost claustrophobic chapels are linked by dark, labyrinthine corridors that promise to lead into some magnificent central nave, but never do. There is so little room inside the church that on great feast days, services were held outside on Red Square.

IVAN THE TERRIBLE

Born in 1530, Ivan IV—"The Terrible"—was just three when he was crowned king and 16 when anointed first Tsar (emperor) of Russia. Professing himself a devout Christian, he nevertheless enjoyed personally torturing his many prisoners. However, the creepy legend that he blinded the architects of St. Basil's so that they could never build anything as brilliant again is unfounded: Posnik Yakovlev went on to build the cathedral of Vladimir.

BIET GIORGIS

⚰ ca. 1300   📍 LALIBELA, ETHIOPIA
✍ UNKNOWN   🏛 PLACE OF WORSHIP

There are a dozen rock churches in Lalibela, a remote village named after the Zagwe king who built them. King Lalibela (1181–1221) was made a saint for his efforts. According to enthusiastic members of the local Coptic church, the churches were built under the direction of St. George, with the help of the Archangel Gabriel and a host of lesser, but equally talented angels. The churches, some carved into cliff faces, are one of the glories of Ethiopian architecture and, although little visited, are being restored.

All 12 churches are extraordinary, but Biet Giorgis, or the Ethiopian Coptic Church of St. George's, is the most extraordinary of all. Hewn deep into the ground from a solid block of red volcanic rock, the church sits in a cavernous trench surrounded by caves and niches for monks and hermits. The building measures 40 × 40 × 43 ft (12 × 12 × 13 m), and its entrance is reached through a narrow tunnel carved into the rock. Twelve windows, perhaps representing the apostles, are cut through an upper story; the nine on the first floor are blind, though nicely carved with floral decoration. The interior is, a mysterious space marked by four three-sided pillars and with a domed sanctuary.

Sunken church

The "roof" of Biet Giorgis is not only structural: carved with a triple Greek cross, it is what visitors first see as they make their way to the church.

India and Southeast Asia

T HE EARLIEST CIVILIZATION in the Indian subcontinent was that of
the Indus Valley, the eastern extension of the Fertile Crescent where
Western civilization first emerged. Perhaps not surprisingly, the culture
that arose here—in the ancient cities of Mohenjodaro and Harappa—
had links to, and was in many ways similar to, that of Sumeria.

For reasons that are unclear, the Indus
civilization died out in about 1500BCE.
Examples of Indus writing exist, but
no one knows what they mean. Nor
do we know what their religion was,
nor how they practiced it—and this
in a land that was to become famous
for its exhilarating temples. The Indus
people had certainly disappeared

before Aryan invaders from Central
Asia charged across India.

AN EMERGING CULTURE
Only slowly did these nomads settle
down. It took 1,500 years—until
about 200BCE—before Indian culture
as we recognize it really came into
being. From then on, there were many

KEY DATES

ca. 700BCE Emergence
of the caste system in
India, with the Brahman
priests at the top level

326BCE Alexander
the Great, King
of Macedonia,
briefly invades
the Indus valley

499 The Hindu
mathematician
Aryabhata writes
the "Aryabhatiya,"
the first book
on algebra

657 Jayavarman
I founds the
Khmer dynasty
in Cambodia

500BCE   **1CE**   **500**

ca. 400BCE Panini's
aphorisms, or sutra,
formalize the
Sanskrit language,
an evolution of Vedic

ca. 50 Thomas, the
apostle of Jesus,
visits India and
establishes a
Christian settlement

ca. 602 The
warlike nomadic
tribes of Tibet are
unified under
Namri Songtsen

711 The Arabs
conquer Sindh
and Multan, or
today's Pakistan

influences at work on the development of Indian architecture. There was a distant echo of the Greeks and of Alexander—who fought his way this far from Macedonia—in the 4th-century Mauryan Buddhist empire in the north. The Kushan empire, founded by Central Asian nomads who made their capital at Peshawar, brought together elements of Greek and Chinese cultures. And then, of course, there were the empires of the Mughals and the British, who saw their own cultures transformed, at best, into such magnificent buildings as the Taj Mahal *(see p.220)* and the Viceroy's House, New Delhi *(p.455)*.

In the south of India, though, were the Hindu dynasties—the Pallavas, Cholas, Early Pandyan, Vijayanagar, and Late Pandyan— all seemingly impervious to outside influences. These were the cultures that created the intriguing temples

The sacred Ganges
The sacred river snakes its way through northern India and Hindu culture; the myths surrounding it are depicted in much temple sculpture.

THE BUDDHA

Siddhartha Gautama was a 6th-century BCE Nepalese prince who renounced his privileged background. After long years of contemplation and denial, he achieved a state of enlightenment, or Nirvana. He was named the Buddha—the "Awakened One"— by his disciples. He continued to teach until his death. Neither god, prophet, nor saint, his subtle influence was to spread across the Indian subcontinent and Southeast Asia, shaping distinctive architecture along the way.

Receiving enlightenment
The Buddha is thought to be just one of a long line of Buddhas stretching back and forth in time.

ca. 800 Kingdoms are created in central India and Rajasthan by Rajput warlords	1192 Islamic chieftains from Afghanistan led by Mohammed of Ghor establish a Muslim sultanate at Delhi	1363 Sultan Mohammed Shah founds the sultanate of Brunei in Borneo	1526 Babur captures Delhi from Ibrahim, the Sultan of Delhi, and founds the Mughal empire in India	1600 The British East India Company is established, sowing the seeds of the British Empire

1000 **1500** **2000**

ca. 1150 Angkor Wat temple complex in Cambodia is built by King Suryavarman II of the Khmer empire	*ca.* 1300 The Tamil establish a kingdom in Ceylon, overthrown by the Portuguese in 1619	1431 Siam invades Angkor and destroys the Khmer empire	1565 Spain occupies the Philippines in a complex play of imperial power in the region

Thai Buddha
Shrines such as this carry a
powerful message: gods are
not a race apart, and every
individual has the potential
for supreme enlightenment.

Krishna vanquishes a demon
In myth, Hindu gods engaged with all levels of Indian society and with the natural world. Here Krishna comes to the aid of his boyhood friends—young cowherds swallowed by a serpent demon.

that we associate so particularly with India, characterized by their massively complex towers, or sikharas, and their physical impenetrability. Religious ceremonies were performed around rather than inside them.

This was true, too, of Buddhist temples. Their influence was to stretch out from India and across Southeast Asia, where the sikhara also makes dramatic appearances. Architectural ideas were able to cross mountains, by word of mouth, through trade, by force and, above all, with religion. The Mauryan emperor Asoka sent Buddhist monks on missions to China, Burma, Thailand, and Cambodia, carrying with them ideas about the running and, presumably, design of temples.

MIX OF INFLUENCES

In an area with so many languages and peoples, it was not surprising that a wealth of architectural ideas emerged; yet it is also fascinating to see how these mingled and merged, so that although it is possible to talk of distinctive forms of Buddhist, Hindu, or Mughal architecture, these tended to blur at the margins. Many of the greatest Mughal buildings are infused with Hindu elements. Equally, when the British bought and fought their way into India, they brought their own architecture with them. By the beginning of the 20th century, when Edwin Lutyens and his team were working on the designs for New Delhi, they had finally seen the point —like the Mughals before them—of incorporating Hindu and Buddhist elements into their work.

There are, though, aspects of Indian and Southeast Asian culture that were never assimilated into the architecture of invaders: a love of nature in terms of depictions of plants, animals, and even human lovers, and of buildings shaped in the guise of lingams (phalluses), fruits, and other richly carved, sensuous, and sensual designs.

HINDU TEMPLE ART

Some of the most animated and moving early Hindu art is to be found adorning the walls of cave and rock temples. These temples contain statues and rock carvings of Hindu gods, such as Shiva, but also representations of touching domestic scenes, reinforcing the notion that all life is sacred. Perhaps the finest examples can be found at the Pallava shore temples at Mahabalipuram on the Bay of Bengal. Here, the monuments range from shrines cut into the rock face to full-blown temples.

Carving of Shiva in rock cave
Shiva is a complex Hindu deity, whose oft-portrayed "dance of bliss" symbolizes the cycle of birth, life, death, and rebirth.

INDIAN ARCHITECTURE
ca. 1700BCE–1800CE

Early Indian architecture is, for the most part, the story of how powerful and popular religions celebrated their beliefs through monumental design. Buddhism, Jainism, and Hinduism all played important roles in the development of buildings that, taken as a whole, celebrate the animal kingdom, the earthly pleasures and otherworldly pursuits of humans, and the complex realm of the gods.

Demonstrating a love both for the physical world and for the realm of the spirit, Indian architecture, and especially Hindu temples, are often warm and sensuous, as well as complex and intriguing, structures. Some of the most beautiful and moving of all are the temples at Mahabalipuram, built as early as the 7th and 8th centuries, on the shores of the Bay of Bengal. But this love for nature and its joyous expression in Hindu carving is a feature of temples throughout central and southern India. The earliest of these are often tender homages to the world of early settled peoples, with their loving depictions of domestic animals. As the centuries rolled by, Hindu temples became celebrations of sculpture that moved away from the agricultural to the highly charged and even erotic celebration of human love—which, at a certain level, can be seen as divinely inspired. The sensuality of architecture so informed remains a challenge, and a delight, to foreign visitors to India.

UNDERSTANDING HINDU TEMPLES
To Western visitors, Hindu temple complexes can be confusing. What are you supposed to look at first? Why are their exteriors so richly decorated? The answer lies in the understanding of a religious culture. Hinduism grew out of Brahmanism. There are many gods in Hinduism, and everything—every living organism, every inanimate object—is connected to them in a binding relationship. In short, all is divine. So the tall, stepped towers, or sikharas, of temples across India are celebrations of all things sacred, from calves and cows to gods, lovers, and kings. These buildings are as much sculpture as architecture, each composed of countless interrelated elements.

◁ THE HAWA MAHAL (PALACE OF THE WINDS) AT JAIPUR, RAJASTHAN, WAS BUILT IN 1799. THE SCREENED BALCONIES ON ITS FACADE ENABLED THE WOMEN OF THE ROYAL HOUSEHOLD TO REMAIN UNSEEN WHILE OBSERVING THE STREET LIFE BELOW.

ELEMENTS

Ancient Indian architecture was affected by powerful and profound religious movements—Buddhism, Brahmanism, and Hinduism. Together, these offer the world a rich and sensuous architecture, balancing the earthly with the divine. A love of nature as well as of crafting buildings is evident at every turn, from carved animals to erotic statuary.

△ **Open kiosks**
Open kiosks are used to animate the skyline of Hindu fortresses and palaces. Some are tiny, others large enough to serve as balconies sheltered from monsoon rains and summer sun.

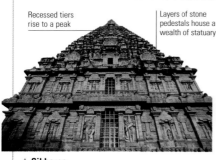

Recessed tiers rise to a peak

Layers of stone pedestals house a wealth of statuary

Rising statuary and abstract carving

△ **Sikharas**
These are the peaks of the "vimanas," or towers, rising from the core of Hindu temples. They vary in shape throughout the country. These towers, such as this one at the temple of Brihadeshvara, Tanjore, are always extravagantly decorated.

△ **Symbolic layers**
The towers of Hindu temples tell stories as they rise skywards. Each has its own distinctive "handwriting" and depicts the concerns of local cults as well as universal themes.

△ **Animal statuary**
To Hindus, all life is sacred and deserving of representation. The shore temples of Mahabalipuram exhibit some of the finest and most tender carvings of animals.

▽ **Stupas**
The stupa is a shrine that represents the sacred Mount Meru, as well as providing a sanctuary for relics of the Buddha. The Great Stupa of Sanchi is the most famous.

A sacred umbrella tops the stupa

Ceremonial gate leads to the shrine

The dome is made of solid brick

MOHENJODARO

🏛 *ca.* 1700BCE 📍 SIND, PAKISTAN ⚒ UNKNOWN 🏛 CITY

The wealth of Mohenjodaro, one of India's earliest cities sited in the fertile Indus Valley, was based on trade in grain; the city's granary was one of the largest buildings discovered in the great brick citadel that forms the core of the settlement. The citadel itself, which featured a large bath as well as other, unidentified public buildings, stood 49 ft (15 m) high. It was separated from the rest of the city by what appears to have been an artificial lake. Beyond the lake lay a grid of residential buildings, facing streets 46 ft (14 m) wide. Two-storied, flat-roofed houses were gathered around wells set in courtyards faced with undecorated walls. In this evidently comfortable and civilized city, many houses boasted bathrooms, complete with plumbing connected to mains sewers.

Urban living
This ancient city with its regular layout was very definitely planned.

HARAPPA

🏛 *ca.* 2550BCE 📍 PAKISTAN ⚒ UNKNOWN 🏛 CITY

Harappa, which with Mohenjodaro is thought to have been one of the first cities of the ancient Indus Valley civilization, was "discovered" in the 1920s. By that time, Victorian railroad engineers had plundered its age-old baked bricks for re-use. However, it is clear that catastrophic flooding over the centuries had done immense damage to this ghost city.

As with Mohenjodaro, Harappa was divided into a citadel and a residential quarter. The gap between the two seems to have been occupied by barracklike housing, which may have been used by workmen engaged in the grain trade. We know little of local culture, nor of the decoration and purpose of individual buildings. The art that has been discovered in the Indus valley remains confined to a small selection of predominantly stone and terracotta statues and rare examples of bronze sculpture.

There has been much speculation regarding the decline of Harappa; whether Aryan invaders devastated the city or whether it was victim of natural disaster no one knows. We do not even know whether the people who once lived here were indigenous or settlers from another culture.

Built in a flood plain
There is little to tell us how the people of this city lived, but their strong bricks have survived millennia.

GREAT STUPA, SANCHI

🖥 100 📍 MADHYA PRADESH, INDIA ✍ UNKNOWN 🏛 PLACE OF WORSHIP

This large and solid-brick hemisphere, constructed on a platform 131 ft (40 m) in diameter as a monument to the Buddha, was rebuilt in the 1st century on the base of an earlier structure erected by the Mauryan emperor Asoka. It would originally have been coated in a thick layer of smooth plaster punctuated by recesses for lamps that would be lit for religious festivals. The monument is surrounded by massive stone railings, punctuated by grand and richly carved gateways offering access to stairs leading up to the ceremonial platform that skirts the stupa's girth.

Protected space
Within the square structure on top is a model of the triple-decked parasol under which the Buddha sat.

RUWANVELISEYA DAGEBA

🖥 137BCE 📍 ANURADHAPURA, SRI LANKA ✍ KING DUTUGEMUNU 🏛 PLACE OF WORSHIP

Anuradhapura was the first capital of Sri Lanka. This majestic dageba, or Buddhist stupa, some 300 ft (90 m) in diameter and 330 ft (100 m) high, was constructed by King Dutugemunu (167–137BCE), the first great hero of the Sinhalese. He had originally wanted it to be twice its present size, but was persuaded by courtiers that he would not live to see its completion. Rocks brought by soldiers formed the foundations, which were trampled by elephants to ensure their firmness. The stupa itself was made of bricks covered in a rough cement, which, in turn, was pasted with mercury sulfide and then draped tightly in a sheet of thick gravel. Over this went sheets of copper, resin dissolved in coconut water, arsenic dissolved in sesamum oil, and sheets of silver. In the relic chamber, the king placed a five-branched Bo tree made of jewels, its roots of crafted coral and sapphire. The stem was made of pure silver, and it was adorned with leaves and fruits of gold. Monuments rarely came more precious than this.

Stupendous dome
The bubble-shaped structure was restored in the early 1930s, when a new gemstone, through which the sun shines, was set on the pinnacle.

CHAITYA HALL, KARLI

🏛 70   📍 MAHARASHTRA, WESTERN INDIA   ✎ UNKNOWN   🏛 PLACE OF WORSHIP

A chaitya hall is a Buddhist temple carved into a rock face and housing a stupa. This, thought to be the largest in India, is a particularly fine example. Through a carved, horseshoe-shaped entrance adorned with 50 ft (15 m) columns crowned with lions and flanked by carvings of elephants, and beyond a softly lit anteroom, lies a truly mysterious hall, or nave, complete with aisles lined with bulbous columns topped with bell-shaped capitals that, in turn, support pedestals stepped on by fierce stone beasts. Above these, a barrel-vaulted timber roof rises into the gloom of the cave. In an apse at the far end of the hall looms a fine and domineering stupa. These cave temples are part of a culture, not exclusively Buddhist, characteristic of the Mauryan period (322–188BCE) and continued

afterward. Rock-cut temples and tombs were part of a tradition extending from Persia and found also at Petra *(see p.119)*. Here, though, the building feels almost animal- or vegetablelike, a rich organic design very different from the quest for straight lines and 90° angles favored west beyond the Indus Valley. It is thought that the Chaitya Hall at Karli was used for secular as well as sacred purposes.

Religious carvings
The rock face is richly worked with Indian Buddhist symbols, while massive columns and statues diminish human importance.

PARASURAMESHVARA TEMPLE, BHUBANESHAWAR

🏛 *ca.* 600   📍 ORISSA, NORTHERN INDIA   ✎ UNKNOWN   🏛 PLACE OF WORSHIP

This is the best-preserved and oldest of a spectacular cluster of Hindu temples found at Orissa, on the east coast of northern India. Its design marks the beginning of a long tradition of temples built in the form of vegetablelike towers encrusted with layer after richly articulated layer of exotic stone carving. The intricate construction, by which structure and decoration are unified, is encoded with symbolic religious meaning. Here, there are carvings of elephants and processions of horses among more abstract designs. A rectangular hall—doubtless a later addition to the tower —is embellished with carved stone windows.

Shrine to Shiva
The temple is dedicated to Shiva, one of the three great Hindu gods.

EROTIC TEMPLES

Can architecture ever be truly sexy? Not really, but India's Hindu temples are a glorious exception. No one knows why some of these buildings are so overtly sensual. One theory suggests that Indra, the thunder god and a keen voyeur, would never strike at such delightful peep shows. Others claim that physical pleasure is key to self-knowledge, and this tantric message found its way on to temple walls.

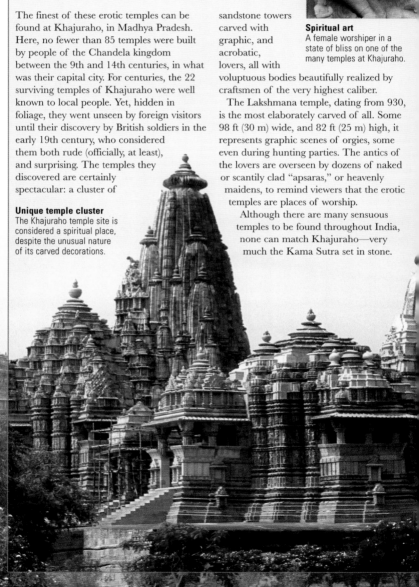

Spiritual art
A female worshiper in a state of bliss on one of the many temples at Khajuraho.

The finest of these erotic temples can be found at Khajuraho, in Madhya Pradesh. Here, no fewer than 85 temples were built by people of the Chandela kingdom between the 9th and 14th centuries, in what was their capital city. For centuries, the 22 surviving temples of Khajuraho were well known to local people. Yet, hidden in foliage, they went unseen by foreign visitors until their discovery by British soldiers in the early 19th century, who considered them both rude (officially, at least), and surprising. The temples they discovered are certainly spectacular: a cluster of sandstone towers carved with graphic, and acrobatic, lovers, all with voluptuous bodies beautifully realized by craftsmen of the very highest caliber.

The Lakshmana temple, dating from 930, is the most elaborately carved of all. Some 98 ft (30 m) wide, and 82 ft (25 m) high, it represents graphic scenes of orgies, some even during hunting parties. The antics of the lovers are overseen by dozens of naked or scantily clad "apsaras," or heavenly maidens, to remind viewers that the erotic temples are places of worship.

Although there are many sensuous temples to be found throughout India, none can match Khajuraho—very much the Kama Sutra set in stone.

Unique temple cluster
The Khajuraho temple site is considered a spiritual place, despite the unusual nature of its carved decorations.

BRIHADESHVARA TEMPLE (GREAT TEMPLE)

🖵 1010   📌 TANJORE, INDIA   ⚒ RAJARAJA CHOLA   🏛 PLACE OF WORSHIP

This phenomenal granite temple is an architectural masterpiece, built during the Chola Empire of Tamil Nadu, in southern India. Said to have been conceived by giants, and finished by jewelers, the temple is crowned by a 13-story, 217 ft (66 m) tower. Its sides record contributions made to it by Rajaraja Chola and his sister, Kundavai, in a huge, 107-paragraph inscription.

The imposing, Dravidian temple (built by native peoples of southern and central India) stands within a wide, rectangular enclosure inside a fort last rebuilt in the 16th century. It was described by the Indian art historian, B. Venkataraman, as "a sculptor's dream, a historian's mine, a dancer's vision, a painter's delight, and a sociologist's scoop rolled into one."

A giant carving of Nandi, the sacred bull ridden by Shiva, weighing some 25 tons, guards the gateways leading to the temple in which there are many more depictions of Nandi, either carved or in frescoes. The inner court, paved with brick and stone and

RAJARAJA CHOLA

Rajaraja (985–1014), and his son, Rajendra (1012–1044), were the most powerful rulers of the Chola empire. The Cholas came to power in the 9th century and ruled most of southern India until the late 13th century. Their main center was Tanjore, in the southeast of what is now Tamil Nadu. Active patrons of the arts, they constructed huge complexes of temples decorated with fine carvings, paintings, and many richly finished portable bronze statues.

measuring approximately 492 x 246 ft (150 x 75 m), is adorned with fine carvings of Shiva as well as lingams—phallic images of the god Shiva. These carvings would have been richly colored at the time of the temple's completion.

The tower, crowned with an 80-ton stone, is the temple's most dramatic feature, but the design of the whole is unified by carving, statuary, and inscriptions. These are remarkably detailed and show the temple as more than a place of worship: it was the heart of the regal city above which it rose.

Civic center
This giant temple was once the hub of an empire—a treasury, public record office, and meeting hall, and a place of worship.

CHENNAKESHAVA TEMPLE

⚱ 1117   📍 BELUR, KARNATAKA, SOUTHERN INDIA   ✍ JAKKAMA ACHARI   🏛 PLACE OF WORSHIP

The architectural pinnacle of the Hoysala empire, the Chennakeshava Temple at Belur is famed for the stunning carvings adorning its many surfaces. The extraordinary degree of detail in these sculptures is taken to such delightful extremes as individual drops of water wrung from a maiden's freshly washed hair. Dedicated to Lord Vishnu, the main temple stands in a spacious courtyard with a pond enclosed by a wall, where it is attended by four lesser, if no less joyously carved,

temples. A soapstone warrior fighting a soapstone tiger represents the Hoysala king, Vishnuvardhana, who began building the Hindu temple after a great victory over the Chola empire at Talakad. The great gray-green stone temple was, perhaps understandably, only finished 103 years later.

A plethora of images
The temple's carvings include some 650 magnificent animals—elephants, horses, lions, tigers, birds—along with warriors and sensual "celestial dancers."

JAIN TEMPLES, MOUNT ABU

⚱ 11TH–13TH CENTURIES   📍 RAJASTHAN, INDIA
✍ UNKNOWN   🏛 PLACE OF WORSHIP

Rising from among the mango trees and wooded hills of Rajasthan's only hill station are five beautiful Jain temples, built of marble and famed for their lucid forms and rich yet elegant carving. Two stand out, the temple of Vimala Vashi (1031) and that of Luna Vashi (1230). The first stands in an open courtyard surrounded by a corridor punctuated by many miniature temples containing idols. The beautiful domed main hall is supported by 12 decorated columns, each featuring a carved female figure playing a musical instrument. The Luna Vashi temple, although 200 years younger, is remarkably similar in style, gathered around a domed hall supported by ornamented columns and ringed with a band of 360 miniature Jain monks. The temple's much loved Hathishala, or Elephant Cell, is host to ten beautifully carved and highly realistic stone elephants. Both temples are filled with light and, because of their gleaming marble construction, feel almost ethereal.

JAIN TEMPLES, RANAKPUR

⚱ 1439   📍 RANAKPUR, INDIA   ✍ RANA KUMBHA
AND DHARNA SAH   🏛 PLACE OF WORSHIP

This remote three-story white marble temple, the most ambitious built by the Jains, is famous not just for its scale but for the intricacy of its design. Rows of small attendant shrines and intriguing carving aside, the interior of the temple is a treasure trove of, supposedly, 1,444 carved columns supporting more domes than any Baroque city might dare to boast, yet so disposed as to allow glimpses in all directions of statues of the first Jain, Trithankara Adinath, the revealer of truth. The lofty, spired temple complex is enclosed by a 200 ft (61 m) wall.

PUBLIC BATHS, BENARES

⛲ 14TH CENTURY 📍 VARANASI, UTTAR PRADESH, INDIA ✍ UNKNOWN 🏛 BATHS

For its millions of bathers, pilgrims, and tourists, the Ganges River represents one of the spiritual hearts of India, a microcosm of life, spirit, ritual, and history. The route to the river's sacred waters at Benares (modern Varanasi) lies through the ghats, the broad public bathing steps that stretch for 3 miles (5 km) along the banks of the holy river. These steps have for many centuries witnessed ritual cremations by Hindus, who believe that by ending their lives here, or even just by bathing in the waters, they will escape the cycle of reincarnation and rest eternally in Heaven. There is no doubt that the desire to live or die on the banks of the Ganges has created a very particular and special waterfront, architectural in character and giving great strength and individuality to the city's spectacularly busy waterside. At certain points, old palaces lean out over the great stone steps, giving parts of this fascinating city a fairytale appearance.

GIANT BUDDHAS, BAMIYAN

⛲ ca. 700 📍 BAMIYAN, NORTHERN AFGHANISTAN ✍ UNKNOWN 🏛 MONUMENT

Once among the largest and finest images of the Buddha in the world, the Giant Buddhas of Bamiyan are now confined to history. Destroyed by the Taliban in 2001, only rubble remains of the two colossal rock-hewn carvings. Influenced by Indian tradition, the vast sculptures, which stood 115 ft (35 m) and 187 ft (57 m) tall, were chiseled into the cliffs that tower over the valley of Bamiyan, northwest of Kabul, at the heart of the cultural, religious, and artistic kingdom of Kushan. The sculptures would have been painted in luminous gold, covered with ornaments, and attended by saffron-robed monks from ten monasteries.

POTALA PALACE

⛲ 1695 📍 LHASA, TIBET ✍ UNKNOWN 🏛 MONASTERY

This great set piece, against its mountainous backdrop, evokes the image of an impossibly exotic fortified medieval hill town. A rare example of traditional Tibetan architecture balanced with Indian and Chinese aesthetics, the beautiful Potala Palace seems to grow naturally from a hill above the Lhasa plains

Formidable sight
The 1,000-room Potala Palace covers a breathtaking 3,875,000 sq ft (360,000 m²), and rises 660 ft (200 m) against a hillside.

to climb 624 ft (190 m). The 13-story timber and stone monastery is in two parts, the White and Red Palaces. These house the traditional living quarters of the Dalai Lama (exiled since 1959) and the remainder of the monastery with its places of worship, cells, kitchens, and stores. Imposing externally, with grand sloping walls, golden roofs, bell-towers, and watch-towers, the palace contains richly decorated sanctuaries and state rooms, one supported by 50 columns.

SOUTHEAST ASIA
ca. 500–1500

It was through Buddhism and Hinduism that Indian building traditions were introduced to Southeast Asia. They spread so rapidly that by the 13th century, the architecture of the stupa, the stepped sikhara, and the lotus-bud tower stretched through Burma, Cambodia, and Thailand to Indonesia. Much of this later fell into a ruinous state, and was resurrected only in the 19th and 20th centuries.

The greatest achievements of historic Southeast Asian architecture were undoubtedly those of Angkor Wat, in Cambodia *(see p.154)*, and the Stupa at Borobudur, Java, Indonesia *(see p.153)*—two very different temples that both represent Meru, the cosmic Buddhist mountain. While Angkor Wat contains many rooms and chambers, Borobudur is all exterior—like the stepped pyramids of Mesoamerica, it has the magnificent brooding presence of an artificial mountain. And where Angkor Wat is a celebration of the art of rock-solid construction, Borobudur is almost otherworldly, its stupa laden with layers of meaning. One of these is the building's association with the five Buddhist elements: the square base of the stupa represents earth; the round dome is for water; the cone on top of the dome is fire; the canopy above this is air; and the volume of the stupa as a whole is space. The result is a work of architecture that guides us through the principal elements of our lives. This superb building is a glorious contradiction, trying its best to lift us up to a spiritual plane while being a richly worked, tactile, sensuous object rising, in solid stone, from a jungle clearing.

A SPATE OF TEMPLE-BUILDING
The construction of temples dominated architectural efforts in Burma, so much so that, in the capital of Pagan alone, there were said to have been no fewer than 5,000 stupas and temples, all of them, great or small, richly adorned with the finest works of local craftsmanship. This temple fever spread out across Thailand and Indonesia, too. Their construction, as well as their rise and fall, also tells the story of how the spread of Buddhism was gradually replaced by the rise and triumph of Hinduism.

◁ **ANGKOR WAT WAS THE FUNERARY TEMPLE OF THE KHMER KING SURYAVARMAN II (1113–50). AFTER THE DECLINE OF THE KHMER EMPIRE, IT REMAINED OVERGROWN BY FOREST FOR HUNDREDS OF YEARS UNTIL ITS CHANCE REDISCOVERY IN 1856.**

ELEMENTS

As Buddhism spread into Southeast Asia, so did the influence of Chinese architecture. The result, over a long courtship, was a marriage of very different design traditions that gave birth to building styles as varied as the stupas of Burma, the temple cities of Cambodia, and the palaces of Bangkok.

Intersecting roofs derived from pagoda form

Sensuality fused with spirituality

◁ **Elaborate reliefs**
Relief carvings are elements of temples and palaces throughout Southeast Asia. Most are highly naturalistic, yet were intended to lead the viewer to the contemplation of higher, otherworldly things.

△ **Small attendant spires**
Even palaces owed a debt to the design of stupas. Here, the complex crossing of the Throne Room of the Royal Palace, Bangkok, shows echoes of ancient Buddhism, as well as Hindu and Chinese precedent.

◁ **Miniature pagodas**
Miniature and richly decorated gold pagodas, here encircling the Shwe Dagon stupa in Burma, served to exaggerate the enormous scale of the main bulk of a shrine; here, the spire rises to a height of 370 ft (113 m).

△ **Gold leaf**
Gold leaf was used extensively, not only inside but also on the exteriors of temples, shining with the sun and gleaming in rainfall.

▽ **Bell stupas**
The great bell stupas that emerged through the region owed much to the design of these conical-hatted royal tombs and shrines at Ayudhya in Thailand.

Disclike ribbed construction

Spires raised on colonnaded drums

Dome often at least partially solid

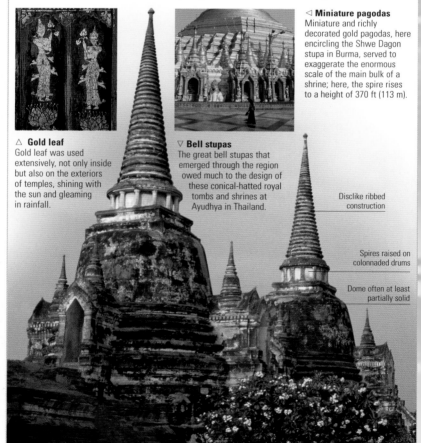

BOROBUDUR

ca. 842   JOGYAKARTA, JAVA   UNKNOWN   PLACE OF WORSHIP

This stunning lava-rock stupa is a representation of Buddhist cosmology spiraling around the axis of the mythical sacred Mount Meru and leading the faithful up from everyday concerns of earthly life to Nirvana, a state of transcendental nothingness or absolute purity.

The 31.5m (103 ft) high shrine is arranged in three parts over nine tiers. These frame open-air galleries decorated with 1,460 narrative bas-reliefs and 432 niches that once contained statues of the Buddha.

The square tiers that form the base are decorated with scenes from everyday Javanese life, incorporated into stories from the life of the Buddha. Above these, three circular tiers are set with 72 miniature bell-shaped stupas, each containing a statue

AERIAL VIEW

of the Buddha. The huge, topmost stupa was probably always empty.

These three levels represent the Buddhist division of the universe. In the lowest Sphere of Desire, the human spirit is chained to greed. In the middle Sphere of Form, the human spirit is not yet able to transcend the material world. At the top, in the Sphere of Formlessness, the spirit has left earthly considerations behind.

THE BUDDHA

Buddha means the "Awakened One" and refers to anyone who has discovered enlightenment. It also refers to the Buddha—Indian-born Siddhartha Gautama. Siddhartha was a teacher and guide who believed that there was no intermediary between humankind and divinity, and that Nirvana was the gift of all beings. Buddhists believe he was one of many Buddhas, in the past and in the future.

Repeated use of the stupa shape
Borobudur contains many stupas but is itself one enormous stupa, representing a universe containing many other universes.

ANGKOR WAT

🗓 *ca.* 1150   📍 SIEM REAP, CAMBODIA   ✍ DIVAKARAPANDITA   🏛 PLACE OF WORSHIP

Abandoned and largely forgotten for half a millennium, the breathtaking ruins of Angkor Wat are one of the true wonders of the architectural world: a deeply ambitious temple complex, built on the scale of the Egyptian pyramids, with the sculptural subtlety of the Parthenon and the detail of a medieval cathedral.

From their citadel, Angkor, the kings of the Khmer empire ruled by divine decree over a vast domain stretching north from southern Vietnam to Yunnan in China and west to the Bay of Bengal. Their wooden palaces, public buildings, and houses have long gone, yet ruins of their great stone temples remain. A funerary temple for the Khmer king Suryavarman II (1113–1150), abandoned after its conquering and sacking by the Thais in 1431, today Angkor Wat is alive with camera-toting tourists. This impossibly imposing Hindu temple, crowned with five lotus-bud towers, rises on a series of colonnaded platforms set behind tiers of arcaded walls fronted by a moat 2.5 miles (4 km) long. The complex is approached across the water via a causeway bordered on either side by giant balustrades in the form of serpents associated with the Hindu creation myth. The walls of the lower terraces are rich in relief sculpture: 2,635 ft (800 m) of carvings tell tales of the Mahabharata and the Ramayana, legendary Indian epics.

STONE HEADS LINING THE CAUSEWAY

Above rise the five towers, including the king's sepulchre. Angkor Wat was a kind of model of the universe; its appeal is certainly universal today.

THE REDISCOVERY OF ANGKOR

In the centuries following its abandonment, Buddhist monks, explorers, and other travelers occasionally stumbled across the ruins of Angkor Wat in the jungle, but it was not until 1858 that Henri Mouhout, a French naturalist, brought them to the world's attention. The French government launched a restoration project in 1908 that, though interrupted by brutal wars and social upheaval, continues today.

Fit for a king
Occupying a site measuring 5,100 × 4,600 ft (1,550 × 1,400 m), Angkor Wat was 30 years in the making.

PRE RUP TEMPLE

🏛 961   📍 SIEM REAP, CAMBODIA   ✎ UNKNOWN   🏛 PLACE OF WORSHIP

The dusky red "temple-mountain" of Pre Rup—symbolizing Mount Meru, home of the Hindu gods—was crafted, mostly from brick and stone, in the late 10th century as the state temple for the Khmer king Rajendravarman II. The temple is a three-tiered stepped pyramid crowned with five towers. The lowest tier hosts a dozen small, east-facing sanctuary towers, each containing lingas. Worship of the Lingam (the divine phallus, or cosmic column of fire) was the state religion, and the Lingam was also associated with the power of the king, who identified himself with Shiva. The third tier, constructed of sandstone, is intricately carved, as are the two stairways ascending the pyramid, flanked by stone lions. The temple has long been regarded by the Cambodians as a site of funerals: the name "Pre Rup" means "turn the body," referring to a cremation ritual thought to have taken place at the base of the temple. Pre Rup lies within the 102 sq mile (400 km²) Angkor World Heritage Site.

Divine symmetry
The five towers, of which this is the central one, have their entrances on the east side and, on the other sides, false doors carved into the sandstone.

BANTEAY SREI TEMPLE

🏛 967   📍 SIEM REAP, CAMBODIA   ✎ UNKNOWN   🏛 PLACE OF WORSHIP

Located in a mountainous region about 12 miles (20 km) from Angkor, the miniature temple of Banteay Srei, meaning "citadel of the women," is one of the region's best-loved architectural treasures. The temple is appreciated not only for its unusually small size—the central tower is only 30 ft (9 m) high, and the sanctuary chamber measures just 5½ft (1.7 m) by 6 ft (1.9 m)—but also for its unusual pink sandstone (quartz arenite) walls; these are carved, with spectacular intricacy, with floral patterns, stories from religious myths, and superbly modeled images of Hindu deities.

The temple comprises three enclosures defined by simple walls reached by

a processional way bordered with decorative statues. Its overall state of preservation is remarkable, as is the exquisite quality of its decoration. It was built by Yajnyavaraha, a Brahmin of royal descent who was a spiritual teacher to the Khmer king Jayavarman V. It is one of approximately 100 Khmer temples in the Angkor area and, like the Pre Rup temple, slightly predates Angkor Wat. Carved pediments from the temple can be found in the National Museum of Cambodia, Phnom Penh, and the National Museum of Asiatic Art, Paris.

Khmer art
Carvings from the period are often high relief. They depict mythical figures combining human and sacred characteristics.

Angkor Wat
The holy city of Angkor is surrounded by a moat 600 ft (183 m) wide, protecting it and enhancing its beauty. The elevated towers, covered galleries, and courtyards of this great temple are built on, and around, a vast stepped pyramid.

SHWE DAGON PAGODA

🕉 ca. 1700 📍 RANGOON, BURMA ✍ UNKNOWN 🏛 PLACE OF WORSHIP

Often referred to as one of the forgotten wonders of the world, the 370 ft (113 m) high golden Shwe Dagon pagoda and stupa on Singuttara Hill dominates the skyline of Rangoon. Built and rebuilt over many centuries and influenced by both Chinese and Indian architectural and religious traditions, the pagoda is a solid stupa, or reliquary shrine dedicated to the Buddha. It has no interior. It does, though, have four doors, which are still said to be protected, somewhere inside mysterious passageways, by sinister swords that scythe in the darkness. So, stay resolutely outside and enjoy the stunning view. The gold-plated and jewel-encrusted stupa rises from a cluster of 64 smaller pagodas, with four larger ones marking the four cardinal points of the compass. These house sanctuaries adorned with statues of lions, elephants, yogis, serpents, ogres, and angels. The whole construction is eye-boggling, lavish, and magnificent.

Solid structure
The stupa has survived eight major earthquakes and a potentially devastating fire in 1938.

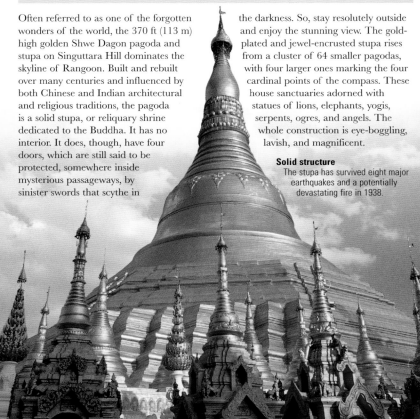

ANANDA TEMPLE

🕉 ca. 1105 📍 PAGAN, BURMA ✍ UNKNOWN
🏛 PLACE OF WORSHIP

With its whitewashed brick walls, delicately tiered roofs, and tapering golden spires, the gorgeous Ananda Temple marks the zenith of classical Burmese architecture. Its plan is a Greek cross, each arm of the cross rising to a large gabled entrance. Above the center of the cross, six terraces rise upward from a stupa to the temple's 171 ft (52 m) gilded teardroplike spire, or "sikarah." Inside are two dark ambulatories, in one of which visitors are greeted by four 30 ft (9 m) Buddhas housed in recesses carved from the deep walls. The temple is girded with extensive walls and rises from a courtyard rich with shady trees.

SHIVA TEMPLE, PRAM'BANAM

🕉 855 📍 PRAM'BANAM, JAVA ✍ UNKNOWN
🏛 PLACE OF WORSHIP

The temple of Shiva is part of a complex of over 150 shrines discovered at Pram'banam, representing the decline of Buddhism and the revival of Hinduism in 9th-century Java. Cruciform in plan, on a square base, with four broad formal staircases and a central chamber measuring 112 ft (34 m) square at its base, the temple reaches a height of 154 ft (47 m). It has much fine sculpture and is particularly noted for a gallery containing 42 bas-reliefs illustrating the Hindu morality epic of Ramayana, depicting Lord Vishnu in his human incarnation, Rama.

WAT PHRA SRI SARAPET

📷 *ca.* 1500 📍 AYUDHYA, THAILAND ✍ UNKNOWN 🏛 MONUMENT

A cluster of enchanting bell-like stupas capped with conical spires, like wizards' hats, Wat Phra Sri Sarapet is the most impressive temple in the historic and once extensive and densely populated Thai city of Ayudhya, founded in the mid-14th century. Erected as royal funerary monuments, the stupas contained secret chambers decorated with frescoes and filled with votive objects in honor of dead kings. Each of the stupas is symmetrical, with stairs rising up the stone "bells" to gabled doors, one at each cardinal point of the compass. Each stupa is decorated with rings carved through the stonework to the very tops of the spires, creating enchanting patterns of shifting light and shade during the day. The temple, one of many in the area (although none is so well preserved) was first built in the reign of King Boromtrilokanath. Ayudhya was sacked in the 18th century, with invaders looting many of the treasures of the great temple.

Royal ruins
Fragments of the royal palace and monastery surround the three pointed stupas.

TEMPLE OF LITERATURE

📷 *ca.* 1400 📍 HANOI, VIETNAM
✍ LY THANH TONG 🏛 UNIVERSITY

The Temple of Literature, dedicated to Confucius, was founded in 1070 by Emperor Ly Thanh Tong. In 1076 it became part of Vietnam's first university, Quoc Tu Giam, established to educate the country's administrative and warrior class. Parts of the university date from this time, although the extensive complex has undergone many changes over the centuries. Recent archaeological study indicates that the architecture stems primarily from the Ly (1010–1225) and Tran (1225–1400) dynasties. The complex is sited in a park in the heart of Hanoi and contains many red and gold temples with strong Chinese characteristics set around paths, gardens, and a central pond. Two of the shrines shelter 82 stone memorials carried on the backs of giant stone tortoises. These record the names of the 1,306 students awarded doctorates here between 1443 and 1788.

PHA THAT LUANG

📷 1566 📍 VIENTIANE, LAOS
✍ LOUIS DELAPORTE 🏛 PLACE OF WORSHIP

This extraordinary Buddhist stupa is the most important historic monument in Laos. In legend, it was founded in the 3rd century BCE to enshrine a breastbone of the Buddha. But although there was a Khmer monastery here in the 12th century, the shrine in fact dates from 1566, when King Setthathirat moved his capital from Luang Prabang to Vientiane. Covered in gold leaf, it was plundered by invaders from Burma, Siam (now Thailand), and China. The present structure is a French reconstruction dating from the 1930s.

East Asia

Snaking 4,160 miles (6,700 km) through the mountains north of Beijing, the 2,000-year-old Great Wall of China has come to symbolize Western notions of Eastern culture. Designed to defend, this huge barrier also had the effect of isolating China, just as, for centuries, Japan sealed itself off from the rest of the world.

With imperial rule coming to an end as recently as 1911, the history of China over the last 2,000 years is the story of its dynasties. For much of this time, China was, to Western eyes, a mysterious world, strictly regulated by imperial law and with a vast laboring class capable of works of construction as impressive as the Great Wall *(see p.167)* and the Forbidden City *(see pp.172–3)*.

Chinese culture, boxed-in partly by its self-imposed isolationism, and partly by its beautiful but distinctive writing system, gave rise to an architectural tradition that was often self-referential and hermetic. However, China was not entirely impervious to outside influences.

Terracotta warriors
This famous army of 10,000 life-size figures guards the tomb of the first Chinese emperor, Qin Shi Huangdi (259–210BCE), who completed the Great Wall.

Chinese calligraphy
In use for four millennia, the Chinese written language has barely changed in the last 2,000 years, unifying Chinese society.

KEY DATES

50 Buddhism is introduced to China, and the first stupas are built

105 Ts'ai Lun invents paper, revolutionizing the way information is presented, stored, and transported

220 Han dynasty ends and China enters a period of conflict and fragmentation; artistic cultures diverge, but flourish

500 Japan adopts the Chinese alphabet

1

500

581–618 Sui dynasty reunites North and South China

538 The Korean kingdom of Paekche dispatches a delegation to introduce Buddhism to the Japanese emperor

607 The Horyu-ji Buddhist temple complex is built, one of the earliest after the spread of Buddhism from China to Japan

725 Xi'an becomes the most populous city in the world, dwarfing European contemporaries

1000

1045 Bi Sheng invents the printing press, 400 years before it appears in Europe

Buddhism made its way into the country early on, bringing with it Indian styles of architecture; and China's famous Silk Road trade route, through Central Asia to Istanbul, brought traces of Persian and even Greek design. In turn, Chinese ideas began to percolate back to the West, just as they had made their mark in the East by traveling to Japan

EDO-PERIOD JAPAN

The height of Japanese isolationism came during the Edo period (1603–1868) established, by force, by Tokugawa Ieyasu, who set up his government in Edo, today's Tokyo. In 1633, his successor, Shogun Iemitsu, forbade foreign travel and foreign books, and greatly reduced trade contacts. Society was divided into five rigid classes, with the samurai, or warrior caste, at the top and the untouchables at the bottom. Despite these strict restrictions, art and culture became richer and more popular than ever before.

Samurai warriors
A member of the warrior caste is challenged in battle by a chivalrous commoner (a folk hero) in this print that dates back to the 1850s.

via Korea. Here they met a feudal society—Japan—which maintained its isolation from the rest of the world well into the modern era. While the West began to appreciate the art and erudition of Chinese society, Japan remained an enigma, a realm in which, in popular myth, fighting between warlords was tempered only by the rituals of religion. Yet it was to be the almost supernatural serenity of Japanese architecture that eventually had the greater impact on the Western world.

1103 Architect Li Jie publishes *Yingzao Fashi*, setting out Chinese building methods and standards

1227 Zen Buddhism is introduced in Japan by the monk Dogen

1200

1264 The Mongols conquer China; Kublai Khan founds the Yuan dynasty with his capital in Beijing

1274 The Mongols of Kublai Khan try to invade Japan but are repelled by *Kamikaze*

1368 Founding of 300-year Chinese Ming dynasty by former Buddhist monk Chu Yuanchang

1394 Yi Song-gye's Choson dynasty sees establishment of Korean capital at Seoul

1400

1467 Japanese civil war sees shogunate split into very many rival feudal fiefdoms

1549 The Catholic missionary Francis Xavier reaches Japan

1603 The emperor of Japan moves the government to Edo (Tokyo) and founds the Tokugawa dynasty of shoguns

1600

CHINA
ca. 25–1700

The vastness of China and its many climates should have created a plethora of architectural styles. While there are regional differences, driven by religion and locale, there are also set styles that, emerging early, spread across the country with ritualistic aplomb. In 1103, a government publication called *Yingzao fashi* ("Building Method") was disseminated throughout China to achieve a consistency of style.

Chinese architecture cannot be understood without recourse to a copy of *Yingzao fashi*. This illustrated codification of Chinese building methods and standards, compiled over three years by the architect Li Jie, made several key recommendations on the design, structure, and decoration of timber buildings that were to stay in vogue for many hundreds of years. One of these insisted that there should be no extraneous or applied decoration. Another stated that buildings had to be earthquake-proof, so they must be constructed using mortise-and-tenon joints that would move as the buildings shook from side to side. In addition, they were to be built without foundations, so that, again, they would shift with movements in the earth rather than keel over. They should be made from standardized components—in other words, lengths and proportions of timber that could be repeated on any site. There was also a strict color code: walls, pillars, doors, and window frames of palaces and temples were to be painted red; roofs were to be yellow; blue and green were for the underside of eaves and ceilings. When grouped, buildings were to be arranged axially and symmetrically.

DIVERSITY AMID CONFORMITY

Remarkably, visitors to Chinese temple, monastery, and palace complexes will find the early-12th century demands of *Yingzao fashi* still very much in evidence. Whether in the Forbidden City in Beijing *(see p.172)*, or at the Hanging Monastery at Hunyuan *(see p.169)*, the same elements can be seen, with the same colors and the same sense of near-timeless serenity. It is in the design of such singular buildings as the pagodas of China *(see p.171)* that the visitor is more able to discern differences in architectural style.

◁ THE TEMPLE OF HEAVEN, BEIJING, WAS BUILT DURING THE MING DYNASTY (1368–1644). THE TEMPLE IS ROUND BECAUSE HEAVEN WAS BELIEVED TO BE ROUND; IT SITS ON A SQUARE BASE, SYMBOLIZING THE EARTH.

ELEMENTS

Traditional Chinese architecture exhibits what appears to be a remarkable consistency not just of design, planning, and structure, but also of use of color and decoration. This reflects an early insistence—perilous to disobey—from the imperial court in Beijing that there should be common standards in what was seen as a unified culture.

△ **Decorative finials**
Finials—carvings that bring roof ridges to a logical and satisfying aesthetic conclusion—are often elaborately decorated, with snakes, dragons, and other fierce creatures protecting the buildings they adorn.

△ **Rooftop statuary**
The decoration of Chinese buildings tended to follow the form of their structure, yet these idiosyncratic ceramic dragons squatting on a curved eave seem happily gratuitous, a law unto themselves.

△ **Bright roof tiles**
Brilliantly glazed roof tiles typify the strong use of color throughout Chinese architecture. Typically, buildings were color-coded in uniform shades, depending on the purpose or nature of the building.

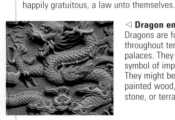

◁ **Dragon emblems**
Dragons are found throughout temples and palaces. They were the symbol of imperial China. They might be made of painted wood, jade, stone, or terracotta.

△ **Lion statues**
Lions guard the entrances to many palaces and temples and are a notable feature of the Forbidden City in Beijing. Usually curly-maned, they are always fierce.

Protective rooftop menagerie

Yellow-tiled roof signifying a palace

Abstract flower decoration

◁ **Elaborate gateway**
There was a high degree of standardization in Chinese architecture. This ceremonial gateway in the Forbidden City is charmingly decorated yet is built to strict laws of proportion and displays the ritual color coding that announced its purpose and laws.

Red paint indicates exclusive palace entrance

GREAT WALL OF CHINA

📺 AFTER 214BCE 🏴 CHINA ✂ UNKNOWN 🏛 FORTIFICATION

Snaking across the northern border of China, the largest military structure in the world makes its way from Shanhaiguan in the east to Jiayuguan in the west. The Great Wall is an amalgamation of ancient walls belonging to over 20 states and dynasties. It became one united defensive system in 214BCE, under the rule of Emperor Qin Shi Huang.

WATCHTOWER

The earliest remains of the wall have been found on the south bank of the Yellow River and are thought to date from 680BCE. These earthwork structures were replaced with stone slabs during the Qin dynasty in the 3rd century BCE. The reconstruction continued, using many kinds of local materials, for almost 1,500 years, until 1210—when the Mongols, led by Genghis Khan, poured over the supposedly unbreachable barrier and conquered China. With the arrival of the Ming Dynasty in 1368, new work began on the wall, which was completed in *ca.* 1500.

The wall varies in height from 20 to 33 ft (6 to 10 m), with an average depth of 21 ft (6.5 m) at its base, tapering to 19 ft (5.8 m) at its top. It has 20,000 watchtowers, with one sited every 328 ft (100 m). The strong parapets have the ability to withstand gunpowder, cannon, and musket shot. Of the original 3,728 miles (6,000 km), only 1,616 miles (2,600 km) remain.

CONSTRUCTION AND DESTRUCTION

Thousands of convicts, slaves, soldiers, and local people gave their lives in the construction and reconstruction of the wall; many of them were buried within the wall, and it was long viewed by the Chinese people as a symbol of tyrannical oppression. Much damage has been done over the centuries by poverty-stricken farmers, who used the wall as a quarry. The wall has more recently been worn down by the feet of millions of tourists.

Symbol of power
Built to withstand the incursion of barbaric northern tribes, the Great Wall of China is now a World Heritage Site.

YUNGANG GROTTOES

🪦 *ca.* 500 📍 DATONG, SHANXI, CHINA ✍ UNKNOWN 🏛 GROTTOES

When Buddhism spread east from India along ancient caravan routes, it left a lasting mark on Chinese culture. The Yungang Grottoes, carved into the sandstone cliffs of the Wuzhou mountain range in the northern part of Shanxi province, constitute a collective masterpiece of early Chinese Buddhist art.

The 53 grottoes, dating from the 5th-century Northern Wei dynasty and varying considerably in design, are home to some 51,000 statues and a riot of carvings of gods, demons, and animals. The excavation of the Yungang caves began in 453, under the auspices of the noted monk Tan Yao. Over a period of some 50 years, twenty major caverns and numerous smaller caves were carved into the sandstone cliffs. Originally, the entrances to large caves were covered by wooden temples several stories high and one room deep. Only two survive.

CARVED AND PAINTED BUDDHA

FAR-FLUNG INFLUENCES

Even at this early time, China was a great trading nation, and its early art was influenced by many sources. Some caves, with their orderly Greek-like columns and stone porticos, allude to Indian chattris and even Roman basilicas. But the heavy decoration —dragons and phoenixes, curved roofs supported by elaborate brackets, and serpentine carvings—shows Iranian and Byzantine influences.

Buddhist monks on pilgrimages used the caves, or grottoes, as places for lodging, centers of worship, and repositories for documents, sacred works, and works of art. Significant repairs to the caves were made during the 11th and 17th centuries. By the early 20th century, travelers to the area reported that the caves had fallen into a state of neglect. Much damage has been done to the interiors of the cave temples by industrial pollution: Datong is one of China's most intensive coal-mining districts.

Niches for carvings
The caves range in size from 68 ft (21 m) deep to little more than recesses to hold carvings.

HANGING MONASTERY, XUANKONG SI

🪦 586 📍 HUNYUAN, SHANXI, CHINA ✎ UNKNOWN 🏛 MONASTERY

Like some fantastic bird's nest, Xuankong Si, the "Hanging Monastery," is perched precariously 164 ft (50 m) above ground at the foot of Hengshan Mountain and above the fast-flowing Golden Dragon River. Admired for its superb workmanship, perilous construction, ingenious engineering, daring cantilevers, and extraordinary beauty, the monastery is approached over a bridge and up a stone staircase chiseled from the rock face. Although originally built during the Northern Wei dynasty, much was reconstructed during the Ming (1368–1644) and Qing (1644–1911) dynasties. Despite being built upon one of China's four most

sacred Taoist mountains, the monastery is famous for its Three Religions Hall, where statues of the Buddha, Confucius, and Laotzu (the founder of Taoism) sit side by side. Inside many of the caves there are images of the Buddha made of copper, iron, terracotta, and stone, most of them, like the buildings, vividly colored. In the depths of winter, with no tourists, yet protected from winds, the monastery is silent.

Precarious perch
Over 40 wooden pavilions and caves cluster here, including six main halls with brilliantly colored tiled roofs, linked by winding corridors and bridges supported by beams driven into the cliff face.

TEMPLE OF HONAN

🪦 479 📍 LOYANG, CHINA ✎ UNKNOWN 🏛 PLACE OF WORSHIP

This is the Shaolin temple seen in many a Chinese kung fu movie, and the one used in the long-running *Kung Fu* series of the 1970s starring David Carradine. More importantly, this is where Buddhist scriptures were first translated into Chinese. Located in Loyang, a small mountain town southwest of Beijing, the temple, badly damaged during the Boxer Rebellion of 1900–1, was restored by the Chinese government in the mid-1970s. Today, it is a mecca for martial arts enthusiasts, and many of the resident "monks" are, in fact, actors. In its long heyday, the temple was home to senior monks of the Shaolin Order. It was

commissioned during the Northern Wei dynasty by the emperor Hsiao Wen. Enclosed by a wall, the temple complex comprises a gateway, porch, successive halls, and a sanctuary containing a statue of the Buddha with seats around it for the monks. Beyond are offices, kitchens, vast libraries, and rooms full of art and sculpture, all arranged according to the ancient laws of *feng shui* and housed under elegantly dramatic roofs. Originally, the temple had 12 upper and lower courts and was ringed almost completely by mountains, festooned with bamboo, cassia, and cedar trees, and laced with waterfalls.

ZHENHAI TOWER

⚑ 1380   📍 GUANGZHOU, CHINA
🔨 UNKNOWN   🏛 FORTIFICATION

This bright red tower, known to locals as the Five-Story Pagoda, was built on top of Yuexiu Hill by Zhu Liangzu, Yongjia Marquis of the Ming dynasty. The broad, tall tower, with green glazed tiles and stone lions to guard its doorway, was later incorporated into Guangzhou's city wall as its northernmost watchtower.

The tower rises from a stone base with battlements. When pollution levels are low, it commands magnificent views of a city that has changed out of all recognition. The city wall has gone, and the tower now stands alone in the pretty location of Yuexiu Park—an oasis of lakes, bridges, pagodas, birds, fish, and trees, created north of downtown Guangzhou in 1952.

Over the past 600 years, the tower has been destroyed five times and reconstructed five times, most recently in 1928. It is now in use as Guangzhou Museum, housing relics and documents relating to the ancient city's 2,000 years of checkered history.

HUMBLE ADMINISTRATOR'S GARDEN

⚑ 1513   📍 SUZHOU, CHINA
🔨 UNKNOWN   🏛 GARDEN

One of the most famous private gardens in China is the "Garden of the Humble Administrator." Built during the reign of Emperor Zhengde (1506–21) for a retired court censor, it covers an area of about 10 acres (4 ha).

Zigzag pathways traverse magnificent ponds that stretch to the feet of pavilions and terraces, so that the whole garden seems to be floating. Architectural techniques are used to frame views in pavilion windows, or arrange glimpses of distant pagodas along geometrically precise avenues.

TEMPLE OF THE SLEEPING BUDDHA

⚑ 629   📍 BEIJING, CHINA   🔨 UNKNOWN   🏛 PLACE OF WORSHIP

Located on the eastern side of the Fragrant Hills, this beautiful temple was first built in the 7th century, during the heyday of the Tang Dynasty (618–907), and subsequently rebuilt many times. Standing within the grounds of Beijing's Botanical Gardens, with a glorious mountain backdrop, it comprises four halls and courtyards. Three arches in

sculpted marble mark the entrance to the complex. The arches are separated by vermilion stucco walls with panels enameled in yellow, green, and blue.

Beyond are three handsome, classical Chinese buildings: the Mountain Gate Hall, the Hall of the Heavenly Kings, and the Hall of the Buddhas of the Three Worlds, all clustered under deeply eaved and heavily tiled roofs. The fourth building —the Hall of the Sleeping Buddha—is the largest in the temple and accommodates a very special 17 ft (5.3 m) long, 54-ton bronze reclining Buddha, cast in 1321.

Sakyamuni
This early forebear of Buddhism in China lies on his deathbed, giving instructions to his 12 clay disciples.

PAGODAS

Pagodas emerged in China, from India, as shrines for
Buddhist relics. The very earliest were variations on the
theme of the Indian stupa (a dome-shaped earth mound).
The multiple stories of Chinese pagodas were designed to
impress and delight. Their hollow structures, giving access
to balconies under swooping roofs, initially rose over
underground chambers for Buddhist relics.

Garden building
An 18th-century Chinese-
style pagoda is a landmark
at Kew Gardens, in London.

Pagodas soon began to appear in, or on top
of, palaces as decorative features, and their
construction became increasingly complex.
The oldest surviving timber pagoda in
China is that of the White Horse Temple
(founded 68CE, rebuilt in the 13th
century), in Luoyang. There were so
many in the area that the Tang dynasty
poet, Du Mu, wrote, "480 Buddhist
temples of the southern
dynasties/uncountable towers and
pagodas stand in the misty rain." The
northern dynasties began building brick
and stone pagodas to standard designs
from the end of the 4th century.

Buddhists took
pagodas to Japan,
probably in the
7th century. There, most were built of wood.
The tallest (until its destruction by fire) was
the seven-story, 354 ft (108 m) high pagoda
of Shokokuji, Kyoto. Although vulnerable
to fire, wooden pagodas are built to absorb
the impact of destructive forces of nature—
they swing and sway around a columnar
core, but almost never collapse. Pagodas in
Japan have survived massive earthquakes
and typhoons: the pagoda of Horyu-ji *(see
p.181)*, in the ancient capital of Nara, is
1,300 years old and remains stable.

Yakushiji Temple
The East Pagoda of
Yakushiji, from 7th-
century Japan, has
three stories plus
three lean-to roofs.

FORBIDDEN CITY

🖥 1420 📍 BEIJING, CHINA ✎ UNKNOWN 🏛 PALACE

The Forbidden City, to the north of
Tiananmen Square, was the Imperial palace
for over 500 years. Surrounded by a 20 ft
(6 m) deep moat and a 33 ft (10 m) high wall,
the palace is arranged on a north–south axis
stretching 5 miles (8 km). It covers 180 acres
(73 ha) and was designed to contain 9,999
rooms. Construction began in 1407; the
outer wall is brick but most of the buildings
are of wood. The Forbidden City is divided
into two parts: the southern section, or
Outer Court, was the seat of government.

HALL OF SUPREME HARMONY

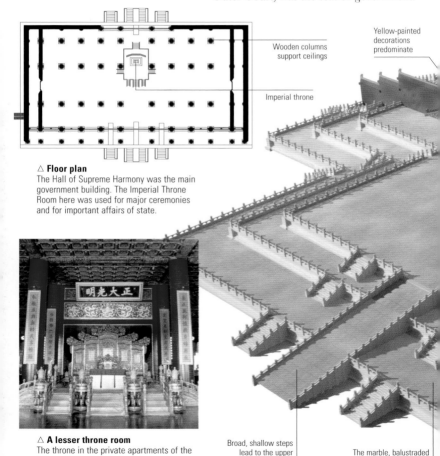

Wooden columns
support ceilings

Imperial throne

Yellow-painted
decorations
predominate

△ **Floor plan**
The Hall of Supreme Harmony was the main
government building. The Imperial Throne
Room here was used for major ceremonies
and for important affairs of state.

△ **A lesser throne room**
The throne in the private apartments of the
Palace of Heavenly Purity was used for
routine business and Imperial audiences.

Broad, shallow steps
lead to the upper
terrace and the main
entrance doors

The marble, balustraded
precinct rises in three
tiers to 26 ft (8 m) high

The northern section, or Inner Court, was the home of the Imperial family. The central building is the Hall of Supreme Harmony *(see below)*, in the Outer Court, which includes the ceremonial throne of the emperors; yellow, symbolic of the royal family, is the dominant color. From 1420 until the 20th century, 24 emperors lived there. In 1924, the last emperor was driven out as China became a republic.

△ **Imperial guardian lion**
A carved lion, with curly mane and grasping a ball, is the traditional guard at doors in the palace.

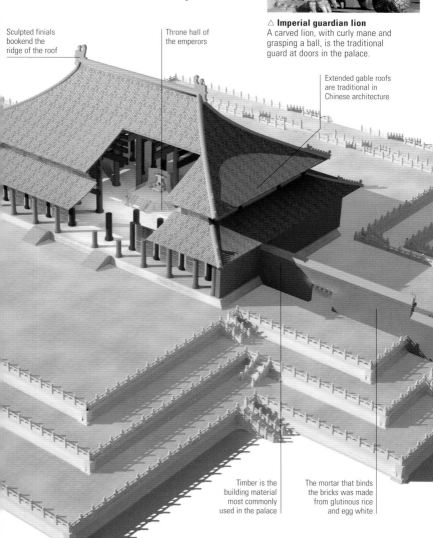

Sculpted finials bookend the ridge of the roof

Throne hall of the emperors

Extended gable roofs are traditional in Chinese architecture

Timber is the building material most commonly used in the palace

The mortar that binds the bricks was made from glutinous rice and egg white

SUMMER PALACE

🏺 *ca.* 1200   📍 BEIJING, CHINA   ✎ UNKNOWN   🏛 PALACE

Comprising myriad bridges, pagodas, gardens, lakes, and streams covering 726 acres (294 hectares), the original imperial residence here was begun during the Jin dynasty (1115–1234) and named The Garden of Clear Ripples. It is the largest of China's imperial gardens. Long secret, it was opened to the public in 1924.

The palace began to assume its present shape in the late 18th century, but was destroyed by British and French forces during the Second Opium War, in 1860. Rebuilt by the Dowager Empress Cixi with funds embezzled from the Chinese Navy, and renamed the Summer Palace, it was ransacked by foreign troops again in 1900, during the Boxer Rebellion. Today, wholly restored, it is a wonderful escape from central Beijing, boasting shops, cafés, boats, magical views, and an idyllic mountainous backdrop. Centered on the Tower of Buddhist Incense (Foxiang Ge), the palace consists of over 3,000 structures including pavilions, towers, bridges, and corridors, and the halls of Dispelling Clouds, Sea of Wisdom, and Moral Glory. The arrangement of its

BRIDGE OVER KUNMING LAKE

buildings was inspired by Taoist legends of immortal islands in the middle of misty lakes. Three-quarters of the gardens are water, so the forms of buildings and bridges are reflected many times. Most of the pavilions are linked together by a 2,300 ft (700 m) covered walkway adorned with paintings.

THE OLD SUMMER PALACE

Lying close by as a more or less total ruin is the old imperial palace, which was very different from its successor. Far from being designed in classical Chinese style, it was laid out according to Baroque principles by Jesuit architects, led by Giuseppe Castiglione, during the reign of the 18th-century emperor Qianlong, whose aim was to outdo the gardens of contemporary French and Italian palaces.

Idyllic setting
Located in Haidian District, some 7 miles (11 km) northwest of central Beijing, this fantastical palace has been a World Heritage Site since 1998.

ANCESTOR TEMPLE, FOSHAN

👥 1085   📍 FOSHAN, CHINA   ⚒ UNKNOWN
🏛 PLACE OF WORSHIP

Continuously added to over the centuries, today this complex is a curious, if charming, amalgam of the much-rebuilt original place of worship, richly colored as are most old Chinese buildings. A Confucian temple was added from 1911; shops and restaurants mingle with fragments of ancient art and craft. Highlights include the Pavilion of Truth Celebration; theatrical drum and bell towers; and a southern courtyard dominated by a large and colorful covered stage once used for Guangdong Opera, a local art form first developed in Foshan. Elsewhere, stone carvings depict caricatures of Europeans made during the Qing dynasty.

LINGYIN TEMPLE

👥 326   📍 HANGZHOU, CHINA
⚒ HUILI   🏛 PLACE OF WORSHIP

Lingyin temple is one of the largest and wealthiest in China. At its zenith in the 10th century it comprised 18 pavilions and 77 palaces and halls, with over 1,300 rooms accommodating around 3,000 monks. Although first built in the early 4th century, it has been rebuilt at least 16 times since then. Despite some damage inflicted by Red Guards in 1968, during the Cultural Revolution, the temple and grounds escaped much of the wholesale destruction inflicted on religious monuments elsewhere in China because of the direct intervention of the Chinese premier, Zhou Enlai. Laid out like a city, its halls are vast: the Mahavira or Daxiongbaodian Hall boasts a triple-eaved roof and stands some 115 ft (35 m) high. The Hall of Five Hundred Arhats (Buddhist disciples) houses, as its name promises, 500 life-sized bronze statues. The Chinese name Lingyin is commonly translated into English as "Temple of the Soul's Retreat."

TAIMIAO ANCESTRAL TEMPLE

👥 1420   📍 BEIJING, CHINA   ⚒ UNKNOWN
🏛 PLACE OF WORSHIP

Taimiao, the imperial ancestral temple of the Ming and Qing dynasties, runs parallel to the north–south axis of the Forbidden City. A magnificent set piece of traditional imperial Chinese architecture, its principal buildings consist of three main halls, two gates, and two subsidiary shrines. The main structure is the two-tiered Hall for Worship of Ancestors, built in 1420 but frequently repaired ever since. The temple complex is surrounded by high walls and tall, mature trees. The two much narrower flanking halls seem almost austere from a distance, but close up they are richly and imaginatively decorated.

DRUM TOWER, XI'AN

👥 1380   📍 XI'AN, CHINA   ⚒ UNKNOWN
🏛 CIVIC BUILDING

Erected in 1380, the great rectangular, triple-eaved, 112 ft (34 m) high Drum Tower is the counterpart of the Bell Tower in the Muslim quarter of Xi'an, a walled city in the heart of China. Equipped with an enormous drum, it was used not only for timekeeping but also as an alarm in time of danger. Today, the second of its two floors is an antiques shop, but the first floor is surrounded by colorful drums and contains a fascinating drum museum. An enormous brick and timber structure, the Drum Tower is pierced by an archway that carries a street through it. This muscular monument is very much isolated today, flanked by such ugly modern buildings as the Century Ginwa department store.

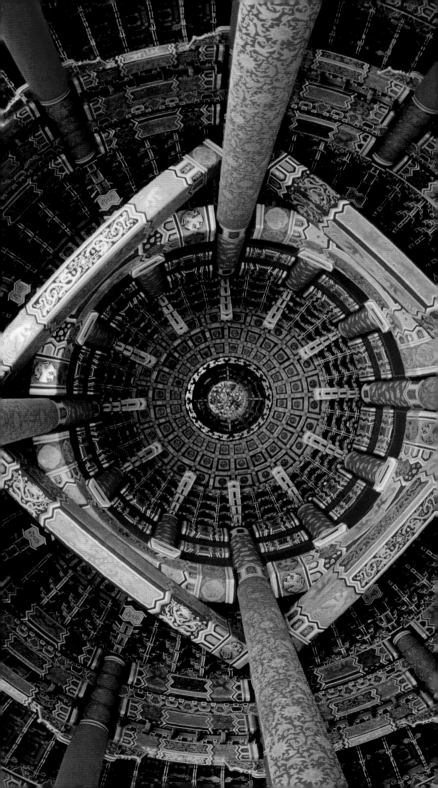

TEMPLE OF HEAVEN, BEIJING

⚑ 1530 📍 BEIJING, CHINA
✍ UNKNOWN 🏛 PLACE OF WORSHIP

The Temple of Heaven was built during the Ming dynasty. Covering a staggering area of 1 sq mile (2.6 km²), the temple now stands in Tiantan Park, in Beijing.

The complex is enclosed within a wall. Its entire architecture and layout are based on elaborate symbolism and numerology. In accordance with principles dating back to pre-Confucian times, the buildings in the Temple of Heaven are round, like the sky; the foundations and axes of the complex are rectilinear, like the earth. The north part of the wall is semicircular

THE HALL OF PRAYER FOR GOOD HARVEST

(Heaven); the south part is square (Earth). The finest of the many exquisite buildings in the complex are the Circular Mound Altar, with three terraces of white marble where the emperors offered sacrifice to Heaven at the Winter Solstice; the Imperial Vault of Heaven, looking like some great blue-and-gold parasol; and the Hall of Prayer for Good Harvest. The latter has a round roof with three layers of eaves; inside, the ceiling is symbolically decorated.

The buildings are connected by a wide bridge called Vermilion Steps Bridge, or the Sacred Way; the emperor had his own solitary way across the bridge, and to other temple buildings in the compound.

Hall of Prayer for Good Harvest
Posts in the roof represent the seasons, months, and 12 two-hour "shichens" of each day; colored glazes symbolize heaven, earth, and all on the earth.

MING AND QING DYNASTIES

These dynasties together lasted from 1368 to 1911. Throughout this entire period, emperors would offer sacrifice in The Temple of Heaven, according to the ancient traditions. As the emperors called themselves "The Sons of Heaven," they dared not build their own dwelling—the Forbidden City (see pp.172–3)—larger than the dwelling they built for Heaven. These practices came to an end after 1911, with the establishment of the Republic of China.

WUXIANGUAN TEMPLE

⚑ 1378 📍 GUANGZHOU, CHINA
✍ UNKNOWN 🏛 PLACE OF WORSHIP

Wuxianguan, the Taoist temple of the Five Immortals, is purported to be the site of the visit of five heavenly beings celebrated in the foundation myth of the city of Guangzhou. The myth says that long ago, these immortals came to the region riding on the backs of five goats or rams. They brought with them five rice plants and gave the secret of rice cultivation to the people; Guangzhou is still known as "Goat City" (yangcheng) or "Rice City" (suicheng). When the immortals returned to heaven, their goats turned to stone and can be found here at this delightful red temple.

The temple includes a huge bell tower, which dates back to the Ming dynasty, and a main hall in front of the tower built in Ming-dynasty style. A pond to the east of the main hall features a huge foot-shaped depression said to be the footprint of one of the immortals.

TEMPLE OF AGRICULTURE, BEIJING

⚑ 1420 📍 BEIJING, CHINA
✍ UNKNOWN 🏛 PLACE OF WORSHIP

This temple is a complex of altars covering an area of 1.2 sq miles (3 km²). It fell into a state of disrepair when used as a factory during the 20th century, but has since been restored. At the start of the agricultural season, emperors of the Ming and Qing dynasties performed rituals in honor of Xiannong, god of agriculture, to ensure that nature provided a bountiful harvest. In the handsome red-and-blue Temple of Agriculture, emperors really did put on new clothes: they changed, in the Dressing Hall, into farming costume to conduct ritual plowing to show respect to the god.

JAPAN AND KOREA
ca. 500–1900

Korea provides the link between Chinese and Japanese architecture.
The timber buildings of the Karayo period (918–1392), despite certain
differences in detail, are essentially Chinese designs that made their
way along the Korean peninsula. Re-emerging across the sea in Japan,
however, they underwent a subtle transformation, gradually taking wing
with gloriously exaggerated roofs and a spirit of creative adventure.

Traditional Japanese architecture
is much admired for its delicacy,
serenity, refined proportions, and the
ways in which buildings are set in
perfectly poised gardens. There are
many reasons, beyond the stylistic, as
to why this is so. Like China, Japan is
beset by earthquakes, so it was never a
good idea to build weighty structures
that might collapse as the earth shook.
Even hundreds of years ago there was
a paucity of land, with the majority
of the Japanese population required to
live on the fringes of this mountainous
country. Consequently, land was used
sparingly, and well—even the smallest
temple, house, or garden could become
a place of quiet contemplation. What
seems remarkable to western visitors
is the fact that many of the "ancient"
buildings they see are not, in fact, very
old at all. At least, they might be in
terms of design and layout, but their
timbers will have been replaced many
times. Famously, Shinto temples are
wholly, and ritualistically, rebuilt every
20 years or so. In part, this reflects the
nature of the Shinto gods, who only
visit earth for brief spells, so have no
need of permanent homes.

ENDURING TRADITIONS
Building traditions evolved with the
coming of Buddhism, when temple
complexes became elaborate and
extensive, but they were ultimately
harmonized during the Edo period
(1603–1868), when strict measurements
were laid down to determine the
proportions of temples, monasteries,
houses, and their interiors. The result
was a very distinctive Japanese style of
architecture, which had little need to
change until the middle of the 19th
century, when Japan began to open
up to the Western world. In Korea,
architecture retained its Chinese
characteristics until the modern era.

◁ **THE ARCHITECTURE AND BRIGHT COLORS SPORTED BY THE PAGODA OF THE KIYOMIZUDERA (CLEAR WATER)
TEMPLE IN KYOTO REFLECT THE CHINESE ARCHITECTURAL STYLES THAT CAME TO JAPAN WITH BUDDHISM.**

ELEMENTS

Traditional Japanese architecture
represents a triumph of timber
construction. Designed to be earthquake-
proof, if not fireproof, temples, palaces,
and other buildings achieved a sense of
serenity in both their structure and their
design. Although rooted in Chinese
design, they quickly gained their own
distinctive characteristics.

△ Manicured gardens
Japanese architecture is often inseparable
from the highly designed and manicured
landscape, or garden, its rises from. Nature
and artifice are held in fine balance.

Screens act as doors
and windows

Carved finials show
fine carpentry skills

Bargeboard protecting eaves
extends up through ridge

◁ Forked finials
These intentionally evoke the
construction of early Japanese
temples—simple structures
made of logs or branches. They
are in fact elaborately carved
bargeboards rising through the
ends of a reed-thatched roof.

◁ Elaborate joinery
The more important temple
and palace buildings were
characterized not by more gold
fittings or precious stones, but by
demonstrations of elaborate and
highly sophisticated timberwork.

△ Tea ceremony pavilions
The tea ceremony is an ancient Zen
ritual encouraging a sense of quiet and
contemplativeness in the simplest of the
day's artefacts and rituals. It has always
required a special building of its own.

Curved lintels
distinguish later
gateways

△ Myojin torii gateways
A more stylized refinement of "shimmei torii" *(see right)*, "myojin
torii" gateways, such as at the Itsukushima Shrine, feature double
lintels whose curves echo the eaves of the temples they serve.

△ Shimmei torii gateway
The early "shimmei torii" is a
simple temple gateway of two
plain pillars, driven straight into
the earth, and two horizontal
beams, one bracing the structure
and one acting as a lintel.

HORYU-JI TEMPLE COMPLEX

👤 607 📍 NARA, JAPAN ✍ UNKNOWN 🏛 PLACE OF WORSHIP

The Horyu-ji temple complex is one of the most important early architectural developments resulting from the spread of Buddhism from China via Baekje—a Korean kingdom with close cultural links to Japan. Emperor Yomei began building it, hoping that his devotion would help him recover from illness. He died before the complex was finished.

FIVE-STORY PAGODA

Destroyed by fire in 670, the Horyu-ji temple complex was quickly rebuilt. Four ancient wooden buildings that predate written Japanese history survive: a five-story pagoda in the central grounds, the Golden Hall *(see below)*, a timber gateway, and a wooden corridor wrapping around the central precinct of the complex.

The design, delicate structure, and detailing of these buildings were probably the work of architects and craftsmen from Baekje; they demonstrate the beginnings of classical Japanese architecture, with its sense of graceful order.

The complex is home to other, later buildings—notably the Dream Hall of Prince Shotoku, an octagonal structure dating from the 8th century. A bell-tower and Great Lecture Hall were rebuilt in the 10th century; other buildings date from the 13th to the 19th centuries. Between 1933 and 1953, all were dismantled, restored, and rebuilt to ensure longevity.

JAPANESE TEMPLE ARCHITECTURE

In 7th-century Japan, the pagoda was the principal temple building. Japanese pagodas were derived from Korean and Chinese traditions that, in turn, had developed from early Indian Buddhist stupas—domed earth mounds built to house sacred relics.

Where many Chinese pagodas were of brick and brightly painted, Japanese pagodas were built of wood and remained calm and uniform in color, often in quiet shades of gray.

Strength and beauty
The Golden Hall, or "Kondo," is probably one of the oldest surviving wooden buildings in the world.

ISE SHRINE

☒ 690   🏴 UJI-YAMADA, JAPAN   ✍ UNKNOWN   🏛 PLACE OF WORSHIP

More or less every 20 years since the 7th century, this pair of picturesque Shinto shrines—one dedicated to Toyouke, goddess of grain or harvest, the other to the sun goddess, Amaterasu, from whom the Japanese royal family claim descent—have been rebuilt in a ritual of renewal known as "Shikene Sengu."

This act of architectural renewal embodies the essence of Shinto architecture and represents the deep-rooted Japanese belief in regeneration. While Chinese influence can also be seen here in the glittering metal rail ornaments and the brightly colored glass balls and gilded doors adorning the main sanctuary, essentially the shrines are elemental structures, classical in form, yet utterly without pretension and seen as an extension of nature, rather than as something apart from it as most architecture is. In this sense they might be seen as the oriental counterparts of occidental primitive Greek temples. The Inner Shrine is a modest

TORII GATE TO MAIN SANCTUARY

building constructed of Japanese cypress. Barge boards, the most dramatic feature of the building, thrust up and out from the roof ends like a pair of crossed swords, although this might also be read as a fork or some other tool used to gather the harvest. Still sacred sites rather than marketing-driven tourist attractions, the Iso shrines are hidden well away from the febrile daily life of modern Japan. The 62nd reconstruction of the shrine is due in 2013.

SHINTO ARCHITECTURE

Shintoism lays great stress on the power of *kami* (the sacred power). *Kami* is found in ancestor worship and also in nature, but the worship of images and the use of elaborate temple buildings is not called for. Nevertheless, the design of early Japanese temples is heavy with symbolism. The large, stylized logs that rest so heavily on the roofs recall a key structural feature of primitive Japanese houses, and of traditional storehouses for grain in particular.

Shinto simplicity

The Ise Inner Shrine is surprisingly small, measuring just 36 ft (10.9 m) wide by 18 ft (5.5 m) deep. The roof is thatched with thick-stemmed reeds.

BYODOIN TEMPLE

🏛 1053 📍 UJI, KYOTO, JAPAN ✍ UNKNOWN 🏛 PLACE OF WORSHIP

This elegant Buddhist temple reflected in an ornamental pond on the west bank of the Uji River was originally a grand villa given to a powerful local nobleman, which was converted into a Buddhist temple by his son. Only the central hall survives—the rest of the buildings were burned down during the Civil War of 1336. Many temples of this era still had a distinctly Chinese look, seen here in the elaborate detailing and colors. However, the monastery, with its domestic and vernacular origins, represents an early stage in the development of a truly Japanese architecture. Completed in 1053, the central Phoenix Hall, so named because its roof is ornamented with two of the mythical birds, enshrines a striking gilded wooden statue of Amida Buddha sculpted by the distinguished artist, Jocho.

Common currency
The temple is well known in Japan because its image is stamped on the back of the 10-yen coin.

KIYOMIZUDERA KONDO

🏛 1633 📍 KYOTO, JAPAN ✍ UNKNOWN 🏛 PLACE OF WORSHIP

The main hall of the Kiyomizudera—"Pure Water"—temple is set in the wooded hills of eastern Kyoto on an open-latticed timber frame. So, the temple, the crowning part of a religious and urban complex dating from the 8th century, is lifted well above ground in this steep, rocky location. This makes symbolic as well as practical sense, as the building is dedicated to Kannon Bodhisattva, the Buddhist goddess of compassion, traditionally associated in Japan with rocky landscapes and depicted with eleven faces and 1,000 welcoming arms. The outer sanctuary is simple, although decorated with paintings donated by tradesmen during the reconstruction of the temple after the fire of 1633. The inner sanctuary is a blaze of gold-leafed images set on raised black-lacquered platforms. The centerpiece is the image of Kannon carved by the artist Enchin. You must time your visit here carefully if you wish to see her: the image is only shown once every 33 years. She will be on view next in 2010. Behind the main hall, the Jishu Shrine is said to bring good fortune to those in search of romance.

Sweeping roofline
The central hall is housed under three interlocking hipped and gabled cypress roofs.

KINKAKUJI GOLDEN PAVILION

🏛 1397 📍 KYOTO, JAPAN ✍ UNKNOWN 🏛 RESIDENCE

Covered in the finest gold leaf, sealed in Japanese lacquer, with its exquisite form reflected in a pond, the Golden Pavilion is one of the most magical sights Kyoto has to offer. Although first built as part of a villa for a retired shogun, what became a Zen Buddhist temple after his death in 1408 was torched by a disturbed monk in 1950. The present reincarnation of this jewel-like design dates from 1955.

Ashikaga Yoshimitsu, third shogun of the Muromachi era (1338–1573), abdicated in favor of his son to take up the religious life. This he would conduct from his beautiful new golden villa. Originally, Kinkakuji, or the Golden Pavilion, was part of a much larger complex of buildings, including two pagodas, but these were burned down during a civil war in the Onin era (1467–77). Although they were rebuilt, they were destroyed again 90 years later. Only the Golden Pavilion and a small annex survived. The pavilion, a lovely play on Japanese architectural history and culture, is a square three-storied structure covered, in the thinnest of layers, in 106 lb (48 kg) of gold

BRONZE BUDDHA IN LOTUS POSITION

JAPANESE ARCHITECTURAL STYLES

Fascinatingly, the Golden Pavilion features three distinct Japanese architectural styles, one on each floor. The first floor, a large room surrounded by a veranda (called the Chamber of Dharma Waters), is designed in Shinden-zukuri—the palace style of the 11th century. The third floor, The Tower of Sound Waves, is in Buke-zukuri, or samurai house style, while the fourth floor is in Karayo, or Zen temple style.

leaf. Each floor houses statues of Buddhist divinities. The roof is topped by a gilded phoenix and is covered with Japanese shingles. The temple was completely restored, with much thicker lacquer than before, in 1987. The garden, with its classic teahouse, or Sekka-tei, remains much as it would have been in the 14th century. A short walk from the pavilion is Ryoanji, Japan's most famous Zen rock garden, laid out for contemplation in the 15th century.

Gold and green
The effect of the glittering gold leaf covering the walls and verandas of the Golden Pavilion is offset by a background of dense, managed planting.

JAPANESE GARDENS

The Japanese garden is an interpretation and idealized conception of nature that began with Buddhist notions of quiet contemplation. Gardens follow certain rules, but each is the work of an individual creator. And, although the idea of miniaturization was always important, many of the finest Japanese gardens are extensive landscapes.

Japanese gardens encourage delight in the smallest detail. The 16th-century teamaster Sen-no-Rikyu created a garden enclosed by a tall hedge that blocked the view of the sea from the house that stood within its walls. When the client first walked through the garden, he was unhappy, until he bent to wash his hands in a stone water basin. As he lifted his eyes from the refreshing water, the sea was clearly visible through a precise gap in the hedge. The client smiled. He understood, intuitively, the clever connection Sen-no-Rikyu had made between the water in the basin and the waters of the ocean beyond, and so between himself and the

infinite universe. The essential elements of a Japanese garden are water, plants, stones, waterfalls, trees, and bridges, and their

Bonsai tree
Nature controlled and miniaturized is a recurring theme.

precise arrangement and immaculate presentation are crucial factors. There are five key types of garden: the Strolling Garden, Natural Garden, Sand and Stone Garden, Tea Garden, and Flat Garden. Architecture is intimately connected with the gardens. The garden is a journey, and the journey is as important as the destination, which is why gardens contain so many small pleasures. These are not gardens for joggers or those who like decking, loud outdoor music, and barbecues.

Toji Temple, Kyoto
Manicured gardens and koi ponds provide a reflective and spiritual setting for the five-story pagoda here, a potent symbol of ancient Japan.

SHUGAKUIN IMPERIAL VILLA

🖥 1659   📍 KYOTO, JAPAN
✍ UNKNOWN   🏛 RESIDENCE

At the base of Mount Hiei, the largest of Kyoto's imperial villas commands sweeping views of the city, notably from The Cloud Touching Arbor (a tea ceremony pavilion) in its Upper Garden. Designed for the retired emperor Gomizuno (1596–1680)—a man of culture and learning but hemmed in by the power of shoguns—the villa is set in glorious gardens and comprises three fine residences of modest and quiet beauty, designed according to strict rules of proportion and propriety. Although more than 300 years old, they seem remarkably modern; they were to have a profound influence on early Modernist design in Europe.

SOKKURAM GROTTO

🖥 751   📍 BULGUKSA, KOREA
✍ KIM TAESONG   🏛 SHRINE

The granite cave shrine of Sokkuram, famous for its serene Buddha surrounded by bas- and haut-reliefs of gods and disciples, was originally constructed during the reign of the Silla king Kyongdok, and was probably designed either by or for his first minister, Kim Taesong. An entrance foyer leads into a short vestibule ending with two thick pillars with lotus-flower bases. Beyond is a dome-capped rotunda carved from granite. As Buddhism fell into disfavor, the shrine was abandoned and in 1913–15 was dismantled by the Japanese authorities controlling Korea. During this process an ingenious natural air-conditioning system built in the rocks was misunderstood and blocked, causing the stones to sweat and threatening the sculptures. The problem was solved more recently: under the auspices of UNESCO, modern air conditioning was installed.

HIMEJI CASTLE

🖥 1614   📍 HIMEJI, JAPAN
✍ UNKNOWN   🏛 FORTIFICATION

Himeji—or Shirasagijo, "the White Heron" —Castle is the best-preserved samurai fortress and a particularly beautiful building, designated a national treasure in 1931. Although its white walls and winged roofs evoke a heron about to take flight, Himeji was designed and constructed very much as a machine for making war by a fierce, ritualistic warrior caste. Covering an area of 58 acres (23 ha), this hill castle was expanded—by soldiers, farmers, and slave labor—at a time of national unification under the direction of Ikeda Terumasa (1564–1613) in the era of the first matchlocks and other guns previously unknown in Japan. So, it was built massively: a main donjon, or

THE SAMURAI

For much of the 12th to 19th centuries, Japan was dominated by *daimyos* (military barons) who, with their samurai (warriors), established a military dictatorship under a shogun (great general). The samurai were a privileged and loyal elite who followed a rigid code of honor, known as *bushido*. From the 17th century, their military duties became largely ceremonial. In 1867, the last shogun resigned, and the samurai were abolished.

keep, attended by three subsidiary towers, surrounded by a moat, and designed to a complex plan, with many secret passages running between the towers, to ensure that even if its security was breached, the castle could be defended

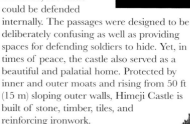

internally. The passages were designed to be deliberately confusing as well as providing spaces for defending soldiers to hide. Yet, in times of peace, the castle also served as a beautiful and palatial home. Protected by inner and outer moats and rising from 50 ft (15 m) sloping outer walls, Himeji Castle is built of stone, timber, tiles, and reinforcing ironwork.

DECORATIVE TILES ON THE ROOF EAVES

The walls of the theatrical superstructure are plastered. The maze-like interior boasts fine timber galleries and rooms with *fusama* (sliding screens) and geometrically arranged *tatami* (straw matting). The principal seven-story tower is 155 ft (47 m) high and rises from an inner court; on the southeast corner is an area called *harakiri-maku* where disgraced samurai would ritually disembowel themselves. Perhaps the strangest thing about this magnificent castle is that, after all the ingenuity that went into its laborious construction, it was never attacked.

Picture perfect
Himeji Castle features in as many Japanese souvenir calendars as Neuschwanstein (see p.412) does in Germany, or Windsor Castle in England.

The Islamic world

PERHAPS MORE THAN any other faith, Islam has spread widely across the world, absorbing influences from diverse cultures. Its different schools of thought, from the mystic to the ascetic, have inspired art and architecture—both religious and secular—that span the range from the puritanical to the sensual and defy easy categorization.

The Islamic tradition has its roots in the Arabian peninsula— the birthplace of the prophet Mohammed, a wealthy merchant from Mecca. From the 7th century onward, Arab forces, inspired by the prophet's teachings, extended the influence of Islam through the Middle East, and then into north Africa, India, Central Asia, Spain, and beyond. Architectural traditions from the Arabian Peninsula were adapted to suit the local climates and building materials of these lands.

"Khusran sees Shirin in the bath"
This miniature illumination for the 16th-century Persian manuscript poem "Khamza," by Nizami (1141-1209), is a richly colored model for secular architectural decoration.

adapted, certain strands became universal throughout the Islamic world. For example, the grace of Arabic script and the richness of the literature—especially the key texts of the Koran—were expressed in the opulent ornamentation of Islamic buildings, and certain religious and secular forms became widespread.

The most recognizable of all Islamic structures— the mosque—has a basic plan that was derived from Mohammed's home compound where the prophet's first followers

A CUMULATIVE TRADITION

Early Islamic architecture was strongly influenced by the styles of Byzantium, especially as embodied in the Hagia Sophia (see pp.126–7), and by the Sassanian art of pre-Islamic Persia. Later, influences from Afghanistan, northern Africa, China, and, increasingly, northern areas of Europe became evident; and as these various styles were absorbed and

Prayer niche
Decorated with dazzling gilded floral motifs, this prayer niche, or mihrab, in the wall of a mosque shows the direction of prayer toward Mecca.

KEY DATES

570 Birth of Mohammed, prophet and founder of Islam, at Mecca, Arabia

632 Death of Mohammed; Muslims capture Jerusalem six years later

ca. **696** Arabic becomes the official language of the Islamic world

825 The Persian mathematician Khwarizmi founds algebra and refines Arabic numerals

600

800

1000

630 Mohammed and his armies conquer Mecca, which becomes the spiritual center of Islam

ca. **655** The Koran, the sacred book of Islam revealed to Mohammed, is finalized by his disciples

711 Tariq ibn Ziyad conquers southern Spain from the Visigoths of King Roderic; Córdoba is his capital

848 The Great Mosque at Samarra is completed, the largest Islamic mosque in the world at that time

gathered to pray. This design comprises an enclosed courtyard, surrounded by arcades, with a building or shady area at one end for prayer. Another key religious form is the madresah, or seminary, which is derived from Sassanian architecture; in this building, an eyvan—two-story hall—is added into each side of the arcades surrounding the mosque courtyard. Perhaps the most

Calligraphic ornamentation
Koranic inscriptions decorate the Dome of the Rock *(see p.197)*. Ceramic tiles are surrounded by mosaics of smoothed cubes of marble and glass.

1187 Saladin, Islamic Sultan of Egypt, reconquers Jerusalem from the Christians

1453 The Ottoman Turks under Mehmet II capture Constantinople—or Byzantium—and rename it Istinpolin

1492 The Christian kingdoms, under Ferdinand and Isabella, reconquer all of Spain

1571 The defeat of the Ottoman navy by Christian forces at the Battle of Lepanto halts Islamic expansion

1200

1400

1600

1100 Timbuktu, a desert oasis in Saharan north Africa, is founded by Muslim traders

1258 The Mongols destroy the Abbasid caliphate of Baghdad, killing 800,000 people

1475 The world's first coffee shop, "Kiva Han," opens in Istanbul

1529 The Ottomans besiege Vienna, creating panic throughout Europe

16th C. City of mud-brick "skyscrapers" built at Shibam, Yemen

distinctive feature of Islamic architecture is the dome, the earliest surviving example of which is the Dome of the Rock *(see p.197)*, developed from early Christian tradition. From the single dome, architects of the great Ottoman Empire later went on to develop a style in which a central dome was surrounded by arcades set with smaller domes and semidomes, notably at the Istanbul Suleymaniye Mosque *(see p.206)*.

The elegant, pointed minarets, often in pairs or groups, which are a common feature of eastern mosques, developed in 16th-century Persia and have been absorbed entirely into the Islamic tradition.

At its best, Islamic architecture is the most beautiful and sensuous to be found anywhere. Color, in particular, is an important part of architectural

decoration, frequently in the form of glowing glass-and-gold mosaics: ceramic tiles in rich blues, greens, reds, and yellows are used externally as well as internally. On religious buildings, the three-dimensional representation of living beings is considered idolatrous, so glorious geometric designs dominate, reflecting the long Arabic history of mathematical development. The curves and swoops of the calligraphic style derived from the script and illuminations of Koranic texts are used both in painting and stonework to decorate mosques, minarets, and secular buildings.

EARTHLY DESIGNS

In secular architecture, Islamic tradition centered for centuries on royal pleasures, mercantile riches, and a lavish use of space. At the Alhambra Palace, Granada *(see pp.204–5)*, for example, the buildings were meant to be a representation of Paradise on earth for the privileged and powerful. Over many centuries, Islamic architects developed magnificent water gardens within which they set their buildings. In the case of the Alhambra, water flowed from gardens and courtyards directly into rooms leading off them— a clear reference to oases, and their paramount significance in arid lands.

Muslim palaces were often more like small townships than single buildings, similar in concept to the later medieval castles of western Europe. They were, however, almost always far more joyous designs, awash with daylight, smelling of roses, almond, lemon, and orange blossom, and resounding to the play of water. Their complexity had much to do with Muslim ritual and belief. The separation of the sexes in certain aspects of daily life required special living quarters for men and women,

MOHAMMED (570–632)

Mohammed was a religious warrior. In his lifetime, he conquered Arabia and fused the disparate Arab tribes into one nation, with one religion. After his death, Islam quickly became a world power. The weakness of the Byzantine Empire – no matter how glorious its architecture – as well as the rivalry between Greek and Latin Christian churches and the weakening power of Persia, were all gifts to the vigorous, sword-wielding Muslims.

Ascension of Mohammed
Rich coloring characterizes this 16th-century Ottoman depiction of the winged horse that carried Mohammed to heaven.

Alhambra, a Moorish paradise
Water in still pools, running canals, and sparkling
fountains is part of the living architecture of this
palace in the sun-baked hills of southern Spain.

taken to an extreme in the harems.
Equally, palaces could be seats of
learning as well as armories and
barracks. Because religion played such
an important role in the development
of Islamic architecture, many palaces,
hunting lodges, and other grand
residences adopted elements from
mosques, including domes and
minarets. However, unlike mosques,
their interiors were sometimes covered
in rich and even sensual mosaics.
Many spectacular early Islamic
palaces crumbled away because they
were not meant to outlast those who
built them; the Alhambra Palace,
preserved by Christian monarchs,
is one of the great exceptions.

ISLAMIC INFLUENCES

Medieval European architects had a
great deal to learn from their Muslim
counterparts. Just as Muslim invaders
digested the glorious architectural
legacy of Greece and Rome in
Constantinople, western European
architects—via the Crusades to the
Holy Land—learned the secrets of
the pointed arch, and of Gothic
design. The achievements of Muslim
architects came to be recognized
down the ages by many men of true
learning. In his history of Westminster
Abbey (1713), Christopher Wren
(*see p.326*) noted: "This we now call
the Gothick manner of architecture...
tho' the Goths were rather destroyers
than builders I think it should with
more reason be called the Saracen
style; for those people wanted neither
arts nor learning."

THE FIRST MOSQUES
ca. 650–1600

There are many architecturally magnificent mosques, designed by
supremely skilled architects like Mimar Koca Sinan *(see p.207)*, yet
though these are often inspiring, there is something starkly and deeply
moving about the very earliest mosques, rising from scorching deserts or
green oases and climbing, via their minarets, into blazing skies where
diamond-hard light conceals the face of a divine and demanding god.

Perching precariously on top
of the minaret at Samarra
in central Iraq, the visitor once had
views of the ruins of the gigantic
mosque below, of the city fanning out
beyond, and of the desert stretching
into a shimmering horizon. This spiral
minaret is one of those buildings that
haunts the architectural imagination,
and this is true, too, of many of
Islam's great buildings, fanning out
from its birthplace to North Africa,
Spain, Persia, India, and Central Asia.

OUT OF THE DESERT
Early Islamic architecture was infused
with all the infectious energy of a new
religion. It drew on the traditions of the
two earlier great monotheistic faiths,
Judaism and Christianity, yet, emerging
from the sands of Arabia, it had a
very different character: warriorlike,
masculine, demanding submission. As a
result, many of the first great mosques

reflect a missionary and militaristic zeal.
Some seem based on the plans of
Roman barracks or parade grounds.
Others, like the beautiful white mosques
of Jerba, a Tunisian island-oasis of date
palms and olive trees (and, today, tourist
hotels), are so understated and tranquil
that they evoke Gustave Flaubert's
description of the summer breeze that
breathes almost silently across the island
—"so soft that it hinders death." There
are nearly 300 of these often exquisitely
simple mosques on an island with a
population of only a few hundred
thousand. According to legend, the
Mosque of the Night (Jamaa Ellile)
outside the village of Guellala
miraculously appeared overnight, as
the builders who were to start on its
construction the next day slept. This
story is not just delightful, but recalls
the astonishing speed of the spread of
Islam across North Africa, and the
rapid construction of early mosques.

◁ LIGHT FILTERING THROUGH PORTAL WINDOWS ILLUMINATES THE MOSAICS INSIDE THE SULEYMANIYE
MOSQUE, ISTANBUL, TURKEY—ONE OF THE GREATEST WORKS OF THE ARCHITECT SINAN.

ELEMENTS

Forbidden by religious law to depict the human figure, much less the face of God, Islamic artists and architects developed highly distinctive and beautiful forms of ornamentation; the result is a profound unity of decoration and architecture.

△ **Calligraphy**
Rarely has lettering had such a profound impact on architecture. Islamic calligraphers wrote their chosen texts, from the books of teachers and philosophers, into the buildings.

Blues, turquoise, and greens are characteristic colors

Elaborate window tracery is set into a complex play of surfaces incised with floral and geometric designs

△ **Colored tiles**
In both Persia and Spain, architects worked with craftsmen on the design of exquisite tiles; sometimes these covered entire buildings.

△ **Horseshoe arches**
Looking as much like headdresses as horseshoes, these striking arches were hugely distinctive and widely distributed.

△ **Elaborate arches**
Multicentered tracery like this made elaborate ritual of the windows of mosques. It was also important in European Gothic design.

△ **Pointed arches**
The pointed arch was to be one of Islamic architecture's great gifts to European design, forming the basis of Gothic architecture.

◁ **Spiral minarets**
The spiral minaret was one of the great inventions of Islamic architects, first appearing at Samarra; this is the minaret of the Ibn Tulun mosque in Cairo.

The path to Heaven is never easy: with each turn, the staircase narrows

These minarets have triple balconies, each reaching for the sky

△ **Rocket-shaped minarets**
Sinan, the great 16th-century architect, surrounded the mightiest mosques with sky-piercing minarets to great effect; this is the Suleymaniye Mosque, on one of the highest points in the city of Istanbul.

QUBBET ES-SAKRA (DOME OF THE ROCK)

🔲 691 📍 JERUSALEM ✍ UMAYYAD KHALIF & CALIPH ABD AL-MALIK 🏛 PLACE OF WORSHIP

Although commonly called a mosque, Qubbet es-Sakra, the earliest monument of Islamic architecture, is a "mashhad"—a shrine with no orientation toward Mecca. Built over the rock from which Mohammed is said to have ascended to Heaven and spoken to Allah, it stands on the site of the Temple of Solomon.

The structure is of Syrian Byzantine design, and its plan is octagonal. The building's interior plan, Roman columns, and rich mosaics are thought to emulate those of the Holy Sepulchre nearby. The great golden dome has a diameter of 66 ft (23.7 m) and rises to an apex more than 115 ft (35 m) above the Prophet's rock. Its double-skin structure comprises cross-braced inner and outer timber frames, covered with gilded copper plates. The dome rises from a drum supported by an arcade of columns gleaned from ancient Roman sites. Two concentric ambulatories (walkways) intended for ritual processions, one circular, the other octagonal, are formed by colonnades.

Sacred site
This important destination for Muslim pilgrims is also a holy site for Jews and Christians.

MOHAMMED

Mohammed (meaning "highly praised") was the name taken by Halabi, the son of a merchant born in Mecca *ca.* 570. At the age of about 40, while in solitary contemplation, he experienced a vision of the angel Gabriel, who instructed him to write the verses of the Koran. The teachings of Islam began from here, and Mohammed became known as the founder of Islam and "God's last prophet." He fought a holy war from Medina and died in 632.

The Koranic verse "Ya Sin" is inscribed around the crest of the exterior of the octagon, below the drum, in deep blue tiles, commissioned in the 16th century by the Ottoman sultan, Suleyman the Magnificent. Below, the shrine is clad in marble up to its round-headed windows, which have pierced marble and ceramic lights. Above is an exquisite architectural carpet of Turkish blue-and-gold tiles. The dome has been reconstructed as closely as possible to the original design.

GREAT MOSQUE, DAMASCUS

715 DAMASCUS, SYRIA CALIPH AL WALID PLACE OF WORSHIP

Damascus reached its "golden age" during the first decades of Islam in the 7th century. Steeped in the cross-currents of emerging new cultures, politics, and religions, it became the capital of the Umayyad Empire, and the magnificent Great Mosque was built. Fires have caused the mosque to be rebuilt several times, but the basic plan has remained unchanged.

The Great Mosque has a complex history. It encompasses the former Byzantine church of St. John the Baptist, itself built on a Roman temple dedicated to Jupiter, which, in turn, was constructed on the site of an Aramaean temple to the god Hadad. Parts of the southern wall of the Roman temple survive and form a structural part of the mosque, surrounded by a courtyard flanked by arcades.

SHRINE IN PRAYER HALL

CALIPH AL WALID

Born in Medina, *ca.* 668, al Walid came to power in 705 as sixth caliph of the Umayyad dynasty. A devoutly orthodox Sunni Muslim, he built some of the largest and most important mosques in the world. He also greatly extended Islamic territory by funding, although not personally fighting, wars in central Asia, north Africa, and southern Spain. As well as mosques, he built the Qusair Amra, or "little red castle," in what is Jordan today, as a pleasure dome and hunting lodge. He died in 715.

The mosque itself comprises three airy aisles, forming a great basilicalike space interrupted only by a transept cutting across its center. The lower arcades are composed of handsome Corinthian columns. Above a second tier of arcades, the pitched timber roof is exposed. The crossing of the transept is crowned with the 118 ft (36 m) Nisr dome, or Dome of the Eagle, originally made of timber, but later of stone, and rebuilt in its present form in 1893. The main prayer hall also contains a shrine that, depending on the tradition, holds either the head of Zechariah—the father of St. John the Baptist—or the head of Hussein, the son of Imam Ali, who was the son-in-law of Mohammed the Prophet.

Safe haven
The domed treasury building stands on Corinthian columns in the courtyard of the mosque.

GREAT MOSQUE, SAMARRA

🏛 AFTER 848   📍 SAMARRA, IRAQ   ✎ CALIPH AL-MUTAWAKKIL   🏛 PLACE OF WORSHIP

The Great Mosque at Samarra was once the largest Islamic mosque in the world. Buttressed by semicircular towers, the burned brick walls protect an arcaded courtyard that measures a massive 509 x 787 ft (155 x 240 m). It was designed to hold 80,000 worshipers, who could enter the courtyard through one of 23 gates.

The internal structure, filled with aisles, mud-brick piers, and timber roofs, has long vanished, but the most dramatic and evocative feature of the mosque remains—the monumental spiral minaret, al-Malwiya. Standing 180 ft (55 m) tall, on a square base 10 ft (3 m) high at the north wall of the courtyard, and designed in the form of a ramp winding five times, anticlockwise, up an ever-diminishing tower, the minaret is an exceptional structure. Although derived, in part, from Mesopotamian stepped ziggurats such as those at Babylon (see pp.48–9), the architectural use of a circular tower is thought to be a primarily Islamic characteristic. To walk up the spiral ramp of the minaret in the heat of an Iraqi noon is a remarkable experience, but be careful as you climb; there are no handrails on the outer side of the ramp to catch you if you fall, and the iron handrail that is attached to the inner wall, when fired by the sun, has been known to burn unsuspecting hands.

High point
This distinctive minaret is one of the most beautiful of Iraq's many ancient treasures.

GREAT MOSQUE, QAIROUAN

🏛 836   📍 QAIROUAN, TUNISIA   ✎ CALIPH AL-MUTAWAKKIL   🏛 PLACE OF WORSHIP

One of the principal architectural consequences of the Arab invasion of North Africa was the construction of vast and often magnificent mosques constructed around military-style courtyards along the south coast of the Mediterranean. Among the earliest of these is the 9th-century mosque at Qairouan, which comprises a large prayer hall, a dome, an arcaded courtyard, and a three-story tower believed to be the oldest standing minaret in the world. Flanking the courtyard are the horseshoe-shaped arches that are characteristic of Islamic architecture, supported by Corinthian columns that trace their stylistic origin back to ancient Greek temples. In fact, many of the columns and stones forming the structure of the building were plundered from ancient Roman buildings in and around Qairouan. The interior of the prayer hall, however, is adorned with detailed painted and carved ornamentation of distinctly Islamic origin, including motifs based on designs from the natural world, such as acanthus, vine, and palms.

Changing faces
The large, square minaret tapers in stages at the top, and is facing toward the south, which is unusual.

MOSQUE OF IBN TULUN

🏛 879   📍 CAIRO, EGYPT   ✍ UNKNOWN   🏛 PLACE OF WORSHIP

With its spiral minaret, vast scale, and sophisticated architectural references, this great mosque, built for Ahmed Ibn Tulun, son of a Turkish slave of the Abbasid caliph al Ma'mun (later governor of Cairo and then of all Egypt), is clearly based on the gigantic mosque at Samarra *(see p.199)* in what is northern Iraq today.

In fact, the Ibn Tulun mosque may well have been the work of architects and craftsmen from Samarra, for Ibn Tulun was born there. The 283,285 sq ft (26,318 m²) mosque, constructed of well-fired red bricks rendered in stucco, is more or less as it would have been in the late 9th century. The off-center spiral stone minaret, however, was rebuilt by Sultan Ladjin in 1296, after many years of neglect, while a major and controversial restoration completed in 1999 has seen the courtyard paved, its old fountain refaced in black marble, and much new plasterwork. The mosque sits within an enclosure that measures 387 × 453 ft (118 × 138 m). Its walls are surmounted with military-style but purely

Recently restored
The meda, or fountain for ritual washing of feet before prayer, is in the center of the courtyard.

> ### ISLAMIC CAIRO
>
> Tucked away amid modern urban Cairo lies one of the world's oldest and most extensive traditional Islamic cities, with its famous mosques, madrassas, hammams, markets, fountains, merchants' houses, and fortified gateways. Founded in the 10th century, it became the new center of the Islamic world, reaching its golden age in the 14th century. It includes the City of the Dead, a cemetery where families live, quite legitimately, in medieval tombs.

decorative crenellations. Although the mosque seems at first glance rather ascetic in design, it proves to be richly, if subtly decorated. Below the crenellations, for example, the inner arcades are decorated with a floral frieze, while above the arches are fine Kufic inscriptions of the Koran said to run to a total of 1.25 miles (2 km). The 128 windows of the mosque's external walls feature intricate stucco patterns, each different from the other.

MOSQUE OF AL-AQSA

🖥 1033   📍 JERUSALEM   ✍ CALIPH AL-WAHID   🏛 PLACE OF WORSHIP

Shortly after the completion of the Dome of the Rock *(see p.197)*, construction began on the vast congregational Mosque of Al-Aqsa, which was intended to be the center of worship and learning for the Muslims of Jerusalem. The mosque holds 5,000 worshipers who overflow on Fridays into the courtyards of the huge open expanse of the Noble Sanctuary, an extensive garden of prayer that includes the Dome of the Rock and other religious buildings. The form of the present structure has remained essentially the same since the original wooden mosque was reconstructed by Caliph Al-Dhahir in 1033. It incorporates part of the former Crusader palace known as The Temple, and its western wall is the "Wailing Wall" revered by Jews. It has been modified several times to protect it from earthquakes and to adapt to changing needs. The style of the mosque reveals Christian Byzantine influence, if not ideologically, then in construction and design: Muslims took much architectural inspiration from existing sources, notably from Byzantine churches. Since 1967, Al-Aqsa has been the target of attempts to destroy or burn it, including several aimed to bring about its collapse through underground excavation.

Public function
Al-Aqsa is the most ancient gathering point for Muslim worshipers and for Islamic study in Jerusalem.

AL-MUSTANSIRIYE MADRASSA

🖥 1234   📍 BAGHDAD, IRAQ   ✍ UNKNOWN   🏛 UNIVERSITY

Although much restored during the 1860s, this fine courtyard building on the banks of the Tigris is an important link with a culture that was all but destroyed by the Mongol invasion of 1258, when the famous circular "City of Peace," founded in 762, and its population were crushed. This Baghdad was the capital of the Abbasid dynasty (750–1258), which saw the cultural heart of the Islamic world shift from Syria to Iraq. This Sunni culture was deeply influenced by Persian art and learning. The Al-Mustansiriye madrassa shows the influence of Persian design, with its pointed arches, as well as that of the great mosque at Samarra *(see p.199)*, the most ambitious of early Abbasid monuments. The madrassa was built around a courtyard measuring 348 x 158 ft (106 x 48 m) during the rule of Caliph Al-Mustansir (1226–1242), for the study of theology, literature, medicine, mathematics, and jurisprudence, and to unify the four orthodox Sunni law schools, Hanbali, Shafii, Maliki, and Hanafi. Hallways and rooms extend from the court through pointed-arched entrances leading to a kitchen, prayer hall, living quarters, and baths. Much neglected since the 15th century, the building has been used as a market, hospital, and army barracks.

Detailed decoration
The madrassah is built of the soft yellow brick that characterizes the buildings of Baghdad, the brickwork then carved with intricate decoration.

MADRASSA OF QAITBAY

📅 1474 📍 CAIRO, EGYPT ⚒ SULTAN QAITBAY 🏛 PLACE OF WORSHIP

Within a maze of medieval alleys in the old Islamic quarter of Cairo stands the Madrassa of Qaitbay, a fascinating early example of what today would be called a "mixed-use" building—it is a mosque, mausoleum, minaret, Koranic school, and public well. Although restored over the centuries, the Madrassa remains unchanged and intact, and is a remarkable example of Mameluke design.

This elegant, even delicate, structure is easily found in the labyrinth of old Cairo, as its slender minaret soars exotically above the surrounding rooftops. The richly carved design of the Madrassa is carefully balanced by its tall, pointed dome. On almost every roundel, lintel, and corner column of the building there is a glorious array of arabesque patterns, blue-and-white marble, and carved moldings. In contrast, the interior walls of the mausoleum are mostly unadorned, and the building offers a cool and welcoming space.

In this calm and beauty, it is hard to think that the Mamelukes, a dynasty of former Turkish and Kurdish soldier slaves, were famed for their love of cruelty: impalement was the standard form of public execution and a favorite public entertainment. In his 1968 book,

SULTAN QAITBAY

Al Ashraf Abou Anasr Saif El Din Qaitbay was born *ca.* 1423 in Kipchak, on the Volga River. He came to Egypt in 1435 as a soldier slave in the retinue of the Mameluke Al Ashraf Bersbay. After Bersbay's death, he was given his freedom, becoming head of the army and, in 1468, sultan. He went on to rule Egypt and Syria for 28 years. Qaitbay was passionate about architecture and commissioned many important buildings in Mecca, Medina, Cairo, and Jerusalem. He died in 1496.

Great Cairo: Mother of the World, the travel writer and historian Desmond Stewart describes "the coexistence of cruelty with piety, of barbaric display with exquisite taste." Today, in the stones of this intriguing religious building, only the exquisite taste and piety remain.

Fine detail
The dome of the Madrassa is lavishly carved with arabesque curvilinear designs.

GREAT MOSQUE, CÓRDOBA

🪑 987 🏴 CÓRDOBA, SPAIN ✍ ABD AR-RAHMAN 🏛 PLACE OF WORSHIP

Under the 8th-century rule of the Syrian prince Abd ar-Rahman (756–88), Córdoba was transformed from a relatively unimportant town into a prosperous city. At its heart he built the Great Mosque: 200 years in construction, it has undergone many subsequent changes—reflecting the rise and fall of the Umayyads in Spain—yet its interior remains a magical place.

PRAYER HALL

The Great Mosque in Córdoba is concealed behind massive stone buttressed walls that give little indication of the glories within. The cavernous prayer hall is filled with 850 granite, jasper, and marble columns supporting red-and-white brick-and-stone striped arches that appear to interlock infinitely and in every direction. Sunlight filters in through the windows, creating ever-shifting jewel-like patterns across the immense floor, originally only supplemented by the flickering light of a thousand small oil lamps. It is like being inside a surreal architectural puzzle; it is an unforgettable experience and a demonstration of how the interior of a building needs no decoration, much less furniture, in the hands of master architects and craftsmen. The rhythm of the arches is broken only by the eye falling on the marble-and-gold mihrab—the arch that indicates to worshipers the direction for prayer—adorned with Byzantine mosaics.

When Córdoba became Christian, the mosque was rededicated to the Virgin Mary, and many incongruous additions were made, the most elephantine being the gigantic Gothic cathedral built into its heart in the 16th century.

THE UMAYYADS IN SPAIN

Abd ar-Rahman was the only surviving prince of a massacre in Damascus, in 750, of the ruling Umayyad dynasty by the rival Abbasids. Fleeing Syria, he seized power in Córdoba, Spain. In 929, Córdoba was proclaimed a Caliphate—independent from that of the Abbasids in Baghdad—by Abd ar-Rahman III, under whom Islamic Spain became an important center of learning. In 1236, the Caliphate was overthrown by the Christian King Ferdinand III of Castile.

Dual purpose
The Great Mosque, with its traditional Islamic exterior, contains the startling addition of a Christian cathedral.

COURT OF LIONS, ALHAMBRA

⚑ ca. 1390   📍 GRANADA, SPAIN   ✐ UNKNOWN   🏛 PALACE

The Alhambra is one of the finest of all architectural achievements—a great, fortified palace from the last of Spain's Muslim dynasties, and a building complex that cannot be separated from its many gardens, nor from the water that flows through them. From the Court of Lions, water from a fountain surrounded by stone lions flows through stone channels, north, south, east, and west across the courtyard and into domed rooms awash with daylight

COURT OF LIONS AS IT IS TODAY

Pools continue right into the rooms of the palace

Water emerges here, from a stone fountain

Pools lie under the north and south canopies

△ **Prolific color**
Geometric patterned tiles in brilliant colors, along with decorated stucco work, cover every surface around the courtyard.

◁ **Floor plan**
The courtyard is laid out on a rectilinear plan and is surrounded by horseshoe arches. The stone channels carry water to the four cardinal points of the compass.

Horseshoe arches are typical of Islamic buildings

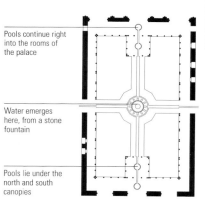

△ **Every surface decorated**
Light filters in through richly decorated arches, so that the palace rooms are integrated with their paradisiacal gardens.

△ **Relief detail**
Much of the carving on the walls and arches is curling and intricate, showing the finest craftsmanship.

reflected on rippling water. The walls of this and other courts are covered with decoration. Many of the arches are "false"—that is, purely decorative—providing symmetry to the arcades. Islam bans the representation of figures, but geometric shapes, flowers, and calligraphic decoration used throughout the palace are highly imaginative.

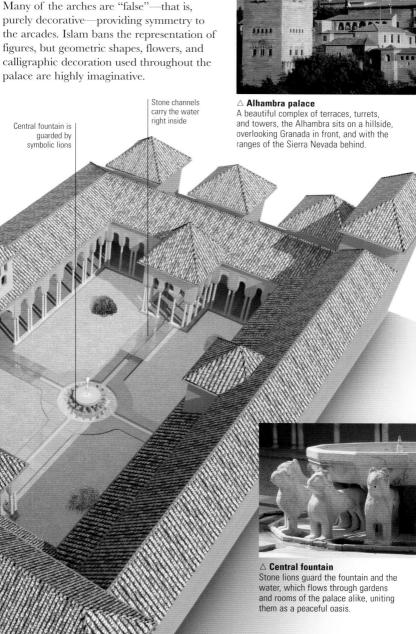

Central fountain is guarded by symbolic lions

Stone channels carry the water right inside

△ **Alhambra palace**
A beautiful complex of terraces, turrets, and towers, the Alhambra sits on a hillside, overlooking Granada in front, and with the ranges of the Sierra Nevada behind.

△ **Central fountain**
Stone lions guard the fountain and the water, which flows through gardens and rooms of the palace alike, uniting them as a peaceful oasis.

CHINLI KIOSK, TOPKAPI PALACE

🏛 1473   📍 ISTANBUL, TURKEY   ✍ UNKNOWN   🏛 PALACE

This delicate Persian pavilion in the grounds of the Topkapi Palace—commissioned by Sultan Mehmet, who conquered Istanbul (then Constantinople) in 1453—was to have a great influence on succeeding Ottoman architecture. Its plan is a square cruciform capped with a central, shallow dome, with the spaces between the arms of the cross filled with self-contained suites of rooms, all of which give on to fine colonnaded

verandas. Consequently, the building feels light and delicate, especially so given that the colors used in its elaborate decoration—principally green and turquoise—are those of the nearby Sea of Marmara.

Topkapi, home to most of the Ottoman sultans until the reign of Abdulmecid I (1839–61), is not a single, massive or even particularly imposing building, but an architectural organism that has waxed and waned over the years. After the establishment of the Republic of Turkey in 1923, it was restored and opened to the public as a museum. The Chinli Kiosk or Tiled Pavilion, the earliest building of Topkapi, became a ceramics museum, where the finest examples of Turkish ceramics from the 12th century to the present day are on display.

Charming colonnades
This essentially modest and low-lying building has world-famous tilework.

SULEYMANIYE MOSQUE

🏛 1557   📍 ISTANBUL, TURKEY   ✍ SINAN   🏛 PLACE OF WORSHIP

This mid-16th century mosque, with its great dome and pencil-thin minarets, dominates the skyline of the west bank of the Golden Horn, the crescent-shaped estuary that divides Istanbul. Its plan is based on Justinian's Hagia Sophia *(see p.126–7)*. The interior of the building is simple: the visitor steps into a giant cube, topped with a hemispherical dome and lit by streams of sunlight filtered through stained glass. The architect Sinan combined an architectural structure of intense

geometric rigor with an equally intense use of decoration inside and out, also rooted in rigorous geometry. Ceramic tiles from Iznik (Nicea) are in abundance, at their best in the octagonal courtyard mausolea of Suleyman the Magnificent, his wife Roxelana, and Sinan, their brilliant architect, who achieved a sense of serene monumentality here.

City bustle
The Suleymaniye dominates a crowded skyline, above city mosques and bazaars.

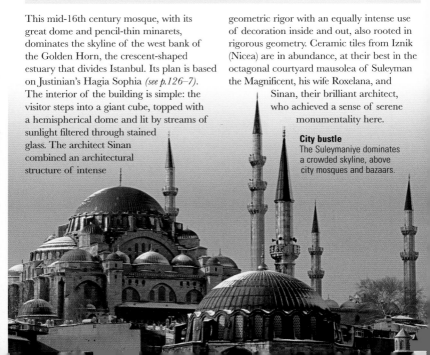

SELIMIYE MOSQUE

🏛 1574   📍 EDIRNE, TURKEY   ✍ SINAN   🏛 PLACE OF WORSHIP

Work began on what Sinan would call his masterpiece in 1569, when the architect was 80 years old. Its monumental domed prayer hall, over 98 ft (30 m) in diameter, and rocketlike minarets, 272 ft (83 m) high, crown the city of Edirne —formerly Hadrianopolis and, until the conquest of Constantinople in 1453, the capital of the Ottoman Empire.

WHITE SCRIPT ON TILING ABOVE LATTICED WINDOW

Seen from below, the dome, carried on eight lofty pillars incised into the walls, braced internally by four surrounding semidomes, and rising to a height of 138 ft (42 m), appears to float within the building. The structure allows for the maximum amount of uninterrupted floor space: it feels extraordinarily light and capacious. The building is entered

through a modest doorway leading into a courtyard surrounded by shady loggias, their bays covered by a small dome supported on curved overhangs. From here, the dome of the mosque itself seems remarkably modest; it is only when you enter the building that its sheer scale tells. The entire surface of the underside of the dome is decorated with abstract painted designs that diffuse the monumentality of the structure they adorn.

Splendid isolation
The mosque was built on an artificial hilltop; standing high above Edirne, it is visible from every corner of the city.

SINAN

Mimar Koca Sinan (1489–1588) was born, a Greek Christian, in Anatolia. Drafted as a soldier, he served first as a cavalry officer, then as military architect. From then on his work for Suleyman the Magnificent was prodigious: he designed some 360 buildings, including 84 mosques, 35 palaces, 48 caravan-serais, harems, hospitals, fountains, aqueducts, and bridges. With the Selimiye mosque, he felt he had outshone the Hagia Sophia (see p.126).

SULTAN AHMED MOSQUE

🗓 1616　📍 ISTANBUL, TURKEY　✍ SEDEFKAR MEHMET AGA　🏛 PLACE OF WORSHIP

Also known as "the blue mosque" because of the 21,043 Iznik tiles that cast an almost mystic blue glow inside, the Sultan Ahmed mosque is located on a prominent site alongside the former Roman hippodrome, adjacent to the Hagia Sophia *(see pp.126–7)*; its construction marks the end of the Classical period of Ottoman architecture.

Distinguished by its six minarets, the mosque is surrounded on three sides by a soul-stirring marble courtyard. Here, the Sultan commanded his architect (and poet) Sedefkar to include an imperial lodge and double-height shops as well as a theological college. The central dome of the mosque, attended by four lesser half-domes, rises from four enormous piers; it has a diameter of 77 ft (23.5 m) and is 141 ft (43 m) high. No fewer than 260 windows, originally filled with stained glass, light the interior of the mosque; they are helped by hundreds of hand-blown glass oil lamps hanging at little more than head height throughout the immensity of the internal space.

From certain angles, the mosque and its subservient buildings appear to form one great sea of domes punctuated by the soaring minarets; the majority of the lesser domes cover the bays of the courtyard. Backed by the sea, the Sultan Ahmed mosque is a truly beautiful place.

Sea of domes
The fervently religious Ahmed I spared no expense in constructing his elaborate mosque, with its stained glass, marble paving, and exquisite tiling.

BEEHIVE VILLAGE, ALEPPO

🗓 16TH CENTURY　📍 NORTHERN SYRIA　✍ UNKNOWN　🏛 VILLAGE

These extraordinary and beautiful conical houses, which date back in form and purpose to the earliest human settlements during the Stone Age, are examples of true vernacular architecture at its most enduring and endearing. Some 10,000 years ago, settlers on the Anatolian plains chiseled out hollows from pillarlike volcanic rocks and made secure, remarkably comfortable homes inside,

complete with built-in furniture and storage. The tradition continued, and continues, with these mud-brick beehive houses found in villages around Aleppo. Although built of mud rather than stone, they are a logical solution to the combination of desertlike local weather conditions, where unrelenting heat and cold winters are the order of the day, and where the need for a simple form of construction using local materials is paramount. The thick tapering limestone mass of the buildings forms both walls and roof, absorbing the beating sun during the day and slowly releasing its warmth and energy during cool nights.

Weather wise
Any rain runs off the beehive shape so quickly that it has little chance to damage the mud walls.

MUD MOSQUE, DJENNE

🗓 1240 📍 DJENNE, MALI ✍ UNKNOWN; REBUILT BY ISMAILA TRAORE 🏛 PLACE OF WORSHIP

The sensational mosque at Djenne, a center of Islamic learning and pilgrimage, dominates the busy market square. Though it incorporates architectural elements found throughout the Islamic world, it is distinguished by its daring mud construction. The mosque was originally built in 1240, but the building, funded by the French, was completely rebuilt in 1907. Maintenance of the structure is continuous, the replastering of the walls a major, much-enjoyed annual event. The enormous tapering walls are deep to keep the prayer hall cool. Bundles of palm branches built into the walls reduce cracking caused by the frequent drastic changes in humidity and temperature. The protruding ends of

these branches give the mosque its curious appearance. The huge external mass of the building makes for an unusual interior: rows of immense plastered brick piers joined by arches occupy almost as much space as they create.

Bristly exterior
Protruding palm branches serve as scaffolding when repairs are needed.

SHIBAM

🗓 16TH CENTURY 📍 SHIBAM, YEMEN ✍ UNKNOWN 🏛 CITY

Shibam, the "Manhattan of the desert," is a *Tales of 1001 Arabian Nights* city, a dreamlike cluster of tall, mud-brick towers that appears at first sight to be more mirage than real. Surrounded by a 23 ft (7 m) fortified wall with just one gate, this 2,000-year-old city, largely rebuilt in the 16th century, is a remarkable example of early high-rise urban planning. This evolved from the constraints of a narrow but fruitful and ultimately wealthy location in an oasis surrounded by

hostile desert and barren mountains. The height of the 500 or so remaining mud blocks varies between six and ten stories; most of the houses were designed for extended patriarchal families, and the majority are still occupied today.

The mud-brick towers use traditional Yemeni building techniques: their bricks are whitewashed with a layer of protective limestone or crushed gypsum to repel water. Despite this, houses that have stood on the same stone foundations for five centuries have to be continually rebuilt because of the inherent instability of mud walls. Today, many of the towers have been in danger of collapse as the owners have filled them with modern gadgets, especially washing machines and dishwashers that leak water into the walls. Shibam was designated a World Heritage Site in 1982.

Desert dwellings
The towers of Shibam may resemble high-rise apartment blocks, but each building is still only occupied by a single family.

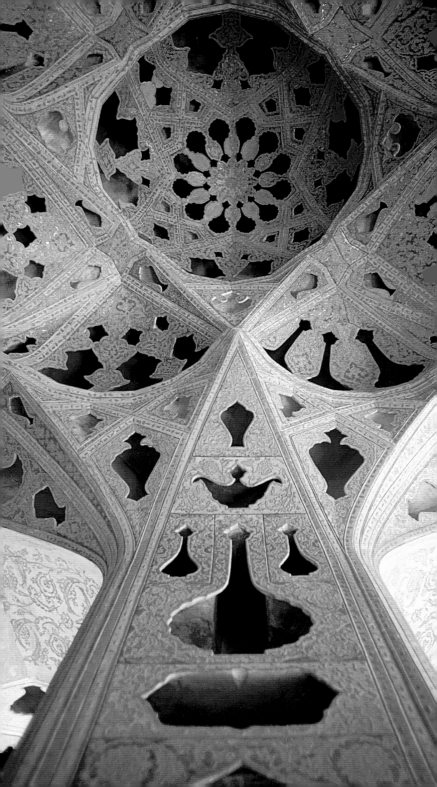

PERSIA AND MUGHAL INDIA
ca. 900–1650

Persia was conquered by Muslim warriors in 637, just 5 years after the Prophet Mohammed's death. The country was later invaded by Seljuk Turks and Mongols, yet finally reasserted its cultural hegemony during the reign of Shah Abbas I, who came to the throne aged 16 in 1587. Abbas made the urban oasis of Isfahan his capital and, in so doing, shaped one of the world's most beautiful cities.

Isfahan, with its gorgeous blue-and-turquoise-tiled buildings, had a subtle influence on some of the finest and most sensual buildings and cities across Europe and Central Asia. It also embodied a form of design that emerged at much the same time as the Islamic Mughal (Persian for Mongol) empire reached its creative peak in northern India. The styles of Isfahan are evident in the works of Shah Jahan (r.1628–58), such as his great monuments—the Red Fort and the Taj Mahal *(see pp.220–1)*—and also in the gardens he created.

MUGHAL INDIA

The Mughal Empire began when Babur the Tiger (r.1526–1530) entered India from Turkestan. Equipped with firearms, his small army of 12,000 soldiers swept through Hindustan. The Portuguese, however, had already gained a foothold in Goa, in southern India:

even as the Mughals established their rule, European usurpers were closing in. By the 1760s, the British effectively controlled the length and breadth of India, although it took them a while to fall in love with the sublime architecture, decoration, and landscape design that dominated Mughal India and Muslim Persia. Although Mughal design owes much to Persia, and thus, via the Silk Route and the Mongol conquests, to China, it did enjoy a very brief time when its patrons seemed on the verge of creating a new world order. During his long reign, the emperor Akbar not only created a brand-new city, Fatehpur Sikri *(see p.218)*, but also invented his own religion, Din-i-ilahi, an amalgam of Islam, Hinduism, Jainism, and Zoroastrianism. Fatehpur Sikri was abandoned due to water shortages, but it remains one of the finest examples of an architecture that, at its height, had an almost transcendental quality.

◁ THE CARVED NICHES, LACQUERED STUCCO CEILINGS, AND SHELL VAULTS OF THE ALI QAPU PALACE IN ISFAHAN TYPIFY THE SUBTLETY AND OTHERWORLDLINESS OF THE FINEST WORKS OF MUGHAL INDIA AND MUSLIM PERSIA.

ELEMENTS

In a complex historical journey, Persian architecture moved across Central Asia and, much influenced by the tenets of Islam, finally came down into the Indian subcontinent at the time of the Mughal invasions. Then, in turn, Mughal architecture began to pick up on themes established long before by Hindu and Buddhist buildings.

△ **Chattris**
A roofline feature of much Mughal architecture clearly based on earlier Hindu Indian precedent, the open kiosk, or chattri, was to be a part of Indian architecture under British rule, too. This one is at Fatehpur Sikri.

△ **Fine marble**
The tradition of working in rich marbles was well established among Mughal architects, who brought their skills to India. It would reach its apogee with Shah Jahan's Taj Mahal.

Deeply recessed marble facades screen interior of building

△ **Deeply recessed windows**
At the Tomb of Humayun, Delhi, the recesses are dug as deep into the facades as they are in the monuments of Isfahan, creating pools of cool shadow—a more than useful feature in the heat.

◁ **Perforated screens**
This delicately carved, sunlight-diffusing marble screen from the Tomb of Humayun shows the influence of Arabic and Persian design on a new Indian architecture.

▽ **Swelling domes**
The beautiful blue-tiled and breastlike dome of the Masjid-i-Shah, Isfahan, was a major influence on Mughal design.

Islamic crescent rises from dome

△ **Interior of dome**
Beautifully tiled dome undersides with stained glass windows (here at the Lotfollah Mosque, Isfahan) showed the influence of Hagia Sophia *(see p.126)* on rich Persian craftsmanship.

Glazed tiles glitter in the sunlight

GUNBAD-I-QABUS TOMB

⚱ 1007   📍 GURGAN, IRAN
✎ UNKNOWN   🏛 TOMB

The Gunbad-i-Qabus tomb is in the north of Iran by the Caspian Sea. It is regarded as the most influential 11th-century tomb tower, and one of the first buildings in Iran associated with the Central Asian Turks.

It is a cylindrical brick tower, tapering to a height of 157 ft (51 m), strengthened by ribs, and topped with a perfect conical roof. In plan it is a ten-sided star. The tomb exterior is remarkably plain. Two bands of inscriptions, and the two pendentives—overhanging, curved, triangular surfaces—that support the tear-shaped half-dome above the entrance are the only ornament on an otherwise unadorned brick facade.

QUWWAT-UL-ISLAM MOSQUE

⚱ 1225   📍 DELHI, INDIA
✎ QUTB-UD-DIN AIBAK   🏛 PLACE OF WORSHIP

This was the first great mosque to be built in northern India. Local construction methods are clear in the corbeled arches and vaults—supported by projecting blocks of stone, often elaborately carved—under the domes. In plan, however, it alludes to Persian designs, and Islamic character is expressed in elegant pointed arches, crowned by Arabic calligraphy with texts drawn from the Koran. The sandstone screen facade and ornamental balconies are finished in bands of shallow relief. The prayer hall is modest, with unusually low domes. The southeast gateway is decorated with red sandstone and white marble.

KALYAN MINARET

⚱ 1127   📍 BUKHARA, UZBEKISTAN   ✎ ARSLAN KHAN   🏛 PLACE OF WORSHIP

Bukhara has a proud history of religious architecture: the downtown area is home to almost 1,000 mosques, though many are now in varying stages of decay, as the population of 250,000 cannot support them.

The Kalyan Minaret, at 154 ft (47 m), is the most impressive of Bukhara's monuments and was the only substantial structure to remain intact after the Mongol invasion of 1220. The minaret stands in the grounds of the 16th-century Kalyan (meaning "Great") Mosque, which has a capacity to hold 12,000 worshipers and dominates the city skyline. Its construction is of baked bricks, with narrow ornamental bands of brickwork in varying, unrepeated patterns decorating the tapering cylindrical shaft. A blue-glazed frieze with Koranic inscriptions wraps around the minaret.

The minaret is topped by a rotunda with 16 arches, from which the muezzins give the call to prayer. In times of siege or war, warriors are said to have used the rotunda as a watchtower. The mosque's foundations are over 33 ft (10 m) deep, cushioned on stacks of reeds as a protection against the region's earthquakes.

Second attempt
The minaret had to be rebuilt after the first construction collapsed before completion.

GUR-I-AMIR

🜚 1404   📍 SAMARKAND, UZBEKISTAN   ⚒ UNKNOWN   🏛 TOMB

Most of the architectural attractions of
Samarkand are the work of Timur
(1336–1405), or Tamerlane, the great
nomadic warrior who fought as far north as
Moscow and who, at the time of his death,
was planning to invade China. During his
lifetime, Samarkand was Central Asia's
economic, cultural, and
intellectual powerhouse.
Gur-i-Amir is a powerful,
colorful, but now partly
demolished funerary
complex dedicated to
Muhammed Sultan,
grandson and heir of
Timur, who died at the
battle of Ankara in 1402.
The mausoleum was also
the resting place of
Timur himself.

Enormous inscriptions
are carved into the high
drum of the large and
bulbous double-skinned

dome. Originally, this dome would have
risen from a cluster of smaller domes and
other structures, but these have long since
gone. The walls and surfaces of the tomb,
which was built with a madrassa (a religious
college) and a caravanserai (a resting place
for traveling merchants), are faced in
ceramics, brick, and
marble. The use of
mosaic both internally
and externally is thought
to have influenced the
design of the Taj Mahal
(see pp.220–1). Restoration
of the dome took place
during the 1950s, and
further repairs to this
funerary complex were
made from 1967 onward.

Tiled dome
The large ribbed dome over
the main chamber of the
mausoleum stands 121 ft (37 m)
high and is brilliantly tiled.

MASJID-I-JAMI

🜚 1127   📍 ISFAHAN, CENTRAL IRAN   ⚒ UNKNOWN   🏛 PLACE OF WORSHIP

One of the foremost Islamic monuments in
Isfahan, the Masjid-i-Jami is the result of
continual construction, reconstruction,
additions, and renovations from 771 to the
end of the 20th century, with the primary
structure completed in 1127. Archaeological
excavation has discovered that there was an
Abbasid hypostyle mosque here by the 10th
century. Later Buyid work added a facade
around the courtyard and two minarets,
making it the earliest example of a mosque
with more than one minaret. Construction
under the Seljuqs added two brick iwans
(domed recesses), for which the mosque is
renowned. The south iwan was built to
house the mihrab in 1086–7 by Nizam al-
Mulk, vizier of Malik Shah, and was the
largest of its time. The north iwan, built a
year later as a riposte by Nizam al-Mulk's
rival, Taj al-Mulk, is a hugely complex piece
of brickwork. It was to set a style for Islamic
architecture in Persia for centuries, as did
the mosque's total of four iwans, which
became the norm rather than the exception.

Magnificent mosque
Painted in gorgeous
yellows and blues,
the Masjid-i-Jami
has courtyards, four
magnificent iwans,
and a wealth of rich
structural elements.

MASJID-I-SHAH

⚰ 1638   🏴 ISFAHAN, CENTRAL IRAN   ⚔ UNKNOWN   🏛 PLACE OF WORSHIP

In 1598, Shah Abbas I of the Safavid dynasty moved the Persian capital from Qazvin to Isfahan. He reorganized the city into a series of linked squares, the largest being the Maidan, 1,640 x 525 ft (500 x 160 m). On one side is the opulent Masjid-i-Shah mosque, reached through a vast gateway with 112 ft (34 m) high minarets.

With its high drum and bulb-shaped dome, its blue-tiled minarets, and its elaborate gateways, the Masjid-i-Shah mosque is a marvel of Safavid art. So that the mosque aligns with Mecca while maintaining the integrity of the square, it is set at a surprising angle of about 45° to the main gateway. The building largely follows the four-iwan plan established in the Masjid-i-Jami, with each iwan leading to a domed hall and flanked by double-story arcades with pointed niches. Beyond the iwans east and west of the courtyard are

MOSAIC DETAIL ON DOUBLE-STOREY ARCADE

madrassas. Minarets are paired at both the entrance to the mosque and the entrance from the square. The 177 ft (54 m) high dome is covered in blue and turquoise tiles, evoking the colors of a peacock's tail. Elsewhere, there are tiles of yellow, pink, and green, and much floral decoration, set off against the warm brickwork.

SHAH ABBAS I

Isfahan, 211 miles (340 km) south of Tehran, is an oasis in a vast expanse of rock and sand. It is largely the work of Shah Abbas I (r.1588–1629), who built many new mosques, palaces, bridges, avenues, and parks. He also welcomed European merchants (to build up the economy), diplomats (to secure allies against the Ottomans), and artists (to enhance the culture of his city). To sum up the city's splendor, Persians would say, "Isfahan is half the world."

Ambitious project
Construction of the Masjid-i-Shah mosque began in 1612; the building is said to be made of more than 18 million bricks.

PAVILION OF ALI QAPU

⚰ 1597 🏴 ISFAHAN, IRAN
⚒ UNKNOWN   🏛 PALACE

Overlooking the Maidan—or royal polo ground—and superimposed onto an earlier structure, the impressive gatehouse of the Ali Qapu palace is known as the Pavilion of Ali Qapu, or the Sublime Gate. Its high balcony, fronting a complex eight-story building with a large central reception hall, served both as a symbolic entrance to the palace and as a place from where members of the court could watch the passing world below. The building features fine lacquered stucco ceilings and exquisite shell-vaulted rooms. The finest of all is the sixth-floor music room.

PAVILION OF CHEHEL-SOTUN

⚰ 1645 🏴 ISFAHAN, IRAN ⚒ UNKNOWN
🏛 PALACE

This six-story structure, built by Shah Abbas II, is one of the garden pavilions that formed the complex of the old royal palace in Isfahan. Sited at the end of a long pool, the high and wide veranda of the pavilion is carried on 20 slender columns. The effect of their reflection in the pool gave the temple its name, Chehel-Sotun, or Palace of Forty Columns. As with the Pavilion of Ali Qapu, walls and columns were originally covered with frescoes, paintings, and mirror mosaics. The main reception hall is a domed room lined with murals. However, the pavilion has suffered over the many years of Isfahan's decline since the capital was moved to Tehran in 1788, and mosaics are now found only in the alcove at the rear of the portico. The pavilion was used for receptions and entertainments: the shah would receive dignitaries and ambassadors, either on the terrace or in one of the stately chambers decorated with exquisite marble, gilding, frescoes, and statues.

CITADEL OF BAM

⚰ ca. 1700 🏴 BAM, IRAN ⚒ BAHMAN ESFANDIYAR   🏛 FORTIFICATION

Considered virtually impregnable when first built some 2,000 years ago, the Citadel of Bam—now close to Iran's border with Pakistan—was a military garrison that commanded important trade routes, notably the Silk Route. The modern city, wrecked by a devastating earthquake in 2003, lies to its southwest. The chiefly mud-built citadel was also largely destroyed within seconds of the cataclysm. It had been divided into quarters, walled around and watched over by guards housed in 38 towers. On the southern side there were four ramparts, and to the northeast, another colossal rampart. The citadel had largely been rebuilt by the Safavid dynasty between 1502 and 1722, so inside its protective earthwork rings was a remarkably civilized, well-serviced city—not quite Isfahan, perhaps, yet complete with two-story houses, many with private baths, along with a palace, shops, bazaar, caravanserai, mosques, military base, public baths, and gymnasium.

Earth fortress
The "mud" citadel was built mainly with baked bricks, wool, and straw.

TOMB OF HUMAYUN

⚰ 1566   🏴 DELHI, INDIA   ✍ MIRAK MIRAZA GHIYAS   🏛 TOMB

The first example of Mughal architecture in India is the tomb of Humayun, son of the first Mughal Emperor, Babur Shah, a descendant of Timur, who forced his way across the Punjab to Delhi in 1526. Standing on a high square platform, the tomb is the centerpiece of a beautiful garden inspired by Persian design.

Construction was begun on the tomb by Humayun's widow, work continuing under the reign of his son, Akbar. The architect was Persian, and his country of origin is clear not just from the tomb's pointed archways and dome, but from the layout of the garden. Essentially a large and perfect grid divided first into four, then again into nine, it is intended to be an earthly representation of the gardens of Paradise. The flat surfaces are separated by ornamental streams, paved pathways, and avenues of trees. The architecture is inspired by a combination of the Hindu idea of enclosed sanctuary, and the Iranian

PERSIAN GARDENS

The word Paradise derives from the ancient Persian for an enclosed garden. The Persian garden, nurtured as a retreat from the desert as early as 4000BCE, evokes an image of an enchanted place where walls shut out the desert and enclose a sacred geometrical space cut through with narrow canals and groves of flowering almonds, pomegranates, and damask roses. The Persian style was widely copied with the spread of Islam, from Moorish Spain to Mughal India.

use of sequences of interconnecting rooms and galleries. The finely proportioned elevations rising from a massive red arcaded base are composed of irwans, arches, arcades, pinnacles, and kiosks. Following Islamic tradition, the mausoleum comprises domes, vaults, pointed arches, and arabesques. Square in plan, the central octagonal chamber containing the cenotaph, or tombstone, is encompassed by octagonal chambers at the diagonals and arched lobbies on the sides, their openings protected with perforated screens.

PERSIAN POINTED ARCHES

Spectacular symmetry
The Tomb of Humayun is crowned by a white marble dome that measures 140 ft (42.5 m) in height.

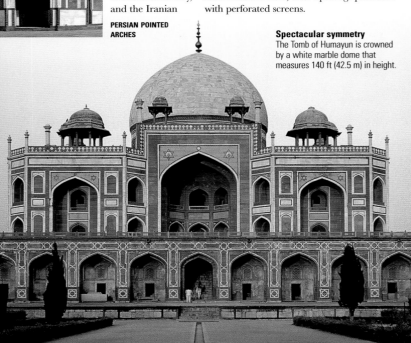

FATEHPUR SIKRI

ca. 1580 · UTTAR PRADESH, INDIA · UNKNOWN · CITY

Meaning "Town of Victory," Fatehpur Sikri is Mughal architecture's most ambitious monument. Constructed at the height of the Emperor Akbar's building activity to honor the birth of his son, Jahangir, the city was abandoned only 15 years later. It may have been magnificent, but there was no water to fill its wells. Today it rests in a near-perfect state of preservation.

WOODEN COLUMN THAT SUPPORTED THE THRONE

With a boundless supply of sandstone and marble and an army of craftsmen, building the royal citadel, Fatehpur Sikri, was not so very difficult. Its location, however, 25 miles (40 km) west of Agra, on a rocky peninsula, was improbable. Possibly due to a shortage in the water supply, only 15 years after its initial inhabitation, Fatehpur Sikri became the most magnificent of all ghost towns.

At every turn, there are superbly crafted and imaginatively designed monuments. There is, of course, a Great Mosque, its courtyard measuring 360 x 425 ft (110 x 130 m), surrounded by arcaded cloisters with a frieze of Hindu chattris running along the top. Its finest part, though, is the sensational Buland Darwaza or southern gate, rebuilt by Akbar as a monumental entrance. A steep pyramid of stairs leads up to the gateway, through an impressive irwan, into a half-octagon lobby, and so through to the courtyard of the mosque itself. From the stairs, visitors have a fine view of the city, principally of the Panch Mahal, or Palace of Five Stories—wonderfully complex red sandstone pavilions linked by bridges and boasting treasuries, harems, bath houses, reception rooms, stables—all the usual bare necessities of life as a Mughal emperor.

THE EMPEROR AKBAR

The Mughal Emperor Akbar (1542–1605) was illiterate and a fierce and even savage warrior, building towers from his enemies' heads, but he took a keen interest in literature, architecture, and the arts. At Fatehpur Sikri he blended Islamic and Hindu elements in his new buildings, as he did in his own religion, Din-i-ilahi. He also had Jesuit priests at his court, along with his 300 official wives and a harem of 5,000 women from across the world.

Monumental error
Despite its elegant, formal reflecting pools, the lack of an adequate water supply was Fatehpur Sikri's downfall.

RUKN-I-ALAM

🏛 1324   📍 MULTAN, PAKISTAN   ✍ TUGHLUQ I   🏛 TOMB

Built by Tughluq I, a medieval Turko-Mongol governor of Depalpur in the lower Punjab, this mausoleum is a fascinating example of pre-Mughal architecture. It still dominates Multan, a city founded in the Bronze Age. Now in central Pakistan, Multan was first conquered by Alexander the Great and then by Muslim invaders in around 712. The octagonal, polished red-brick tomb of Rukn-i-Alam, surmounted by a high, hemispherical dome with a diameter of 56 ft (17 m) and a height of 148 ft (45 m), is supported by massive buttresses that narrow as they climb into Multan's hot and dusty sky. The dome rises from a second octagon around which is a passage from where the muezzin could call the faithful to prayer. The materials used are brick bonded at intervals with carved shisam wood—an indigenous form of construction dating back to the ancient Indus Valley civilization—faced in terracotta and glazed blue, azure, and white tiles. The tomb is decorated with floral and calligraphic patterns.

Local landmark
Standing high on an artificial mound, the domed mausoleum can be seen from up to 25 miles (40 km) away. It was beautifully restored in 1977.

TOMB OF JAHANGIR

🏛 1630   📍 LAHORE, PAKISTAN   ✍ UNKNOWN   🏛 TOMB

This long, low, single-story arcaded structure, set in an ornamental garden northwest of Lahore across the Ravi River, holds the tomb of the fourth great Mughal emperor, Jahangir, who ruled from 1605 to 1627. The red sandstone and white marble building is the first in a series of major architectural achievements during the "Reign of Marble" of the next Emperor, Shah Jahan (1628–58). Four octagonal minarets, new to India yet incorporating traditional Indian elements, stand at each corner of this elegantly restrained tomb, which is set in formal gardens—representing Paradise—and contained within a high walled compound. The building is fairly simple, yet the manner in which it has been carved and inlaid with semiprecious stones gives a glimpse of a craft that would find its peak in the Taj Mahal (see p.220–1) some years later. Here you can spot lapis lazuli, onyx, jasper, topaz, carnelian, and variously colored marbles. The tomb is approached from the garden through four corridors, three of which are dressed in intricate marble. The outer entrance to the tomb opens into a courtyard that served as a caravanserai during the Mughal era.

Valued monument
An image of the tomb of Jahangir can be seen on Pakistan's highest-denomination banknote, the 1,000-rupee note.

TAJ MAHAL

🪦 1653   📍 AGRA, INDIA   ⚒ SHAH JAHAN   🏛 TOMB

Sheathed in shimmering white marble and standing at the foot of a long reflecting pool, the Taj Mahal (Crown Palace) represents the pinnacle of Mughal architecture. Commissioned by Emperor Shah Jahan in memory of his favorite wife, Mumtaz-i-Mahal, this fine tomb took 20,000 workers 22 years to build. Its beauty lies in its calm solemnity, and the marble's subtle colors as it reflects the changing sky above.

Built on a terrace beside the Jamuna River, the Taj Mahal complex is enclosed by a high wall with broad octagonal pavilions at each corner that can be seen from the emperor's palace in the Agra Fort. The tomb itself rises on a high red sandstone platform, 187 ft (57 m) square, its corners marked by four slender 154 ft (47 m) high minarets. These emphasize the considered proportions of the tear-shaped, double-

MUMTAZ-I-MAHAL'S CENOTAPH, TOMB CHAMBER

shelled central dome, the inner shell of which is 79 ft (24 m) high with a diameter of 59 ft (18 m). The dome, whose shape is derived from both Hindu temple design and Persian Timur architecture, is flanked by four smaller domed chattris (roof pavilions). The plan is a rationalization of Delhi's Humayun Tomb (see p.217): an octagonal chamber surrounded by a series of interlocking

SHAH JAHAN

Born in 1592, Shah Jahan (r.1628–58) was the great builder of the Mughal Empire. His finest works include the Red Fort and the Jama Masjid at Delhi, but he is most famous for the Taj Mahal. He was deposed in 1658, after a power struggle among his sons. Prince Aurangzeb imprisoned his father in the Agra Fort's Octagonal Tower—one of Shah Jahan's own commissions—and he died there in 1666.

corridors, with a subsidiary octagonal chamber at each junction. The beautiful, rather pure elevations have little decoration. The interior of the building is dimly lit through delicate marble lattices. The bodies of the emperor and his wife remain in a vault below the building.

The Taj Mahal does not sit, as convention at the time dictated, at the center of its surrounding garden, but to the back of it, with the rear elevation facing the river. According to one story, it overlooks the Jamuna because the emperor had planned to build a corresponding tomb, in black marble, on the other bank.

Jewel in the crown
The Taj Mahal has been described as "having been designed by giants and finished by jewelers."

RED FORT, DELHI

🏆 1648 📍 DELHI, INDIA
✍ SHAH JAHAN 🏛 PALACE

The Red Fort, so called because of its massive red-sandstone perimeter walls, is a fortified palace complex built by Shah Jahan when he moved his capital from Agra to Delhi. The main entrance—the imposing Lahore Gate—leads to such attractions as the Hammams (royal baths), the Shahi Burj (the Shah's private office), and the Moti Masjid (Pearl Mosque). The Rang Mahal (Palace of Colors), crowned with gilded turrets, housed the emperor's wives and mistresses.

EMIN MINARET

🏆 1778 📍 TURPAN, XINJIANG, CHINA
✍ IBRAHIM 🏛 PLACE OF WORSHIP

This 144 ft (44 m) high minaret, near Turpan on the ancient Silk Road, is the only Islamic tower in China. Construction was begun in 1777 by Turpan's ruler, Emin Khoja, and completed a year later by his son, Suleman. Designed by the Uygur architect Ibrahim in local sun-dried gray brick, the strongly tapered, circular minaret is decorated with 16 different geometrical and floral patterns. The play between the confident climb of the minaret and the simple horizontality of the Song Gong mosque alongside is a delight.

Medieval
Europe

THE TIME BETWEEN the fall of Rome in the 5th century and about
1000 is often called the Dark Ages. Yet these sketchily documented
centuries were not the intellectual and artistic shadowlands they are often
painted. Embers of creativity still glowed amid the gloom, and medieval
architecture eventually burst forth, fully armored, in a blaze of glory.

The conquering Germanic tribes, such
as the Goths and Franks, that migrated
throughout western Europe in the wake
of the Roman empire were not always
the brutal pagan warriors of popular
imagination. Most were either Christian
or became converts to Christianity,
and some admired the achievements
of the empire they had undermined.

Nevertheless, they retained many of
their customs, ways of life, and forms
of social organization, and with their
arrival western Europe entered into a
prolonged state of cultural and social
flux and political instability. During
this time, much of the infrastructure
developed by the Romans, such as
roads and water supplies, fell into ruin.

An age of war
Europe's great new cathedrals housed
those who fell in the Crusades and
the Hundred Years' War, among
innumerable conflicts; this is
the tomb, in Canterbury,
of Edward (1330–76),
England's "Black Prince."

KEY DATES

800 Charlemagne crowned first Holy Roman Emperor by the Pope on Christmas Day

988 Grand Duke Vladimir of Kiev becomes a Christian; the conversion of Russia follows

1066 Conquest of England by William of Normandy as Anglo-Saxon army under King Harold fails

1096–99 The First Crusade, led by Godfrey of Bouillon, captures Jerusalem from the Saracens

800   **900**   **1000**   **1100**

851 Major earthquake in Rome destroys many buildings

976 Simplified Arabic mathematical symbols introduced to Europe, challenging Roman numerals

1088 The first European university opens

1163 Pope Alexander III lays the foundation stone of Notre Dame cathedral in Paris

Illuminated manuscripts
Religious texts, such as this Book of Hours (a prayer book), were painstakingly illustrated by monks.

The Christian Church, the only international force at work in Europe during the early medieval era, at least provided a thread of social unity in the region's former Roman colonies. In these turbulent times, the monasteries acted as repositories of learning and havens for the arts. (One of the only significant architectural drawings to have survived from before the Gothic era is a plan of an ideal Benedictine monastery, from the abbey of St. Galle, Switzerland.) It was a role that did not go unrewarded: as western Europe's new rulers became more powerful and willing to learn, the Church benefited from their wealthy patronage.

AGE OF CONFLICT

As Europe adjusted to the vacuum left by the demise of Rome, rivalries and power struggles between local, regional, and national leaders led to war after war after war—so much so, that it is difficult to see the history of medieval Europe, from the Dark Ages to the 15th century, as anything other than a long series of bloody battles.

These medieval power struggles were not just secular ones. In the 13th century, the Church in Rome gained religious supremacy over western Europe with the ruthless crushing of the Cathar, or Albigensian, "heresy." This was a form of Christianity that

HOLY GRAIL LEGEND

The Grail was a holy object associated with Christ and sought by the legendary knights of medieval Arthurian romance tales. It was most commonly depicted as the cup or platter used by Christ at the Last Supper, and later by Joseph of Arimathea to catch the blood from Christ's wounds as he hung on the cross. Medieval poets and storytellers ascribed life-restoring powers to the Grail.

Perceval and the Holy Grail (1286)
In the earliest stories, Perceval was the Grail-seeker; in later versions, Sir Galahad was the hero.

1200	1300	1350	1400
1315 First accurate public dissection of human corpse performed by Italian surgeon Mondino de Luzzi	**1337–1453** The Hundred Years War rages between the emerging superpowers of England and France	**1378–1417** The Great Schism between the rival Popes of Avignon and Rome ends with Roman supremacy	**1402** Work starts on a massive, late-Gothic cathedral in Seville, which would be the world's largest when completed
1271 Marco Polo, explorer, soldier, and writer, leaves Venice for his sojourn in China	**1321** Death in Ravenna of Dante Alighieri, author of *The Divine Comedy*	**1347–51** The Black Death, or bubonic plague, wipes out one-third of the population of Europe	*ca.* **1386** Geoffrey Chaucer begins writing *The Canterbury Tales*, the first great literary work in English

emerged in the Languedoc around Albi, southern France, in the 12th century and was seen as a threat to the established Roman Church. When the Cathars were eventually brought under the Papal yoke, an immense, fortresslike cathedral was built in Albi to emphasize the Pope's authority.

Political stability gradually returned to western Europe, and by the end of the Middle Ages, the key European nation states either had emerged—such as England, France, Spain, Sweden, and Portugal—or were recognizable among the principalities and grand duchies that comprised Germany, Italy, and the Low Countries.

MEDIEVAL ARTS

With political stability came economic and cultural revival, including a great flowering of architecture. This resulted in some of the world's finest buildings, in the form of the medieval cathedrals and monasteries, and some of the most enchanting local architecture, in the guise of the many thousands of parish churches that bloomed across Europe; those in England are one of the greatest collective works of vernacular art to be found anywhere in the world.

Great rose window, Sainte-Chapelle, Paris
The art of stained glass reached its peak in the 13th and 14th centuries, flooding the interiors of Gothic cathedrals and churches with color and light.

THE CRUSADES

In 1095, Pope Urban II launched a military campaign to reclaim Jerusalem's Christian holy places from the Seljuk Turks who ruled the Holy Land. This was the first of many such campaigns, or "crusades" in the Middle Ages that aimed to retake control of the Holy Land. Any gains they made were eventually reversed by the continued growth of Islamic states. Crusades were also waged against pagan lands and heretical Christian groups.

The Fifth Crusade
This detail from an illustrated manuscript shows the Crusader knights taking Damietta, Egypt, in 1219.

As well as great buildings, the Middle Ages also produced magnificent art, exquisite literature and book production, wonderful sagas, such as that of the quest for the Holy Grail, resplendent armor, imaginative structural engineering, and a revival of ancient learning—largely through contact with Islamic scholars in Spain who had kept alive the writings of Plato, Aristotle, and others.

Despite all the color we see in illustrated prayer books and Books of Hours, in the stained glass windows of Gothic cathedrals, and in the battle flags and plumed helmets of knights, there was a darkness at the heart of the medieval world. Not only was it a time of more or less

Medieval mass
Standing in awesome isolation, Mont St. Michel in France looms high over its tiny island base.

continual conflict, but Europe also underwent a major change of climate during this period. The medieval era that began with citrus fruit growing in England descended into a miniature Ice Age during the first decade of the 14th century, leading to the Great Famine of 1315–17, which decimated many towns and cities.

Hard on the heels of this tragedy came the Black Death of 1347–51: an outbreak of bubonic plague that began somewhere along the Silk Road and ended up killing up to a third of the population of Europe. Numerically, it would be 150 years before Europe recovered. The economic and social effects were profound: when the Black Death receded, there were far fewer workers, so wages rose, peasants revolted, and the feudal system broke down. This was the end of serfdom in western Europe, although not of the plague, which broke out again, though with lessening virulence, throughout the rest of the 14th century.

Amid all this death and warfare, chaos and strife, medieval architecture must have been truly inspirational, lifting people high above the pestilent mire of daily life. Today, it remains one of the crowning glories of the art of building.

ROMANESQUE
ca. 800–1100

The classic Romanesque church, a development of the Roman basilica, was sponsored by powerful abbots and kings hoping to recreate the might and architectural splendor of ancient Rome. Early Romanesque became the "house style" of Charlemagne, or Charles the Great, king of the Franks from 768 to 814, and was widely adopted after Pope Leo III crowned Charlemagne the first Holy Roman Emperor.

Charlemagne, a patron of art and learning, was a great defender of the City of Rome, and it was for this that he was rewarded with an emperor's crown on Christmas Day 800. From then on, Romanesque architecture spread across Italy (including Sicily), France, Germany, Scandinavia, and England with power and aplomb. The style, which despite regional variations is remarkably consistent, was also pushed along by dynamic religious forces such as the Cluniac order. The order built some of the greatest pilgrimage churches of the era, including the French churches of St. Martin at Tours and St. Sernin, Toulouse, and Santiago de Compostela *(see pp.234–5)* in Galicia, Spain.

CHARACTERISTICS OF ROMANESQUE
Romanesque churches were typified by their cruciform (Latin cross) plans, by ambulatories (walkways) around the apse, where pilgrims could file past reliquaries, and by hefty stone vaults carried on vast columns and extremely thick walls. Architects and masons (the two were often synonymous) had yet to learn how to develop the light and airy vaults of the coming Gothic era, so their buildings appear massive and usually rather dark. To build with strength and height required deep walls with small windows, although this was rather appropriate for an architecture nurtured and developed by warrior kings—not only Charlemagne in the 9th century, but also William of Normandy, who conquered England in 1066. William knew full well the power of architecture as a sign of control and domination. Nevertheless, although his tough regime began with the construction of fortresses, it was to lead to such Romanesque marvels as the nave of Durham Cathedral *(see p.240)*. Might could, after all, do right.

◁ **THE INTERIOR OF THE DUOMO IN PISA, ITALY, FORMS A LATIN CROSS, DIVIDED INTO FIVE NAVES BY 68 GRANITE COLUMNS. LIT FROM ABOVE, IT IS ENLIVENED BY FRESCOES, GEOMETRIC PATTERNS OF COLORED MARBLE, AND THE COFFERED CEILING.**

ELEMENTS

Characterized by castlelike solidity, Romanesque was the style of Christian warrior-kings who wished to emulate the fortunes of legendary Roman emperors. They adopted some of the forms of Ancient Rome, while developing many more of their own, influenced by both the Islamic and Christian architectural traditions.

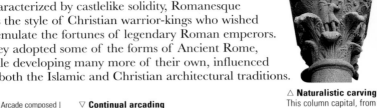

Arcade composed of high, round-headed arches

▽ Continual arcading
Arcading was taken to extremes around the famous leaning tower, or campanile, of Pisa Cathedral, Italy. This was a feature of many Romanesque churches; the design is mirrored in the nave at Pisa.

△ Naturalistic carving
This column capital, from Monreale Cathedral, Sicily, is based loosely on classical Corinthian design, but enlivened by the carved figure of a shielded knight wrapped around with typically frondlike decoration.

△ Blind arcading
This was a distinct form of decoration aimed at relieving otherwise blank walls, and far cheaper and easier to construct than openings for glass windows. It was rare at this time.

△ Carved columns
The massive, rubble-filled columns at Durham Cathedral, England, are lightened by zigzag carving, which brings a play of light and shadow into the heart of the muscular nave.

Strapwork contrasts with structural stone

◁ Strapwork
Stone strapwork, an interlacing decoration that resembles straps, was a key feature of Anglo-Saxon churches, such as All Saints Church in Earls Barton, England.

Carved zigzag surround

Figurative carving in center of tympanum

Columns huddled closely together

△ Sculpted tympanum
Like the pediment of a Roman temple, the tympanum—the area between the top of a door or window and the arch above it—of a Romanesque church was filled with relief sculpture.

BAPTISTERY, PARMA

AFTER 1196 **PARMA, ITALY** **BENEDETTO ANTELAMI** **BAPTISTERY**

Benedetto Antelami's baptistery in Parma is a lavish affair. Between the bluff buttresses at the angles of the walls, themselves topped by open lanterns, four square-topped arcades encircle the building. These, in turn, have an elegant round-headed arcade above them. The three entrances, or portals, are unusual for their relief sculptures, unique in Italy at the time; they are thought to be the work of Antelami himself. The sculptures are an echo of contemporary developments in France, not least in their subjects: the Virgin and the Last Judgement.

The 16-sided interior bears other signs of French influence: it is articulated by half-columns that rise to almost the height of the building. The columns are topped by pointed arches and, importantly, a ribbed vault. In addition, the lowest level of the interior has an applied arcade surmounted by resolutely round-headed arches.

A medieval masterpiece
Parma's exquisite pink marble baptistery (to the right of the 12th-century Duomo) is one of the finest buildings of the Italian Romanesque.

GARISENDA AND ASINELLI TOWERS

c.1100 & 1119 **BOLOGNA, ITALY**
GARISENDA & ASINELLI FAMILIES **TOWERS**

Bologna allegedly once had 180 structures like the Garisenda and Asinelli towers. Nominally watchtowers, these immense free-standing structures were statements of the power of the families that built them. Square and brick-built, with just a handful of small windows, they are architecturally unremarkable, but, built in an age when calculating forces and loads was largely a matter of guesswork, they are technically exceptional. The Asinelli is 318ft (97m) high, the Garisenda, reduced for safety reasons in 1360, is 154ft (47m). Due to subsidence, neither is vertical; the Garisenda is as much as 10½ft (3.25m) out of true.

SANT'AMBROGIO CHURCH

AFTER 1080 **MILAN, ITALY**
UNKNOWN **PLACE OF WORSHIP**

With its unadorned brick construction, enclosed atrium (forecourt), and two-story gabled façade pierced by hefty round-headed arches, Sant'Ambrogio is rather austere and backward-looking. Inside, however, are some technical breakthroughs. The moldings of the nave arches carry down into the supporting piers, providing a visual link between arch and pier, and the nave ceiling is articulated by shallow transverse and diagonal rib-vaults—one of the earliest uses of such devices. The resulting system of bays into which the nave is divided hints at later Romanesque and Gothic developments.

MONREALE CATHEDRAL

🏛 1182   🗺 NEAR PALERMO, SICILY   ✎ WILLIAM II   🏛 PLACE OF WORSHIP

Monreale Cathedral is an overwhelmingly lavish building and the supreme example of Norman-Arab architecture: a synthesis of 12th-century Western church building and Arab decorative patterning. There are strong Byzantine influences, above all in the glittering mosaics of the nave, aisles, and apses.

Monreale Cathedral is a flat-roofed basilica, with a broad nave, and spacious aisles leading to three shallow apses at the east end. A half-dome, from which a fearsome Byzantine mosaic Christ gazes down, covers the high altar. The interior is most striking for its expanses of mosaics.

All that links the building with the parallel developments of the Gothic style in northern France are the pointed arches of the nave. Externally, the most remarkable feature is the main apse: a confection of applied, overlapping, pointed arches, and discs, the whole studded with colored marble set in precise geometric patterns. The overall effect is of elaborate surface decoration with clear Islamic influence.

The craftsmanship is continued in the 42 biblical scenes on the striking bronze doors of the main entrance. The cloisters, all that remain from the original Benedictine

THE INTERIOR, SHOWING MOORISH INFLUENCES

monastery outbuildings, contain 228 twin columns supporting Moorish arches. Many of the columns are twisted, and are carved with elaborate figures and vegetation; a number are inlaid with glass mosaics.

WILLIAM II

The construction of the opulent Monreale Cathedral by the Norman ruler of Sicily, William II (r.1166–89), was more than an act of piety: it was a political necessity. It was a deliberate attempt to eclipse not just the existing cathedral in Palermo but its English-born archbishop, Walter of the Mill, who was a staunch supporter of Pope Innocent II, himself a long-time opponent of the Normans in Sicily.

High over the town
The cathedral dominates the town of Monreale, southwest of Palermo. It is a fine Christian church decorated by craftsmen trained in Muslim traditions.

SAN NICOLA, BARI

🏛 AFTER 1087 📍 BARI, ITALY ✎ UNKNOWN 🏛 PLACE OF WORSHIP

The church of San Nicola, in the Puglian town of Bari in southeastern Italy, stood as evidence of the energy, and wealth, of its Norman builders, creating what would prove to be a surprisingly enduring local style. The southern tower was never finished, but the exterior of the church displays a calm symmetry.

The central, gabled bay, accented by a projecting porch, is strongly vertical. Two pilasters—rectangular features in the shape of pillars but only barely projecting from the wall—emphasize the lines of the porch. The central bay reflects the presence of a substantial nave behind it, just as the flanking bays, each with its own arched doorway, make clear the aisles to which they lead. The arcading that follows the roofline is surprisingly delicately carved.

Inside, the flat-roofed nave is spanned by three transverse arches, and precisely defined by an arcade of double columns. Above, there is a sizeable passageway, or triforium, lit by high clerestory windows.

A perfect prototype
The strong Romanesque church of San Nicola was the first of a series in this style built across southern Italy. It displays a clear sense of its own worth.

The aisles are handsomely spacious under substantial cross vaults characterized by sharp-edged diagonal groins formed by the intersection of two barrel vaults. The ground plan is simple: a straightforward rectangle animated only by the apse behind the altar, and two smaller flanking apses.

PISA CATHEDRAL

🏛 AFTER 1063 📍 PISA, ITALY ✎ BUSCHETTO DI GIOVANNI, RAINALDO & OTHERS 🏛 PLACE OF WORSHIP

Few buildings highlight more clearly than Pisa Cathedral just how different Italian Romanesque and Gothic architecture were from counterparts elsewhere in Europe. In part this was a celebration of local architectural traditions, in part it reflected the country's Classical heritage; both worked against the adoption of non-Italian styles.

The cathedral sits at the heart of one of the most imposing architectural complexes in Europe, comprising the cathedral itself, the more or less contemporary baptistery, and the campanile (the Leaning Tower). All three are sheathed in brilliant white banded marble and are deliberate, almost overwhelming, statements of Pisan civic pride. Begun in the 11th century, the

Traditional influences
Renaissance-style arches form a kind of superimposed double-pedimented temple facade.

cathedral was later extensively remodeled, mostly in the 13th century when the nave was extended and the facade added.

The latter is a prime example of the Tuscan "proto-Renaissance:" an arcaded first floor, which extends around the entire building, topped by four tiers of carved arches, the lower two extending the full width of the building, the upper two only to the width of the nave.

Cathedral of Santiago de Compostela, Spain
Completed in 1211 at a major center of medieval
Christian pilgrimage, the Romanesque interior of
this great church remains largely preserved. The
much later facade, however, was constructed in
the Spanish churrigueresque style *(see p339)*.

NOTRE DAME LA GRANDE

🏛 *ca.* 1145   📍 POITIERS, FRANCE   ✎ UNKNOWN
🏛 PLACE OF WORSHIP

Well into the 13th century, France's political
fragmentation favored the development of
regional architectural styles, of which Notre
Dame La Grande is an impressive example.
Despite its vivid sculptural decoration and
idiosyncratic beehive spires, this church has
a robust, muscular quality. The facade lacks
the obsession with the vertical so evident in
churches further north. The nave has neither
triforium nor clerestory; rather, the arcade's
round-headed arches almost abut a stone
barrel vault supported by plain transverse ribs.

SAN MIGUEL DE ESCALADA

🏛 AFTER 913   📍 NEAR LEÓN, NORTHWEST SPAIN
✎ KING GARCIA   🏛 PLACE OF WORSHIP

Mozarabic buildings—Christian in function
but Moorish in detail—are a key feature of
early Spanish Romanesque architecture. San
Miguel de Escalada was built in the 10th
century largely by Moorish craftsmen left
behind after the expulsion of the Arabs from
northern Spain. In plan a simple rectangle
with aisles as wide as the nave, a rudimentary
crossing, and three apsidal arches at the east
end, San Miguel's Moorish influence is most
obvious in the horseshoe arches of the nave
and portico, and the ornate wooden roof.

MARIA LAACH ABBEY

🏛 AFTER 1093   📍 RHINELAND, GERMANY
✎ UNKNOWN   🏛 PLACE OF WORSHIP

Bold and massive, this imposing Benedictine
abbey church stands in an idyllic lakeside
location on the southwest bank of the
Laacher See, near Andernach, south of
Cologne. Along with the cathedrals at
Speyer, Mainz, and Worms, Maria Laach
ranks as one of the finest specimens of
German Romanesque architecture.
Although heavily influenced by northern
Italian and Carolingian styles, its boldly
grouped structures and sheer scale are an
emphatic statement of the power of a
reinvigorated Church.

Built mainly of local lava, Maria Laach's
most obvious external features are its towers,
three at the west end and three at the east.

ST. BENEDICT

The Benedictine order (based on St. Benedict's Holy
Rule, "Pray and work") was the most successful
monastic order of the Middle Ages. Little is known of
the Roman-born Benedict (*ca.* 480–550), but tradition
claims he fled the depravity of the city to become a
hermit and then a monk. His strict, humane
order was crucial in the establishment
of Christianity in northern Europe
following the collapse of Rome.

The central and largest tower at the west end is square—the roof areas between its gables form diamond-shapes, or "helm" roofs—while that over the crossing is octagonal.

CAPITAL DETAIL FROM OVER WEST DOOR—THE DEVIL NOTES WORSHIPERS' SINS

Although the building strongly emphasizes the vertical, contrast is provided by horizontal courses supported by round-headed arcades, which are a consistent visual motif. Paired round-headed arches, mainly in the towers, repeat this pattern. The west end is also marked by a dominant apse and, contained within the circular towers, a western transept. Less usual is the cloistered atrium at the western end, which leads to the main entrances in the circular towers. Three apses also mark the east end.

The interior of the abbey is strikingly sparse and echoing, with the massiveness of the construction everywhere apparent. Decorative relief is provided by the naturalistic carving on some of the capitals. A typical Rhineland touch is the use of half-columns on the square piers of the nave and aisles—a suggestion, if nothing more, of the emerging Gothic style. The vaulting bays of the nave and aisles are the same width —another hint of things to come.

Bold and massive
The German Romanesque placed an unmistakable premium on substance over subtlety.

CASTLES

Although cloaked in legends, quests, and chivalric fantasy, the medieval castle, for all its blazing fires, fluttering banners, banquets, damsels, and knights-in-armor, would have been a trying place to live. These were machines for defending territory, and for killing.

The race to build castles across Europe during long centuries of war developed into a competition to create imposing structures, especially when seen from a distance. The powerful castles built across Wales by Edward I are stark reminders of how effectively the Norman invaders subdued and contained an entire people. Other castles, however, are surprisingly beautiful because they were created by those who were more used to building or adorning cathedrals, such as Alonso de Fonseca, Archbishop of Seville, who commissioned Spain's finest medieval castle, the 15th-century Coca

Castillo de Loarre, Aragon, Spain
Its commanding position and awesome construction gave this castle psychological and strategic dominance over its surroundings.

Castle in Segovia *(see p.269)*, an impressive mix of Moorish and medieval European architecture. The medieval castle was also notably luxurious in its heyday and was used as much as a palace as a fortress. In terms of their function, castles finally lost out to gunpowder and modern weaponry, but some that continued to develop long past their role as military machines have gained a charm of their own over the centuries, such as William of Normandy's 11th-century White Tower *(see p.240)*, the handsome keep at the heart of the Tower of London.

Conwy Castle, Wales
The estuary of the Conwy River, directly below the castle, provided a natural barrier that further strengthened the defensibility of the fortifications.

KRAK DES CHEVALIERS

AFTER 1142 **HOMS, SYRIA** **KNIGHTS HOSPITALLERS** **FORTIFICATION**

Krak des Chevaliers is by some way the most impressive of the castles built in the Middle East during the Crusades, evoking the long and brutal fight for possession of the Holy Land. It is also a prime example of the way in which Muslim military architecture was adopted almost entirely unchanged by the West.

This castle was one of five built to safeguard the strategic Homs Gap in Syria. Its three key features are its location on what was already a natural strongpoint, its huge size and massive construction, and its use of concentric rings, studded with circular defensive towers around its keep, the heart of the castle. The site itself is formidable—a mountainous spur of rock, from which the ground slopes steeply. The gatehouse in the outer curtain wall leads to a typical Crusader device, the "bent entrance:" assuming they had been able to storm the outer wall, attackers were then forced to follow a winding path where they were subjected to further enemy fire. The inner wall is also defended on its more vulnerable south and west sides by an

THE KNIGHTS HOSPITALLERS

Officially founded in 1113, when their charitable work in the Holy Land was recognized by Pope Paschal II, the Knights Hospitallers rapidly became a dominant military force in the Near East, while still continuing their traditional role of tending the sick. The Order left the Holy Land in 1291 with the fall of Acre, settling first in Cyprus, and then from 1530 in Malta.

SEAL OF THE KNIGHTS HOSPITALLERS

enormous "glacis"—an unscaleable sloping wall, in places over 82 ft (25 m) thick. The principal function of castles such as this was not merely to secure conquered territory but to resist attack while supporting a huge garrison: the contemporary Crusader castle at Margat, Syria, could support 1,000 men for a siege of up to five years. But having successfully resisted 12 sieges, the Krak finally fell, in 1271, through treachery.

Mountain stronghold
The defenses at Krak des Chevaliers were supplemented by ditches, the construction of which involved the removal of hundreds of tons of rock.

WHITE TOWER, LONDON

🏛 AFTER 1078   📍 LONDON, ENGLAND
✍ WILLIAM THE CONQUEROR   🏛 FORTIFICATION

The Norman Conquest of England in 1066 was emphatically underlined by the construction of no fewer than 70 castles at key sites across the country. The White Tower was one of the largest; a rectangular, stone-faced structure, with towers at the corners, shallow buttresses along the walls, and small, slitlike windows placed high up. In the late 17th century, Christopher Wren added the elegant turrets on the towers and enlarged most of the windows.

ST. LAURENCE, BRADFORD-ON-AVON

🏛 ca. 1050   📍 BRADFORD-ON-AVON, WILTSHIRE, ENGLAND
✍ UNKNOWN   🏛 PLACE OF WORSHIP

Only about 50 Anglo-Saxon buildings survived the Norman conquest. This was no accident: the obliteration of every facet of Anglo-Saxon England was a priority for the new French rulers. St. Laurence is one of those rare survivors. Externally, it is plain, almost crude: three small, interlinked gabled structures—porticus (entry way), nave, and chancel—in roughly dressed stone, topped and partly animated by a round-headed blind arcade. If only by virtue of its age, the rough-hewn, cramped interior is oddly moving.

DURHAM CATHEDRAL

🏛 AFTER 1093   📍 DURHAM, ENGLAND
✍ BISHOP CARILEPH   🏛 PLACE OF WORSHIP

The ruthless military and political energy that drove the Norman conquest expressed itself in an astonishing burst of construction. Castles may have been the most immediate legacy, but in time it was the Norman genius for church building that would prove most enduring. Nowhere is this better embodied than in Durham Cathedral, built during the reign of William II (r. 1087–1100). This is a building exactly cast in the mold of its creators: austere, daring, and imposing.

Durham Cathedral is perhaps the supreme monument to the technical mastery of its late 11th-century Anglo-Norman builders,

WILLIAM DE ST. CARILEPH

This Norman Benedictine monk became Bishop of Durham in 1081. In 1093, he demolished the Anglo-Saxon cathedral and began work on its Romanesque replacement and a Benedictine abbey. His links with Scotland's King Donald III made him unpopular with King William II. Called before the king at Windsor in 1095, the sick bishop died soon after his arrival.

Commanding view
The city of Durham is dominated by the cathedral and the nearby castle—the ancient home of the powerful "Prince Bishops" of Durham.

who for almost half a century were the most accomplished engineers in Europe. It was the first building in Europe to use pointed rib vaults. Ribbed vaults had been used before, notably at Speyer in Germany after 1082, but never in this way—or to such dramatic effect. This was more than just a matter of being able to enclose a huge space with a stone roof, impressive though this was. Visually, the upward thrust of the giant shafts lining every second bay was forcefully extended up and across the roof. The result was an interior of exceptional unity and

BRONZE DOOR KNOCKER (_CA._ 1140), NORTH DOOR

power, a building with an astounding sense of its own monumentality. It was also an early hint of the coming Gothic style.

Despite Gothic touches, Durham is overwhelmingly Romanesque. The piers in the nave, which are decorated with precisely incised geometrical patterns, are massively solid, while their equally assured curved arches are rhythmically dynamic. The exterior is scarcely less impressive, in part the result of its dramatic setting high above the banks of the Wear River. In more ways than one, this was a high point of Anglo-Norman architecture.

ØSTERLARS CHURCH

🏛 1150   📍 BORNHOLM ISLAND, DENMARK   ✍ UNKNOWN   🏛 PLACE OF WORSHIP

In the years between 800 and 1050, Scandinavia influenced much of northern Europe, as the Vikings and Norsemen conquered and colonized lands from Russia to the Mediterranean, including much of eastern England and northern France. From the mid-11th century, as Scandinavia was Christianized, so the process was gradually reversed. The result was a fusion between local and Christian traditions, nowhere more obvious than in church building. On the Baltic island of Bornholm, for example, a distinctive tradition of stone-built circular churches developed, similar to the centrally planned churches of the Crusader Knights of the Temple. The fortresslike quality is deliberate: the building was intended as a strong point against raiding Baltic pirates, as much as a place of worship.

Fused styles
Østerlars's hefty sloping buttresses were added at a much later date.

BORGUND CHURCH

🏛 1150   📍 SOGNE FJORD, NORWAY   ✍ UNKNOWN   🏛 PLACE OF WORSHIP

Borgund church is the best known of Norway's "stave" churches. Its exotic external appearance seems part pagoda, part Viking funeral pyre, but the interior of the church is derived from the centrally planned churches of Byzantium, evidence of the far-flung nature of the Viking world.

As originally built (the apse at the east end is a later addition), it consisted of an arcaded central space beneath a high tower, whose soaring wooden construction suggests a link with the development of the Gothic in France. Stave construction refers to the timbers (or "staves")—logs split vertically, the curved side facing outward, flat side facing inward—that were butted together. Though a long-established means of construction in Scandinavia, the technique had never before been used on such a scale.

The exterior of the church lingers in the mind for its steep-pitched, weathered roofs and for the carved dragons' heads crowning the gables – reminders of past pagan traditions in the area.

Synthesized traditions
The church is a meeting of traditional building methods and the needs of Christian worship.

LUND CATHEDRAL

🏛 1103 📍 LUND, SWEDEN ✍ DONATUS 🏛 PLACE OF WORSHIP

Where the local, Scandinavian roots of the churches at Østerlar and Borgund are immediately obvious, in stark contrast the cathedral at Lund is fully in the mature Romanesque tradition, particularly as it was developed in Germany. Except for the absence of a western apse and double transepts, it is a building that would not look out of place among those in the Rhineland.

The western facade is dominated by two square towers animated by a complex series of round-headed arcades, arranged over three stories and topped by roofs sufficiently steeply pitched as to hint at spires. The upper story of the gabled central bay is given a similar series of arcades over

three much larger, round-headed windows. The tympanum (the space between the lintel and the arch) over the principal entrance is vigorously carved. Inside, the arcades of the nave are arranged in double bays, an innovation pioneered at Speyer, in Germany, not long before. Again, there is much rich carving, especially of the capitals of the nave piers. The east end is strongly marked by the deep transepts and apse.

The building is heavily restored, but Lund emphatically signaled the emergence of Scandinavia into the mainstream of Romanesque ecclesiastical architecture.

Romanesque statement
The most impressive feature of Lund is its dynamic facade, above all the two flanking towers.

HEDDAL STAVE CHURCH

🏛 1250 📍 TELEMARK, NORWAY ✍ UNKNOWN 🏛 PLACE OF WORSHIP

Heddal's is the largest surviving stave church in Norway. Over 1,000 are estimated to have been built, of which 28 are still in existence. By any measure, Heddal Stave Church is an imposing structure: a great heaping up of steep-pitched wooden roofs, gables, and towers, generating a strongly repetitive and rhythmical mood that rises to a climax in the square turret at its apex.

A near-pagan sense of grandeur is particularly obvious in the richly carved interior. Its impact is reinforced by the dim lighting, a characteristic of all stave churches. There are few windows, and these are small and set high up in the walls, often right under the eaves.

The building underwent extensive restoration in the mid-19th century, when Norwegians developed a greater awareness of their architectural heritage. As with many

Scaling the summit
In order to maintain the wooden church, a regular program of tarring is necessary. This is carried out by local mountaineers, who scale the steep roofs.

19th-century church restorations, the work was based on a rather flimsy understanding of the building's history. It was accordingly re-restored to something much closer to its original condition in the early 1950s.

GOTHIC
ca. 1150–1500

The architecture of the great medieval Gothic cathedrals is one of the glories of European civilization. Here was an attempt to lift everyday life up to the heavens—to touch the face of God—using the highest stone vaults, towers, and steeples permitted by contemporary technology. Here were buildings that owed as much to the vision of client and architect as they did to the handiwork of skilled masons and craftsmen.

High above the naves of these shiplike structures, and often well out of range of the human eye, we find expertly carved angels, demons, fronds, and finials: nothing was too good for the all-seeing eye of the Heavenly Father. The Gothic style emerged in France at the time of the bloody Crusades: despite its dark beginnings, it led to some of the most inspiring and daring buildings of all time.

THE FLYING BUTTRESS

The essence of High Gothic style is the flying buttress, which allowed medieval masons to transfer weight away from cathedral walls; the higher the walls, the greater the span of the decorated buttresses. Using flying buttresses, the cathedral builders were able to construct sensationally high and elaborate stone vaults and create ever bigger windows as they gained mastery of this new device. The windows began to take over from the walls, as in the example of Chartres (see p.250). Filled with colored glass telling the stories of the Old Testament and the lives of Christ, his apostles, saints, and martyrs, these churches were the medieval equivalent of movies or television. The contrast between these ambitious and lavish structures and the clay-and-wattle hovels that most people lived in could not have been more extreme. No wonder, then, that the church was able to keep people in a state of awe. If the French aimed high with their vaults, the English and the Germans competed for the tallest spire. The spire of Salisbury Cathedral (see p.256) rises 404 ft (123 m), while that of Ulm Münster (see p.262), completed as late as the 1890s to the designs of the original medieval architect, Matthäus Böblinger, reaches 525 ft (160 m). Gothic architecture was beautiful, and extreme.

◁ THE GOTHIC VAULTING IN THE CHAPTER HOUSE AT WELLS CATHEDRAL HAS A PALMLIKE EFFECT, EXPLOITED TO THE FULL BY THE 32 RIBS THAT SPRING FROM THE CENTRAL COLUMN.

ELEMENTS

Soaring skyward, Gothic was one of the most remarkable adventures in architecture. Pointed arches, high vaults, and flying buttresses lifted abbeys, churches, and cathedrals high into the medieval heavens. Structural ingenuity and the finely honed skills of stonemasons were matched by the lively imaginations of craftsmen, who made these Gothic buildings sing.

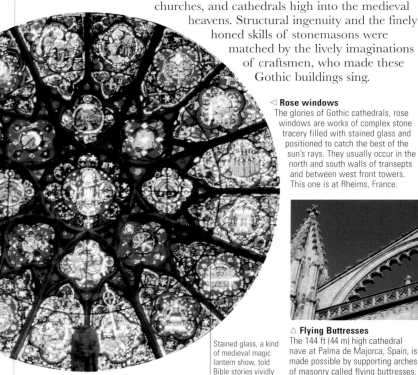

◁ **Rose windows**
The glories of Gothic cathedrals, rose windows are works of complex stone tracery filled with stained glass and positioned to catch the best of the sun's rays. They usually occur in the north and south walls of transepts and between west front towers. This one is at Rheims, France.

Stained glass, a kind of medieval magic lantern show, told Bible stories vividly

△ **Flying Buttresses**
The 144 ft (44 m) high cathedral nave at Palma de Majorca, Spain, is made possible by supporting arches of masonry called flying buttresses.

△ **Gothic arches I**
These simple pointed, or lancet, Gothic windows, dating from the late 12th century, illuminate the nave of Ripon Cathedral, Yorkshire, built by Roger of Pont L'Eveque, Archbishop of York.

△ **Gothic arches II**
The late-13th-century window tracery at Amiens Cathedral, France, designed by Thomas and Regnault de Cormont and Robert de Luzarches, illustrates the division of window arches into two.

△ **Gothic arches III**
Arches within arches: this 14th-century example at St. Hermes, Ronse, Belgium, shows the increasingly complex subdivision of Gothic windows and the elaboration of tracery.

△ **Gothic arches IV**
This English four-centered, or Perpendicular Gothic, arch at St. George's Chapel, Windsor, shows how an entire wall could be transformed into one gigantic window. The chapel dates from 1475.

Pinnacles peppered with crockets and weather vanes

Spirelike pinnacles send lines of tower soaring

△ Pinnacles

The vertical thrust of Gothic towers is continued and exaggerated by pinnacles, shown here on the late-15th-century bell-tower overlooking the cloister of Magdalen College, Oxford. Gothic pinnacles were often decorated with crockets—carved leaf motifs.

△ Interlaced stone tracery

The continual arcading, with an ogee design of interlaced stone tracery, around the *piano nobile* of the Doge's Palace (built 1309–1424) in Venice, Italy, is wholly distinct, and known as Venetian Gothic.

△ Groined vaulting

This superb groin vault, formed where two barrel vaults meet, is at Amiens Cathedral. As vaults grew lighter, higher, and slimmer, the windows in the walls of cathedral naves became larger and more daring.

△ Fan vaulting

This final development of the Gothic vault was an English invention. Here, stone vaults fan out like the tops of palm trees in a masterful design of 1515 by John Wastell at King's College Chapel, Cambridge.

Some gargoyles represent real animals, while others are mythical creatures

Gargoyles ▷

Among the many wonders of Gothic cathedrals and churches are the grotesque roof figurines called gargoyles. Some are water spouts, others have heraldic meaning, and then there are the winged and fanged beasts designed to scare away evil spirits. The most famous, seen here, peer over the west front of Notre Dame, Paris.

SAINTE CHAPELLE, PARIS

🪦 1248   📍 PARIS, FRANCE   ⚔ LOUIS IX
🏛 PLACE OF WORSHIP

Designed to be more sumptuous than any church in medieval Christendom, this building is a deliberate statement of the piety and prestige of the French monarchy. It was built as the resting place of holy relics, including the crown of thorns and a fragment of the cross, purchased by Louis IX from Baldwin II of Constantinople. The exterior makes it immediately clear that this is a building whose accents are vertical: the buttresses are topped by elaborately worked finials; the steeped-pitched gable at the west end is flanked by equally precipitous towers; and a delicate tapering flèche rises from the pitch of the roof. Inside there are two chapels. One is a rather gloomy, cryptlike affair; above this is the Sainte Chapelle itself, a vertiginous space articulated by brilliantly painted columns that soar to the vault. Between the columns are huge windows—in effect, the walls are given over entirely to glass. The creation of these shimmering walls of light in a wholly unified interior represents a supreme moment in the evolution of Gothic architecture.

Glistening chapel
The Sainte Chapelle is a startling Gothic tour de force, a building that seems more insubstantial than real.

NOTRE DAME, PARIS

🪦 AFTER 1163   📍 PARIS, FRANCE
⚔ BISHOP DE SULLY   🏛 PLACE OF WORSHIP

The imposing bulk of Notre Dame is a fine example of the new architectural language of Gothic, whose impact reverberated throughout western Christendom from the mid-12th century onward. Notre Dame was made possible by more than just a happy meeting between technology and finance. Like the cathedrals of St. Denis, Sens,

RAYONNANT ROSE WINDOW, WEST END OF NOTRE DAME

Laon, and Noyon—its immediate predecessors in northern France (the new intellectual heartland of Europe)—Notre Dame was a response to a major theological imperative in the newly assertive Christian Europe: the creation of buildings that were earthly echoes of God's kingdom. It was, literally, intended as a New Jerusalem.

Almost all the technological advances of the period were used in the construction of Notre Dame. The vault over the nave, more than 100 ft (30 m) high, is crossed and recrossed by stone ribs that are not only structural but also provide strongly unifying visual elements. Outside, flying buttresses, used here almost for the first time, make possible an upper story—the clerestory—containing windows that fill the interior with light. The stern, rational facade is studded with statues, dominated by an immense rose window, and heroically set off by two commanding towers. The transepts and their elaborate rose windows, threaded with tracery, were added in the mid-13th century. The flèche is a 19th-century addition.

BISHOP DE SULLY

Born of humble parents near Orléans at the beginning of the 12th century, Maurice de Sully became Bishop of Paris in 1160. He commissioned Notre Dame and ensured that much of it was built in his own lifetime. A skilled politician, he was one of the guardians of the Royal Treasury during the Crusade of 1190. He was a supporter of Thomas à Becket, Archbishop of Canterbury, against King Henry II of England. He retired to a monastery and died in 1196.

Island cathedral
In part, the impact of Notre Dame stems from its dramatic location on the Ile de la Cité in the Seine.

CHARTRES CATHEDRAL

🪦 1230　📍 CHARTRES, FRANCE　✍ UNKNOWN　🏛 PLACE OF WORSHIP

Construction of this first great Gothic cathedral began after a fire destroyed its predecessor in 1020. Much of it, except for the west front, was destroyed by another fire in 1194, and begun again. The result was a magnificent building, harmonious and all of a piece. The vast nave, the porches adorned with richly animated sculpture, the superb stained glass windows, and the fascinating labyrinth set into the floor that conveys worshipers on a virtual pilgrimage to Jerusalem

CHARTRES CATHEDRAL FROM THE EAST

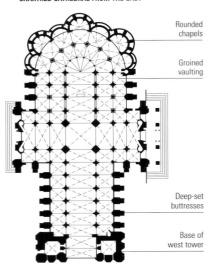

Rounded chapels

Groined vaulting

Deep-set buttresses

Base of west tower

△ **Floor plan**
The nave is 427 ft (130 m) long and 54 ft (16.5 m) wide. The plan is typical of French Gothic cathedrals and very similar to those of Reims and Amiens, differing from the English plan in its use of height, light, and an undivided nave and choir.

△ **Vaulted ceiling**
The innovative use of flying buttresses at Chartres cathedral allowed this ceiling, a soaring 112 ft (34 m) high, to be supported by what are virtually entire walls of stained glass.

Rose windows decorate the west front and two transept facades

△ **Stained glass, detail**
In total, over 32,292 sq ft (3000 m²) of medieval stained glass bathes the cathedral's interior in colored light.

◁ **Sculpture**
In the recessed triangular space of a pediment over the porch, a sculpture depicts Christ in glory surrounded by saints and angels. The work, richly detailed and three-dimensional, is continued throughout the cornices.

are just some of the beautifully executed elements of this great architectural and spiritual achievement. The cathedral was raised on the site of a holy well (which can be seen in the crypt) revered by Druids and Romans alike. It was the first to be dedicated to the Blessed Virgin Mary and was built, in part, to house the tunic that she was said to be wearing when she gave birth to Christ.

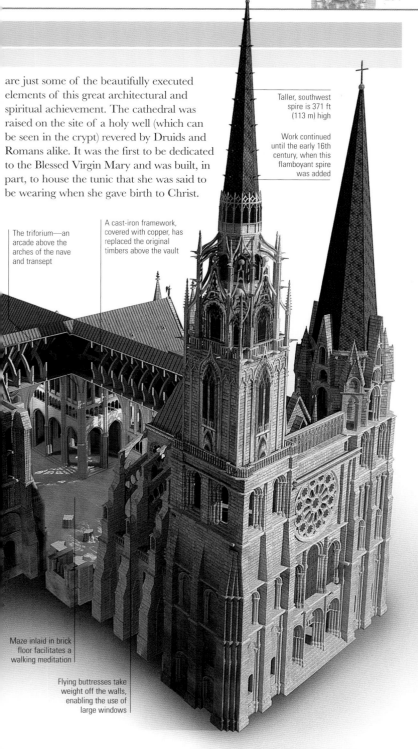

Taller, southwest spire is 371 ft (113 m) high

Work continued until the early 16th century, when this flamboyant spire was added

The triforium—an arcade above the arches of the nave and transept

A cast-iron framework, covered with copper, has replaced the original timbers above the vault

Maze inlaid in brick floor facilitates a walking meditation

Flying buttresses take weight off the walls, enabling the use of large windows

BEAUVAIS CATHEDRAL

🏛 AFTER 1247   📍 BEAUVAIS, FRANCE   ✎ UNKNOWN   🏛 PLACE OF WORSHIP

Beauvais, begun in 1247, represents the final stage in a direct line of the architectural evolution of the Gothic style that began at St. Denis in 1144. It is here that the High Gothic in France climaxes. Or rather, it is here that it might have climaxed. For Beauvais was not only never finished; its glory, the choir—at 157 ft (48 m), the tallest ever built in France—collapsed in 1284. Although it was rebuilt largely to the original designs by 1337, albeit with additional piers prudently added, the nave was never even started, as ambitious projects such as this became simply too expensive to undertake. Nonetheless, the sense of soaring, dizzy height in the choir is remarkable.

Vaulting ambition
Beauvais cathedral is the supreme example of the French Gothic's quest for verticality.

ALBI CATHEDRAL

🏛 AFTER 1282   📍 ALBI, SOUTHWEST FRANCE   ✎ UNKNOWN   🏛 PLACE OF WORSHIP

Albi presents a startling contrast to the near-contemporary High Gothic cathedrals of northern France. Externally, it more resembles a fortress than a church—its base slopes outward, as though to repel attackers; its windows, in stark contrast to the expanses of stained glass in the northern French cathedrals, seem mere attenuated slits; in place of flying buttresses, there are semi-circular buttresses bulging out from the rose-colored brick walls. In fact, the building's fortresslike quality reflects more than a regional variation, and it was quite deliberate: an unambiguous assertion of the control of

the Church, backed by royal power, extended into the Languedoc for the first time.

The great hall-like interior presents a contrast to the simplicity of the exterior. It consists of a single nave, at 59 ft (18 m) the widest in France. Along both walls are a series of deeply recessed chapels, 22 in all, formed by substantial internal buttresses that project inward. The internal decoration, including a magnificent rood screen, dates from the 14th and 15th centuries and includes lavish frescoes, murals, and statues. The cathedral also contains one of the most impressive organs in France.

Christian stronghold
Albi Cathedral was, literally, the Church Militant made real—Christian orthodoxy in brick form.

CARCASSONNE

🏛 ca. 1350 📍 AUDE, FRANCE ⚒ UNKNOWN 🏛 TOWN

Despite its extensive 19th-century restorations, Carcassonne, overlooking the Aude River in the Languedoc-Rousillon in southwestern France, is among the most complete and best-preserved medieval fortress towns in Europe. Its most striking feature is the wall studded with steep-pitched towers that encircles it. Though partly 1st-century Roman and partly 5th-century Visigothic, the majority is 13th-century, built by Louis IX and his successor, Philip III, after the city had fallen to Simon de Montfort in 1247 and then passed to the French monarchy. As such, it became a key defensive point against the expansive Spanish kingdom of Aragon to the south. From the 15th century onward, its military importance bypassed, Carcassonne gently declined. In 1835, when it was visited by the poet Prosper Mérimée, its dilapidation was such that, galvanized by a determination to restore the city to its medieval glory, he arranged for Viollet-le-Duc to oversee what amounted to a near complete rebuild.

Restored to glory
However heavily reconstructed, Carcassonne is the most striking medieval fortress town in France.

HÔTEL DE VILLE, ARRAS

🏛 AFTER 1502 📍 ARRAS, FRANCE ⚒ UNKNOWN 🏛 CIVIC BUILDING

Whatever the prosperity of late medieval France, it claimed relatively few civic buildings of distinction. In general, as the surge of cathedral and church building that had begun in the 10th century faded, the most prestigious architectural projects were the building of palaces and other châteaux. Certainly, there are few civic buildings of note comparable to those in late medieval Italy and the Low Countries. The Hôtel de Ville, or town hall, in Arras is a notable exception. Arras is not only geographically close to the Low Countries; when the Hôtel de Ville was built in the early 16th century, it was in effect ruled by Hapsburg Spain, whose rule also included the Low Countries. Arras's Hôtel de Ville bears a marked resemblance to the Cloth Halls in Bruges and Ypres *(see p.254)*.

The building is deliberately ornate, a conscious expression of civic pride. The first floor is given over to an arcade, above which are traceried windows that light the main hall on the first floor. The steep-pitched roof is studded with three levels of dormer windows. An enormous belfry rises 250 ft (76 m) into the sky.

Civic pride
Today's building was reconstructed after the original was destroyed in World War I.

CLOTH HALL, YPRES

🔲 AFTER 1214   📍 YPRES, BELGIUM   ✎ UNKNOWN   🏛 CIVIC BUILDING

Of all the major medieval secular buildings in the Low Countries—in Antwerp, Ghent, Bruges, Louvain, and Brussels—the most impressive, indeed most overwhelming, is the Cloth Hall in Ypres. In part, this is a matter of simple scale. The building is 443 ft (132 m) long, substantially more than most cathedrals of the period, for example. Just as much as the Cloth Hall at Bruges, this is a building that can only be read as a temple to trade.

Also as at Bruges, Ypres Cloth Hall is crowned by a bell-tower that rises from the ridge of the steep-pitched roof and climaxes in a delicate central lantern. Further vertical emphases are provided by the turrets at either end of the facade. Yet it is the horizontal that predominates. The facade itself is otherwise simple: a first-floor of rectangular openings under two floors of arched windows, those on the first floor round-headed, the larger ones on the third floor pointed. Together, they establish a repetitive, rhythmic regularity that gives the building an astonishing sense of assurance and certainty.

Temple of commerce
Ypres Cloth Hall was rebuilt in the 1930s, after the original was destroyed in World War I.

CLOTH HALL, BRUGES

🔲 AFTER 1282   📍 BRUGES, BELGIUM   ✎ UNKNOWN   🏛 CIVIC BUILDING

"The full might of late medieval commerce" is made clear by the Lakenhalle, or Cloth Hall, in Bruges. The hall was the center of the cloth trade in Bruges, a leading Hanseatic city and among the richest in Europe. Bruges was typical of the urban centers that emerged in northern Europe and Italy after 1000. Made rich by trade, they had a burning sense of civic worth. Architecturally, this partly found expression in new types of buildings—markets, warehouses, town halls, and guild halls—intended both to facilitate trade and to project their cities as impressively as possible. The dominant feature of the Cloth Hall is a tower, 260 ft

(80 m) high, that looms over the sturdy three-story brick-built hall itself. In its sheer massiveness it rivals the Cloth Hall in Ypres, or indeed Antwerp Cathedral. The latter comparison is apt. Though in no sense antireligious, the trade-rich cities of northern Europe in the high Middle Ages were conscious of their new status and determined to give it expression in buildings that were fully the equal, in opulence as much as size, of the most magnificent cathedrals. The tower's lower half was built after 1282, after the original hall burned down; the upper half, an octagonal lantern, was added between 1482 and 1486.

WELLS CATHEDRAL

🖵 AFTER 1180   📍 WELLS, SOMERSET, ENGLAND   ✎ UNKNOWN   🏛 PLACE OF WORSHIP

With Lincoln and Salisbury *(see p.256)*, Wells is traditionally considered one of the first three great and indisputably English (as opposed to French-influenced) cathedrals. Practically every prime feature of this first phase of mature English Gothic—Early English—is present. As with all such monastic foundations, the building sits in a spacious close; it values length over height; it has double transepts and a square east end; the principal entrance on the west front is diminutive. More unusually, the west front is rich in sculptures. Internally, the most remarkable features are the inverted "strainer" arches at the crossing, built in 1338 to support the central tower.

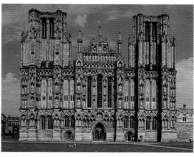

Wide-screen view
The curiously two-dimensional expanse of the west front acts as a screen on which to display the cathedral's many fine sculptures.

ELY CATHEDRAL

🖵 AFTER 1080   📍 ELY, CAMBRIDGESHIRE, ENGLAND   ✎ UNKNOWN   🏛 PLACE OF WORSHIP

Ely is among the most remarkable and arresting of England's cathedrals, both for its great size and the range and variety of its architecture, which spans every period from 11th-century Norman to 14th-century Decorated Gothic. Its most unusual and memorable feature is the eight-sided crossing at the meeting of nave and transepts, added between 1322 and 1340, above which rises an equally exceptional wooden octagonal lantern. Both are unknown in Gothic architecture elsewhere in Europe. The nave and transepts are resolutely Norman, and at least as impressive as their counterparts in Durham, with sturdy round-headed arches marking the arcade, triforium, and clerestory alike. By contrast, the ornate choir, supported externally by rare (for England) flying buttresses, dates from the 14th century. The Lady Chapel, built in 1321–49, is an astounding confection of luxuriant carving.

Towering presence
The vast bulk of Ely is made more dramatic still by its central tower and the tower over the west front.

SALISBURY CATHEDRAL

🪦 1258   📍 SALISBURY, WILTSHIRE, ENGLAND   ⚒ ELIAS DE DEREHAM   🏛 PLACE OF WORSHIP

Salisbury, serene and substantial, surrounded by unquestionably the most beautiful cathedral close in the country, is perhaps the most typically English of cathedrals, for many the embodiment of England at its most beguiling. Spire, cloister, and above all the building's huge length constitute an exemplar of English Gothic in the 13th century.

VAULTED NAVE

Salisbury is unique not just for having been built from scratch (rather than on the foundations of an earlier building, as was the case with most other major cathedrals), but for having been built in only 38 years. Other than the spire, added almost 100 years later, it has scarcely been changed since. Accordingly, it is the most complete and revealing example of early English Gothic, almost a template of the style. The comparison with contemporary French buildings is telling. Whereas Amiens—as representative of the French Gothic as Salisbury is of the English —is conceived as a unified whole, with its facade logically introducing the interior and the stress throughout on the vertical, Salisbury is just as obviously conceived as a series of individual elements in which the horizontal dominates. Typically, the facade, certainly the least satisfactory element of the building and crowded with restored 19th-century sculpture, is wider than the church itself. Inside, the emphasis in the nave naturally leads the eye to the distant Lady Chapel in the east end rather than up to the vaults: the vault shafts, for example, extend downward only to the arches of the triforium rather than being carried all the way to the floor. As at Wells (see p.255), double transepts are used, reinforcing the sense of separate, compartmentalized spaces. The overall impact, continued in the remarkable Chapter House, is cool rather than compelling.

ELIAS DE DEREHAM

It is not generally helpful to talk in terms of the "architects" of medieval buildings. Though the names of a handful are known, very little else is. In general, projects were directed by churchmen and executed by teams of masons. At Salisbury, this administrative role was played by Elias de Dereham, a Canon of the cathedral, though the extent to which he designed the building is uncertain. De Dereham died in 1245, before the cathedral was completed.

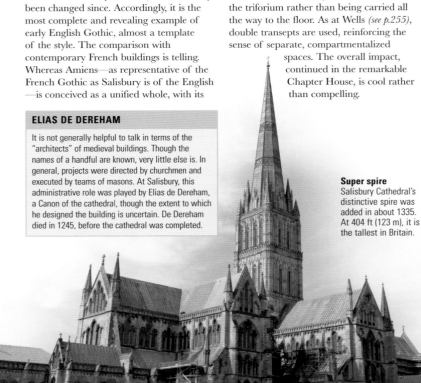

Super spire
Salisbury Cathedral's distinctive spire was added in about 1335. At 404 ft (123 m), it is the tallest in Britain.

KING'S COLLEGE CHAPEL

🏛 1515   📖 CAMBRIDGE, ENGLAND   ✍ HENRY VI   🏛 PLACE OF WORSHIP

King's College Chapel, begun in 1446, is the supreme example of the Perpendicular, the final flowering of English Gothic (and a style unique to England). In plan, it is simplicity itself, a rectangle 289 ft (88 m) long, 40 ft (12 m) wide; it is 80 ft (24 m) tall; in short, a single, unified space, with no aisles, divided along its length only by an elaborate early Renaissance wooden rood screen, which never disrupts the interior's overwhelming sense of unity.

The wonder of the building is partly the result of the immense, identical windows—12 to each side, lining the nave and, in effect, reducing the walls to little more than the slim piers between them—and partly of the amazingly

Perfect Perpendicular
The solemn grandeur of King's College Chapel stems from its combination of simplicity of plan and elaboration of detail.

elaborate decoration. This climaxes in the luxuriant fan-vaulting of the roof. An exuberant exercise in geometry, the chapel is no less remarkable in the profusion of carved heraldic devices and beasts that crowd the lower walls and piers. Externally, the dominant features are the narrow buttresses between the windows, pinnacled along the skyline, and the even more commanding pinnacled towers at each of the four corners of the chapel.

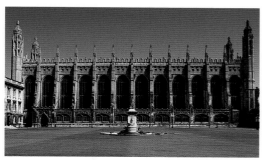

WESTMINSTER HALL

🏛 1399   📖 LONDON, ENGLAND   ✍ HENRY YEVELE & HUGH HERLAND   🏛 PALACE

With the Jewel Tower on the opposite side of the road, Westminster Hall is the only part of the medieval Palace of Westminster to have survived the fire of 1834 (which subsequently saw the building of the present

Houses of Parliament). The body of the hall was the work of master mason Henry Yevele, who, in a reflection of the changing status of late medieval artists, can almost be considered an architect in the modern sense.

Yet the most remarkable feature of the building is Hugh Herland's wooden hammer-beam roof. Medieval England was unique in developing a variety of wooden roofs, of varying degrees of complexity. While the majority are in churches, the grandest by some way is that in Westminster Hall: fully 230 ft (70 m) long by 66 ft (20 m) wide. It is not only a technical tour de force, with a double system of oak arches supported by projecting hammer-beams, but also a triumph of Perpendicular decoration. The massive timbers are exceptionally richly carved with delicate tracery and, most memorably, at the ends of the hammer-beams themselves, giant angels.

Dramatic medieval engineering
Westminster is one of the largest medieval halls of Europe with a roof unsupported by pillars.

CONWY CASTLE

🏛 1289　📍 CONWY, ABERCONWY & COLWYN, NORTH WALES　✍ EDWARD I　🏛 FORTIFICATION

Along with its fellow Welsh castles of Harlech, Beaumaris, and Caernarvon, Conwy Castle was built by Edward I as a brutal statement of the reality of the English conquest of Wales. These forbidding fortresses represent the high point of the medieval castle: within not much more than a century, the introduction of gunpowder would render them largely obsolete. They highlight a significant shift in castle-building. Whereas in the 12th century, a castle's defenses were arranged from the outside in, becoming progressively

stronger toward the keep, here the defenses are concentrated on the outer wall, which at Conwy is studded with eight immense, self-contained round towers. As a further defense, the courtyard is divided in two, with an outer and an inner ward.

Strategic design
Conwy's towers are self-contained: if any part of the castle was conquered, the remainder could still be defended.

STOKESAY CASTLE

🏛 1305　📍 STOKESAY, SHROPSHIRE, ENGLAND　✍ LAURENCE DE LUDLOW　🏛 FORTIFICATION

Whereas Conwy Castle was built as an expression of state power, Stokesay is an altogether more modest structure, in effect a manor house whose location close to the border with Wales made it necessary that it should be defensible. Today, the most obvious military aspect of the building is the tower at its southern end. Originally, however, the entire castle was moated;

similarly, much of the outer wall has disappeared, while the original gatehouse was replaced in the early 17th century. However, the Great Hall, 52 ft (16 m) long and 31 ft (9.5 m) wide, makes clear that the prime purpose of the building was domestic rather than military, the seat of a merchant rather than of a warrior.

Protected against attack
The tower at the southern end of Stokesay gave all-around views of its border territory. To the left is the rear of the Great Hall.

MEDIEVAL INNS

Travel through medieval Europe was widespread, although largely confined to soldiers, merchants, pilgrims, and, in particular, priests. The Catholic church united Europe at the time, more so than the EU does today, and it established the first chains of hostelries and inns.

Pilgrim arriving at a monastery
Throughout Europe, the use of Latin as a common language aided travel by priests and pilgrims.

One of the biggest pilgrim, or tourist, attractions of medieval Europe was Canterbury Cathedral, where the archbishop, St. Thomas à Becket (1118–70), had been cut down during a service by knights from Normandy, on what appear to have been the orders of King Henry II. The sheer number of pilgrims coming here from across Britain and Europe in the ensuing centuries would have put great pressure on the abbey, which traditionally was a source of lodgings for travelers. Finally, Prior Goldstone (1449–68) erected a handsome, and doubtless very profitable, timber inn around a courtyard,

called "the Bull." Lodgings arranged in groups over first-floor shops were gained by separate staircases, as in the arrangement found in the medieval colleges of Oxford and Cambridge. Many of the original details of this 15th-century inn survive. It is, though, pre-dated by another English inn, The Angel at Grantham (now The Angel and Royal), a stone hostelry built by the Knights Templar in 1212. Seven English kings have stayed at The Angel, including King John of Magna Carta fame.

Travelers' rest
The most impressive of these prototype hotels, the 15th-century George Inn, Glastonbury, *(see p.260)* features a dignified late Gothic street front.

GEORGE INN, GLASTONBURY

🗓 *ca.* 1480   📍 SOMERSET, ENGLAND
✎ UNKNOWN   🏛 INN

Until it fell into ruin after Henry VIII's dissolution of the monasteries in the 1530s, the Benedictine abbey of St. Mary near Glastonbury, Somerset, was one of the oldest in England, and one of the richest. Its importance was such that, in addition to a guest house for pilgrims and other visitors in the abbey itself, it also had a large and lavishly built inn at Glastonbury. Now known as the George and Pilgrims Hotel, it is arranged over three floors, with the principal public rooms on the second floor, which, accordingly, has the largest windows. The exterior has molded courses above all three floors, and the roof line is topped by bold crenellations. Strong mullions between window lights provide vertical accents and give the building something of a checkerboard feel. A shallow, four-centered arch in the center of the facade leads to a courtyard behind.

TITHE BARN, BRADFORD-ON-AVON

🗓 *ca.* 1350   📍 WILTSHIRE, ENGLAND
✎ UNKNOWN   🏛 AGRICULTURAL

This stone-built tithe barn is strongly reminiscent of a church, although one of simple construction. Gabled at both ends, it has a steeply sloping roof, two gabled porches, and substantial buttresses along each wall. It is this robust construction that has enabled such an otherwise unexceptional building to survive. The barn was central to local life, being used to store a tenth of all agricultural produce (hence the term "tithe"), which was paid as a tax by the tenants of church lands.

COLOGNE CATHEDRAL

🗓 AFTER 1248   📍 COLOGNE, GERMANY
✎ GERHARD OF COLOGNE   🏛 PLACE OF WORSHIP

The glorious medieval choir of Cologne Cathedral rises to 150 ft (46 m), with slender, soaring piers extending unbroken from the floor to heavenly vaults. The arcade and the huge, glazed clerestory are of near identical proportions, and the extension of the clerestory windows behind a shallow passage above the arches of the nave and choir results in an almost continuous area of glass stretching from the passageway to the vault. This form of design reflects French Gothic

VAULTED CEILING OF COLOGNE CATHEDRAL

influences from Beauvais Cathedral (see p.252) and Amiens. However, only this towering choir and the nave actually date from the Middle Ages; much of the cathedral is of a later date.

At the eastern end, another area is strongly French in origin—the rounded apse is surrounded by a passageway, off which spring seven chapels. However, the transepts at Cologne project more strongly than those in comparable French cathedrals, to a width of 275 ft (84 m) across the double aisles.

Outside, at the western entrance, two giant, open-work towers rise in tiers of extravagant tracery to reach no less than 500 ft (152 m). Clearly to echo the original design for the choir, these were built between 1824 and 1880, after the original plans for the building were rediscovered.

MASTER GERHARD OF COLOGNE

Gerhard of Cologne was typical of the master masons of the Middle Ages. Unlike his more famous contemporary, Villard de Honnecourt, whose notes and drawings provide an extraordinary insight into the builders of Europe's medieval cathedrals, none of Gerhard's notes have survived. However, it is clear that he traveled extensively in France and certainly visited and was inspired by Beauvais and Amiens, both then under construction, and also Notre Dame and St. Denis in Paris.

Extravagant facade
The exterior of
Cologne Cathedral
positively revels in its
extravagant use of
flying buttresses,
tracery, pinnacles, and
lofty, gabled porticos.

ULM MÜNSTER

🏛 AFTER 1377   📍 ULM, GERMANY   ✏ ULRICH VON ENSINGEN & OTHERS   🏛 PLACE OF WORSHIP

Ulm Münster, in Bavaria, is a cathedral that includes parts of a much older parish church. The grand scale and showy ornamentation of the cathedral are a reflection of the increasing power and mercantile wealth experienced by towns and cities in central Europe during the 14th and 15th centuries, the ravages of the Black Death (1347–51)

notwithstanding. Ulm not so much embraces the Late Gothic tendency toward increasing decoration, but positively flaunts it. The effect is a slightly overheated statement of the new status of the burghers of Ulm.

From the outside, the church is a riot of delicate, lacy masonry, elaborate flying buttresses topped by airy pinnacles, and slender, precisely carved moldings. Towering above all this at the west end is the massive single spire, which rises a startling 528 ft (161 m) into the sky—not completed until 1890, but still the tallest church spire in the world.

Ulm Münster epitomizes the Late German Gothic belief that more is always better. But, however striking the building, it is in many ways rather unsatisfactory, not least because there are no transepts—the building is a simple basilica. In addition, the body of the church (nave, chancel, and choir) is disproportionately small, almost as if it has been crushed by the sheer weight of the tower above.

Vaulted ceilings
Ulm Münster's double aisles, 68 ft (21 m) high, are covered by ornate net vaulting.

CUSTOMS HOUSE, NUREMBERG

🏛 1502   📍 NUREMBERG, GERMANY   ✏ HANS BEHEIM   🏛 CIVIC BUILDING

Nuremberg retains its allure as one of the most appealing medieval cities in Germany —a wonderful tribute to restoration work, since 90 percent of the medieval buildings are reconstructions, following the near complete destruction of the city by Allied bombing in World War II.

As a free imperial city within the Holy Roman Empire, answerable only to the emperor, medieval Nuremberg developed as an important trading city and a leading center of craftsmanship and manufacturing.

The commanding bulk of the Customs House (originally built as a grain store) is evidence of the city's medieval prosperity. The building's most remarkable feature is its steeply pitched roof, which is broken by an exceptional array of windows arranged over five stories. Each of the high gable ends displays a further, triangular cluster of windows under pointed arches, making six stories. On one side of the roof, a huge dormer punches out into the sky. The body of the building, arranged over three floors, is somewhat austere.

CHURCH OF ST. ELIZABETH, MARBURG

🏛 ca. 1283 📍 MARBURG, GERMANY ✍ UNKNOWN 🏛 PLACE OF WORSHIP

St. Elizabeth expresses both local German church-building traditions and the influence of the French High Gothic, which was already making itself felt in Cologne Cathedral *(see p.260)*. Like many German churches of the Gothic period, St. Elizabeth is a hall-church: that is, both the nave and aisles are the same height. The result is a large, uniform interior, rather than the French High Gothic idea of a vertical space that rises to a crescendo in the nave vault. The three-tier internal elevation of the French High Gothic (arcade, triforium, and clerestory) is also dispensed with, and there is no need for flying buttresses. The east end and the transepts terminate in apses, a form of design harking back to German Romanesque. However, much of the detailing, especially the molding of the nave piers and their extension upward and into the nave and aisle vaulting, is clearly of French origin, as is the window tracery.

Twin spires
The spires at St. Elizabeth show a strong parallel with contemporary developments in French architecture.

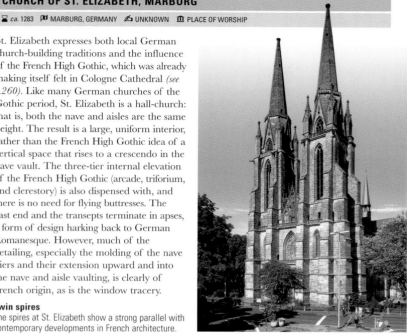

MALBORK CASTLE

🏛 AFTER 1276 📍 MALBORK, POLAND ✍ TEUTONIC KNIGHTS 🏛 FORTIFICATION

In 1233, backed by the Holy Roman emperor and the pope, the Teutonic Knights began the enforced conversion to Christianity of huge areas of central Europe. Originally a fortified monastery, Malbork Castle was taken over by the Knights and grew into Europe's largest medieval brick-built castle. With a system of multiple defense walls, gates, and towers, it covers 80 acres (32.4 hectares). The castle was substantially enlarged when it became the residence of the Teutonic Grand Master in 1309. There were several building phases: the Upper Castle was first, followed by the Middle Castle, and then, between 1382 and 1399, the Palace of the Grand Master, an exceptionally lavish four-story brick-built structure. Severely damaged during World War II, it has since been carefully restored.

Teutonic fortress
The Palace of the Grand Master is visible on the left; to the right is the heavily fortified Upper Castle.

ST. MARTIN, LANDSHUT

📷 1498   📍 LANDSHUT, BAVARIA, GERMANY   ✍ HANS VON BURGHAUSEN   🏛 PLACE OF WORSHIP

The church of St. Martin is typical of the hall-churches of much of central and southern Germany that developed in the Late Gothic period: at Freiburg, Nuremberg, Mainz, Marburg, and Munich, to take only better-known examples. With nave and aisles of equal height, the effect is to transform the interior into a single columned hall lit, not via the clerestory, but by aisle windows, typically arranged in either a single story or in two stories. That said, there is no lack of vertical emphasis: the church has a striking sense of soaring space, reinforced by the narrow windows and by the absence of transepts. The single western tower, 436 ft (133 m) high, is characteristically Late Gothic, but—whereas in French cathedrals of the 13th century such verticality reinforces a strong west–east axis—here, the effect is rather to allow the eye to wander up and across, as much as to draw it to the east end. The lower roof over the choir subtly divides this area from the nave, without interrupting the glorious sense of open space within the church.

Inspiring reverence
Full-height pillars draw the eye upward, creating a sense of light and awe.

SIENA CATHEDRAL

📷 AFTER *ca.* 1226   📍 SIENA, ITALY   ✍ UNKNOWN   🏛 PLACE OF WORSHIP

Italian architecture was notably resistant to the development of Gothic architecture that took place in northern France. Echoes of antiquity and a vigorous tradition of Romanesque building led instead to an architecture largely unique in Europe.

Siena Cathedral, among the largest and most prestigious Italian medieval churches, is a case in point. The west facade has superficial similarities to contemporary French buildings: the three portals; the use of sculpted figures; the central rose window. But the differences are much more striking, above all not just the coloring but the unmistakable horizontal emphasis provided by the vivid stripes of marble. This marble banding is continued in the interior, its decorative effect reinforced by a later inlaid marble floor. Yet the most unusual feature is the hexagonally shaped crossing topped by that most un-Gothic of forms, a dome. Rising over the south transept is a square bell-tower, itself banded in marble. In short, the lucid priorities that drove the Gothic in France are subsumed by a curious blend of Classical, Romanesque, and local traditions of Northern Italy.

French influence
The lower half of the cathedral's facade was built between 1285 and 1295, the upper half completed in 1376.

SANT'ANTONIO, PADUA

🏛 1307 📍 PADUA, VENETO, ITALY ⚒ UNKNOWN 🏛 PLACE OF WORSHIP

The curiosities, not to say confusions, of the Italian Gothic are nowhere more obvious than in the church of Sant'Antonio in Padua. French Gothic, Lombard Romanesque, and—oddest of all—Byzantine influences

combine to create a startling hybrid. That there should be Byzantine influences in Padua is no surprise given the proximity of Venice. Much more surprising is their use in what, in plan, is essentially a French Gothic church of nave, aisles, transepts, and choir—the last terminating in a chevet east end with nine radiating chapels.

From the outside, the confusion of styles is exaggerated by the slender, lantern-topped, circular towers that rise at intervals from the center of the nave roof. Equally unusual are the gables to either side of the nave, separated by substantial buttresses that extend at right angles to the aisles.

The delicate, gabled facade is the most obvious Romanesque element of the building. Four large pointed arches flank a smaller round-headed central arch, the whole below an arcaded gallery.

Eastern influence
An arcade of Byzantine-style pointed arches rises on slender columns, to extend along the south side of the church below the dome.

SANTI GIOVANNI E PAOLO

🏛 1385 📍 VENICE, ITALY ⚒ UNKNOWN 🏛 PLACE OF WORSHIP

In size, Latin-cross plan, and soaring internal height, Santi Giovanni e Paolo—traditional burial place of the doges (the rulers of Venice) —clearly belongs to the northern Gothic tradition, a fact reinforced by its pointed arches, rib-vaulting, and high clerestory. In practically every other respect, the church is unmistakably the product of native Venetian traditions. The giant columns of the stark nave are widely spaced, in the process tending to dissolve the distinction between nave and aisles and to create instead a single internal space whose emphasis, despite the great height of the building, is as much lateral as longitudinal. Additionally, rather than being supported externally by flying buttresses, the building is held together internally by the relatively much more crude method of "tie beams." The much-praised brick-built facade, with a central gabled bay rising dramatically between and, as it were, in front of a second shallower gable formed by the aisles, dates from 1430. The dome over the crossing is much later.

Internally braced
Wooden tie beams, or crosspieces, running across the interior pull the walls and columns inward.

DOGE'S PALACE

🏛 ca. 1438   🏴 VENICE, ITALY   ⚒ GIOVANNI & BARTOLOMEO BUON   🏛 PALACE

This elegant and exotic Gothic building was the residence of the Doge, the chief magistrate and leader of the Venetian Republic, and housed a number of political institutions. However, the Doge's Palace is something of an anachronism: by the time of its completion, Gothic was already being overtaken elsewhere in Italy by a rediscovered Classicism. That said, to call the Doge's Palace Gothic is almost to miss the point, since this is a form of Gothic without parallel outside Venice. The lacelike tracery of the second-floor arcade, the exuberantly sculpted main entrance (the Porta della Carta), and the remarkable tiaralike stone "crest" of the roofline are all untypical of the Gothic style. Perhaps the building's most

remarkable feature is that above the two decorative lower floors is a great mass of wall space. One might expect that the result would be a building that is visually top-heavy, but the impact is actually quite different— supremely graceful and, despite its serious public purpose, almost playful. The first floor is devoted to an airy arcade of pointed arches, while the third floor contains the Grand Council Chamber, one of Europe's finest and largest public rooms.

Colorful facade
The 164 ft (50 m) long facade of the Doge's Palace is faced with pink-and-white marble.

CA D'ORO

🏛 1440   🏴 VENICE, ITALY   ⚒ GIOVANNI & BARTOLOMEO BUON   🏛 PALACE

The Ca d'Oro on Venice's Grand Canal may be the most magnificent of the city's late medieval domestic buildings, but it contains features common to all the city's palaces. Its arcades and central courtyard were more than decorative—they were intended to ventilate the building in the summer. The large first-

floor arcade reflected the building's function as part warehouse and office, and part residence; the upper floor, or *piano nobile*, was the site of the grandest public rooms. Nonetheless, it is as the finest expression of Venice's distinctive brand of fantasy Gothic, heavily influenced by Byzantine and Arab models, that the building is chiefly notable. It is exceptionally sumptuous: its name, House of Gold, derives from the fact that it was originally covered in gold leaf. The arches on all three floors have elaborate, highly detailed tracery; the unusual undulating spires above the facade betray an obvious Arabic influence.

Accidental asymmetry
Ca d'Oro's asymmetry is not deliberate: a flanking wing was originally intended on the left of the facade.

PALAZZO PUBBLICO, SIENA

🖥 1309 🏳 TUSCANY, ITALY ✍ DOMENICO DI AGOSTINO & OTHERS 🏛 CIVIC BUILDING

Standing austere yet elegant at the top of the fan-shaped Piazza del Campo in the heart of Siena, the Palazzo Pubblico was the impressive seat of government of this former city-state. A fine example of Pointed Gothic, the Palazzo Pubblico has a softer, less militaristic feel than many municipal palaces of the time. Even the crenellations that animate the skyline seem more decorative than defensive.

Originally an adaptation of the customs house, the Palazzo Pubblico was enlarged several times, including by the annexation of the local prison. Only the upper floors are brick, while the first floor is faced with handsome travertine limestone, pierced by substantial openings and windows under pointed arches. To the left of the main facade is the Torre del Mangia, a powerful symbol of municipal authority that surges 334 ft (102 m) skyward. At the base of this bell-tower is a large and intricately decorated portico—the Capella di

Piazza, designed by Domenico di Agostino—that rises to the height of the second-floor windows. The tower and portico aside, the building is noteworthy for its symmetry, with a central four-story block flanked by two three-story blocks, each three bays wide. Inside the Palazzo Pubblico is a network of offices, chambers, and living quarters, many frescoed by leading artists of the day. The building now houses Siena's Civic Museum.

DOMENICO DI AGOSTINO

An Italian sculptor and architect, Domenico di Agostino is known to have been working between 1300 and 1347 in Siena. Here, he married Lagina di Nese, who was possibly a sister of the sculptor Cellino di Nese of Pistoia. Their two sons, Giovanni and Domenico, both became sculptors and master builders, but Agostino himself seems to have been the most significant artist in the family. He is best known for his work on Siena's Palazzo Pubblico.

Tall tower
Soaring over the Piazza del Campo, the Torre del Mangia is the tallest of all the municipal towers in Italy.

ST. THOMAS'S CHURCH, AVILA

🏛 1493 📍 AVILA, SPAIN ✏ MARTIN OF SOLOZANO 🏛 MONASTERY

This handsome monastic church just outside Avila is laid out on a Latin-cross plan and was used as a summer retreat by King Ferdinand and Queen Isabela of Castille. They chose it as the burial place for their only son. Ferdinand successfully persuaded the Pope to allow his church as the seat of the Inquisition in Spain, and it became the headquarters of the infamous General Inquisitor, Tomás de Torquemada (1420–1498), who is buried here. Under him, thousands of Jews, suspected witches, and Christian heretics were cruelly murdered. It later became a monument to the reconquest of the Spanish mainland when the Moors and Jews were ousted in 1492.

Set well back in a courtyard, the west front of this overtly simple church is stamped with the coats of arms of Ferdinand and Isabela, set between wonderfully fierce lions. Inside

the choir, the 73 walnut seats are said to have been carved by a Moorish prisoner in exchange for his life. Above them are five scenes depicting the life of Saint Thomas, painted by Pedro Berruguete. The wide nave features low, four-centered arches, and there are three shady cloisters: the Cloister of Novices, the Cloister of Silence, and the Cloister of Kings.

A royal retreat
The monastery church was originally founded by King Ferdinand and his Queen, Isabela, as a serene location outside the city's defensive walls.

SEVILLE CATHEDRAL

🏛 1520 📍 SEVILLE, SPAIN ✏ UNKNOWN 🏛 PLACE OF WORSHIP

In the Middle Ages, Seville Cathedral was the world's largest church. In part, this was because the cathedral was built on the foundations of one of the largest mosques in the Muslim world. It also reflects a determination to reinforce the Christian reconquest of Spain by building a church at least as big as the mosque it replaced.

The result is a curious fusion: a church that is Gothic in its details but not in its

rectangular ground plan. The large nave is flanked by immense double aisles that lead to equally wide side chapels. Externally, the most dramatic features are the triple flying buttresses and the 322 ft (98 m) Giralda tower, the adapted minaret of the original mosque now pressed into Christian service.

Size dominates
The wide, shallow stairs inside the Giralda tower are designed to allow access to horses and their riders.

SEGOVIA CATHEDRAL

⚑ AFTER 1525 📍 SEGOVIA, SPAIN
🖉 JUAN GIL DE HONTAÑÓN 🏛 PLACE OF WORSHIP

Almost 100 years before Segovia's Gothic cathedral was started in the early 16th century, Italian architects had begun the rediscovery of the antique. The classical conquest of European architecture that they launched would endure for at least a further three centuries. The day of the Gothic, which, in various forms of increasing elaboration, had dominated European architecture since the mid-12th century, was clearly drawing to a close. It survived mainly in the extremities of Europe.

In Spain, a combination of local traditions and the fierce pieties of medieval Christendom meant that Gothic was still seen as the "true" style of Christian architecture. In a country that had seen the final expulsion of the Moors only in 1492, and where the need to assert the superiority of the Christian West accordingly remained a priority, Gothic generally retained its central role well into the 16th century. Segovia Cathedral is a prime instance of this final Gothic flourish in Spain: a vast, lofty structure, encrusted with carvings that fuse Moorish and Gothic elements in equal measure.

COCA CASTLE

⚑ AFTER 1453 📍 SEGOVIA, SPAIN
🖉 ALONSO DE FONSECA 🏛 FORTIFICATION

The huge brick-built bulk of Coca Castle, 30 m (45 km) northwest of Segovia, is among the most impressive late-medieval castles in Europe. It was designed largely following the principles of castle building that developed in Christendom during the Crusades—a central keep surrounded by massive concentric outer fortifications studded with towers and other strong-points.

The construction itself was the work of Moorish master-masons. Combined with its huge size, the result was remarkable: Western in its planning, Moorish in details.

BURGOS CATHEDRAL

⚑ AFTER 1221 📍 BURGOS, SPAIN
🖉 UNKNOWN 🏛 PLACE OF WORSHIP

Burgos Cathedral is almost a textbook guide to every phase of Gothic architecture seen in Spain. The nave, transepts, and choir, which are the earliest parts of the building, are all clearly derived from French Gothic models. Externally, the flying buttresses and the lower part of the west front were also designed in the French manner.

However, the immense lantern over the crossing, the staggeringly rich side chapel at the east end, the Capilla del Condestable, and the open-work spires towering over the west end are all much later and testify to the elaboration of the late Gothic in Spain.

SAN PABLO, VALLADOLID

⚑ 1276–1492 📍 VALLADOLID, SPAIN
🖉 UNKNOWN 🏛 PLACE OF WORSHIP

The facade of the late 15th-century church of San Pablo is described as exuberant or overheated, according to taste. It was probably the work of a German, Simon of Cologne, begun after 1486, and is among the most extreme examples of Spanish late-Gothic "Isabeline" decoration, named after Isabel the Catholic (r.1474–1504).

The central bay of this tall, narrow building positively writhes with sculptured decoration—figures, coats-of-arms, spires, and arches—the whole against a background of elaborate geometrical patterning of clear Moorish inspiration.

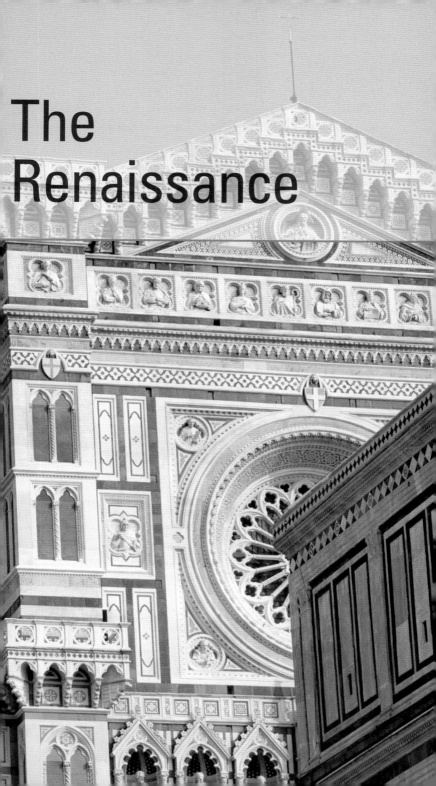

The Renaissance

A WATERSHED IN THE STORY of architecture, the Renaissance saw an upwelling and dissemination of new ideas as never before, facilitated by a revolution in printing. Books spread knowledge and literacy beyond the confines of court and clergy, leading to a challenge to the Church's authority and the rise of great secular artists and patrons.

It is hard to pinpoint exactly when the Renaissance began. Muslim scholars and Christian monks had preserved Classical learning throughout Europe's Dark Ages, while as early as the mid-14th century, the Italian priest-scholar and poet Francesco Petrarch (1304–74) was leading the way to a rediscovery of Greek and Roman authors. Indeed, he may well have coined the phrase "Dark Ages" to describe the gap he saw between Classical civilization and

his own, reawakening European world. Even before Petrarch, there was Dante Alighieri (1265–1321); in the early parts of the *Divine Comedy*, Dante's guide through the circles of Hell is the epic Roman poet, Virgil.

If Petrarch's Dark Ages had been the province of the Devil, and the late

Sistine Chapel ceiling, Vatican, Rome (1508–12)
Invigorated by a new respect for human dignity, Renaissance art became more lifelike. This fresco by Michelangelo shows God infusing life into Adam.

KEY DATES

1469 Donatello's bronze statue of David is first freestanding sculpture since ancient Rome

1485 Publication of Leon Battista Alberti's *De re aedificatoria* (Ten Books on Architecture)

1475

1492 Christopher Columbus sails for Asia but ends up in the Caribbean, having crossed the Atlantic

1502 Donato Bramante completes the Tempietto San Pietro in Montorio, setting the standard for Renaissance architecture

1500

1517 Martin Luther nails his 95 theses to door of Wittenberg Cathedral, sparking the rise of Protestantism

1522 Magellan completes the first circumnavigation of the world, signaling global trade

1525

1534 Henry VIII establishes the Church of England, putting an end to Papal power in England

1563 Council of Trent ends under Pope Pius IV, leading to the Counter-Reformation led from Rome

1550

1547 Ivan the Terrible becomes the first emperor, or tsar, of all Russia

THE PRINTING REVOLUTION

Johannes Gutenberg (1398–1468) of Mainz, Germany, made crucial advances in printing technology, including Europe's first practical printing press and typecasting —producing large amounts of movable, reusable metal type cheaply and quickly. Previously, books were written by hand, and it might take a whole year to copy a single Bible; Gutenberg's press could produce several hundred copies a year.

Literature on the production line
Type was assembled in a frame, inked, and the press screwed down to print the text onto paper.

medieval world the realm of God, Renaissance Europe witnessed the ascent and triumph of man, who was now, in the words of the Greek philosopher Protagoras (*ca.* 485–420BCE), "the measure of all things." This was the basis of Humanism, the assertion of personal independence and individual expression.

Italy was the hub of the Renaissance, its first architectural expression the dome of Florence Cathedral (1436) by Filippo Brunelleschi *(see p.280)*, which represents an aesthetic break from medieval design. Brunelleschi was one of the first architects to use perspective drawing.

PRINTING AND THE SPREAD OF IDEAS

With the invention of practical printing presses, books became a revolutionary new medium for the spread of ideas. The first important architectural treatise of the Renaissance was *De re aedificatoria*, by the Florentine architect Leon Battista Alberti (1404–72), which was written in 1452 and published in 1485. The following year saw the publication of the writings of Vitruvius, the 1st-century Roman architect, which would become a bible, of sorts, for architects for the next 400 years.

Vitruvian Man **(*ca.* 1490)**
Leonardo da Vinci drew this figure as a study of the proportions of the (male) human body described by the Roman architect Vitruvius.

Image of an ideal city
The idealized buildings in this Renaissance painting from the Palazzo Ducale at Urbino, Italy, were thought to embody both the human and the divine.

Alberti's book was a revelation, setting out in mathematical detail the principal elements of architecture—the square, cube, circle, and sphere—and the ideal proportions for a building. These proportions were thought to be in harmony with music and nature, and also with those of the idealized human body. So, just as humanity was created in the image of God, a building could represent the image of the creator if Alberti's proportions were followed.

Even though the Renaissance would be characterized by Humanism and increasing challenges to religious authority, the Roman Church remained all-powerful for at least another century. Many of the greatest buildings of the early Renaissance were commissioned by ambitious popes and wealthy clergy.

Alberti's sacred geometry, however, was highly influential in the making of the Renaissance mind: man was no longer impotent in the face of an omnipotent God, but increasingly an independent agent able to carry out God's will by shaping the world through the arts. The role and self-image of the architect was thus greatly enhanced. He was no longer the largely anonymous designer-mason of the Gothic world, but a stand-in for God. No wonder that, ever since, so many architects have had such brazen egos!

Other important architectural books followed, including works by Sebastiano Serlio (1475–1554) in 1537 and Giacomo Barozzi da Vignola (1507–73) in 1562. The next most significant work after Alberti and the printed translations of Vitruvius was *I quattro libri dell'architettura* (1570) by Andrea Palladio *(see p.288)*, one of the greatest and most influential of all late Renaissance architects. The first major architectural book in English was almost contemporary: Sir John Shute's *First and Chief Groundes of Architecture*, published in 1563.

With books came the desire to draw buildings to comparable scales and to publish accurate plans, sections, and elevations. From now on, ideas could travel independently of the architect himself, so he was no longer a slave to the construction site.

URBAN PLANNING

Renaissance architecture and urban planning went hand-in-hand, or colonnade-in-piazza. Both were intended to be rational and humane, as shown by the painting in the Palazzo Ducale, Italy *(see above)*. This famous image, possibly by Piero della Francesca, depicts the new architecture in an idealized setting. It is bereft of people, which is how most architects have presented their buildings ever since. This is not because people would have spoiled the view, but because of Alberti's belief—a fundamental of Renaissance architecture—that the buildings themselves represented both human and divine images through their perfect proportions.

The Palazzo Ducale painting is also an important image because it shows that architects had begun to think of planning cities on a rational basis. Soon, the ideal Renaissance city, with its gridiron, radial, and star pattern of streets, would spread across the Italian landscape and out, via printed books and new learning, to the rest of the Western world.

PROTESTANTISM

The Roman Church faced not only the external challenge of Humanism, but also an internal threat from clergy and scholars who protested that the Church needed to reform. These "protestants," such as Martin Luther (1483–1546), believed that the Church had become corrupt and too rich, and had slipped away from Christian ideals set down in the Bible. Their reforms included a return to simple ceremonies, less emphasis on priestly intervention, and services in local languages rather than in Latin. Protestantism's growth was aided by printing. The Church was slow to act, so the protestants, backed by certain kings and rulers, made their own Reformation by creating an alternative Protestant Church.

Martin Luther
Luther, a priest and university teacher, wanted people to find their own personal faith in God through individual Bible study.

ITALIAN RENAISSANCE
ca. 1420–1550

In 15th-century Italy, the rise and rise of wealthy city states *(see p.275)*, pumped up with profits from banking and new-found capitalist ventures, encouraged a rich new spate of private, commercial, and civic buildings. Each city state competed, and fought, with the other, constantly seeking to outdo its rivals in terms of the splendor of its architecture and its public places. The results were a revelation.

The earliest ideal Renaissance buildings realized in stone and marble include the Pazzi chapel in the cloisters of the Franciscan church of Santa Croce, Florence, and the mid-15th century palazzi built for the Florentine families Pitti, Riccardi *(see p.281)*, and Strozzi. In one sense, these hugely grand townhouses were still medieval, since they were fortified and secretive. Although they boasted details drawn from antiquity, such as the superb cornice that divides stone facade from sky in the Palazzo Strozzi, they were not quite the models of reason and light that would emerge half a century later in the work of Donato Bramante (1444–1514) in Rome. Bramante represents the High Renaissance in Italy, the era of magnificent buildings that confidently reinterpreted ancient prototypes. Many of the architects who designed these buildings were archetypal Renaissance men—sculptor, painter, poet, engineer, playwright, and soldier all rolled into one dynamic person.

BRAMANTE'S TEMPIETTO
Strangely, the most influential building in this glorious outburst of creativity was Bramante's Tempietto *(see p.282)*, a modest affair shoehorned into the cloister of the church of San Pietro in Montorio, Rome. Loosely based on the Temple of Vesta in Rome *(see p.108)*, it was the inspiration for Michelangelo's dome on St. Peter's *(see p.282)*, the dome of Wren's St. Paul's in London *(see p.326)*, and that of the US Capitol, Washington *(see p.368–9)*. With a colonnade in which the sun could play and people could stroll, this small design spoke of reason and civility, rather than religious domination and fear. Amid the new churches and palazzi, a fresh brand of civil architecture was emerging from the long-buried ruins of ancient Rome.

◁ **MICHELANGELO'S MAGNIFICENT DOME IN ST. PETER'S BASILICA, ROME, RISES ABOVE THE SITE OF THE SAINT'S TOMB. MICHELANGELO TOOK OVER AS ARCHITECT ON THE BUILDING AT THE AGE OF 72.**

ELEMENTS

The Renaissance witnessed architects plundering ancient Roman sources with energy and imagination. The result was a profusion of new styles that responded to the needs of a widening client base. It was no longer just church and court that could afford to indulge in bravura design, but also an ever-increasing number of wealthy private individuals with a taste for self-aggrandisement.

Wavelike scroll supporting pediment of Santa Susanna

△ **Doric order**
Archaeologically correct use of Doric order, with entablature, can be seen in the circular colonnade of Bramante's Tempietto at Montorio, Rome, which was built in 1502.

◁ **Ionic order**
This chaste example of Ionic order is from the magnificent Palazzo Farnese, Caprarola. The entablature is adorned with fine incised Roman script.

△ **Corinthian order**
Corinthian order can be seen in pilasters on the pediment of Santa Susanna, Rome. This device was used with increasing vigor in the facades and interiors of Renaissance churches.

▽ **Grand Late Renaissance colonnade**
Here is Bernini in full flight with the glorious sweeping colonnade of the Piazza of St. Peter's, Rome, begun in 1656; this set the pace for numerous copycat colonnades across Europe.

Statuary along balustraded rooftops became commonplace

Curves of dome balance an angular facade

The facade climbs through layers of pediments to the dome and lantern

△ **Symmetrical plan**
The ideal Renaissance villa was wholly symmetrical; Palladio achieved this in the design of the Villa Capra, Vicenza.

◁ **Superimposed pediments**
A magnificent play of Classical forms, one on top of the other; this work of subtle genius, Il Redentore church in Venice, is by Palladio.

△ **Rusticated stonework**
This gave the base of buildings a powerful and rugged look. Seen here is the Palazzo Medici-Riccardi in Florence, designed by Michelozzo.

◁ **Fountains**
Renaissance architects and designers liked to show off their prowess at hydraulic engineering. This is the Ovato Fountain at the Villa d'Este, Tivoli.

The colonnade curves around and embraces the oval piazza

Strong use of Doric order suggests the power of the Vatican behind

DUOMO, FLORENCE CATHEDRAL

📺 1436   📕 FLORENCE, ITALY   ✍ FILIPPO BRUNELLESCHI   🏛 PLACE OF WORSHIP

The mesmerizing dome of the cathedral of Santa Maria del Fiore marks the beginning of the great revolution in architecture we label Renaissance. With this structural tour de force, Brunelleschi made the giant architectural leap away from the Gothic world. In addition, the architect as signature artist was born.

The question of how to build a dome, or cupola, over the crossing of the medieval cathedral had long vexed the Opera del Duomo, or board of works. If it could be built, it would have to span a diameter of 150 ft (nearly 46 m), something that had never been done before. Finally, in 1418, the challenge was put out to a competition. Brunelleschi won it; work began in 1420. Brunelleschi's inspired solution was to build a double-skinned brick dome that

FRESCOES ON THE INSIDE OF BRUNELLESCHI'S DOME

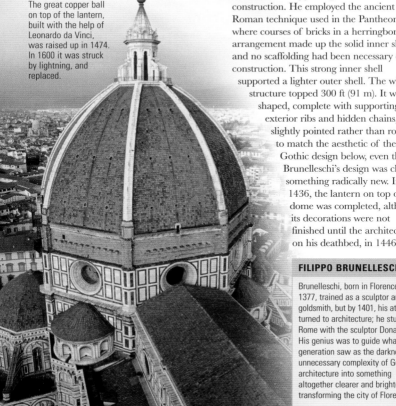

Final achievement
The great copper ball on top of the lantern, built with the help of Leonardo da Vinci, was raised up in 1474. In 1600 it was struck by lightning, and replaced.

would be self-supporting while under construction. He employed the ancient Roman technique used in the Pantheon, where courses of bricks in a herringbone arrangement made up the solid inner shell and no scaffolding had been necessary during construction. This strong inner shell supported a lighter outer shell. The whole structure topped 300 ft (91 m). It was shaped, complete with supporting exterior ribs and hidden chains, to be slightly pointed rather than rounded to match the aesthetic of the Gothic design below, even though Brunelleschi's design was clearly something radically new. In 1436, the lantern on top of the dome was completed, although its decorations were not finished until the architect was on his deathbed, in 1446.

FILIPPO BRUNELLESCHI

Brunelleschi, born in Florence in 1377, trained as a sculptor and goldsmith, but by 1401, his attention turned to architecture; he studied in Rome with the sculptor Donatello. His genius was to guide what his generation saw as the darkness and unnecessary complexity of Gothic architecture into something altogether clearer and brighter, transforming the city of Florence.

OSPEDALE DEGLI INNOCENTI

🏛 1445 📍 FLORENCE, ITALY ✍ FILIPPO BRUNELLESCHI 🏛 CIVIC BUILDING

The pretty external loggia facing Piazza Santissima Annunziata is the most important part of this influential early Renaissance design; its widely spaced arches raised on delicate Corinthian columns with terracotta medallions decorating the spandrels between them, and extensive areas of unadorned flat walls above, were soon to be found in many later Renaissance buildings. Brunelleschi's architecture here was humane, creating a light and gentle home, spaced around two cloisters, for the city's *innocenti*, or orphans—the first institution of its kind in Europe, sponsored by the Guild of Silk Weavers. A lack of funds stopped building from 1430 to 1436, by which time Brunelleschi had become far too busy with the Duomo. He appointed Francesco della Luna in his place. The Ospedale was fully restored in 1966.

Famous facade
The children's dayroom above the celebrated loggia arcade is now a small art museum.

PALAZZO MEDICI-RICCARDI

🏛 1459 📍 FLORENCE, ITALY ✍ MICHELOZZO DI BARTOMMEO 🏛 RESIDENCE

Commissioned by Cosimo de Medici, work began on this broad-shouldered city palace in 1444. Its asymmetrical plan is organized around a square courtyard from which a staircase connects the various living quarters and the exquisite Cappella dei Magi, frescoed by Benozzo Gozzoli. The fortress-like facade of jutting, rusticated stone lessens in severity as the building climbs from sidewalk to cornice, with each floor decreasing in height and structural bombast. In contrast, the internal courtyard is gentle-spirited and an almost exact copy of Brunelleschi's loggia at the Ospedale degli Innocenti; Michelozzo (1396–1472) succeeded Brunelleschi as surveyor of works to Florence Cathedral immediately after the latter's death. The palace was sold to the Riccardi family in 1642, and the original design was modified, in keeping with Michelozzo's work, in 1680, when a further six window bays were added. Although presenting a formidable fortified face to the city street, this civic-minded palace has five generous stone benches set into the base of its wall for anyone and everyone—Medici enemies aside—to rest on.

Cloistered calm
The graceful arcade of the internal courtyard has Corinthian capitals and spandrels adorned with Medici symbols.

TEMPIETTO SAN PIETRO IN MONTORIO

1502　ROME, ITALY　DONATO BRAMANTE　PLACE OF WORSHIP

This exquisitely proportioned, domed Doric rotunda was built to commemorate the alleged spot where St. Peter, the first Pope, was crucified, upside-down, some years after the death of Christ. St. Peter's crypt can be seen in a hole in the center of the floor of the small, templelike structure, known as a "tempietto." The chapel stands in a small courtyard in the cloisters of the church of San Pietro in Montorio.

This is the first major architectural work of Donato Bramante (1444–1514) and shows how a new, restrained sensibility was emerging in early Renaissance architecture. Bramante can be seen playing subtly with ancient Roman forms: a circle of strict Doric columns decorated in the Roman style is topped with the semicircular dome characteristic of a Christian shrine.

Bramante's first masterpiece, known to the Renaissance world outside Italy through Andrea Palladio's *I Quattro Libri dell'Architettura* (1570), was a huge influence on Classical architects over the following 400 years.

Combining influences
The bringing together of Classical and early Christian architectural styles for this tempietto created a model for the Renaissance world.

ST. PETER'S DOME

1591　ROME, ITALY　MICHELANGELO BUONAROTTI　PLACE OF WORSHIP

The crowning element of St. Peter's was given over to Michelangelo Buonarotti (1475–1564) when, in his seventies, he became cathedral architect, 40 years after work had first begun on the hugely ambitious Papal basilica. Working in honor of God, Michelangelo refused payment for his heroic design. His solution was to adopt much the same technique as Brunelleschi had in Florence Cathedral *(see p.280)*.

The massive dome, 138 ft (42 m) in diameter, is built up from two skins of brick and stone, one inner, one outer. From the outside it appears to rise from a handsome drum punctuated by projecting pairs of coupled Corinthian columns set

between massive blind windows. Viewed externally, the dome seems to be far more of a hemisphere than it really is; seen from underneath, it proves to be quite pointed, although the effect is cleverly lessened by the heavy decoration adorning the underside of the dome.

The mighty structure, supported by four massive 52 ft (16 m) deep piers and bound by hidden iron chains, is topped with a crownlike lantern that is in turn capped with a ball and cross, 450 ft (137 m) above the sidewalk. The work was executed between 1588 and 1591 after the death of Michelangelo.

Vertical delineation
Ribs on the dome link columns supporting the drum to those around the lantern.

DOMES

The sky, especially by night, was often described by ancient observers as a celestial vault. It seemed as if the Earth was covered by a giant dome; beyond were the Heavens. From the Pantheon *(see p.110–1)* onward, the dome was a model of the universe as well as a magnificent architectural device.

A flatter dome
The dome of the Four Courts, Dublin *(see p.359)* has a more simplified outline.

Domes made their appearance under the Romans and, because of Justinian's spectacular Hagia Sophia *(see p.126–7)*, with its massive saucer-shaped dome, became a key element in Islamic architecture. During the Italian Renaissance the dome prevailed: the very name for an Italian cathedral —"duomo"—speaks for itself. Beginning with Brunelleschi's dome spanning the crossing of Florence Cathedral *(see p.280)*, Italian architects became increasingly confident as they devised new techniques to raise increasingly higher and more expansive structures. St. Peter's, Rome, for example, boasts a double-shelled dome.

In London, Sir Christopher Wren went one step further and created a triple-shell design for St. Paul's Cathedral *(see p.326)*. The external lead dome begins where the internal brick dome ends. The outer dome is a lightweight lead-and-timber structure attached to a brick cone rising above the internal dome and bearing the weight of the lantern and ball and cross on top of the external dome. This complex design allows the dome of St. Paul's to rise up like a Renaissance interpretation of a Gothic tower and spire: it is lofty and broad, and a long way, in terms of the impact it makes on the city skyline, from the concrete dome crowning the Pantheon.

Double domes
The two domes at Santa Maria della Salute, Venice, *(see p.319)* cover large, linked central areas of the church.

PALAZZO FARNESE, CAPRAROLA

📷 *ca.* 1560 📍 NEAR ROME, ITALY ✍ GIACOMO BAROZZI DA VIGNOLA 🏛 RESIDENCE

MAIN FACADE

This palatial villa, which dominates the local landscape to the north of Rome, was designed by the painter-turned-architect Giacomo Barozzi da Vignola (1507–73). It was an utterly spectacular rebuilding of an earlier pentagonal fortress by Sangallo the Younger. Hugely ambitious, part of the neighboring town was demolished to accommodate it, but it was never completed. Given its military origins, the Palazzo Farnese

△ **Hall of the Angels**
Rich frescoes by Giovanni del Vecchio on the walls and cupola ceiling depict the fall of rebel angels.

△ **Palatial approach**
The villa is approached up a pair of ramps, and then a monumental double stairway, between which an ornate stream cascades.

Powerful double-height *piano nobile* above the fortresslike main entrance

Main entrance above the rusticated base reached by zigzag stairways can be seen as a Renaissance interpretation of a fortified medieval house. It sits on high ground and is approached by a series of huge stairways and terraces that completely obscures the moat and bastions at the base of the structure. The interior is equally grand in conception.

△ **The Sala d'Ercole (Hall of Hercules)**
The Palazzo Farnese is famed for the quality of its interior frescoes. This fine hall, on the *piano nobile*, is frescoed in part by Federico Zuccaro (1541–1609) and has a grotto-style fountain at the far end.

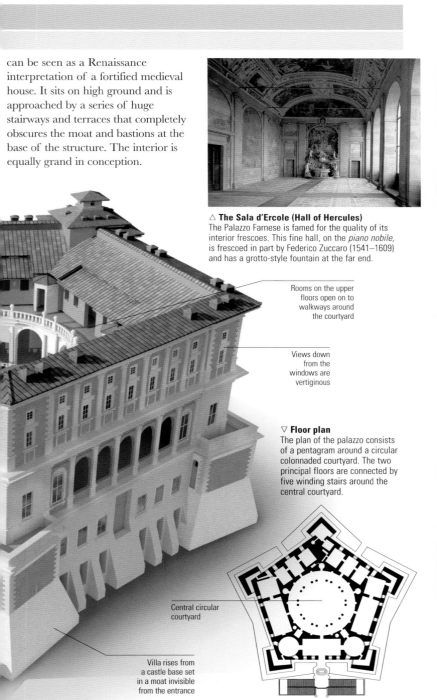

Rooms on the upper floors open on to walkways around the courtyard

Views down from the windows are vertiginous

▽ **Floor plan**
The plan of the palazzo consists of a pentagram around a circular colonnaded courtyard. The two principal floors are connected by five winding stairs around the central courtyard.

Central circular courtyard

Villa rises from a castle base set in a moat invisible from the entrance

PALAZZO DEL TE

🏛 1535   📍 MANTUA, ITALY   ✍ GIULIO ROMANO   🏛 PALACE

A grand summer island retreat for the
Duke of Gonzaga and his mistress, Palazzo
del Te is the masterpiece of Giulio Romano
(*ca.* 1499–1546), a pupil of Raphael whose
playful and imaginative style we know as
Mannerism. Although its wilful facades and
eccentric interiors are highly mannered, the
palace is built on the simplest of plans. The
shell of the building was completed in just
18 months; what took time was the fantastic
interior decoration: frescoes portray
Olympian banquets and charging horses
and become astonishingly three-dimensional
in the Sala dei Giganti (Hall of Giants).
Guests bathed under cascades of water in
the shell-encrusted Casino della Grotta.

Palazzo plan
At del Te, four Classical ranges, including one with
an open loggia inspired by Palladio, are gathered
symmetrically around a central courtyard.

VILLA D'ESTE

🏛 1572   📍 TIVOLI, ITALY   ✍ PIRRO LIGORIO   🏛 RESIDENCE

The palatial gardens at the Villa d'Este are
among the most ambitious, beautiful, and
influential of the 16th century. Laid out
by Pirro Ligorio and Alberto Galvani,
the Renaissance villa and gardens were
commissioned by Cardinal Ippolito d'Este,
governor of Tivoli, who lived here in
splendor until his death in 1572—when the
project was almost complete. The Cardinal
was inspired both by fantasy illustrations of
the Hanging Gardens of Babylon and by
Hadrian's Villa *(see p.117)*, sited close by. He

wanted, if anything, to outdo the ancient
Roman emperor in his deployment of water,
designed to play through hundreds of
ingenious fountains. When these are working,
Villa d'Este is inspiring as an architectural
and horticultural wonder of the Renaissance.

Rising splendor
The villa and its gardens
were laid out over a
series of terraces
beneath what was
once a monastery.

GIULIO ROMANO'S HOUSE

⚰ 1546 📍 MANTUA, ITALY ✍ GIULIO ROMANO
🏛 RESIDENCE

All Giulio's important architectural works
are in Mantua, where he ruled as architect,
designer, and painter from 1524 until his
death in 1546. He built himself this highly
theatrical house, breaking many of the
accepted rules of Classicism in doing so:
few, if any, architects before him would have
thrust the entrance portico of the house up
into the line of the heroically grand *piano
nobile* above it. The sheer scale of the
building shows how well Giulio did for
himself. Here he kept his designs for the
Palazzo del Te, the reconstruction of
Mantua cathedral, the church of San
Benedetto, and the renovation of the Ducal
Palace in a cupboard, showing them to
Giorgio Vasari when the latter was writing
his famous *Lives of the Artists*. Giulio also
made pornographic drawings that he had
hoped to get away with as frescoes in the
Vatican. He is the only contemporary artist
mentioned by name by Shakespeare
(*A Winter's Tale*, Act V, Scene 2).

ST. MARK'S LIBRARY

⚰ 1553 📍 VENICE, ITALY
✍ JACOPO SANSOVINO 🏛 LIBRARY

Sansovino's stirring Classical library with its
white stone facades and handsome interiors
is as magnanimous as it is a delight. A loggia
running the length of its 21-bay-long east
side serves as a handsome sheltered public
walkway, while the whole composition, at
once modest in scale yet mellifluously
decorated, acts as a polite foil to the Gothic
immensity of the Doge's Palace across St.

Mark's Square *(see
p.266)*. The loggia
is lined with Doric
half-columns, while
the *piano nobile*
housing the library
itself is adorned with
Ionic half-columns set
between round-topped
windows, where finely
carved "victories" and
sea-gods disport
themselves between
and over the arches.

PALAZZO MARINO

⚰ AFTER 1558 📍 MILAN, ITALY
✍ GALEAZZO ALESSI 🏛 RESIDENCE

This ambitious townhouse was designed
for the Genoese banker Tommaso Marino,
a senator in the Spanish government that
ruled Milan; he lent money to both the
Holy Roman Emperor and the Pope, and
he collected local taxes. His extensive
household included a squad of 27 men
authorized to circulate in the city fully
armed and "licensed to kill." Suitably
muscular, the facades of the Palazzo are
nevertheless decorated in an exuberant
manner, borrowing from Michelangelo
and Giulio Romano. The palazzo became
Milan's town hall in 1861.

BASILICA, VICENZA

⚰ 1617 📍 VICENZA, ITALY
✍ ANDREA PALLADIO 🏛 CIVIC BUILDING

Asked to remodel Vicenza's medieval town
hall, Palladio transformed it, with real
genius, from 1549, into his own idea of what
a contemporary Roman basilica might be.
The new arcaded architecture wraps around
and supports its 15th-century predecessor
while in the process creating one of the most
eye-catching yet subtle civic buildings of the
Italian Renaissance. The first floor arcade is
Doric, the second floor Ionic. Both are
characterized by the architect's signature
openings—used in doorways, windows, or,
as here, in arches—composed of a round-
topped arch supported by a column on
either side, with both columns further
supporting entablatures designed to allow
a narrow, vertical opening between column
and wall. The parapet of the basilica is
populated with statuary, while the powerfully
expressed copper-clad roof of the enclosed
medieval council chamber rises up behind it.
Palladio's facades and arcades run around
three sides of the old building only.

CHURCH OF SAN GIORGIO MAGGIORE

🪑 1610   📍 VENICE, ITALY   ✍ ANDREA PALLADIO   🏛 PLACE OF WORSHIP

Achingly beautiful, the costly Benedictine church of San Giorgio Maggiore in Venice is one of the great set pieces of European architecture. At once picturesque and rigorously geometric, romantic and urbane, built on an island yet addressing the center of a city, it is both deeply civilized and sublime.

Fusing subtle geometry with noble forms, San Giorgio owes its calmly profound design to Andrea Palladio, one of the most influential architects of all time. Instructed to build a traditionally cruciform church, he concealed the essentially Gothic or medieval nature of the plan with a grand pedimented white marble facade that, even though an architectural smoke screen, still expresses the form of the red-brick building behind with its tall nave and lower attendant aisles. The facade is articulated with four three-quarter Composite columns linked by festoons (decorative loops) and raised on high pedestals framing the entrance. Statues in niches and

ANDREA PALLADIO

Trained as a stonemason in Padua and educated in Rome, Andrea Palladio (1508–80) settled in Vicenza. The farmhouses he built there, his Venetian churches, and his book *I Quattro Libri dell'Architettura* (1570) have all had a profound effect on architecture in countries as far apart as Russia, Great Britain, and the US.

handsome inscriptions hark back to the architecture of ancient Rome. The bright, white nave, inspired by Roman baths, is barrel-vaulted, lit by semicircular windows, and crowned with a lantern-topped dome. Part of an originally 10th-century monastic complex added to and rebuilt by Palladio, the church was completed well after the architect's death.

ANDREA PALLADIO

Opposing view
San Giorgio Maggiore displays an impressive facade to the Piazzetta di San Marco across the water.

IL REDENTORE

🪦 1592 📍 VENICE, ITALY ✍ ANDREA PALLADIO
🏛 PLACE OF WORSHIP

Widely considered to be Palladio's finest church, Il Redentore looks for all the world like a great red ship come to berth between the packed houses of the Giudecca, at a diagonal across the water from St. Mark's. Its design is traditional in many ways, with a long nave—flanked by chapels lit by lunettes (semicircular windows) and supported by deep external buttresses—and a crossing capped with a simple dome. The white stone facade is remarkable, a brilliant play of grouped pediments set one within another: this is the high game of architecture played out geometrically and joyously, yet modestly.

BRIDGE OF SIGHS

🪦 1600 📍 VENICE, ITALY
✍ ANTONIO CONTINI 🏛 BRIDGE

This white limestone bridge, veering on the Baroque, earned its name not because visitors sighed at its beauty, but because it was the link between the Doge's Palace and the city prison. In fact, the darkest days of cruel punishment in Venice were over when this pretty, enclosed bridge with its two passageways was built. Its facades with their curved pediments are decorated with scrolls representing the swell and sway of the sea, while stone heads of grim-faced patriarchs glare down at tourists in their gondolas today.

PALAZZO PORTO BREGANZE

🪦 ca. 1605 📍 VICENZA, ITALY
✍ ANDREA PALLADIO 🏛 RESIDENCE

Palladio was dead by the time this ambitious palazzo began to be built under the direction of Vincenzo Scamozzi. Only two of the seven monumental bays were realized, yet these have great power, and the unfinished building remains a tantalizing delight today. Palladio's design was for a grand house arranged around a suitably imposing courtyard. The street facade boasts massive Corinthian half-columns, their capitals linked with rich festoons, rising from massive and lofty bases. To give an idea of the sheer scale of the building, the tops of the windows of its piano nobile reach higher than the dormer windows lighting the fourth-floor attics of the happily mundane building alongside. The building is little more than a facade, however; a glance at its side walls shows that more floors have been squeezed behind it than Palladio ever intended. The interiors are unexceptional.

TEATRO OLIMPICO

🪦 1585 📍 VICENZA, ITALY
✍ ANDREA PALLADIO 🏛 THEATRE

Palladio's recreation of a Roman outdoor theater, the sole surviving theater of its period today, was built with archaeological precision. The wooden theater, its half-oval auditorium quite out of keeping with contemporary fashions in stage design, is constructed inside a simple brick box but is designed to look and feel as if it is outdoors, with its sky-blue painted ceiling and garden-like statues. Steep tiers of seats facing a rectangular proscenium stage are encircled above by a corniced wooden colonnade.

RENAISSANCE BEYOND ITALY
ca. 1500–1700

Ten years before the consecration of Bramante's Tempietto in Rome *(see p.282)* in 1502, Christopher Columbus "discovered" the Americas. With Europe being fed by the riches of Latin America, and Portuguese explorers opening up trade routes to the East, the West's view of the world began to change dramatically. Shot through with radical ideas from Italy, a new flowering of Renaissance buildings bloomed.

The Renaissance spread through books and trade, although it took some while to infiltrate outlying European countries such as England. King's College Chapel, Cambridge *(see p.257)*, for example, a Perpendicular Gothic masterpiece, was completed more than a decade after Bramante's Tempietto. Gradually, though, English patrons began to adopt Italian design, as their French counterparts had earlier, but to begin with, only in decorative details. Crude versions of Doric, Ionic, and Corinthian pilasters abounded, accompanied by carved angels, dragons, grotesques, and demons, giving the impression that the medieval and Renaissance worlds were locked in a battle for supremacy. England's first truly Classical buildings were designed by Inigo Jones (who had traveled through Italy) for the court of King James I, such as the Queen's House, Greenwich *(see p.302)*.

RENAISSANCE HYBRIDS

This slow adoption of Italian ways led to the flowering of some fascinating architectural hybrids across western and northern Europe in the 16th and 17th centuries. Local styles in the Low Countries, Scandinavia, Scotland, and England merged with those arriving from Italy. In France, the Château de Fontainebleau *(see p.294)* became a center of the arts, producing a rich Mannerist style seen in the design of the glorious Loire châteaux *(see p.293)*. In the Netherlands, artist Hieronymus Bosch kept alive, nightmarishly, the tradition of Gothic design into the 16th century. Rough-and-ready forms of Renaissance design also made their way across the Atlantic with explorers and conquerors from Spain and Portugal. Eventually, the effects of Renaissance design were felt worldwide as new European empires spread their wings and seized much of the world.

◁ **THE GUILD HOUSES IN THE GRAND PLACE, BRUSSELS, SEEK TO OUTDO EACH OTHER IN THE RICHNESS AND INVENTIVENESS OF THEIR DECORATION, WHICH IS TYPICAL OF FLEMISH BUILDINGS DURING THE LATE RENAISSANCE.**

ELEMENTS

As the Renaissance spread beyond Italy,
so it encountered earlier design traditions
elsewhere. The merger between these
gave rise to hybrid styles of architecture,
sometimes gloriously imaginative, at other
times a muddle—though even these were
rarely less than charming.

△ **Pediments with stone scrolls**
This popular device imported directly
from Rome is here seen cast on to the
front of the Church of Val-de-Grace,
Paris, by Lemercier.

Wealth of Renaissance detail
pasted over essentially
medieval designs

◁ **Elaborate gables**
It was easy to adopt the detail of
Renaissance buildings rather than their
rigorous plans and sections. Fanciful
facades abounded beyond Italy.

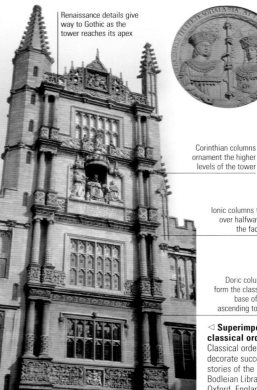

Renaissance details give
way to Gothic as the
tower reaches its apex

Plaque sculpted or
engraved with heraldic
emblems or portraiture

◁ **Cartouches**
These essentially Classical
decorative plaques became
popular on buildings
throughout northern Europe.

Corinthian columns
ornament the higher
levels of the tower

Ionic columns take
over halfway up
the facade

Doric columns
form the classical
base of the
ascending tower

◁ **Superimposed
classical orders**
Classical orders
decorate successive
stories of the
Bodleian Library,
Oxford, England.

△ **Elaborate dormer
windows**
These rooftop windows at
Château de Chambord, in
France, are studded with
Italian details, if not informed
by Italian proportions.

CHÂTEAU DE CHENONCEAUX

🏚 1576 📍 CHENONCEAUX, FRANCE ✐ PHILIBERT DE L'ORME 🏛 RESIDENCE

Philibert de l'Orme (*ca.* 1510–70) was the first professional French architect to have studied in Italy, after which he was made surveyor to the Royal works. The main part of the château at the historic Chenonceaux estate was a rectangular block with four towers, built on piles in the Cher. River. It was rebuilt between 1513 and 1523, in a medieval-meets-early-Renaissance manner. De l'Orme's remarkable contribution was the building of a slim and graceful new wing over a five-arched bridge across the river. De l'Orme's extension is a meticulously balanced composition reflected dreamily in the river passing through the arches of the bridge. Massive buttresses on

either side of the arches are lined up with the windows of the three floors above them. The Mannerist windows in the attic story are a later addition by Jean Bullant (*ca.* 1520–78), dating from 1576 when Catherine de Medici, Queen of France, owned the house. Despite many changes of ownership, and threats of destruction at the time of the Revolution, this is, after Versailles, the most visited house in France.

A house in a river
Gothic turrets on the original house give way to Renaissance symmetry in the wonderful bridge wing.

CHÂTEAU DE CHAMBORD

🏚 1547 📍 CHAMBORD, FRANCE ✐ DOMENICO DA CORTONA 🏛 RESIDENCE

The plan of François I's breathtaking Château de Chambord alludes to medieval castles, complete with deep walls, gatehouses, and a central keep, and flanked by turrets at each corner capped with conical roofs. However, the building is adorned with early Renaissance carved stone detailing and has the most intriguing internal design of all the French châteaux of this prolific era. Designed by the Italian architect Domenico da Cortona, possibly with help from

Leonardo da Vinci, the keep—also known as a "donjon"—features a spectacular double-helix stone stair at its heart; based on the same idea as the crisscross arrangements of escalators found in modern department stores, this allowed guests to climb up and down stairs without passing one another.

Strong protection
Not only is the château fortified and protected by a moat, it also sits in gardens surrounded by a 22 mile (35 km) long wall.

PALAIS DE FONTAINEBLEAU

📷 1586   📍 NEAR PARIS, FRANCE   ⚒ GILLES LE BRETON   🏛 PALACE

A rebuilding of an existing palace, Fontainebleau is important architecturally for the works carried out here for François I by Gilles Le Breton in the 1530s and 40s. This former medieval hunting lodge had been used by the kings of France since the 12th century. François, however, wanted to make it a part of his vision of a "New Rome," with all the grandeur the term implies. François's Italianate transformation of the palace combines Renaissance and French artistic traditions. The house itself is remarkably sober, given its scale and ambition; inside, though, there are spectacular Renaissance rooms, principally the Galerie de François I, an enormously long room with elaborate painted and stucco decoration by the Italian painter Rosso Fiorentino (1494–1540). As the house became more self-consciously artistic, the role of architect after Le Breton's death in 1553 was taken on by the painter Francesco Primaticcio (1504–70).

Rural retreat
Surrounded by an immense park and glorious landscaped gardens, the palace is sited within the forests of Fontainebleau.

PAVILLON DE L'HORLOGE, LOUVRE

📷 ca. 1640   📍 PARIS, FRANCE   ⚒ JACQUES LEMERCIER   🏛 PALACE

The old buildings of the Louvre, originally built as a fortress in 1190 and rebuilt as a palace for Charles V in the 14th century, were demolished by François I in 1527. Construction of a new royal palace on the site began under the direction of Pierre Lescot (1500–78) in 1546, shortly before the king's death, and was to continue over many generations. Lescot established the grand, if rather bulbous French Renaissance style forever associated with the old Louvre courtyards from his study of slightly earlier Renaissance Loire châteaux: close-coupled columns, carved stone detail piled upon carved stone detail, pediments set within pediments, massive pitched or curved roofs, and promiscuous statuary. The Pavillon de

L'Horloge was a later addition by Jacques Le Mercier, architect of the Sorbonne, who took over building work at the Louvre in 1624. His was the last ripe, even over-ripe flowering of the French Renaissance style. He had many heated exchanges with the painter Nicholas Poussin, who thought Lemercier's approach to decoration was overwrought and heavy-handed.

French grandeur
Lemercier designed the Pavillon d'Horloge in the style of Lescot, under the direction of Cardinal Richelieu, for whom he later built a separate palace.

PLACE DES VOSGES

🏛 1612 📍 PARIS, FRANCE ✍ CLAUDE CHASTILLON 🏛 RESIDENCES

An elegant enclosed square of red-brick, stone-dressed houses built under the patronage of Henry IV, Place des Vosges (formerly Place Royale) was a revolution in French urban design: here were houses rather than palace buildings forming a residential square in the center of Paris. And very fine they are too. Each well-planned and well-lit house is set behind, and rises above, a uniform arcade running around all four sides of the garden square; each, though, has a distinct roofline, creating a sense of individuality within order. The square measures exactly 460 x 460 ft (140 x 140 m); the garden at its center was laid out in 1680. At either end of the square are two

substantial houses secreted behind openings in the arcade; these were originally called the houses of the King and Queen, although no monarch ever lived in them. However, Place des Vosges was not without its celebrities: among its many famous residents were Cardinal Richelieu and Victor Hugo, and Madame de Sévigné was born here. Fully restored today, it remains a prestigious Parisian address.

Regal entrance
The King's and Queen's houses are two pavilions that form the northern and southern gateways to the square.

GUILD HOUSES, BRUSSELS

🏛 1700 📍 BRUSSELS, BELGIUM
✍ WILLEM DE BRUYN 🏛 RESIDENCES

Erected by various city guilds and private owners, these delicious houses gathered around Brussels' Grand Place were built in the 1690s after the French bombardment of August 1695. Though highly individualistic and a riot of Renaissance decoration, the houses form a more or less cohesive group. Adorned with extravagant statuary, phoenixes, urns, atlantes, horses, lunettes, fluted pilasters, scrolls, and other lacelike details too prolific to list, the houses are, mostly, showpieces of master builders' art and carpenters' skills. Today they have many uses, from apartments to offices and restaurants. All have rich histories: Marx and Engels stayed in rooms above La Maison du Cygne restaurant in 1847, when meeting with the Deutsche Arbeiterverein (German Labourers' Union). The large building looking like a late-17th century department store on the south side of the square is in fact several houses behind one grand facade designed by Willem de Bruyn.

ONZE LIEVE VROUWEKERK

🏛 1627 📍 SCHERPENHEUVEL, BELGIUM
✍ WENCESLAS COBERGER 🏛 PLACE OF WORSHIP

The seven-sided pilgrim church of Our Lady was built to house a supposedly miraculous statue of the Virgin Mary discovered in a nearby oak tree in around 1300, but it is best known for its magnificent dome, the very first of this scale and quality built in the Low Countries. The church, approached along an avenue, from a distance appears to be set between a pair of Classical pavilions. The dome, however, dominates everything, even though the overall design of this centrally planned church is notably fine. Coberger, court architect to the Catholic Hapsburg rulers of the then Spanish Netherlands, worked with great aesthetic restraint here, which is remarkable given that the church was intended to be a bulwark of Catholic Counter-Reformation dogma in this Protestant part of Europe. The design of the church is based, possibly, on a study Coberger may well have made of the church of San Giovanni dei Fiorentini, Rome.

TOWN HALL, ANTWERP

🏛 1566 📍 ANTWERP, BELGIUM ⚒ CORNELIS FLORIS 🏛 CIVIC BUILDING

Occupying one side of Antwerp's Grote Markt, this is a grand early Renaissance design by the architect and sculptor Cornelis Floris (1514–75). Here, Floris, who was much influenced by illustrations in Sebastiano Serlio's *l'Architettura* (published from 1537), mixed the latest Italian styles with those of Flemish and Netherlandish tradition. Beneath a great pitched roof crowned with impressive chimneys, Floris designed the central section of the facade as a sequence of triumphal Roman arches rising in four tiers and topped with a pedimented gable flanked by elongated obelisks. Slightly set back from this feast of Doric, Ionic, and Corinthian pilasters, with decorative shields and statues representing Prudence and Justice, are flanking wings remarkably modest and free of decoration. The rusticated first floor housed 45 shops.

Welcoming visitors
The fourth floor, immediately under the eaves of the roof, is an open-air gallery.

MAURITSHUIS

🏛 1640 📍 THE HAGUE, NETHERLANDS ⚒ JACOB VAN CAMPEN 🏛 RESIDENCE

Dutch architecture in the mid-17th century was heavily influenced by the work of the Italian Renaissance architects Palladio and Scamozzi. The Mauritshuis, a grand town house, was built for Jan Maurits van Nassau, governor of Dutch Brazil, and designed by Jacob van Campen with Pieter Post. The more-or-less square plan, with main reception areas flanked by private suites, is clearly derived from Palladio's Venetian villas. The brick facade, dominated by Ionic pilasters and low-relief sculptural details, is derived from Italy, but the steeply sloping roof, once dominated by tall chimneys, is conspicuously Dutch. The pediment over the entrance facade is underplayed: in fact, it might as well not exist. The building was severely damaged by fire in 1704 and rebuilt in 1720. For a while, under French occupation, it served as a prison, but since 1822 it has housed the Royal Cabinet of Paintings, a magnificent collection of works by, among others, Vermeer, Steen, Rembrandt, and Frans Hals. The Mauritshuis played a major role in the development of a new domestic architecture in the Low Countries and in England.

Classical influence
The formal Mauritshuis was much admired by Christopher Wren, the greatest British architect of the era.

TOWN HALL, ENKHUIZEN

🚢 FROM 1686   📍 IJSSELMEER, NETHERLANDS   ✎ STEVEN VENNEKOOL   🏛 CIVIC BUILDING

In the 17th century, the picturesque and prosperous northern Dutch town of Enkhuizen was a seaport, home to a 400-boat herring fleet and the hugely wealthy offices of the East and West India Companies. In many respects it rivaled the commercial might of Amsterdam.

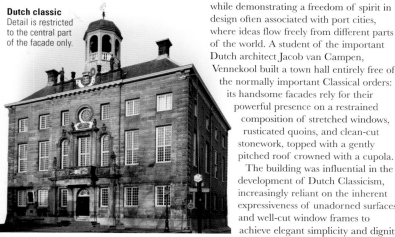

Dutch classic
Detail is restricted to the central part of the facade only.

The new Town Hall—begun in 1686 and designed by Steven Vennekool, from Amsterdam—reflected the town's stature while demonstrating a freedom of spirit in design often associated with port cities, where ideas flow freely from different parts of the world. A student of the important Dutch architect Jacob van Campen, Vennekool built a town hall entirely free of the normally important Classical orders: its handsome facades rely for their powerful presence on a restrained composition of stretched windows, rusticated quoins, and clean-cut stonework, topped with a gently pitched roof crowned with a cupola.

The building was influential in the development of Dutch Classicism, increasingly reliant on the inherent expressiveness of unadorned surfaces and well-cut window frames to achieve elegant simplicity and dignity.

LOGGIA, WALLENSTEIN PALACE

🚢 1631   📍 PRAGUE, CZECH REPUBLIC
✎ ANDREA SPEZZA   🏛 PALACE

The Wallenstein Palace and Gardens was commissioned in 1626 by one of the wealthiest and most powerful Czech noblemen, General Albrecht Vaclav Eusebius, to compete with Prague Castle itself. Its grand facades, around four great courtyards, combine late Italian Renaissance and contemporary northern European elements, while the interiors are similarly rich and eclectic. The highly theatrical loggia, facing an avenue replete with writhing statuary, is more purely Italian. Monumental in scale, it consists of three giant arches rising from double columns and appears to belong to an even bigger palace than Wallenstein. It leads out to a grand architectural landscape of stables, grotto, fountain, aviary, and Italian garden. Work was completed in 1631. The palace became the Ministry of Culture in 1950, but since 1994 it has been home to the senate of the Parliament of the Czech Republic. Restoration work still continues.

PALACE OF CHARLES V

🚢 1568   📍 GRANADA, SPAIN
✎ PEDRO MACHUCA   🏛 PALACE

This ambitious building with its sensational central court designed for bullfights was never completed. But what majesty, what grandeur the royal architect, a pupil of Michelangelo's, envisaged! The central court is ringed around with tiers of austere Doric and Ionic columns, punctuated by deeply recessed doorways, creating starkly defined patterns of light and shadow. The court sits within the square box of the palace, which is adorned externally with rich marble facades and some wonderfully powerful rustication.

EL REAL MONASTERIO DE SAN LORENZO DE EL ESCORIAL

🏛 1582 📍 EL ESCORIAL, CENTRAL SPAIN ✍ JUAN BAUTISTA DE TOLEDO & JUAN DE HERRERA 🏛 PALACE

The massive and austere El Real Monasterio de San Lorenzo de El Escorial, built for King Philip II, from 1562, in the middle of nowhere, embodies the spirit of its zealous patron as much as it does a particular era of Spanish architecture. Built at the peak of Spanish imperial power and at the height of the Inquisition, the result is one of the most daunting buildings in the world, an austere religious complex on a gridiron plan (the symbol of St. Laurence), which overwhelms the visitor even today with its intensity. Palace, monastery, church, mausoleum, and religious college are grouped around a series of symmetrically arranged courtyards enclosed by imposing and somber five-story walls. The domed church captive within these walls, austere but handsome, reflects the influence of Italian Renaissance design. King Phillip spent his last years here.

Enclosed order
A rectangle of five-story walls in polished yellow granite guards the complex.

METROPOLITAN CATHEDRAL

🏛 1813 📍 MEXICO CITY, MEXICO
✍ CLAUDIO DE ARCINIEGA 🏛 PLACE OF WORSHIP

The first Spanish church here, itself built on the site of an old Aztec temple, was torn down in 1628 while the ambitious new cathedral rose in its place, constructed, in part, from stones ransacked from the last surviving Aztec buildings. The earliest parts of the church include the ethereally dark nave, flanked by double aisles and side chapels. The interior is smothered in gold decoration. The west towers, designed by Jose Damian Ortiz de Castro, date from 1793.

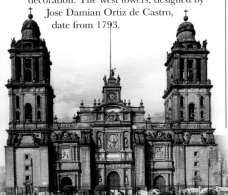

IGLESIA DE LA MERCED

🏛 1737 📍 QUITO, ECUADOR ✍ UNKNOWN
🏛 PLACE OF WORSHIP

One of the oldest and best-preserved South American capitals, Quito was settled in the first millennium and was an Inca city at the time of Spanish conquest. It then became an important center for rival religious missions, each building ambitious churches, all a happy marriage of Spanish, Italian, Flemish, Moorish, and indigenous styles. La Merced is a great white-walled basilica dominated by a massive square tower, with Arabic details and five domes. The entrance features carvings of the sun and moon that would be familiar to Inca worshipers. The foundations were laid in 1701, the tower completed in 1736, and the church dedicated in 1747. The main cloister of the adjoining monastery—a lovely thing— is all dazzling white archways supported by stone pillars and with a fountain with a figure of Neptune playing at its center. A second cloister houses a museum filled with tiles from Seville. The church has survived many earthquakes.

MOSTEIRO DOS JERONIMOS

🖳 *ca.* 1610   📍 BELÉM, PORTUGAL   ⚒ DIOGO DE BOITACA & OTHERS   🏛 MONASTERY

Commissioned by King Manuel I (r.1495–1512), work on this spectacular monastery for the Order of St. Jerome—paid for by a royal tax raised from the spice trade with Africa and the Orient—began in 1501. It was completed about a century later and involved the work, and even entire careers, of architects, artists, and master masons. Its style is one unique to Portugal: Manueline, a richly ornate crossover between late Gothic and early Renaissance design. Here, the style is seen to great effect. The principal facade of the stone monastery is 985 ft (300 m) long, and although fundamentally simple, it bursts with gloriously carved doorways and windows featuring coral, ropes, and other artefacts, natural and man-made, that the Portuguese explorers of the time encountered on their epic sea voyages. Rooms behind this great wall are appropriately monumental: the long refectory is quite magnificent. On the disbandment of all religious orders in 1833 the monastery became a school and was made a World Heritage Site in 1984.

Magnificent resting place
King Manuel is buried in the vaults of the intricately decorated monastery church; buried here, too, is Vasco da Gama, the greatest explorer of the Manueline age.

TORRE DE BELÉM

🖳 *ca.* 1600   📍 BELÉM, PORTUGAL   ⚒ DIOGO DE BOITACA & FRANCISCO DE ARRUDA   🏛 FORTIFICATION

The tower of Belém was built by Manuel I as the last of three fortresses announced by King João II (1455–95), at Cascais, St. Sebastião da Caparica, and Belém. Construction began in the early 16th century under the guidance of the Royal Master of Works, Diogo de Boitaca, at the time also in charge of the nearby Jeronimos monastery. The detailed design, however, was by Francisco de Arruda, who had considerable experience in defensive buildings. Despite the need for immense strength, Arruda created a remarkably pretty building shot through with Moorish and oriental details, including the

pepperbox-shaped cupolas that top the sentry boxes. The tower is decorated with characteristic Manueline detail, including the thick stone rope that girds its base and ends, often soaked in water, in elegantly tied knots. In the 18th century, new battlements and a cloister, designed to ventilate smoke from cannons firing below, were added.

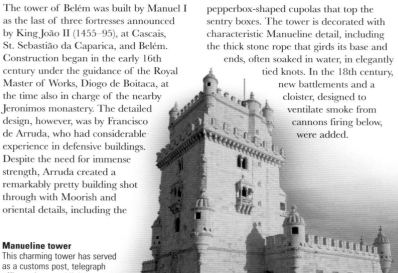

Manueline tower
This charming tower has served as a customs post, telegraph office, prison, and lighthouse, and has been a World Heritage Site since 1983.

HARDWICK HALL

🏆 1597 📍 DERBYSHIRE, ENGLAND ✎ ROBERT SMYTHSON 🏛 RESIDENCE

Clear glass, as used by the Romans, was rediscovered by the Venetians in the 15th century and came to England in the 16th, where the size of windows grew increasingly, where wealth allowed. Nowhere was this as true as at Hardwick Hall, a striking late Elizabethan country house built for "Bess of Hardwick" (Elizabeth, Countess of Shrewsbury), a four-times-married social climber whose monogram "ES" is carved into the building's elaborate balustrades. The long gallery running right across the third floor of the main facade is one of the most dramatic rooms to be found in any English house.

"Hardwick Hall, more glass than wall"
The great windows here reach almost from floor to ceiling; they were as much to demonstrate the immense wealth of the owner as to let in light.

WOLLATON HALL

🏆 1588 📍 NOTTINGHAMSHIRE, ENGLAND ✎ ROBERT SMYTHSON 🏛 RESIDENCE

This imposing house built for Sir Francis Willoughby is the chief work of Robert Smythson (1535–1614). Its construction, funded by wealth accruing to the family during the dissolution of the monasteries, required the destruction of the village of Sutton Passey. Its gloriously elaborate design, though castlelike, is outward-looking: there is no inner courtyard. Its most remarkable feature is the great turreted banqueting hall with its huge late Gothic windows rising from the clerestory of the centrally placed hall. The facades of the house below are

decorated with pairs of Doric, Ionic, and Corinthian pilasters, empty niches, and handsome balustrades, showing the influence of Italian Renaissance architects, notably Sebastiano Serlio. The tops of the towers, peppered with elaborate scrolled pediments, have obelisks at each corner. The original Smythson interior, destroyed by fire, was replaced by designs by Sir Jeffry Wyatville.

High drama
Although the banqueting hall looks as if it has been lowered in by crane onto an existing building, it is very much part of the original Smythson design.

BURGHLEY HOUSE

🖵 1587   📍 LINCOLNSHIRE, ENGLAND   ✍ WILLIAM CECIL   🏛 RESIDENCE

The Renaissance made its first decorative forays into English architecture in the reign of Henry VIII, but even by the end of the long reign of his daughter, Elizabeth I, it was still little more than a plaything for English architects. This great stone country house was built over a Catholic monastery Henry VIII had dissolved by Elizabeth's Chief Secretary of State, William Cecil, later Lord Burghley. If you can imagine stripping away its wonderfully ornate skyline, all turrets, spires, onion domes, obelisks, and elaborate

weathervanes, you will uncover a rather chaste stone building gathered around a large central court. The tall gatehouse and high-roofed great hall are essentially medieval elements that had yet to vanish in the encroaching Renaissance revolution proper. The deer park in which the house sits was landscaped by Capability Brown.

Splendor inside and out
The exterior has remained largely untouched, but the interior was radically remodeled in the 17th century by brilliant craftsmen, including Grinling Gibbons.

BANQUETING HOUSE, WHITEHALL

🖵 1622   📍 LONDON, ENGLAND   ✍ INIGO JONES   🏛 CIVIC BUILDING

The first truly Classical building completed in England was a ground-breaking addition to the medieval palace of Whitehall. The seven-bay building was inspired by ancient Roman basilicas and by the work of Palladio, which Inigo Jones (1573–1652) saw on study tours to Italy. It was built for the enactment of light-hearted court entertainments, many written and designed by Jones himself. The wonderfully simple, infinitely subtle interior is no more and no less than one large double cube, painted white, with a gallery adorned with a ceiling painting by Rubens, and with Ionic and Composite pilasters, columns, and half-columns.

Classical combination
Ionic columns punctuate the pedimented first floor windows, while above, flat-corniced windows are separated by Corinthian columns and pilasters.

QUEEN'S HOUSE, GREENWICH

🏛 1635 📍 LONDON, ENGLAND ✎ INIGO JONES 🏛 PALACE

Built originally for Anne of Denmark, wife of King James I, who died long before its completion, the Queen's House was in fact a hunting lodge straddling the public road to Deptford, which cut through the grounds of Greenwich Palace, separating the house from its gardens. The Queen's House was thus really a bridge, and so, behind its chaste and unrevealing façades, it had an unusual plan.

The Queen's House only really became a home from 1662, when John Webb was commissioned by Charles II to remodel the interior. This was completely restored in the 1980s, and after a six-year closure the House, which had for a long while been part of the National Maritime Museum, was reopened in 1990. It is fitted out in the style of the 1660s and contains a mixture of original and replica furnishings. The idiosyncrasies of the original design are still evident, but so too are its magnificent Palladian spiral stairway, the handsome loggia overlooking the park, and the crab-like stairs leading up to the main entrance.

Palladian proportions
Typically Palladian, the tripartite facade has a central projecting portion, with plain walls crowned by a balustrade surmounting a rusticated first story.

BODLEIAN LIBRARY

🏛 ca. 1615 📍 OXFORD, ENGLAND ✎ UNKNOWN
🏛 LIBRARY

Thomas Bodley, an Oxford scholar and retired diplomat, dedicated his life and fortune to the restoration of the University library, destroyed in 1550 in the turbulent wake of the Reformation. The library reopened in 1602, some years before work started on the tower of the main courtyard. Known as the Tower of the Five Orders, because of the engaged pairs of Tuscan, Doric, Ionic, Corinthian, and Composite columns that climb up its sides, this ceremonial entrance to the library is really a Gothic building dressed in Renaissance frills.

ST. PAUL'S, COVENT GARDEN

🏛 1633 📍 LONDON, ENGLAND ✎ INIGO JONES
🏛 PLACE OF WORSHIP

The first entirely new church to be built in London after the Reformation was severely simple in plan, a basilica installed with broad galleries to allow as many people as possible to hear the scriptures; and, with precious little ornament, it was humble outside, too. Even so, Jones's great east-facing Tuscan portico is powerful stuff, although because the altar is directly behind it, it is not the entrance to the church, which, by right, it ought to be. The barnlike entrance is at the west end of the church, reached through a small city garden.

THE EXCHANGE, COPENHAGEN

🗓 1640   📍 COPENHAGEN, DENMARK   ✍ HANS VAN STEENWINCKEL THE YOUNGER   🏛 CIVIC BUILDING

It is the lantern tower of this building that everyone remembers, a brilliant design by the sculptor Ludwig Heidriffer taking the form of four braided copper dragons' tails. The handsome building below, however, is a fine achievement in its own right. This is Europe's oldest stock exchange, commissioned by the builder king, Christian IV. The two-story brick facade is long and repetitive, but subtle and handsome, too. The reason for the repetitive design is that the building is essentially one long warehouse, where goods were brought after being unloaded from ships from Denmark, Sweden, and Norway; their royal crowns top the pediments rising along the length of the waterfront facade.

Vanishing point
Today the headquarters of the Copenhagen Chamber of Commerce, the otherwise solid Exchange is topped by the thinnest of needlelike spires.

FREDERIKSBORG CASTLE

🗓 1620   📍 HILLERØD, NEAR COPENHAGEN, DENMARK   ✍ HANS & LOUVENS VAN STEENWINCKEL   🏛 FORTIFICATION

Frederiksborg Castle was built originally for Frederick II, King of Denmark and Norway, although it was not until the accession of his son, Christian IV, crowned in 1599, that the palace took on the extravagant form we see today: three brick and stone buildings on three islands set in a lake and linked by a sequence of elegant bridges. This was never going to be an ordinary castle, and, especially with its glorious romantic roofline, it is, happily, nothing of the kind. Christian,

born at Frederiksborg in 1577, was determined to make it into a colorful and pleasurable place. His extensions to Frederick's castle, by two Dutch Renaissance architects, are characterized by joyfully sculptural treatment of the many gables, pinnacles, copper-covered roofs, spiraling steeples, and fine sandstone decorations.

Island life
This fairytale castle, on its three linked islands, lies within gardens that were laid out according to the latest French fashion.

Baroque and Rococo

THE BAROQUE, a name derived from the Portuguese for an irregularly shaped pearl, was the exuberant child of the Counter-Reformation (*ca.* 1545–1650), nurtured by the Catholic Church to fight the Protestant "heresy" spreading across northern Europe. Rococo (from the French *rocaille*, a rock, and *coquille*, a shell) was its frivolous, secular follow-on.

Much of the Counter-Reformation fight took the form of dynamic preaching and industrious teaching by militant new Catholic orders, such as the Society of Jesus, founded in 1534 by the Spanish soldier Ignatius Loyola (1491–1556) and given Papal approval in 1540. Yet it was also evident, and very dramatically so, in the theatrical art and architecture that emerged alongside it in Rome and then spread across Spain, France, Austria, Bavaria, and Latin America—and even in Protestant England, although in a far more sober way. Baroque architecture was thus a means of propagating faith, particularly when commissioned by such powerful and determined patrons as Pope Sixtus V *(see opposite)*, who did much to endow Rome with stupendous new buildings and public places.

Baroque art was sensational, theatrical, pictorial, and illusionistic. In both painting, as in the chiaroscuro canvases of Caravaggio, and architecture, as in almost any Italian

church of the period, Baroque meant a heightened play of light and shadow. In the best and most extreme cases, sculpture seems alive, as in the work of Bernini in Rome or the Asam brothers in Bavaria, and interiors of buildings become otherworldly.

The Palace of Versailles
Baroque art meets Baroque architecture in this theatrical painting of a *bal masque* in the Galerie des Glaces celebrating the marriage of the Dauphin.

KEY DATES

1620 Plymouth, Massachusetts founded by the Pilgrim Fathers	**1643** King Louis XIV of France, the Sun King, begins his 72-year reign at the age of five	**1685** Revocation of the Edict of Nantes by Louis XIV signals an all-out assault in France against Protestants	**1687** *Principia Mathematica* published by Isaac Newton, includes full expanation of principle of gravity
1625	**1650**	**1675**	**1700**
1633 Bernini finishes the *baldacchino* of St. Peter's basilica in Rome.	**1666** The Great Fire of London follows the Great Plague of 1665; the city is rebuilt conservatively	**1685** Births of Johann Sebastian Bach and Georg Frideric Handel, masters of Baroque composition	**1694** The Bank of England is established, marking the beginning of institutionalized national and global finance

POPE SIXTUS V

Sixtus (Felice Peretti, 1520–90) was the powerhouse behind the Baroque. He came from a poor family and had been a swineherd before taking up the priesthood. Hugely energetic, he made the Papacy rich after a period in the financial doldrums, by levying unpopular taxes and selling plum jobs in the Church. He spent much of the money on huge building projects that transformed the city of Rome. In an ambitiously baroque manner, he also hoped to drain the Pontine Marshes, conquer Egypt, crush the Turks, and ship the church of the Holy Sepulchre from Jerusalem to Rome.

1712 St. Petersburg, a new city created by Peter the Great, is made the capital of Russia

ca. 1766 French Rococo artist Jean-Honoré Fragonard paints *The Swing*

1773 The Boston Tea Party: Americans rebel against British rule, destroying tea imported from India

1818 John Nash begins replanning of central London, creating Regent's Park and Regent's Street

1725   **1750**   **1775**   **1880**

1732 Covent Garden Opera House opens in London

1763 France cedes all North American and Canadian territory east of Mississippi to Great Britain

ca. 1760s European Enlightenment appeals to human reason to challenge traditional views about the church, state, monarchy, education, and social institutions.

Many Baroque cathedrals, palaces, churches, and country houses boast grandiose domes, nurseries of cherubs, cinematic paintings, and statuary that verges—as with Bernini's *Ecstasy of St. Theresa*, for example—on the erotic. Many of these same buildings appear to embrace the streets of the squares they face, such as the great arms of Bernini's colonnade fronting St. Peter's, Rome *(see pp.278–79)*, and there are squares, such as Piazza Navona, Rome *(see p.315)*, in which a whole piece of city has been treated as a Baroque stage set, still as thrilling today as anything films can offer in terms of art direction and backdrop.

The Baroque developed in two separate, if overlapping forms. There was the effusive Baroque of the Catholic countries, and the more temperate Baroque of England, the Netherlands, and northern Europe.

The Ecstasy of St. Theresa of Avila
This fevered depiction of the divine vision of St. Theresa by Bernini shows the Carmelite nun being speared by an angel, after which she declared: "[my] soul is now satisfied by nothing less than God."

Bach and his family
The Baroque style pervaded not only architecture, but painting, sculpture, and music, Johann Sebastian Bach being the latter's complex and sublime master.

The masters of English Baroque, Christopher Wren (1632–1723), John Vanbrugh (1664–1726), and Nicholas Hawksmoor (1661–1736), developed a remarkable style of their own that was to echo down through the centuries, not just in Great Britain, but in the United States and elsewhere.

EUROPE: ROCOCO'S PLAYGROUND

Rococo, a playful style of decoration that first blossomed in France, was handmaiden to the Baroque. Colorful, charming, filled with swirling shapes, gilding, a multiplicity of mirrors, Chinoiserie, and decorative tricks galore, Rococo is rarely less than fun. Its essence is captured in the work of contemporary artists like Tiepolo in Italy, and Watteau, Boucher, and Fragonard in France. In Fragonard's most celebrated painting, *The Swing*, a young lady dressed in layers of the lightest silk flies effortlessly into the air in a gloriously lush garden. A young buck, also garbed in silk, poses below her with a view not so much of the Rococo scene, as up the young lady's pretty skirts. This might seem a little

childish, even crude, yet the painting is rather delightful and in much the same spirit as the sparkling Rococo interiors of contemporary French and German palaces, and even, dare it be said, of the spectacularly light-hearted church at Rottenbuch *(see p.335)*, in which cherubs play instruments at every turn and where the decoration seems to waltz before the visitor's eyes.

AN END TO FRIPPERY

Although the Baroque was to spread very successfully as far afield as Russia and Latin America, it was rejected fairly early on in Europe and, perhaps unsurprisingly, in Protestant England. Rococo, too, fell foul of the new mood of severity. Criticized harshly by such influential architect-writers as Jacques-François Blondel (1705–74), who decried the "ridiculous jumble of shells, dragons, reeds, palm-trees and plants" in contemporary interiors, Rococo, immense fun though it had been, ultimately made way for the rigors of Neo-Classicism.

Fragonard's *The Swing*
Look closely: the young woman is being given a push, and scandalously so, by her priest-lover, hiding in the bushes behind her.

BAROQUE
ca. 1600–1725

The exuberant, stage-set extravaganza of Baroque art and architecture is not to everyone's taste—too Catholic for some, too sensuously full-lipped for others. And yet, towns and cities across Europe benefit enormously from Baroque design, which recognizes that they are indeed the stages upon which we play our lives. Baroque buildings are some of the finest props and settings yet invented for the purpose.

H ad they lived today, many Baroque architects would perhaps have made good in Hollywood. The finest Baroque architecture is, after all, highly cinematic. It has movement built into every last curve and scroll. It is full of surprises, tricks of the light, sensation, and unapologetic drama. Naturally, it made the most enemies in Protestant countries, where its exuberance was looked on as something shockingly Papist as well as curvaceously vulgar. Even so, some of the most charismatic Baroque designs, notably those of Sir John Vanbrugh and Nicholas Hawksmoor, were by Englishmen, working for an ebullient aristocracy. The fact that Vanbrugh was a playwright, sometime soldier of fortune, *bon viveur*, and wit made him as Baroque a figure as his stupendous designs for Blenheim Palace and Castle Howard *(see p.329)*.

COMPELLING DESIGNS
You would, though, have to be verging on the puritanical not to thrill to such sights as the dome of St. Paul's Cathedral *(see p.326)* in London, or that of Venice's Santa Maria della Salute *(see p.319)*. And no one I know of who has visited the Benedictine abbey church at Rohr, Bavaria, has ever felt short-changed by the hair-raising sculptural ensemble of the Blessed Virgin Mary ascending into heaven over the heads of larger-than-life followers in the sensational choir, designed and sculpted by Egid Quirin Asam (1692–1750). The Virgin really does appear to be flying. Like all Baroque art, even at its bravura best, such work veers close to kitsch. But the finest Baroque architects, sculptors, and painters knew how to steer a path between moving theatricality and tasteless melodrama. When they succeeded, Baroque architecture was never less than utterly compelling.

◁ THE EXTERIOR OF KARLSKIRCHE, VIENNA, DESIGNED BY FISCHER VON ERLACH, IS AN UNUSUAL BUT NOT ENTIRELY UNSUCCESSFUL AMALGAM OF BAROQUE AND CLASSICAL ROMAN ELEMENTS.

ELEMENTS

The Baroque was architectural theater of the grandest, most imaginative, and opulent style. Although initially developed in Rome, the style, characterized by ambitious domes, ample curves, and tubby cherubs, eventually spread to Protestant countries, too. We know Baroque best for its unerring self-confidence and sheer, swaggering dramatic effect.

△ **Cherubs**
No Baroque church, palace, table, or chair is complete without at least a few cherubs. These playful "putti" can be found in the courtyard of the Palace of Aranjuez, Spain.

Copper is luminescent against the stonework

Gilding highlights dome in sun and rain

Softly rounded dome and lantern capping

△ **Roman fashion**
Domes with decorative ribbing echo St. Peter's in Rome. At Fischer's Karlskirche, Vienna, the lantern and cross above the green copper dome are 236 ft (72 m) high.

△ **Aiming high**
To create a dome that would rise high above Paris, Baroque designer Mansart constructed a two-story drum at Les Invalides, crowning the lantern with a steeple.

△ **Symbolic carving**
Giant, coiled, wavelike scrolls supporting statues buttress the main, galleried dome at Santa Maria della Salute, Venice, by Baldassare Longhena.

△ **Gravity-defying statuary**
Outstanding theatrical altarpiece sculpture at Rohr Abbey, Bavaria; the Virgin Mary really does seem to be flying.

▽ **Tiers of external stairs**
Theatrical stairs were an exuberant feature of grand Baroque buildings. This eye-catching staircase fronts the pilgrimage church of Bom Jesus do Monte, Portugal, a building complex that also incorporates Rococo and Palladian styles.

Contrasting bands of color heighten drama

Church gradually appears as you climb

ST. PETER'S, ROME

🏛 1615   📍 ROME, ITALY   ✍ MICHELANGELO & OTHERS   🏛 PLACE OF WORSHIP

If only by virtue of its extraordinary size, St. Peter's is hugely impressive, a triumphant assertion of the power and potency of the Roman church. Yet the difficulties of constructing such an immense building, exacerbated by frequent political turbulence, ensured that construction was stop-start at best, dragging on for more than a century.

DOME INTERIOR

The building is the work of three principal architects: Michelangelo; Giacomo della Porta (largely responsible for the dome); and Carlo Maderno. In 1546, when Michelangelo was appointed, the rebuilding of the church had already been underway for 40 years to the designs of five architects—Bramante, Sangallo, Fra Giocondo, Raphael, and Peruzzi—each changing his predecessor's plans.

Michelangelo's design was laid out on a centralized, Greek-cross plan. Yet however ideal an architectural solution in Humanist terms, it made little sense liturgically. After his death in 1564, three further architects—della Porta, Fontana, and Vignola—worked on the building, though still largely to Michelangelo's plans (dome aside). In 1606, Maderna added the nave and the facade but abandoned the centralized plan.

MICHELANGELO BUONARROTI

When he was appointed architect of St. Peter's, at almost 72, Michelangelo (1475–1564) was widely revered as the greatest sculptor and painter in Europe. Yet his last years were given over almost entirely to architecture, with St. Peter's —for which he refused to accept payment— his masterpiece. In scale and plasticity, his work there paved the way to the Baroque.

Unusually high facade
Maderno's facade is frequently criticized: its height obscures the dome except from a distance.

SAN CARLO ALLE QUATTRO FONTANE

🖳 1665   📍 ROME, ITALY   ⚒ FRANCESCO BORROMINI   🏛 PLACE OF WORSHIP

Although San Carlo alle Quattro Fontane could fit inside the central piers of St. Peter's *(see p.313)*, it is a church of astounding energy and inventiveness. One of the key works of the Roman High Baroque, it was the masterpiece of its enigmatic, tortured architect, Francesco Borromini.

Despite its tiny size, San Carlo is in fact a monastery church. Behind and to one side of it are a cloister, monastic buildings, and a garden, all on the same diminutive scale as the church. Rightly, however, it is San Carlo, Borromini's first major independent commission, that is the prime focus. It was designed in the 1630s, but financial problems meant that the work was undertaken in two stages. While the interior had been completed by 1641, the facade was begun only in 1665, not long before Borromini's death.

OVAL ROOFED COURTYARD SURROUNDED BY COLUMNS

Both internally and externally, the impression is of a building in an apparently permanent state of restless flux. The ground plan of the church is based on that most characteristic of Baroque devices, the oval. This has the double advantage of bestowing movement and reconciling the otherwise contradictory demands of centrally and longitudinally planned churches. But Borromini added a further, crucial twist, splitting the interior into fragments of interlocking ovals. The result is a superb interior consisting of a series of undulating walls that combine to generate an astounding sense of urgency, further emphasized by the strong lines of the cornice and the clusters of three-quarter columns. The oval motif is echoed externally in the two-story curving facade. This was the Baroque redefined.

Curving facade
The lower story of San Carlo's facade has a concave–convex–concave arrangement; the upper story is concave–concave–conave.

FRANCESCO BORROMINI

Borromini (1599–1667), born in northern Italy but active in Rome from 1617, trained with Maderno before working with Bernini. While the latter was as accomplished a courtier as he was an architect and sculptor, Borromini was reserved and intense—one reason for his relatively small number of major commissions, despite widespread recognition of his exceptional gifts. A difficult life ended in suicide.

PUBLIC SPACES

The flourishing of public building projects during the Renaissance and Baroque periods reflected the desire of the political authorities to flaunt their munificence. Undoubtedly, the most endearing to the public were the grand squares, with their fine statues, fountains, and impressive architecture, where people could promenade freely and enjoy the bustle and pure theater of urban life.

The epitome of a Baroque square is Rome's Piazza Navona. It has everything a grand Italian civic square of its era should have: stupendous fountains by Bernini and Giacomo della Porta, a Borromini church, obelisks, and heroic statuary. And, because the square is so very right in every last aspect of its design, it remains hugely popular with local people as well as tourists. Such squares are the heart of Italian towns and cities. They were gradually adopted around the world, and their appeal is on the increase as urbanism, or the design of our cities, is taken seriously again. At the time of their design in the 17th century, Italian cities competed aggressively to design and build the finest piazzas. They are civic stages, and, as such, they set the tone and pace of the dramas enacted upon them. Piazza Navona itself is an enclosed space, very much an urban theater where the focus remains as it was when first built: on people, sculpture, and architecture rather than, as is so often the case today, on cars, stores, street furniture, advertising, and general clutter. These public squares are some of the finest achievements of the Baroque.

Michelangelo's *David*
This famous statue of 1504 was originally in the Piazza della Signoria, Florence. It had set the pace for competitive statuary in civic spaces.

Fontana di Nettuno
Giacomo della Porta's dramatic fountain in Piazza Navona depicts the god Neptune.

ORATORY OF ST. PHILIP NERI

⛾ 1640   📍 ROME, ITALY   ✍ FRANCESCO BORROMINI   🏛 PLACE OF WORSHIP

Though from the outside strongly reminiscent of a church, the Oratory of St. Philip Neri is in fact the headquarters of the Oratorians, a counter-Reformation religious society founded in 1564 by the subsequently canonized Philip Neri. It is located next to the movement's church, Santa Maria in Vallicella. The interior was designed, from about 1620, by a variety of architects, Borromini among them.

But it is Borromini's facade that provides the real interest. Its importance lies partly in the fact that it is curved—the first example of what would prove a keynote of the Roman Baroque—and partly in the characteristic dynamism and invention that Borromini, the most idiosyncratic of the architects of the Roman Baroque, brings to bear.

Concave facade
The distinctive pediment of straight and curved lines is typical of the endlessly inventive Borromini.

SANTA MARIA DI MONTESANTO AND SANTA MARIA DEI MIRACOLI

⛾ 1677   📍 ROME, ITALY   ✍ RAINALDI, FONTANA & BERNINI   🏛 PLACES OF WORSHIP

The importance of the twin churches of Santa Maria di Montesanto and Santa Maria dei Miracoli lies less in their architectural virtues and more in their impact on the grandiose town planning that increasingly characterized 17th-century Rome. The imperatives of the Counter-Reformation demanded a Rome reborn, the sweeping-aside of the remnants of the shantytown of the medieval city and the creation of a series of huge public spaces and vast new vistas. The result was town planning on an entirely new scale, driven forward by a succession of popes, realized by a succession of equally ambitious architects, and given life by the heroic dynamism of the Baroque. It was a vision that would transform the city. These twin churches were intended as the focal point of the Piazza del Popolo, itself laid out in 1518, at the intersection of three streets created at much the same time. Though similar, they are not identical (the result of awkward sites), though considerable efforts were made to make the bold, domed exteriors as alike as possible.

Twin peaks
Santa Maria di Montesanto is to the left, Santa Maria dei Miracoli to the right.

TREVI FOUNTAIN

🖥 1762 📍 ROME, ITALY ✍ NICOLA SALVI 🏛 FOUNTAIN

Plans for a fountain on this site were being made almost as soon as the aqueduct that feeds it, the Aqua Virginis, was extended in 1453 by Nicholas V. The project was

periodically revived, notably in 1629 when Bernini was commissioned by Pope Urban VIII to design a fountain to exceed any other in the city in size and splendor. Work was abandoned in 1643. Two further attempts to revive the project in the early 18th century similarly foundered until, in 1732, the present fountain was begun to designs by Nicola Salvi. Eight different sculptors were responsible for the sculptures. Nonetheless, it is Salvi's conception that dominates, not least his decision to incorporate the facade of the existing Palazzo Poli as a background, which adds enormously to the grandeur of the work. The fountain is deliberately dramatic: an imposing, statue-studded triumphal arch from which water gushes and cascades into the main basin, across huge blocks of tufo stone strewn seemingly at random.

Divine waters
The giant central figure of the god Neptune, completed only in 1762, is flanked by figures symbolizing Abundance and Health.

THE SPANISH STEPS

🖥 1728 📍 ROME, ITALY ✍ FRANCESCO DE SANCTIS 🏛 PUBLIC SPACE

The idea of linking the church of the Trinità dei Monti with the Piazza di Spagna at its foot had been suggested even before the church itself was completed in 1570. Throughout the 17th century, a series of proposals were put forward, inevitably including one by Bernini. But it was only in 1717, on the insistence of Clement XI, that the project was finally begun. The result was one of the most striking examples of late Baroque town planning in Rome—a sinuously elegant staircase 137 steps high. Its most obvious architectural features are the two major terraces and the expansion and contraction of the staircase along its length, narrowing as it rises toward each terrace, widening as it sweeps past them. The overall impact is strongly rhythmic, with more than a hint of the more gentle accents of Rococo in place of the heroic certainties of the Baroque. The obelisk at the summit in front of the Trinità dei Monti was added by Pius VI in 1786. The Steps have been restored several times, most recently in 1995.

Divine stairway
These impressive steps link church and commerce. At their foot, the Piazza di Spagna runs into one of the most elegant shopping streets in Rome.

SUPERGA CHURCH

🏛 1731   📍 TURIN, ITALY
✎ FILIPPO JUVARRA   🏛 PLACE OF WORSHIP

Juvarra's church of the monastery of the Superga outside Turin is one of the supreme works of the late Baroque by one of the 18th century's most fluent and versatile architects. Though the centrally planned church is not large, it is conceived on the grandest of scales, a triumphant climax to the large and unrelieved monastery buildings to which it is attached. If the main elements—huge, jutting four-columned portico, commanding dome on a massive drum, and flanking, delicately pinnacled campanili— are heroic, their detail is calmly restrained, the whole memorable in every sense.

SINDONE CHAPEL

🏛 1690   📍 TURIN, ITALY
✎ GUARINO GUARINI   🏛 PLACE OF WORSHIP

The dome of the Sindone Chapel in Turin Cathedral is Guarino Guarini at his most breathtakingly innovative. Much of it hardly seems to belong to any recognizable Classical tradition, drawing elements from Gothic and Moorish sources and filtering them through Guarini's own interest in mathematics to produce a building as original as any in Europe. The dome sits on a high drum that rises from a circular cornice whose base is just overlapped in three places by the ribs of the pendentives below. The interior of the drum has six round-headed windows with pedimented niches between them. The dome itself consists of a series of shallow semicircular ribs, each supported by the center of the one below it. Between them are 72 small windows. The apex of the dome is crowned by further ribs, star-shaped and lit from above. The impact is astonishing, almost otherworldly.

CA' PESARO

🏛 1710   📍 VENICE, ITALY   ✎ BALDASSARE LONGHENA   🏛 PALACE

The Ca' Pesaro on the Grand Canal is one of the most exuberant and successful Baroque palaces in Venice, stately and sparkling by turns. Externally, the principal elements of the building are simple: a heavily rusticated first floor surmounted by two further floors, each of equal height and each with seven tall round-headed windows, the whole under a typically Venetian pyramid-style roof. What is remarkable, however, is the quality and richness of the ornamentation. Given the difficulties of building in Venice— cramped sites and unpredictable tidal waters—Venetian architects were almost always obliged to concentrate on otherwise flat facades. Longhena's palace bursts with decorative detail. The first-floor rustication is exceptionally deeply incised; heroic figures and giant heads cluster over the first-floor entrances and around the windows; alternating rhythms of double and single columns articulate and animate the two upper floors and balance the strong horizontals created by the three-floor organization.

Waterfront facade
The unusually heavy cutting of the rustication, creating a kind of sawtooth diamond patterning, is called "bossage."

SANTA MARIA DELLA SALUTE

🖥 1681 🏴 VENICE, ITALY ✍ BALDASSARE LONGHENA 🏛 PLACE OF WORSHIP

Santa Maria della Salute is not just the most important Baroque church in Venice, it is one of the earliest—and grandest—in Italy. Its impact derives partly from its location, at the southern end of the Grand Canal across from the Doge's Palace and St. Mark's Square, but more particularly from its heroic scale and boldly assembled masses.

INTERIOR VIEW

Its commanding dome is not just a precocious statement of Baroque drama but, in tandem with the second, smaller dome over the choir itself flanked by two tapering campanili, produces a skyline that is both daring and authentically Venetian. Added drama is generated by the octagonal first floor plan (unique in Venice), the imposing main entrance, with

giant three-quarter columns rising through two stories, and, most famously, the 16 huge volutes that act as buttresses to the drum of the main dome, the scrolling stonework mimicking waves in a manner quite appropriate to the watery setting. Not the least of Longhena's achievements is that so overwhelmingly Baroque a building complements Gothic Venice so effectively.

BALDASSARE LONGHENA

Baldassare Longhena (1598–1682) was a Venetian who worked mainly in Venice itself, where he was one of the greatest exponents of Baroque architecture of the period. He studied under the architect Vincenzo Scamozzi, and after Scamozzi's death, completed his monumental Procuratie Nuove in St. Mark's Square. Santa Maria della Salute is his best-known work, built to give thanks for the cessation of a plague in Venice.

City landmark

From any number of viewpoints, Longhena's dreamlike domes seem to float above the rooflines of Venetian residences.

PALACE OF VERSAILLES

🏛 1772   📍 NEAR PARIS, FRANCE
✍ JULES HARDOUIN MANSART & OTHERS   🏛 PALACE

There is no clearer proof that Rome had been eclipsed by France as the center of European artistic power than the immense palace of Versailles. The palace is more than a reflection of the obvious dominance of the monarchy in 17th-century France. Its grandeur and huge gardens were imitated across Europe. Given its overwhelming splendor, the origins of Versailles were modest: a hunting lodge built between 1623 and 1631 for Louis XIII. In 1661, Louis XIV decreed that

MANSART'S CHAPELLE ROYALE

this unprepossessing building would become the new French court and seat of government. The scale of the original hunting lodge proved hard to reconcile with the ambition of his vision, and the extensive rebuilding this entailed occupied several distinct stages, which extended well into the late 18th century. The first stage (1661–70) was the enclosing of the original hunting lodge by Louis Le Vau. This created both the Cour d'Honneur—a three-sided courtyard that leads directly to the main (east) facade—and the central portion of the (west) garden facade. At the same time, André Le Nôtre began the creation of the vast formal gardens that extend west of the palace. The second stage

JULES HARDOUIN MANSART

Louis XIV's favorite architect, Mansart (1646–1708) dominated French architecture at the end of the 17th century. His influence was huge, and his intuitive formality, taste for unashamed grandeur, and ability to work on huge scales lingers today in the country's instinct for *grands projets*. Yet whatever his obvious administrative gifts, he was an architect of great ability: Les Invalides, and the Chapelle Royale and the Hall of Mirrors at Versailles have real distinction.

(1678–1708) saw Jules Hardouin Mansart extend Le Vau's garden facade north and south, creating a facade 1,318 ft (402 m) long. Mansart also added the 230 ft (70 m) Hall of Mirrors and the sumptuously beautiful Chapelle Royale. The final stage (1770–72) was undertaken by Jacques Ange Gabriel; its principal legacy was the opera at the end of the north wing. The result was less the creation of a palace, more the building of an immensely formal miniature city.

Regal vision
From its humble beginnings as a hunting lodge, Louis XIV's palace became a magnificent example of French Baroque.

LES INVALIDES

🏛 1706 📍 PARIS, FRANCE ✍ JULES HARDOUIN MANSART 🏛 PLACE OF WORSHIP

No less than Versailles, Les Invalides, the church of the complex built by Louis XIV for veteran soldiers, is designed to impress. By far its most imposing feature is its facade, dominated by a huge dome and topped by a gilt lantern 350 ft (106 m) above the ground. The dome rests on a scarcely less imposing double drum, its upper story buttressed by volutes, its lower story by boldly projecting double columns. The central bay of the facade, arranged over two stories, supported by clusters of immense columns, and surmounted by a pediment, is equally forceful.

PLACE VENDÔME

🏛 1720 📍 PARIS, FRANCE ✍ JULES HARDOUIN MANSART 🏛 PUBLIC SPACE

The Place Vendôme marks a key moment in the drive toward formality in late 17th-century French town planning. It is entirely uniform, a rectangular public space surrounded by harmonious facades with rusticated first floors, giant pilasters on the second and third floors, and mansard roofs with alternating oval and rectangular windows. The beveled corners are pedimented and project discreetly. The column in the center is Napoleonic (though much altered); originally, there was an equestrian statute of Louis XIV on the top.

MELK ABBEY

📅 1736   📍 MELK, AUSTRIA   ✍ JAKOB PRANDTAUER   🏛 PLACE OF WORSHIP

Catholic Austria and southern Germany took to the Baroque with rare gusto. Jakob Prandtauer's Benedictine abbey and church in Melk is a prime example of this uninhibited approach. Its setting, high above the Danube, is deliberately dramatic: its design even more so. A commanding dome topped by an exotic lantern dominates. The curved facade is given emphasis by two campaniles with onion domes. This animated composition is heightened further by the flanking abbey hall and library, themselves linked by lower curving wings.

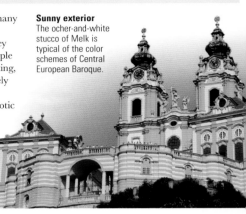

Sunny exterior
The ocher-and-white stucco of Melk is typical of the color schemes of Central European Baroque.

TROJA PALACE

📅 1696   📍 PRAGUE, CZECH REPUBLIC   ✍ JEAN-BAPTISTE MATHEY   🏛 PALACE

This striking example of the spread of the Baroque from its heartlands in western Europe is a remarkably elegant building, Baroque in its disposition of masses yet almost Palladian in its ordered restraint. The central block, five bays wide and three stories high, dominates. To either side, two-story wings lead to flanking wings that project forward. The roofs, steeply pitched, contain modest dormer windows. The most striking architectural element and a significant unifying motif is the giant

Composite pilasters that begin at the level of the first-floor windows in the case of the wings, and at the level of the second-floor windows in the case of the central block, extending boldly to the level of the upper windows. On the garden front, an elaborate double staircase with sculpted figures leads to the French-influenced gardens.

Color contrast
The red-and-white color scheme of Troja contributes importantly to the building's impact and adds drama to an otherwise sober design.

KARLSKIRCHE

🕰 1737   🏳 VIENNA, AUSTRIA   ✍ JOHANN BERNHARD FISCHER VON ERLACH   🏛 PLACE OF WORSIHP

Vienna's Karlskirche expresses all the imperial bombast of the expanding Hapsburg Austria, especially with its heavy debt to Ancient Rome. Yet however impressive, the building is curiously disjointed, an assemblage of individually glorious elements that never entirely mesh and are oddly, though charmingly, out of scale with one another. The basic design is familiar enough within the Baroque lexicon: dome, curved facade, flanking towers, and pedimented portico. Yet of these, only the dome on its tall drum and with elaborate oval windows is truly resolved. The flanking towers, modeled on Trajan's Column in Rome *(see p.116)*, scarcely seem part of the building at all, an effect made all the more obvious by their vast scale. The central portico, modeled on that of the Pantheon *(see pp.110–11)*, here seems dwarfed by these hefty columns and their no less immense bases. To either side are what amount to triumphal arches, themselves much taller than the central portico, topped by decidedly non-Classical towers. They make the facade exceptionally wide, and, as the body of the church is in fact no wider than the central portico, this adds to the sense of dislocation the building generates. The Karlskirche, though, for all these academic faults, is a wonderful example of Baroque drama and theatrical urban stage management.

Thanks offering
The Karlskirche was dedicated to St. Charles Borromeo for the delivery of the city from plague.

FRAUENKIRCHE

🕰 1743   🏳 DRESDEN, GERMANY   ✍ GEORGE BÄHR   🏛 PLACE OF WORSHIP

Dresden's Frauenkirche is among the most compelling Baroque buildings in Germany, all the more unusual for having been built in the Protestant north of the country (albeit in a city unusually rich in Baroque buildings). Destroyed in World War II, it lay in ruins for decades, until restoration was completed in 2005. Though a substantial building, it has an appealing delicacy, like a tabletop ornament on a vast scale. The church is centrally planned, its symmetry broken only by the curved chancel. Externally, the facades have bold, broken pediments supported by no less imposing giant pilasters arranged in pairs. The corners of the building are beveled with shallow, circular pediments, each topped by elegantly elaborate towers. This taut composition is dominated by a curiously steep dome broken by dormer windows and crowned by a substantial open lantern.

Fine recreation
The Frauenkirche combines a bold outline with an unusual delicacy of detailing.

NEW CATHEDRAL, SALAMANCA

🏛 1738   📍 SALAMANCA, WESTERN SPAIN   ⚒ ALBERTO DE CHURRIGUERA & OTHERS   🏛 PLACE OF WORSHIP

The New Cathedral was founded at the behest of King Ferdinand in 1510. Work began, under the direction of Juan Gil de Hontanon, three years later. The building is an exciting marriage between Late Gothic, by Juan de Ribero, and later Baroque design by various members of the Churriguera family, and is crowned with a Baroque dome riding 262 ft (80 m) above the sidewalks. It is intriguing to see how Italian details were gradually added before full-blown Baroque

triumphed completely over late-flowering Gothic design. The most dramatic part of the interior is the choir by Alberto de Churriguera, with elaborate stalls by Jose de Larra and Juan de Mujica, dramatic bas-reliefs of saints, martyrs, and apostles, and a grand organ by Pedro de Echevarria.

Old and new side by side
The New Cathedral, "La Nueva," stands alongside the Romanesque Old Cathedral, or "Catedral Vieja," which was built in the 12th century.

CHURCH OF SAN FRANCISCO XAVIER

🏛 1762   📍 TEPOTZOTLAN, MEXICO   ⚒ LORENZO RODRIGUEZ   🏛 PLACE OF WORSHIP

The grottolike, white limestone facade of this powerfully modeled church, sited close to an Aztec shrine to the god of feasting, is itself a Baroque, or Churrigueresque, feast for the eyes. It is decorated with more than 300 sculptures of angels, saints, cherubs, artichokes, cauliflowers, urns, chicory plants, and people, flanked by tapering pilasters. The interior of the Jesuit church is even richer than the facade and is famous for its florid gilded altarpieces. The facade is divided unevenly into three levels, across which zigzag moldings cast strong shadows in both sun- and moonlight. These shadows obliterate some details while highlighting

others during the course of the day, so that the design is continually changing—a Baroque dance that photographs never quite capture. The overscaled curved gable is crowded with urns. In 1777, secular clergy transformed Tepotzotlan into a seminary for the instruction and "correction" of secular clerics. After long periods of abandonment, the Mexican government returned Tepotzotlan to the Jesuits in the middle of the 19th century. To escape advancing anti-clerical revolutionaries, the Jesuits abandoned the entire complex in 1917. The church has been a part of Mexico's National Museum of the Vice-Royalty since 1964.

PALACE-MONASTERY OF MAFRA

🏛 1770 📍 MAFRA, PORTUGAL ✍ JOÃO FREDERICO LUDOVICE 🏛 PALACE / PLACE OF WORSHIP

The immense palace-monastery of Mafra, 24 miles (40 km) northwest of Lisbon, is an imposingly vast structure, built by the improvident João V of Portugal as a thanks offering for the birth of an heir. It was financed by the money that flooded the country following the discovery of diamonds in Brazil. The vast size of the building was consciously intended to rival the Escorial (*see p.298*) in Spain, built by Philip V 150 years earlier. Some idea of the scale of the project is conveyed by the fact that 45,000 workmen were used, and the building has over 800 rooms and 4,500 doors and windows. Its cost was such as to bring the country close to bankruptcy. The 722 ft (220 m) long facade

is dominated by the monastery church at its center. At either end of the building are enormous projecting wings under flattened, four-sided domes: that to the south contained the rooms of the queen, that to the north, those of the king. Mafra is an enormous building that truly bludgeons you into respect.

Super-sized
The monastery church is a two-story pedimented affair flanked by huge bell towers, each containing 57 bells.

WREN LIBRARY, TRINITY COLLEGE

🏛 1695 📍 CAMBRIDGE, ENGLAND
✍ CHRISTOPHER WREN 🏛 UNIVERSITY

Trinity College Library is the last and in many ways most impressive—and certainly ingenious—of Wren's three buildings in Cambridge. Though the building is a two-story structure—the lower, an arcade; the upper, the library itself—the floor of the library begins not at the level of the second-story windows, as from the outside it appears to, but at that of the lunettes of the arcade. This permits maximum space for the book stacks and, just as importantly, maximum light. Three-quarter Doric columns are used on the first floor, three-quarter Ionic pilasters on the upper floor.

RADCLIFFE CAMERA

🏛 1749 📍 OXFORD, ENGLAND
✍ JAMES GIBBS 🏛 UNIVERSITY

The Radcliffe Camera is one of the most supremely harmonious buildings in England, its assurance stemming from the exceptionally precise articulation of its component parts: base, upper stories, and dome. The heavily rusticated base, with alternating bays of niches and pediments, is not circular but 16-sided; however, it gives way to a genuinely circular structure of two stories, linked by pairs of giant three-quarter Corinthian columns and topped by a massive cornice and urn-studded balustrade. Crowning the building is a dome, heavily ribbed, supported by strongly projecting buttresses and crowned by a lantern.

ST. PAUL'S CATHEDRAL

👤 1710   📍 LONDON, ENGLAND   ⚒ CHRISTOPHER WREN   🏛 PLACE OF WORSHIP

St. Paul's is the high point of the short-lived English Baroque, a style regarded with mistrust in Protestant England because of its association with Catholicism. It is a striking paradox of this supremely harmonious building that Wren was able to persuade a Protestant clergy to accept so obviously Baroque a building.

For all its air of Classical serenity, St. Paul's is the product of compromise—between Wren's hopes to build a centralized church, Classical in every sense, and the Protestant insistence on a longitudinal church with nave, aisles, and choir to suit the needs of Protestant ritual. Yet there can be few longitudinal churches with such unmistakable centralizing tendencies. The nave, for example, is only one bay longer than the choir. Further, the immense crossing under its vast dome, 112 ft (34 m) in diameter and carried on eight huge piers, dominates the interior. There is no sense of these conflicts on the astonishingly rhythmic exterior, the whole arranged over two stories. Yet the upper story of the nave and choir is no more than a screen to disguise the one-story aisles. The dome soars over the building as once it soared over the London skyline.

CHRISTOPHER WREN

Wren (1632–1723), a mathematician and astronomer by training, turned to architecture only when 30. The Great Fire of London (1666) provided his greatest opportunity. His ambitious plan to rebuild the entire city was never implemented, but it did lead to the rebuilding of St. Paul's and 52 other churches.

CHRISTOPHER WREN

True Baroque
The dome of St. Paul's rivals, and in many respects exceeds, anything built in Rome.

ST. MARY-LE-BOW

🏛 1673　🏴 LONDON, ENGLAND　✍ CHRISTOPHER WREN　🏛 PLACE OF WORSHIP

The 52 churches built by Wren in London after the Great Fire are an extraordinary testament to his ingenuity (not least in overcoming often cramped and irregular sites) and industry. The interiors of most are plain (St. Stephen, Walbrook, a virtuoso exercise in the handling of space in which a longitudinal interior is treated as though it were a centralized church, is a conspicuous exception). This was partly a matter of finance, partly of Protestant doctrinal necessity. St. Mary-le-Bow, in common with most of the city churches, is longitudinal, with a broad nave separated from the aisles by substantial piers with half-columns rising to a tunnel vault pierced by spacious windows. The aisles have handsome wooden galleries, a feature of almost all Wren's churches. But the most notable aspect of the building, as again it was in all these buildings, is the tower.

At any rate until the end of the 19th century, Wren's church towers were second only to the dome of St. Paul's as the

dominant feature of the London skyline. As was generally the case, the base of the tower at St. Mary-le-Bow is plain; it is only once it climbs past what would have been the roofline of the surrounding buildings that it turns into a wholly unprecedented and astonishingly elaborate confection, part Classical, part Gothic. The belfry supports increasingly narrow circles of columns, creating one tempietto above another, that climax in a thin three-sided spire.

Towering genius
If only by virtue of their originality and fantasy, Wren's church towers are fully Baroque in spirit.

ST. MARY WOOLNOTH

🏛 1726　🏴 LONDON, ENGLAND　✍ NICHOLAS HAWKSMOOR　🏛 PLACE OF WORSHIP

Where Wren's City of London churches exude calm elegance, the half-dozen built by his former assistant, Hawksmoor, early in the 18th century, have a fierce, almost disturbing energy. No less than the buildings of John Vanbrugh, for whom Hawksmoor also worked, they are startlingly original. Classical in most of their details, Baroque in their heroic self-confidence, they have a thudding, sledgehammer impact all of their own.

The facade of St. Mary Woolnoth is wholly typical of Hawksmoor's style. The lower floor of the building is exceptionally heavily rusticated, its effect heightened by the unusual three-quarter columns on the corners —themselves also

rusticated—and by the continuation of the rustication into the keystones above the arched entrance and the semicircular window above it.

By contrast, the second floor is almost entirely plain, relieved only by three small square windows in its center. Above, there is a tower, with double composite columns to each side and two columns framing an almost louvered window in the center, with blank walls between them. The composition comes to a climax with two small oblong towers, with oversized balustrades resting on a strong entablature.

Extra dimension
Hawksmoor's dramatic handling of masses and contrasting textures gives his work a strongly sculptural quality.

CHRIST CHURCH, SPITALFIELDS

🗓 1729   📍 LONDON, ENGLAND
✎ NICHOLAS HAWKSMOOR   🏛 PLACE OF WORSHIP

Nicholas Hawksmoor (1661–1736) was a conventionally educated architect, highly trained at the Office of the King's Works, but much of his work was distinctly personal in style. He had unrivaled ability to use familiar forms in unfamiliar ways.

At Christ Church, the portico, supported by four Doric columns, is effectively a form of projecting Palladian arch—the main arch being flanked by two square-headed openings. This is echoed in the second floor by what looks from the front to be a solid wall, but is in fact no more than a double screen. Viewed from the side, its boldness is breathtaking. Towering over this mass of Baroque masonry is a Gothic spire.

ST. MARTIN-IN-THE-FIELDS

🗓 1726   📍 LONDON, ENGLAND
✎ JAMES GIBBS   🏛 PLACE OF WORSHIP

Even at his boldest, the Baroque buildings of James Gibbs (1682–1754) anticipate the calmer, more rational architecture of the later 18th century. St. Martin-in-the-Fields is therefore, in many ways, the archetypal English 18th-century church.

It is a simple rectangle, with giant Corinthian pilasters lining the north, south, and east faces; at the west end is a magnificent pedimented portico on six Corinthian columns. An elegant balustrade runs the length of the roofline, interrupted only by the portico. Characteristically, the detailing throughout is exceptionally rich. The coffered ceiling of the portico, for example, is finely carved.

Yet the chief feature of the building, which was much criticized at the time but later proved enormously influential, was the spire. No less elaborate than any of Wren's spires, it is placed directly behind the pediment, with the result that it appears to rise unsupported above the building.

CHATSWORTH HOUSE

🗓 AFTER 1687   📍 DERBYSHIRE, ENGLAND   ✎ WILLIAM TALMAN & THOMAS ARCHER   🏛 RESIDENCE

Chatsworth is one of the largest and grandest country houses in England, with a complex architectural history running well into the 19th century. The yellow stone house stands on the site of an Elizabethan building, overlooking splendid gardens and extensive parkland.

The south facade was designed by William Talman (1650–1719). It is an emphatic, low structure on a heavily rusticated stonework base—with roughened surfaces and recessed joints—above which are two rows of identical windows under heavy keystones.

The three bays at either end are emphasized by giant Ionic pilasters. A balustrade studded with urns animates the roofline. The double-ramped steps were added later.

The west facade, built after 1700 by an unknown architect, is lighter. A substantial pediment supported by three-quarter columns marks the three central bays. The north facade, designed by Thomas Archer (1668–1743)—who also laid out the original gardens—is slightly later still. Its unusual curve disguises the fact that the corners of the building are not symmetrical.

Cunning curves
The west facade at Chatsworth. The bulge in Archer's north facade is just visible to the left.

BLENHEIM PALACE

📅 1724   📍 WOODSTOCK, OXFORDSHIRE, ENGLAND   ✎ SIR JOHN VANBRUGH   🏛 PALACE

The vast sprawl of Blenheim sees Sir John Vanbrugh (1664–1726) at his most audacious. It is a trumpet blast of a building, overwhelmingly sure of itself. This is more than a matter of scale, huge though that is. Rather, Vanbrugh's supremely confident handling of masses—allied to an inventiveness to rival Hawksmoor's *(see opposite)*—produces a building that is deliberately extravagant. The irony is that, even before it was finished, the building, indeed the Baroque in general, was being derided in England precisely for the bombast at which Vanbrugh excelled.

Showcase facade
The boldly projecting central bay and portico of the south front gaze out over extensive ornamental parkland.

CASTLE HOWARD

📅 1712   📍 NORTH YORKSHIRE, ENGLAND   ✎ SIR JOHN VANBRUGH   🏛 RESIDENCE

If smaller than Blenheim, Castle Howard is as grand, and as Baroque in its sweep and exuberance. Designed by a man who was a soldier, then a merchant and a playwright before he came to architecture, this was Vanbrugh's first, astonishing building.

Like Blenheim, the main (north) facade is arranged around a fine reception court. Sweeping wings flank a massive central block, reached by an expansive staircase, with giant pilasters and a highly decorative dome on a high drum. As at Blenheim, outbuildings complete the ensemble. The south front of the building, though equally richly detailed, is treated as a single, flat unit, though the central block, here pedimented, is again prominent. It was behind this facade that the house's principal public rooms were arranged in an interconnecting series—the same arrangement as at Blenheim. Nonetheless, by far the most imposing interior space is the vast hall on the north side, extending the full height of the building.

Swashbuckling exterior
The south front at Castle Howard— Vanbrugh's skylines are action-packed affairs full of unexpected drama.

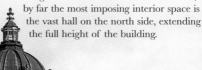

ROCOCO
ca. 1725–1775

Rococo was never exactly an architectural style. It was really a form of enervated Baroque, executed with a light and whimsical touch by a number of brilliantly frivolous French, Italian, and German artists, decorators, and architects. Mostly associated with the reign of Louis XV (1715–74) in France, it reached extraordinary heights in Bavaria: the interior of the church at Rottenbuch *(see p.335)* is overwhelming.

A s much a mood or a fashion, Rococo was a short-lived style of architecture and decoration that fanned out from the royal courts of Europe from the 1730s and 40s. Although its flamboyant and gilded flourishes are most notable in France, Bavaria, and Russia, it was also a style that made remarkable, if unexpected, headway elsewhere in Europe, in towns and cities that, superficially at least, were normally far more conservative in matters of taste. One of these is Dublin, a city rebuilt and extended during the 18th century in handsome, though chaste, brick terraced houses and garden squares. Yet behind the doors of many severe-looking Palladian houses in central Dublin are joyous ceilings writhing with exuberant Rococo plasterwork; this is a bit like finding a fancy silk lining in an otherwise sober custom-made suit.

At its best, Rococo was a happy movement that added a lightness and gaiety to Classical architecture. At its worst, it could be pure kitsch. Externally, it was at its best in the design of extravagant church and palace towers and in the popular fairytalelike grottoes that studded the landscaped gardens of country houses.

ROCOCO MASTERS

Rottenbuch's interior was the work of Josef Schmuzer (1683–1752) and his son Franz (1713–75), both experts in stucco decoration. Equally expert were the Swiss-born Lafranchini brothers, Paul (1695–1776) and Philip (1702–79), who brought a sensational exuberance to a number of Irish Palladian houses. And in Russia, the Italian architect Bartolomeo Rastrelli (1700–71) crafted the sumptuous Rococo masterpiece that is the Catherine Palace, near St. Petersburg *(see p.338)*.

◁ THE GILT DOMES AND BLUE PLASTERWORK OF THE CATHERINE PALACE AT TSARSKOE SELO, OUTSIDE ST. PETERSBURG, RUSSIA, DISPLAY THE BRIGHT EXUBERANCE THAT CHARACTERIZED ROCOCO'S BRIEF EXISTENCE.

ELEMENTS

Rococo was a playful style of design, more associated with interior decoration, painting, and general frivolity than with architecture. Even so, there are definite Rococo flourishes to be found across Europe, from Ireland to the fringes of the Austro-Hungarian Empire.

Decorated mirrors ▷
Rococo designers loved mirrors (the more the better). These playful examples are from Schloss Bruhl in Germany.

Prettily gnarled mirror, smothered in gilding

△ **Playful plasterwork**
Exuberant plasterwork is a characteristic of all Rococo designs, shown here in the ceiling of the outstanding Wieskirche, at the foot of the Bavarian Alps in Germany.

Frolicking cherubs epitomize the lightheartedness of Rococo

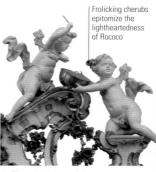

Freestanding gable and statuary animate facade

△ **Cherubs in excelsis**
Rococo cherubs cannot keep still; here a pair is seen playing with a drum high up in the church at Rottenbuch, Bavaria.

△ **Flamboyant classical facade**
The wings of the Palácio de Mateus, Vila Real, Portugal, focus the eye on the spectacular central facade, with its carefully controlled riot of turrets, chimneys, and statues.

▽ **Halls of mirrors**
This extravagant Rococo room, all gilt and mirrors, is in the Amalienburg pavilion at Schloss Nymphenburg, Germany.

ZWINGER

🏛 1722 📍 DRESDEN, GERMANY ✍ MATTHÄUS DANIEL PÖPPELMANN 🏛 PALACE

The Zwinger is a building like no other in Europe, part pleasure-garden, part theater, part art gallery. Yet if its purpose as a place of courtly entertainments is clear, its architecture resists precise definition. It is an astoundingly elaborate confection—a mixture of Baroque and emerging Rococo—in which architecture and sculpture melt and fuse.

STONE CARVINGS ON THE GLOCKENSPIELPAVILLON

The Zwinger was built for the Saxon Elector, Augustus the Strong, to house his art collection and as a venue for staging tournaments—the architect, Matthäus Pöppelmann, called it a "Roman arena." In plan, the Zwinger is simple: an enclosed, largely square garden, with apselike curves at either end housing two-story pavilions that double as entrances. The pavilions are linked by one-story galleries with, at their centers, further two-story entrances in the form of gate pavilions. Topped by urn-studded balustrades, the galleries are relatively sober. The pavilions, by contrast, are exuberant assemblages of sculptured decoration. The Kronentor, for example, is squashed under spreading onion-domes festooned with royal insignia. On the upper floors there are curved broken pediments, a motif echoed on the lower floors except that here the pediments face away from each other. The effect ought to be discordant, yet the precise opposite is the case. These are structures of unfettered *joie de vivre*, heady and joyfully intoxicating.

Formal gardens

Although it was never finished, the Zwinger is nevertheless impressive, its impact heightened by the formal gardens precisely laid out by Pöppelmann.

MATTHÄUS DANIEL PÖPPELMANN

Court architect Matthäus Pöppelmann (1662–1736) was responsible for rebuilding much of Dresden after the great fire of 1685, and also for the reconstruction of the Elector's palace after it too burned down in 1701. The Zwinger is by far Pöppelmann's greatest contribution to the development of the Rococo. His influence in Germany, poised to emerge as one of the most important centers of the Rococo, in secular as much as in ecclesiastical architecture, was immense.

ST. JOHN NEPOMUK, MUNICH

🏛 1750   📍 MUNICH, GERMANY   ✍ EGID QUIRIN & COSMAS DAMIAN ASAM   🏛 PLACE OF WORSHIP

This little church is unusual in almost every sense. It was built as a private church next to their house by the Asam brothers—painter Cosmas Damian (1686–1739) and sculptor Egid Quirin (1692–1750). It is dedicated to a 14th-century Bohemian priest, canonized in 1729, who was reputedly drowned on the orders of Wenceslaus IV; over the entrance, the saint ascends to heaven in a flurry of drapery from the rocky river banks. But it is

the interior that dazzles most. Tall and narrow, it is nonetheless crowded with movement and drama, the whole a startling melange of painting, stucco, sculpture, and architecture, united by a richly somber color scheme that is heightened by hidden light sources above the upper cornice.

Asam style
The facade bears all the hallmarks of the Asam brothers: undulating walls, a curved broken pediment, and strong coloring.

RESIDENZ, WÜRZBURG

🏛 ca. 1722   📍 WÜRZBURG, GERMANY   ✍ JOHANN BALTHASAR NEUMANN   🏛 PALACE

The Residenz in Würzburg was the official palace of the pleasure-loving prince-bishop of Würzburg. The building itself is not without merit, in particular the exceptionally lavish chapel, which is part-Baroque, part-Rococo. However, the Residenz is most noteworthy as a supreme example of the fusion of the arts—architecture, sculpture, stucco work, and painting—that increasingly characterized the Rococo in central Europe. The high points are the grand staircase and the throne room designed by Johann

Balthasar Neumann (1687–1753). Above the framed staircase with its cantilever cupola, Giovanni Battista Tiepolo, the 18th century's pre-eminent frescoist, painted the world's largest fresco—a shimmering vision of the continents. The throne room contains further sumptuous Tiepolo frescoes. The chapel was also built to Neumann's design.

Fit for a prince
Built for the prince-bishop Johann Philipp Franz von Schönborn, the Residenz was allegedly called the "nicest parsonage in Europe" by Napoléon.

ABBEY CHURCH, WELTENBURG

🪦 1724　📍 KEHLHEIM, GERMANY　✎ EGID QUIRIN & COSMAS DAMIAN ASAM　🏛 PLACE OF WORSHIP

The Asam brothers' taste for theatricality in architecture reached an early peak in the abbey church at Weltenburg, on the banks of the Danube. From the outside, the church promises little. Inside, however, is one of the first great German church interiors of the 18th century, representing a key moment in the emergence of full-blown Rococo in the country. The plan is not elaborate: an oval vestibule and nave, and a deep choir giving on to the high altar. But this simplicity is offset by the decoration—above all, the startling statue behind the high altar of a mounted St. George killing a writhing dragon. All is underpinned by theatrical metaphor: the deep,

galleried choir could almost be an auditorium, while the twisting columns on either side of St. George are reminiscent of the proscenium arch that frames a stage. Hidden light sources behind the statue flood it with brilliant light, as if illuminating a stage, in clear contrast to the otherwise shadowy body of the church.

Church as theater
The flamboyant Rococo decoration—all gilt and richly colored stucco—swirls over curved walls that lead the eye to the high altar.

ROTTENBUCH CHURCH

🪦 1747　📍 ROTTENBUCH, GERMANY　✎ JOSEF & FRANZ XAVER SCHMUZER　🏛 PLACE OF WORSHIP

Bavaria's passion for the Rococo is well illustrated by Rottenbuch parish church, an unexceptional 15th-century Gothic building transformed by a riotous Rococo interior. Regensburg's Gothic church of Alte Kapelle received a similar makeover by the Asam brothers, but there the contrast between Gothic and Rococo was never quite resolved. No such reservations apply at Rottenbuch.

AMALIENBURG

🪦 1739　📍 MUNICH, GERMANY　✎ FRANÇOIS DE CUVILLIÉS　🏛 PALACE

The Amalienburg is a pavilion in the grounds of Schloss Nymphenburg, the palace outside Munich built by the Elector Max Emanuel between 1716 and 1728. If the Rococo, as originally developed in France, was first and foremost a style of interior decoration, the Amalienburg is among its purest and most compelling examples, almost a shrine to the sophisticated pleasures of courtly dalliance.

Most of the Amalienburg is given over to a single central room—the oval-shaped Hall of Mirrors. Other than the doors at either end and the windows on one side, the walls are completely covered by oval-topped mirrors. Around, between, and, in places, over them curls a profusion of silver-gilt stucco depicting musical instruments, plants, birds, and cherubs. Where it also spills onto the pale-blue ceiling, it is transformed into a series of delicate landscapes peopled by shepherds and shepherdesses. The effect is mesmerizing.

WIESKIRCHE

🏛 1754   📍 BAVARIA, GERMANY   ✍ DOMINIKUS & JOHANN BAPTIST ZIMMERMAN   🏛 PLACE OF WORSHIP

The Wieskirche, or Meadow Church, is officially the Pilgrimage Church of the Scourged Savior. In meadowland at the foot of the Alps, its architects—the brothers Dominikus (1685–1766) and Johann Baptist (1680–1758) Zimmerman—created a spirited confection of Baroque and Rococo. It is now a World Heritage Site. The church was built on the site where tears were said to have been seen flowing from the eyes of a carved figure of the scourged Christ, and it remains an important place of pilgrimage as well as a major tourist venue.

WIESKIRCHE AND SURROUNDING MEADOWS

The Wieskirche is a joyous place, brilliantly engineered to allow daylight into the nave from a number of concealed sources and to make the most of its rural setting. Externally, straight lines dominate, but internally, it is all swirls and curls. Although as rich as Bavarian cake, the church is rigorously planned. Colors are used symbolically, with red and blue dominating. Red signifies the sacrificial blood, while blue—swirling down from the canopy—represents God's forgiveness and grace. Rich Catholic iconography abounds in the paintings, plaster work, and statuary.

Many levels of roof give a complex exterior profile

Baroque gables echo the shape of the onion dome on the tower

△ **Choir windows**
Richly colored marbled columns, with gilding, are bathed in the light from large windows over the choir.

The tall gilded cross is visible for several miles around

Steep-roofed onion dome, evolved from Byzantine influences

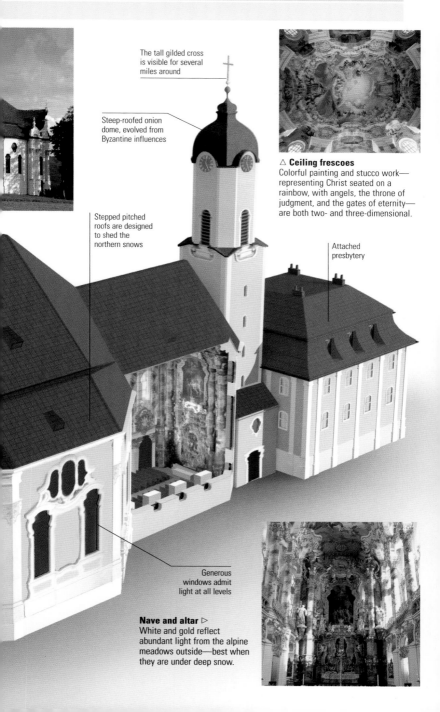

△ **Ceiling frescoes**
Colorful painting and stucco work—representing Christ seated on a rainbow, with angels, the throne of judgment, and the gates of eternity—are both two- and three-dimensional.

Stepped pitched roofs are designed to shed the northern snows

Attached presbytery

Generous windows admit light at all levels

Nave and altar ▷
White and gold reflect abundant light from the alpine meadows outside—best when they are under deep snow.

CATHERINE PALACE

🏛 1756   📍 TSARSKOE SELO, NEAR ST. PETERSBURG, RUSSIA   🏛 FRANCESCO BARTOLOMEO RASTRELLI   🏛 PALACE

The Catherine (or Ekaterininsky) Palace rivals the Winter Palace in St. Petersburg in size and sumptuousness. No less than Versailles, it is a remarkable demonstration of how architecture could be pressed into service to reflect and buttress the power of absolute monarchy. The main facade is 978 ft (298 m) long; the park in which it sits covers 1,400 acres (567 ha).

GILDED ONION DOMES

The palace was built by the Tsarina Elizabeth, who named it after her mother, Catherine I. While it incorporates elements of an existing building, externally at least it is authentically Rococo, a full-blown example of the style at its most imposing. The main, garden facade is broken into a carefully separated, rhythmic arrangement of pedimented bays. The central three bays have a white rusticated base, an elaborate balcony carried on four pairs of double columns, giant three-quarter columns, and a swirling, broken pediment with the royal arms. The same arrangement is repeated on either side four bays away, except that the columns carrying the balcony are dispensed with and the pediment is triangular. But the most immediately obvious aspect of the facade is the color scheme: blue walls, white columns, pediments, and windows, and gilt detailing on capitals, coats of arms, scrollwork, and giant caryatids.

FRANCESCO BARTOLOMEO RASTRELLI

Rastrelli (1700–71) was the son of an Italian sculptor who went to Russia in 1716, one of hundreds of western artists and craftsmen employed in the crash-course building of St. Petersburg. In 1741, after studying in Paris, he became court architect to the Tsarina Elizabeth. His output was substantial. His masterpieces were the Catherine Palace itself and the Winter Palace.

Arrive in style
A broad stairway flanked by statues leads up to the brilliantly colored garden facade.

BOM JESUS DO MONTE

📷 AFTER 1784 📍 BRAGA, PORTUGAL ✍ CRUZ AMARANTE 🏛 PLACE OF WORSHIP

Despite its dramatic location and bold silhouette, it is not the pilgrimage church of Bom Jesus do Monte that provides the real interest but the staircase leading to it. It is an extraordinary structure, a remarkable zigzag of granite steps that climbs a thickly wooded slope to the church at its summit. In part, the impact of the staircase is generated by its successive folding and refolding back on itself to create a precise yet abstract pattern. Seen from below, the effect is astonishing, heightened by the brilliantly white plaster walls that follow the stairs. More particularly, however, what distinguishes the stairs is their increasingly elaborate decoration. Fountains set into the walls represent the senses and, toward the summit, the virtues. Further, there is a series of sculptures, of increasing elaboration, set on each successive level. Although designed in the Rococo era, this remarkable structure also refers back both to the Baroque and to, beneath its ostentatious ornamentation, Palladian architecture.

Unique approach
The most devout pilgrims visiting the church climb the monumental staircase on their knees.

SANTIAGO DE COMPOSTELA

📷 1749 📍 SANTIAGO, SPAIN ✍ FERNANDO DE CASAS Y NOVOA 🏛 PLACE OF WORSHIP

Perhaps only Durham *(see pp.240–1)* rivals the Cathedral Metropolitana de Santiago de Compostela among the great Romanesque cathedrals of Europe. Yet where the exterior of Durham has retained its medieval magnificence, that at Santiago has been smothered under one of the most extreme Churrigueresque façades in Iberia. The term comes from the Churriguera, a family of sculptors and architects from Barcelona, the most important of whom was José Benito Churriguera (1665–1725). It has been suggested that the style was influenced by local art forms in Latin America; certainly, it became hugely popular there. It consists of the piling up of vastly elaborate elements, with a particular fondness for towers, turrets, and finials, over practically every inch of a building to create a vast mass of exuberant, often discordant, always fantastic decoration whose Classical origins are notional at best.

SAN XAVIER DEL BAC

📷 1797 📍 TUCSON, AZ ✍ EUSÉBIO FRANCISCO KINO 🏛 PLACE OF WORSHIP

The Jesuit mission church of San Xavier del Bac *(below)* is among the largest and most impressive of the churches built by the Spanish in what is now the Southwest. Two bold open square towers supported by buttresses dominate the exterior, stark white other than the elaborate red-brick portal under a dramatic curved broken pediment. A small dome, devoid of all decoration other than a cross at its summit, marks the crossing. A heavily emphasized cornice provides a strong horizontal accent in an interior notable for a sense of calm gravity.

Classical revival

WITH THE EMERGENCE of the new science of archaeology and the excavation of sites such as Herculaneum (1738) and Pompeii (1748), western Europe renewed its interest in Classicism. Renaissance, Baroque, and Rococo design gave way to a more archaeologically correct but updated style of ancient Greek and Roman architecture.

This new Classicism was seen as an ideal match for the ambitions both of powerful European states—whether autocratic or experiencing the birth pangs of democracy—and of the young United States of America, for which it provided a symbolic link to the republican ideals of pre-Augustan Rome and the democracy of Athens and the Greek states.

Neo-Classicism was, ultimately, able to serve almost every conceivable architectural purpose, becoming a noble cloak for country houses, town halls, law courts, train stations, and nationalistic monuments alike.

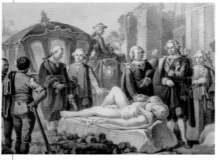

Gustav III of Sweden on the Grand Tour, 1783
It was fashionable for royalty and nobility, as well as artists, architects, and their wealthy patrons, to make a Grand Tour of the antiquities of Rome and Greece.

In England, Neo-Classicism flourished as a reaction to what some architectural purists came to see as the vulgarity of the Baroque. Foremost among these was Richard Boyle (1694–1753), 3rd Earl of Burlington, who became a great fan of the works of Andrea Palladio during three Grand Tours of Italy. In 1723, he designed the facade of a house for General Wade in central London, based on that of a Palladian palazzo. In doing so, he created a chaste, exquisitely proportioned style known thereafter as Palladianism, which spread through Ireland, where Burlington owned land, and across to the United States. This is the style of Georgian Bath, Dublin, and Edinburgh, and of many of the finest English country houses.

In post-revolutionary France, the frivolity of the Rococo, which was associated with the *ancien régime* of the Bourbon kings, was rejected in favor of the heroic imperial nature of Neo-Classical architecture, a suitable

KEY DATES

1755 Winckelmann extols ideal Greek beauty in *Reflections on the Painting and Sculpture of the Greeks*

1757 Giovanni Paolo Panini paints *Ancient Rome*, a heroic work celebrating the key Roman monuments

1762 James "Athenian" Stuart and Nicholas Revett publish *Antiquities of Athens*, encouraging Greek Revival

1769 James Watt and Matthew Boulton patent the first steam engine

1770 Captain James Cook of the Royal Navy charts east coast of Australia

1771 Clement XIV inaugurates the vast Vatican Museum with its huge collection of Classical art

1776 The Declaration of Independence: the United States finally declares itself free of British rule

1786 Death of Prussia's Frederick the Great, the "Enlightened Despot" and patron of Neo-Classical architecture

| 1750 | 1760 | 1770 | 1780 |

style for the new French empire established by Napoleon Bonaparte. Completed in the mid-19th century, the Madeleine *(see p.349)*, a huge Corinthian temple in Paris modeled on the Temple of Castor, Rome, shows how far French design had come in little more than half a century.

Napoleon Bonaparte (1769–1821)
A brilliant civil administrator and military leader, Napoleon made himself Emperor of the French in 1804.

Of the Neo-Classical architects who built relatively little, Frenchman Étienne-Louis Boullée (1728–99) had the most impact. His drawings for a National Library and a Monument to Newton (1784) showed antlike humans attending sepulchral buildings of an almost unimaginable scale. They were to prove fodder for megalomaniac politicians—most famously Adolf Hitler and Albert Speer *(see p.462)*—who believed that brute scale and bombast were all-important.

THE GREEK REVIVAL

The mid-18th century writings on the art of Classical Greece by Johann Winckelmann (1717–68) and on the roots of Western architecture by Abbé Laugier (1713–69) persuaded many that Greece, rather than Rome, provided the best examples of ideal beauty. Over the next century, Greek themes became increasingly dominant in the arts, and major cities witnessed a surge in the construction of Greek-style buildings, graced by porticos, colonnades, and tympanums.

Parthenon, Athens (18th-century etching)
To Greek Revivalists, no architecture was more perfect than that of 5th-century Athens. The acme of Athenian architecture was the Parthenon, which influenced many Neo-Classical buildings.

1789 The Fall of the Bastille marks the beginning of the French Revolution and overthrow of monarchy

1799 Napoleon Bonaparte becomes dictator of France, plunging Europe into years of war

1806 Napoleon commissions the construction of the Arc de Triomphe

1815 Battle of Waterloo: Napoleon is finally defeated, by British and Prussian forces, and sent into exile

1837 Queen Victoria ascends throne of England and begins the long reign that will name an era worldwide

1790   **1800**   **1825**   **1850**

1793 The Reign of Terror begins, a year during which thousands in France are sent to the guillotine

1805 Nelson destroys the French and Spanish fleets at the Battle of Trafalgar

1807 Britain outlaws the slave trade; it is finally abolished in the United States in 1865

1848 Karl Marx and Friedrich Engels publish *The Communist Manifesto*, signifying the rise of Socialism

NEO-CLASSICISM
ca. 1750–1850

From the mid-18th century onward, many European cities began to change out of all recognition as a revival of Classical architecture revolutionized both the way they looked and the way they worked. The result was that, at the time of the first stirrings of industrialism, the very latest ideas in architecture and urban design were rooted, quite bizarrely, in cultures that had reached their peak up to 2,000 years or more earlier.

St. Petersburg, Edinburgh New Town, Helsinki—these were all creations of the Neo-Classical era, each a magnificent fresh start; each somehow pretending that their cold, damp, even icy climates were appropriate for an architecture born under the Aegean sun and nurtured beside Adriatic and Mediterranean seas. Remarkably, the conceit worked: these cities were, to a great extent, glorious things to look at, and their architecture was thoughtfully adapted to make the best of their demanding locations. Fascinatingly, the ancient style of architecture they embodied was considered up to date, even "modern," a word that enters the English language in the 18th century. The crisp and sometimes colorful designs of the streets, palaces, churches, and civic halls of these European cities, so very far from Athens and Rome, do indeed seem modern, or fresh, even today.

CLASSICAL CIVILITY

The true brilliance of Neo-Classicism lies not just in the domes, pediments, colonnades, and mathematically precise proportions of its buildings, but also in their underlying civility. Here are buildings designed to be walked past, or, in the case of St. Petersburg, to be ridden past on horseback or in the seat of a carriage. Even when pompous and overscaled, like the Arc de Triomphe *(see p.348)*, they feel like familiar character actors on the urban stage. By the 19th century, many of the most dramatic Neo-Classical buildings began to display local characteristics. The spired Admiralty building in St. Petersburg *(see p.363)* could only be Russian, while the work of the Glaswegian architect Alexander "Greek" Thomson, such as his Caledonia Road Free Church *(see p.358)*, belongs to a world (now largely demolished) of its own.

◁ LUDWIG I OF BAVARIA BUILT THE NEO-CLASSICAL DORIC TEMPLE OF WALHALLA, NEAR REGENSBURG, GERMANY. STANDING ABOVE THE DANUBE, WALHALLA HOUSES PORTRAIT SCULPTURE OF PROMINENT FIGURES IN GERMAN HISTORY.

ELEMENTS

Neo-Classical architecture was associated not only with the archaeological rediscovery of the glories of ancient Greece and Rome, but also with the ambitions of a new generation of European kings and emperors, who saw themselves as the inheritors of Classical civilization. They built on a titanic scale and with Herculean determination.

△ **Neo-Classical Rome**
The Madeleine is a Roman temple recreated larger-than-life in the heart of Paris for Napoleon Bonaparte, in honor of his Grand Armée. It was eventually consecrated as a church.

Classical-style sculptures represent the progress of civilization

Facade is free of color, unlike an original Greek temple

△ **Neo-Classical Greek facade**
As the monuments of ancient Greece were rediscovered, they became the basis for grand Neo-Grecian facades, such as that of the British Museum, London, which is styled like an Ionic temple.

△ **Severe colonnades**
The chaste and unyielding colonnade of the Altes Museum, Berlin, was hugely influential in Neo-Classical design.

Relief panels based on Roman designs

Prussian winged spirit of victory

Heroic statuary celebrates the glory of France

△ **Triumphal arches**
Commissioned by Napoleon Bonaparte, the Arc de Triomphe, Paris, dwarfs the arches of ancient Rome. The subtle sensibilities of Neo-Classical architects were often overridden by egotistical patrons.

△ **Greek statuary**
The Greek "quadriga" (four-horsed chariot) appears many times in the monumental sculpture of Neo-Classical cities, the most famous being on top of Berlin's Brandenburg Gate.

PANTHÉON, PARIS

🖥 1790   📍 PARIS, FRANCE   ✍ JACQUES-GERMAIN SOUFFLOT   🏛 CIVIC BUILDING

This superb Parisian landmark is the great achievement of Jacques-Germain Soufflot (1713–80), the finest of the early Neo-Classicists, who studied the ruins of ancient Rome assiduously. The Panthéon, which we now know as a secular hall of fame for French heroes and heroines, was originally designed as the church of Sainte Geneviève for Louis XV.

PAINTING INSIDE DOME

The Panthéon's dome was based on that of Christopher Wren's St. Paul's in London. Like St. Paul's, it rises from a church (or what was intended to be a church) with narrow naves and aisles. The high walls give the building a more massive appearance than its plan warrants. This is not a criticism: the resolution of the Greek-cross plan, 361 ft (110 m) long by 279 ft (85 m) wide, and the Neo-Classical facades is masterly. The Corinthian temple-front, based on that of the Pantheon, Rome, is glorious. Inside, the arms of the Greek cross are covered by domes and barrel vaults. Construction of the

building began in 1757, on the site of the 6th-century basilica where Sainte Geneviève, patroness of Paris, was buried. The original windows around the building were filled in after the Revolution, when the building was turned into a shrine to French men and women. In 1806 it became a church again, and then in 1885 a museum. Whatever its purpose, the Panthéon is a building with great presence.

JACQUES-GERMAIN SOUFFLOT

Auxerre-born Jacques-Germain Soufflot attended the French Academy in Rome from 1731 to 1738. In 1755, the Marquis de Marigny gave him control of all royal buildings in Paris. Although a Classicist, Soufflot was also unfashionably fascinated by the brilliant lightness of Gothic construction, and in the design of the Panthéon Soufflot adopted medieval techniques to achieve Neo-Classical ends.

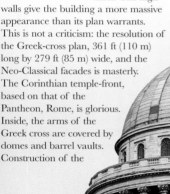

Monumental dome
The 272 ft (83 m) high dome of the Panthéon catches the eye along many of the streets and boulevards of central Paris.

AUX GRANDS HOMMES LA PATRIE RECONNAISSANTE

BARRIÈRE DE LA VILLETTE

🏛 1789   📍 PARIS, FRANCE
✏ CLAUDE-NICOLAS LEDOUX   🏛 CIVIC BUILDING

Now a magnificent folly in a public park, this is one of four surviving toll houses out of 40 that once ringed the walled city of Paris and fed the royal coffers; the rest were demolished during the Revolution. The surprisingly massive building takes the form of a great rotunda rising from a square base fronted by Doric facades stripped of all ornament. This was the architecture that was to inform the work of a number of Adolf Hitler's architects 150 years later.

PLACE DE LA CONCORDE

🏛 1775   📍 PARIS, FRANCE
✏ JACQUES ANGE GABRIEL   🏛 CIVIC BUILDING

A vast square at the west end of the Louvre, stretching along the Seine River and separating the Tuileries Gardens and the Champs-Elysées, the Place de la Concorde was laid out, from 1753, as a modest backdrop for a new equestrian statue of Louis XV. It remains a fine creation, lined on its north side by two identical ranges of palatial buildings flanked with handsome pedimented Corinthian pavilions. These are home to the French Naval Ministry and the Hotel Crillon. The statue of the king was torn down at the time of the Revolution and replaced with a guillotine that severed the heads of 1,300 people here between 1793 and 1795, including those of Louis XVI, Marie Antoinette, Danton, and Robespierre. The guillotine was replaced by the 75 ft (23 m) Obelisk of Luxor, a gift of the Egyptian Viceroy, Mehemet Ali, in 1829. The Pont de la Concorde bridge, 1787–90, by Jean-Rodolphe Perronet, leads out of the Place to the National Assembly.

CHAMBRE DES DÉPUTÉS

🏛 1810   📍 PARIS, FRANCE   ✏ BERNARD POYET
🏛 GOVERNMENT BUILDING

Asked to create a setting for the French revolutionary parliament that was both "noble and religious in style," Bernard Poyet (1742–1824) designed this heroic portico to front the increasingly complex gathering of palace buildings behind it that became the seat of the national assembly. Poyet created a center line that bisects both the Pont de la Concorde directly in front of his facade and the vast Place de la Concorde beyond. Poyet also designed a bizarre device (never built) that would allow citizens to experience zero gravity, by dropping them from a bridge in an iron cylinder—mounted on springs to soften their fall—into the Seine River.

ARC DE TRIOMPHE

🏛 1836   📍 PARIS, FRANCE   ✏ JEAN FRANÇOIS
THÉRÈSE CHALGRIN   🏛 MONUMENT

Commissioned by Napoleon in 1806, shortly after his victory at Austerlitz, this hugely inflated triumphal arch based on ancient Roman precedent was not completed until 1836, 25 years after the death of its architect, Thérèse Chalgrin. At 162 ft (49.5 m) high, it remains the world's largest arch; not for nothing was Chalgrin a pupil of the monumental fantasist, Boullée. It stands at the center of a star-shaped pattern of 12 radiating avenues and is the climax of a vista along the immense length of the Champs Elysées. It features four huge and energetic relief sculptures at the bases of its Herculean pillars, while around the top of the arch are the names of major victories won during the Revolutionary and Napoleonic wars. The names of less important victories, as well as those of 558 French generals, can be found on the inside walls.

EGLISE SAINTE-MADELEINE

AFTER 1842   PARIS, FRANCE   PIERRE-ALEXANDRE VIGNON   PLACE OF WORSHIP

It was meant to be a church, but in 1806 Napoleon decreed that this gigantic new Corinthian building, based on the Roman Maison Carrée in Nîmes *(see p.108)*, should be a Temple to Glory dedicated to his Grand Army instead. It was finally consecrated as a church, dedicated to St. Mary Magdalene, in 1842. Isolated, raised on a 23 ft (7 m) pedestal, and flanked by 66 ft (20 m) columns, the Madeleine is a hugely imposing and utterly convincing building

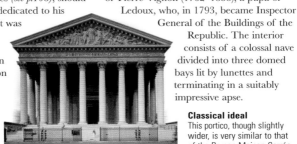

that conveys the power and civic majesty of Roman temples some 1,400 years on from their decline and fall. It is the great work of Pierre Vignon (1762–1838), a pupil of Ledoux, who, in 1793, became Inspector General of the Buildings of the Republic. The interior consists of a colossal nave divided into three domed bays lit by lunettes and terminating in a suitably impressive apse.

Classical ideal
This portico, though slightly wider, is very similar to that of the Roman Maison Carrée.

RUE DE RIVOLI

1855   PARIS, FRANCE   PIERRE FONTAINE & CHARLES PERCIER   CIVIC BUILDING

A handsome arcaded street facing the Tuileries Gardens, and leading from the Marais to the Place de la Concorde, Rue de Rivoli was designed by two of Napoleon's favorite architects, Pierre Fontaine (1762–1853) and Charles Percier (1764–1838). The street's arcades stretch for nearly a mile (1.5 km), protecting strolling Parisians from wind, sun, and rain.

The street took a long time to build. It was easy, however, for successive kings and emperors to justify work on such popular and largely politically neutral projects, and construction continued during the reign of the restored Bourbon monarchs, Charles X

and Louis-Philippe, and Napoleon III. The main Paris sewer was built under the street at the same time.

At the end of World War II, Adolf Hitler gave the order to destroy Paris; the order was disobeyed by Dietrich von Choltitz, German commander of the occupied city, who was captured by Allied troops at his headquarters in the Meurisse Hotel, Rue de Rivoli, on August 25th, 1944. Why would anyone want to destroy such a street?

Civic triumph
This fine example of regulated and civil urban planning was named after Napoleon's victory over the Austrians at the Battle of Rivoli (1797).

Arc de Triomphe
The famous Parisian monument is richly decorated with reliefs. Built for Napoleon, successive governments have added their own marks to it. Beneath the arch, the Tomb of the Unknown Soldier honors the dead of 20th-century wars.

BRANDENBURG GATE

🏛 1793   📍 BERLIN, GERMANY   ✏ KARL GOTTHARD LANGHANS   🏛 MONUMENT

A great Doric gateway based on the propylaea—the ceremonial entrances of the Acropolis, Athens—the Brandenburg Gate was commissioned by Friedrich Wilhelm II of Prussia in 1780 to symbolize peace, although it has always looked more like war. For many years it was one of the most famous sections of the Berlin Wall. The gate stands, 86 ft (26 m) high, at the end of Unter den Linden, the grand avenue of linden trees leading to Wilhelm's palace. It was one of several gates commanding entrances to Berlin. It comprises a central Doric screen with two rows of six columns, flanked by a pair of chaste Doric pavilions. The gate is crowned with a quadriga—a sculpted four-horse chariot—driven by the goddess of victory, holding a laurel wreath aloft. The gate was the first of a long sequence of Classical Revival buildings passing through the center of Berlin that led aesthetes at the time to call the city "Spreeathen," or Athens on the Spree River.

Great gateway
The central Doric screen measures 213 ft (65 m) across and is 36 ft (11 m) deep.

ALTES MUSEUM

🏛 1830   📍 BERLIN, GERMANY   ✏ KARL FRIEDRICH SCHINKEL   🏛 MUSEUM

Icy, perfect, and haunting, the Altes Museum is one of the most important buildings of the Greek Revival, and had a huge influence on the stripped Classical style popular between the two World Wars (in particular, on the work of Adolf Hitler's architect, Albert Speer). Here, Schinkel composed a vast, double-height drum, based on the Pantheon. Raised on a prominent pedestal, the magnificent, Ionic 18-column screen is topped with double-headed Prussian eagles, while the drum, set into a cube, boasts Grecian athletes reining in proud stallions. Here is architecture as Platonic elements, beautifully thought out and executed. Completely restored since the reunification of Germany, the Altes Museum is today a popular gallery and museum.

Modern glazing
The museum's screen is now glazed; the entrance to the galleries—up exposed stairs—was very draughty, and few people today wish to suffer for their art.

COURT GARDENER'S HOUSE, CHARLOTTENHOF

🏛 1829 📍 POTSDAM, GERMANY ✍ KARL FRIEDRICH SCHINKEL 🏛 PALACE

This is a lovely example of Schinkel in a gentle and even playful mood. The gardener's house at Charlottenhof was a remodeling of an older building and shows the influence of the extremely playful, and brilliant, English Neo-Classicist and exoticist John Nash, an architect a generation older than Schinkel. The two had met on Schinkel's trip to London to see the new British Museum in 1826, during which he had been most impressed by gas street-lighting and Marc

Brunel's tunnel under the Thames. This is one of a number of houses that Schinkel rebuilt in the grounds of Charlottenhof, a makeover of an old farmhouse, previously owned by one Charlotte Reventzow, for the crown prince and his consort, Elisabeth. Charlottenhof was a *maison de plaisance*, a house of aesthetic as well as any other delight, and so arranged that its owners could step straight out from drawing rooms into picturesque landscaped gardens. The gardener's house is, in form, a miniature Roman bath, a Roman temple, and a rustic Italianate villa conjured into one singularly happy design. It is sad, perhaps, that so few suburban villas built today have anything like its subtlety and playfulness of design.

Gardener's delight
Charming and intelligently designed, this house represents Schinkel's style at its most approachable.

SCHAUSPIELHAUS, BERLIN

🏛 1821 📍 BERLIN, GERMANY ✍ KARL FRIEDRICH SCHINKEL 🏛 OPERA HOUSE

With the design of Berlin's opera house, Schinkel showed how a revival of Greek design could inform the most ambitious new civic buildings. Schauspielhaus is a bravura performance, a big, bold building that eschews ornamentation in favor of candidly expressed straight lines outlining the great rooms behind them. These are lit by almost continuous bands of windows, and, in this respect, the design of the theater can be seen as a predecessor of the grand Neo-Classical department stores that would appear on European streets three-quarters of a century later. The entrance facade on the Platz der Akademie comprises a noble Ionic portico over which rises a massive pedimented attic story containing the auditorium and topped by

a sculpture of Apollo driving a chariot drawn by griffins. With a great sense of public theater, Schinkel set the building between the fine towers of the German and French cathedrals. Inside, he created a Greek-style amphitheater with the stage jutting into the auditorium. Gutted by fire in 1945, the building finally reopened in 1984.

Cultural landmark
Beethoven's Ninth Symphony made its Berlin debut here, and Wagner conducted the Berlin premiere of *Der Fliegende Holländer*.

CHISWICK HOUSE

🏛 1739 📍 LONDON, ENGLAND ✍ LORD BURLINGTON 🏛 RESIDENCE

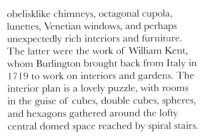

An exquisite villa, Chiswick House was part of a now demolished larger residence. It was designed by Richard Boyle, 3rd Earl of Burlington (1694–1753), an architect, patron, and connoisseur who led the Palladian movement in England—a reaction to what he and his colleagues saw as the gross voluptuousness of late Baroque design. In its place, Burlington recommended more puritanical and geometrically correct design based on the work of Andrea Palladio, which Inigo Jones had introduced to England a century earlier. A play on Palladio's Villa Capra in Vicenza, although not wholly symmetrical, Chiswick House is distinguished by the simplicity of its forms, its clean-cut stonework,

obelisklike chimneys, octagonal cupola, lunettes, Venetian windows, and perhaps unexpectedly rich interiors and furniture. The latter were the work of William Kent, whom Burlington brought back from Italy in 1719 to work on interiors and gardens. The interior plan is a lovely puzzle, with rooms in the guise of cubes, double cubes, spheres, and hexagons gathered around the lofty central domed space reached by spiral stairs.

Building blocks
Balanced forms play a large part in Chiswick House's elegant simplicity.

SOMERSET HOUSE

🏛 1786 📍 LONDON, ENGLAND ✍ SIR WILLIAM CHAMBERS 🏛 GOVERNMENT BUILDING

Occupying a vast site between the Strand and the Thames River, Somerset House was built as a range of government offices. In fact, this was Britain's first purpose-built office block. That it is so palatial is down to its architect, William Chambers (1723–96), who—having trained in Paris and Italy—became architect and tutor to the Prince of Wales, the future George III.

The Strand facade, apparently modest, is just nine bays wide, with

no grand gestures. An archway, however, leads into a magnificent court ranged around with magnificent wings, one of the finest set pieces of post-Renaissance urban planning in England. The 656-ft (200-m) long, Versailles-like river facade is broken up by two pedimented and colonnaded gateways, and a central projecting block crowned with a pedimented attic and shallow dome. This elongated facade stands on a great platform supported by rusticated archways that can

be read as a Palladian bridge. These gave directly onto the Thames until the river was embanked in the mid-19th century.

Riverside offices
Originally government offices, Somerset House is now home to major European collections of art.

ROYAL CRESCENT & ROYAL CIRCUS, BATH

🏛 1775 📍 BATH, SOUTHWEST ENGLAND ✍ JOHN WOOD & JOHN WOOD THE YOUNGER 🏛 RESIDENCES

Resembling a giant question mark seen from the air, the Royal Circus and Royal Crescent form one of the great moments in 18th-century town planning. Here, John Wood (1705–54) and his son John Wood the younger (1728–82) gave new life to Roman design, moving exultantly, always elegantly, from the enclosure of the Circus to the embracing openness of the Crescent.

Both are quite magnificent and remain much-sought-after city homes. The Circus was laid out first, from 1754, by the elder John Wood. Bath had been a Roman city, and Wood was determined to recreate a modern version. The Circus was intended as a sports venue, but given the demand for high-end housing in an increasingly fashionable health resort, the site became a circle of townhouses. This is entered by three streets, one of them, Brock Street, leading to the Crescent. Borrowing from the facades of Rome's Colosseum, Wood designed the honey-colored stone facades of the houses with a hierarchy of Doric, Ionic, and Corinthian orders. The plans of the

ROYAL CRESCENT FROM THE AIR

houses vary, so that seen from behind, the Circus appears anything but perfect; this, though, was a good example of English pragmatism, explaining the enduring appeal of the Circus: it is both rigorously formal and highly adaptable at one and the same time. The Royal Crescent embraces 30 houses in a great sweeping design that again takes its cue from the architecture of the Colosseum. Its quietly detailed facade boasts glorious Ionic columns set on a high base.

THE WOODS

John Wood, son of a Bath builder, designed many of the finest streets and buildings in 18th-century Bath, including Queen Square, North and South Parades, the Circus, and Prior Park. He followed his vision of creating a "New Rome" at Bath unerringly, making urban palaces out of clusters of very English town-houses. His son John completed the Circus, then designed the Royal Crescent and Assembly Rooms. The Woods's mark on Bath remains undiminished.

Open to visitors
No. 1 Royal Crescent has been completely restored as a museum by the Bath Preservation Trust.

CUMBERLAND TERRACE

⚱ 1813 📍 LONDON, ENGLAND
✍ JOHN NASH 🏛 RESIDENCES

This glorious terrace is the finest of several ringing Regent's Park in central London. Its grand stuccoed facade, highlighted by Ionic columns, a freestanding central pediment, triumphal gateways, and statuary, has the feel of a dreamlike palace. In fact, it conceals a large number of houses and apartments. The terrace was heavily damaged in World War II and very nearly demolished in the early 1950s. The facades are beautifully kept today.

Regent's Park, a former royal hunting ground, was created by architect John Nash (1752–1835) for the Prince Regent from 1811. Originally, the prince was to have lived in a new palace in the center, set about by 56 high-class Neo-Classical villas. As it turned out, just eight villas were built, and no palace, although Nash did construct a series of white terraces around the park. Cumberland Terrace was designed to be especially grand, since it would have been visible from the planned palace. In the end, the prince chose to move to what later became Buckingham Palace.

ST. PANCRAS CHURCH

⚱ 1822 📍 LONDON, ENGLAND
✍ WILLIAM & HENRY INWOOD 🏛 PLACE OF WORSHIP

A theatrical delight, St. Pancras is a clever brick-and-stone creation. William Inwood (1771–1843) and his son Henry (1794–1843) transposed entire elements of famous Greek monuments onto the body of a church. At the east end is a pair of caryatid porches borrowed from the Erechtheion (see p.97), and the tower is modeled on both the Tower of the Winds (see p.101) and the Choragic Monument of Lysicrates (see p.98).

BRITISH MUSEUM

⚱ 1846 📍 LONDON, ENGLAND
✍ ROBERT SMIRKE 🏛 MUSEUM

Robert Smirke's (1780–1867) British Museum is in the same severe Grecian spirit as the contemporary designs of Schinkel in Berlin (see pp.352–3). Its facade has an Ionic portico flanked by two projecting wings, all wrapped in a screen of Ionic columns. The galleries behind are arranged around a courtyard; this was filled in 1857 by a copper-domed reading room designed by Smirke's brother, Sydney (1798–1877). More galleries were added throughout the 20th century, and in 2001 the courtyard was given a billowing steel-and-glass roof designed by Norman Foster.

CRONKHILL

⚱ ca. 1804 📍 SHROPSHIRE, ENGLAND
✍ JOHN NASH 🏛 RESIDENCE

This lovely Italianate house, in an estate in the Shropshire countryside overlooking the Severn River, was designed by John Nash, a master of picturesque Classical design. Nash began his career as a speculative house-builder but turned to architecture proper in 1795. At the time, Cronkhill would have seemed revolutionary, with its asymmetrical composition, tall round tower, several pitched roofs, pronounced balustrades, and the second floor set so very far back from the arcaded first floor. Unlike later Victorian houses, Cronkhill is free of decoration and Classically planned, so that it would have been thought unusual, but not wilfully perverse.

The point of houses like Cronkhill is that they gave their owners a sense of living in an idyllic pastoral landscape, like those painted by the great French or Italian masters. With its crisp white walls and big windows, it is also very modern in appearance, and set a precedent for some of the very best English suburban villas of the 1920s and 1930s.

TOWN PLANNING

The designs of the ideal new towns of the Renaissance were high-flying dreams realized in stone and marble, drawn up with joyous abandon. But by the 18th century, the rapid growth of European cities demanded a more considered, coordinated approach to planning.

Peter the Great
Under the rule of Tsar Peter I, St. Petersburg was planned and built as a great Neo-Classical city.

Under the rule of absolute European monarchs—such as in France, Germany, and Russia—rigid, but handsome, plans were often imposed by law. In the early 1700s, Peter the Great of Russia (1672–1725) laid the foundations of a new capital, St. Petersburg. He spent his reign striving to bring Russia technologically and culturally up to date with Western Europe, and as such wanted St. Petersburg to be a match for any European capital. The result was one of the greatest of all Neo-Classical cities. Similarly, Napoleon Bonaparte (1769–1821) dreamed of turning late-18th century Paris into a grandiose city of palaces and public monuments. Many of these were built, but he also modernized the city with sewers, sidewalks, a better water supply, and new markets and slaughterhouses.

In England and the United States, rational urban plans developed by consensus, with city growth in England being still fairly organic. Covent Garden, the first Renaissance square in London, was built for rich merchants and aristocrats wanting to move away from the noise and dirt of the old City of London. A few decades later it, too, had become sullied by the more unsavory aspects of city life, such as prostitution and crime. So the wealthy moved further out to newer, cleaner Georgian squares, and the city grew ever larger.

In the US, Washington, D.C. developed from the end of the 18th century. Its scheme of broad avenues linking key buildings, open spaces, and a grid pattern of streets oriented north, south, east, and west was to prove a model for town and city planners worldwide.

Center point
Commissioned by Napoleon in 1806, the Arc de Triomphe is surrounded by 12 avenues that radiate outward from it like the spokes of a wheel.

ST. GEORGE'S HALL

🖈 1854   📍 LIVERPOOL, ENGLAND   ⚒ HARVEY LONSDALE ELMES   🏛 CIVIC BUILDING

A breathtaking Neo-Classical temple housing several courts of law and a gigantic concert and meeting hall, St. George's Hall is one of the great British buildings of the first half of the 19th century. Harvey Lonsdale Elmes (1813–47) won the competition for the design of St. George's Hall, originally a concert hall, when he was just 23. He also won a competition for the design of a new Assize Court. Work on a revised design combining the two—a muscular temple in the manner of the Prussian architect,

Schinkel (1781–1841)—began in 1842. Elmes fell ill and was replaced as architect by Charles Robert Cockerell (1788–1863).

Standing on a high podium, the building is severe in style, although its massive attic story, over the concert hall, was derived from the hedonistic Baths of Caracalla, Rome *(see p.115)*. The concert hall is barrel vaulted and lavishly gilded. It boasts a colossal organ and a floor carpeted with fine ceramic tiles. The building speaks loudly of prosperity built on trade.

Statement of civic pride
St. George's Hall is the first building passengers see when leaving Liverpool's main train station.

CALEDONIA ROAD FREE CHURCH

🖈 1857   📍 GLASGOW, SCOTLAND   ⚒ ALEXANDER "GREEK" THOMSON   🏛 PLACE OF WORSHIP

The Neo-Classical movement was particularly strong in Scotland in the 19th century, and this is a stupendous, late-flowering Grecian-style church by one of Scotland's greatest architects. The prolific Alexander "Greek" Thomson (1817–75) continued the Classical tradition in his adopted Glasgow long after its influence had waned in England.

Sited in the Gorbals area of the city, this former United Presbyterian church, of which Thomson was an elder, rises on a massive west-front podium supporting an Ionic portico. Alongside, a tall, square, rather bare stone tower rockets up into the

Glaswegian cloudscape. The 1,150-seat nave of the asymmetrical church was originally lit by the many windows in the clerestory.

The church lost its congregation in 1962, at the time of the demolition of the old tenement houses in this part of Glasgow. In 1965 the inside of the building was destroyed by fire. Incomprehensibly—given the magnificence of its design and the fact that the renowned 20th-century American architectural historian, Henry-Russell Hitchcock, described it as one of the finest Romantic Classical churches in the world—the shell has stood forlorn and empty, although floodlit by night, for 40 years.

FOUR COURTS, DUBLIN

🏛 1802 📍 DUBLIN, IRELAND ✍ JAMES GANDON 🏛 CIVIC BUILDING

Influenced by Wren's Greek cross design for St. Paul's Cathedral (see p.326) and by the monumental works of Claude Nicolas Ledoux (1736–1806), the Four Courts is a tour de force by James Gandon (1743–1823), an English architect. The handsome drum surmounting the building is capped with a shallow saucer dome. The four law courtrooms themselves—Chancery, King's Bench, Exchequer, and Common Pleas—are arranged in a diagonal pattern off a great central hall beneath the drum. The roofline sculptures by Edward Smyth represent Moses, Justice, Mercy, Wisdom, and Authority. Much damaged during the Irish Civil War (1922–23), the building has been restored externally but remodeled and rearranged internally.

Impressive entrance
The mighty Corinthian portico faces the Liffey river.

CUSTOM HOUSE, DUBLIN

🏛 1791 📍 DUBLIN, IRELAND ✍ JAMES GANDON 🏛 CIVIC BUILDING

The Custom House has four facades, each different, linked by powerfully modeled corner pavilions. Influenced by Wren's royal hospitals in Chelsea and Greenwich in London, it stands close to the Four Courts. Gandon was offered the job of designing a Custom House, for the collection of excise duty, in 1781. Angry Dublin merchants, fearful that the location of the new Custom House would devalue their own properties by blocking the view, delayed its construction, but it was completed in 1791. The building is essentially plain, but there are fine sculptures along the roofline by Thomas Banks, Agostino Carlini, and Edward Smyth, who carved keystones symbolizing the rivers of Ireland. The interior of the building was destroyed during the Anglo-Irish War (1919–22), when fire melted the dome and cracked the stonework. Restoration was finally completed in the 1980s.

Riverside elegance
The Custom House is an elegant, low-lying building parading effortlessly along the banks of the Liffey river.

CAFFÈ PEDROCCHI

📅 1831 📍 PADUA, ITALY ✍ GIUSEPPE JAPPELLI & ANTONIO GRADENIGO 🏛 COMMERCIAL BUILDING

Designed as a major civic monument and meeting place, Caffè Pedrocchi also provided a delightful new covered walkway through a city famous for its covered walkways. The spacious café has never lost its popularity among locals and tourists.

It was designed by Giuseppe Jappelli (1783–1852) and Antonio Gradenigo (1806–84) in a dramatic Greek style, with elements of Roman decoration. The twin entrances are through a pair of loggias (open galleries) behind heavily Doric porticos, splendid with Roman-inspired carving and decorative ironwork. Between these first-floor entrance loggias, and set well back—enclosing a sort of courtyard at the front of the building—is a further, highly theatrical, two-story loggia in the Corinthian style.

The sides of the building are animated with Corinthian pilasters—tall, rectangular features simulating set-back pillars. The side walls resemble those of handsome public offices and do not prepare the visitor for the drama of the entrance facade. Nor do

Elegant dining
Café chairs and tables arranged in the entrance loggias are under cover, and behind a grand Grecian facade, but still open to the street.

they prepare for the entertaining Neo-Gothic extension, completed in 1842, and known as Il Pedrocchino, at the back of the building. Jappelli later indulged in a number of styles: his Teatro Verdi in Padua is Rococo, while the villas he designed are rooted in the work of Palladio.

UNIVERSITY LIBRARY, HELSINKI

📅 1845 📍 HELSINKI, FINLAND ✍ CARL LUDWIG ENGEL 🏛 LIBRARY

The University Library is one of the key buildings in the redevelopment of Helsinki under the direction of Carl Ludwig Engel (1778–1840), a Berlin-born architect who worked in Tallinn (in what is now Estonia), and St. Petersburg, Russia, before coming to Finland. The library is a substantial yellow-ocher box with three galleried rooms inside, all roofed with decorated semicircular barrel vaults; the central library features a glorious dome with sunken panels. All three

rooms are ennobled with heroic Corinthian colonnades and are beautifully lit, especially when snow lies heavily outside, reflecting the daylight. The exterior of the building is simple, clad on all sides by a parade of Corinthian half-columns and pilasters; these look like columns but are actually set into the walls of the building.

The library fuses the aesthetics of the best contemporary architecture of Prussia and St. Petersburg. It remains almost entirely as it was first built and is a delight to use. The genius of Engel's design is in the way he maximizes the use of daylight, creating a building that glows inside, in a city that can be dark for much of the year.

***Trompe l'oeil* pillars**
A series of half-columns and pilasters against the yellow walls gives the illusion of a colonnaded building.

LUTHERAN CATHEDRAL, HELSINKI

📺 1852 📱 HELSINKI, FINLAND ✍ CARL LUDWIG ENGEL 🏛 PLACE OF WORSHIP

Helsinki's mighty snow-white Lutheran Cathedral is raised on a podium reached by huge flights of granite steps and dominates virtually every view of the city. The narrow central drum, and dome, stare out across the city's harbor and the Baltic Sea. The 203 ft (62 m) high main dome is flanked by four towers with smaller Russian-style domes.

The main body of the cathedral is laid out on a Greek-cross plan, each of the four arms fronted by an identical, Corinthian portico. The interior is filled with light from the many windows. The arms of the Greek cross are lined with columns, while the drum is supported by muscular masonry piers, with Corinthian styling, from which develop arches with sunken panels. Simple box pews create an ordered appearance along the length of the nave; Greek detailing, notably over the pulpit, is sparse but finely executed. Engel began work on the design in 1818, and construction began in 1830. The building was completed by Ernst Lohrmann (1803–70), after the death of Engel in 1840.

Superior position
Looking down from the roof of the cathedral are zinc statues of the Twelve Apostles.

THE OLD CHURCH, HELSINKI

📺 1826 📱 HELSINKI, FINLAND ✍ CARL LUDWIG ENGEL 🏛 PLACE OF WORSHIP

The Old Church, standing isolated in a park in the center of Helsinki, was only intended to be a temporary structure. However, by the time the cathedral designed to replace it was completed, the population of the city had grown to such an extent that both buildings were needed. In fact, while the cathedral can seat 1,300 people, the much smaller Old Church has room for a congregation of 1,200.

The Old Church is particularly beautiful when the snow lies heavily in the park. A generous timber structure, it is animated by four projecting Doric porticos and a square tempietto (templelike structure), with triangular roof ends and capped with a small dome. The interior is simple and awash with daylight flooding in through the well-proportioned windows.

This is the oldest church in Helsinki. The park it stands in was originally a cemetery. The remains of the victims of the Great Famine of 1697 were buried here and were joined by 1,185 victims of the Great Plague of 1710, many of them Swedish soldiers. At the same time as building the church, Engel designed a stone gate at the main entrance to the park, commemorating the plague victims. Planted with elm trees, Old Church Park is a happier place today.

GENERAL STAFF HEADQUARTERS, ST. PETERSBURG

🏛 1829 📍 ST. PETERSBURG, RUSSIA ✍ KARL IVANOVICH ROSSI 🏛 MILITARY BUILDING

These commanding buildings, which formerly housed army offices, sweep in a breathtaking 1,968 ft (600 m) curve around the south side of the immense Palace Square facing the Winter Palace. The massive, complex building is now being converted, in part, into galleries and offices for the Hermitage Museum.

The facades, which disguise old and newer buildings, are essentially simple, yet culminate in a powerful central section in which the rusticated stonework of the base is superimposed with lofty Corinthian half-columns on the first floor. This central section is then shot through by a gigantic coffered (sunken-paneled) archway, allowing a street to pass underneath. This in turn is overarched by a quadriga (a sculpture of a four-horsed chariot) carrying Nike, the winged Greek goddess of victory, high over palatial St. Petersburg.

The central arch is made up of three arches at angles that match the curve of the street. The giant glass dome over one side of

Created to impress
The magnificence of these army buildings creates a powerful impression of the military might of St. Petersburg under Peter the Great.

the building lights the military library below; this is out of bounds to the public, although it houses a priceless collection of age-old military history. The design of the building was by Karl Ivanovich Rossi (1775–1849), a half-Italian born in St. Petersburg, who visited Italy for inspiration in 1804–06.

ST. ISAAC'S CATHEDRAL

🏛 1858 📍 ST. PETERSBURG, RUSSIA ✍ AUGUSTE MONTFERRAND 🏛 PLACE OF WORSHIP

This stupendous Greek-cross cathedral was commissioned by Tsar Alexander I and stands alone in a huge square. The gilded dome dominates the area, while the gallery around its base affords views across the Neva River and around the whole of St. Petersburg. The vast interior of the cathedral,

Engineering support
The weight of St. Isaac's is borne on thousands of wooden piles driven into the marshy ground.

covering 43,000 sq ft (4,000m²), was designed for 14,000 standing worshipers. It gleams with thousands of tons of semiprecious stones, including 14 different colored marbles and 43 other minerals, including malachite, jasper, porphyry, and lapis lazuli. The exterior columns are red granite. For many years after the Russian Revolution, St. Isaac's was used as a Museum of Atheism. It has now been thoroughly restored and houses a large collection of 19th-century art.

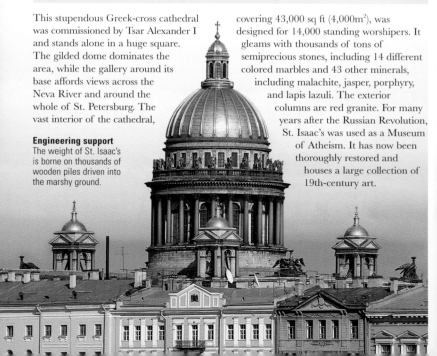

NEW ADMIRALTY

🏛 1823   📍 ST. PETERSBURG, RUSSIA   ✏ ADRIAN DMITRIEVITCH ZAKHAROV   🏛 MILITARY BUILDING

The New Admiralty fuses Classical forms in a truly Russian manner. This imposing military building is the undoubted masterpiece of Adrian Dmitrievitch Zakharov. While training in Paris, Zakharov had clearly been fascinated by the fantasy drawings of Étienne Louis Boullée, whose influence can be seen in the bombastic central gateway beneath the gilded spire of this spectacular design.

The New Admiralty is one of the most original of all Neo-Classical buildings. Zakharov's theme was the sea and Russia's power over it.

The main 1,230 ft (375 m) long facade is divided into a series of pavilions terminating in powerful Doric temple fronts. The entrance tower and sky-piercing spire are 240 ft (73 m) high. Tiered like a wedding cake, the tower has a frieze showing Neptune, the Roman god of the sea, handing Peter the Great his trident of power. Higher up are four statues of ancient military leaders: Achilles, Ajax, Pyrrhus, and Alexander the Great. Higher still, the tower's 28 Ionic columns support a cornice bearing 28 sculptures symbolizing air, earth, fire, and water, the seasons of the year, and the winds of each compass point. The ways of the sea and the Russian navy are here truly captured in stone.

ADRIAN DMITRIEVITCH ZAKHAROV

Russian architect Zakharov (1761–1811) studied at the St. Petersburg Academy of Fine Arts before traveling to Paris in 1782, where, for four years, he was a pupil of Jean François Chalgrin, architect of the Arc de Triomphe. He returned to the Academy as professor and in 1806 was commissioned by Tsar Alexander I to rebuild Peter the Great's original Admiralty. His other major works include the Academy of Science, St. Petersburg.

Naval pointers
A weathervane on the pinnacle of the spire is in the shape of Peter the Great's personal warship.

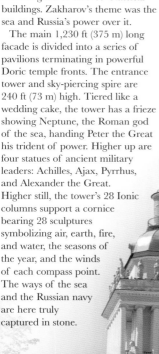

NEO-CLASSICISM IN THE UNITED STATES
ca. 1775–1850

The Neo-Classicism of the United States was affected by a number of factors, among them the prevailing taste of early settlers, the general thrust of 18th-century culture at the time of the Declaration of Independence (1776), and the belief, nurtured by Thomas Jefferson (1743–1826), author of the famous Declaration, that the architecture of Greece and Rome was both inherently civil and democratic.

Despite these noble associations, many of the most original and handsome Neo-Classical buildings in the US were plantation houses built in the South for wealthy slave-owners. Both Greece and Rome had depended on slaves, of course, and so did Jefferson in his home state of Virginia, where this self-taught architect designed the State Capitol in Richmond and the University of Virginia at Charlottesville *(see p.371)*.

STYLE FOR A NEW CAPITAL
Neo-Classicism was favored by revolutionary governments on both sides of the Atlantic, and Congress chose it for the major monuments of Washington, D.C., with the Capitol itself *(see pp.368–9)* eventually looking like a secular St. Peter's, Rome, or St. Paul's, London. The initial city plan was drawn up in 1791 by a French engineer, Major Pierre Charles L'Enfant (1754–1825), who had come to America in 1777 and served with George Washington during the Revolutionary War. The result was a system of intersecting diagonal avenues superimposed on a gridiron plan, based partly on Le Nôtre's garden designs at Versailles *(see pp.320–1)*, and also on the plans of newly Classicized European cities given to L'Enfant by Thomas Jefferson. The broad avenues L'Enfant designed for Washington radiated from the Capitol *(see pp.368–69)* and the White House *(see p.370)*. As the capital of the new nation, Washington, D.C. was intended to be an impressive model for city planning throughout the United States, as well as a symbol of governmental power to be looked upon with suitable admiration by other nations. The plan conceived by L'Enfant is little changed today. It had been a remarkably bold and mature adventure for this infant nation.

◁ JEFFERSON'S ROTUNDA AT THE UNIVERSITY OF VIRGINIA (THE COUNTRY'S FIRST STATE UNIVERSITY) WAS BASED ON THE PANTHEON IN ROME. THE BUILDING, WHICH OVERLOOKS THE UNIVERSITY'S CENTRAL LAWN, HOUSED THE LIBRARY.

ELEMENTS

As the United States began to take its place as the world's most powerful country, its architects turned to Neo-Classical forms to reflect the spirit of ancient Athenian democracy and of republican Rome. Neo-Classicism flourished in New England, applied particularly to sober geometric libraries and government buildings, but also—with a lighter touch—to residences.

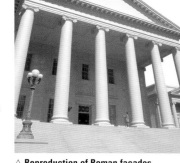

△ **Reproduction of Roman facades**
The State Capitol, Richmond, Virginia, was designed by Thomas Jefferson. Based on the Maison Carrée, Nîmes, a 1st-century Roman temple, it was an idealization of a "republican" building, although the Maison Carrée dates, in fact, from the heyday of imperial Rome.

Balcony for ceremonial salutes by the head of state

△ **Influence of Palladio**
Thomas Jefferson did much to introduce his fellow Americans to the spirit of the Renaissance architect Andrea Palladio. The White House, Washington, D.C., shows Palladian touches—harmonious, symmetrical floor plans and extensive use of pediments and columns are prominent features.

A symbol of power and ambition

△ **Wrap-around Classical porticos**
Perhaps a little ironically, given the ideals of the Founding Fathers, one of the finest uses of "Greek style" was in the exceptionally fine plantation houses designed for wealthy Southern slave-owners. With their shady porticos, these houses were well adapted to the local climate.

A monumental 666 ft (169 m) tall

△ **Neo-Classical city terrace**
Washington Square, New York, was a version of a type of housing development well known in London, Dublin, and Edinburgh. Regular facades with sash windows and doors flanked by Roman columns were the norm.

White granite facing

◁ **Giant obelisk**
An urban gesture greater than Napoleon's Arc de Triomphe, the Washington Monument dominates downtown Washington, D.C. Based on the ancient Egyptian obelisks, it was built to match the scale and ambition of the US capital.

INDEPENDENCE HALL

🏛 1745   📍 PHILADELPHIA, PA   ✍ ANDREW HAMILTON & WILLIAM STRICKLAND   🏛 CIVIC BUILDING

This building is justly famous for the pivotal role it played in US history. It was here, on July 4th, 1776, that the Declaration of Independence was adopted; this document set out the rights "to life, liberty, and the pursuit of happiness" that underpin the theory of government in the US.

The Hall is a characterful Georgian building which emerged over a long period, with several architects contributing to its evolution. The main body of the building is of handsome red brick with white stone dressings; it was completed in 1745, first serving as the State House of the Colony of Pennsylvania. A tower

with a distinctive steeple was added in 1753 but was demolished and rebuilt in 1832 by William Strickland (1787–1854), one of the architects of the US Capitol in Washington.

The architects of Independence Hall were much influenced by Queen Anne-style red-brick houses which, in turn, had been informed by mid-17th century Dutch architecture. Both the Dutch and English were settlers here, and they passed on the tradition for modest yet spirited design. In its time, the Hall has served as a state house, a museum of art and natural history, and a court of law. It was designated a national historic site in 1943.

MONTICELLO

🏛 1809   📍 CHARLOTTESVILLE, VA   ✍ THOMAS JEFFERSON   🏛 RESIDENCE

This ingenious country house was designed by Thomas Jefferson (1743–1826) for his own use. Jefferson—the author of the Declaration of Independence, the US minister to France, and President of the United States (1800–08)—began this mountaintop eyrie as a more or less conventional Palladian design. However, during an extended posting to Paris he absorbed the latest Neo-Classical ideas and reworked Monticello into an altogether more fascinating and intellectually rigorous building. Built and rebuilt in two stages, from 1768 to 1784 and 1796 to 1809,

Monticello had 33 well-lit rooms and no fewer than five indoor privies—in short, a highly desirable residence. It also housed Jefferson's remarkable 6,700-volume library, which was to form the literary foundation of the Library of Congress. In 1923, the house, pavilions, and grounds—once tended by Jefferson's slaves—were sold to the Thomas Jefferson Foundation, which takes care of them to this day.

Impressive entrance
Monticello boasts two main entrances, one under a handsome Doric portico *(below)*, which leads into a fine domed reception room.

CAPITOL, WASHINGTON

🖂 1863 📍 WASHINGTON, D.C. ✍ THOMAS USTICK WALTER 🏛 GOVERNMENT BUILDING

Dozens of government buildings across the United States are modeled on this triumphal design overlooking the Potomac River. The original design by William Thornton (1759–1828), Benjamin Henry Latrobe (1764–1820), and Charles Bulfinch (1763–1844) was begun in 1793 but proved to be inadequate for both practical and political reasons. Walter (1804–87)

VIEW OF THE WEST FRONT

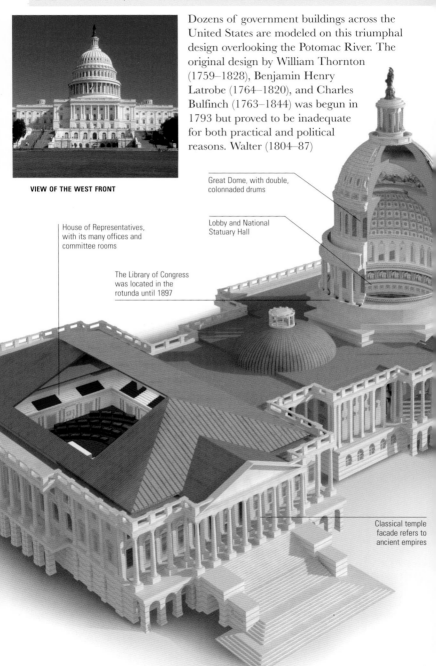

Great Dome, with double, colonnaded drums

Lobby and National Statuary Hall

House of Representatives, with its many offices and committee rooms

The Library of Congress was located in the rotunda until 1897

Classical temple facade refers to ancient empires

created a much bigger building. The south wing contains the chambers of the House of Representatives (the lower House of the legislative assembly). The north wing is home to the Senate (the upper House). The wings meet at the Rotunda, under a grand cast-iron dome lit by 108 windows. Under the dome is the National Statuary Hall, containing an important collection of paintings and sculptures of historic figures.

The Senate moved into its current chambers in the north wing in 1860

△ **Pediment statuary**
Classical-style figures on the pediment over the main entrance of the Capitol represent the themes of liberty, wisdom, and civil government for the American nation.

△ **Dome interior**
Light pours in through the many windows in this huge, fire-proof dome. Neo-Classical symmetry, as seen here, symbolized the pride of an emerging powerful nation.

Georgia marble replaced less robust sandstone in 20th-century renovations

In session ▷
Semicircular seating in the House of Representatives symbolizes democracy, drawing members together as equals. Both Houses also have an upper public gallery.

THE WHITE HOUSE

🏛 1817 📍 WASHINGTON, D.C. ✎ JAMES HOBAN 🏛 GOVERNMENT BUILDING

The official house of the US president and, by extension, one of the most famous buildings in the world, the White House was originally designed in 1792 by the Irish architect James Hoban (c.1762–1831) in the Palladian style and built, in sandstone, by masons shipped from Edinburgh and by local slaves. Porticos were added by B. H. Latrobe in 1807–08. Burned by the British during the War of 1812, the White House was rebuilt between 1815 and 1817 and then gradually remodeled over many decades by such distinguished architects as

McKim Mead & White, who replaced the conservatories in 1902 with an executive office building, the West Wing, for the president and his staff. These were enlarged in 1909 when the famous Oval Room, the president's private office, was added. The house was much rebuilt with a steel frame between 1948 and 1952, when the old timbers holding up ceilings were found to be giving way under the weight of office.

Presidential portico
Until Theodore Roosevelt became president in 1901, the house was known as the Executive Mansion.

WASHINGTON MONUMENT

🏛 1884 📍 WASHINGTON, D.C.
✎ ROBERT MILLS 🏛 MONUMENT

The realization of this soaring monument to the first US president took nearly a century. The first suggestion was for a conventional equestrian statue. Work on the magnificent design finally chosen began in 1848 and, interrupted in 1861 by the Civil War, took nearly 40 years to complete. Built of stone clad in white marble, the 555 ft (167 m) monument was to have risen from a huge circular colonnaded pantheon housing statues of other presidents and national heroes, but the design was simplified as the costs were too much for the public, no matter how highly they regarded their founding hero.

TEMPLE OF SCOTTISH RITE

🏛 1915 📍 WASHINGTON, D.C.
✎ JOHN RUSSELL POPE 🏛 CEREMONIAL BUILDING

This monumental and unexpected building, based on the design of the tomb of King Mausolus—one of the "Seven Wonders of the World"—has been the headquarters of The Scottish Rite of Freemasonry since 1915. It was the first major work of John Russell Pope (1874–1937), who went on to design Washington's National Gallery of Art and the Jefferson Memorial. Up a ritualistic stairway, massive bronze doors are guarded by a pair of huge stone sphinxes representing wisdom and power. Beyond are lavish ceremonial chambers, rich in arcane masonic detail and symbolism.

WESTOVER

🏛 1736 📍 CHARLES CITY COUNTY, VIRGINIA
✍ WILLIAM BYRD II 🏛 RESIDENCE

Westover was built for William Byrd II, the Virginian explorer and writer. It is an exceptionally grand American house for this period: standing on a high bluff overlooking the James River and capped with a high roof and tall chimneys, it was clearly meant to be seen and admired. Its severe red-brick design and structure was based on Drayton Court, an English house Byrd knew well.

This plantation house comprises a central block and two wings, one of which once housed Byrd's impressive 4,000-volume library. This was destroyed during the Civil War, and a replacement wing built in 1900. Westover's grand hall, running the depth of the house, features mahogany elements shipped from London, while marble used in the reception rooms was imported from Italy. A fascinating labyrinthine basement included rooms that were used for Byrd's extravagant store of claret and madeira wines, and a means of escape in the event of raids by Indians.

STATE CAPITOL, RICHMOND

🏛 1788 📍 RICHMOND, VIRGINIA
✍ THOMAS JEFFERSON 🏛 CIVIC BUILDING

Thomas Jefferson designed this building on top of Shockoe Hill, overlooking the falls of the James River, with the French antiquarian and decorator Charles-Louis Clerisseau. They modeled it, loosely, on the Maison Carrée, Nîmes *(see p.108)*, which Jefferson had visited, although they substituted plain Ionic capitols for the fluted Corinthian ones in France. Inside, a proud statue of George Washington stands in a domed rotunda.

UNIVERSITY OF VIRGINIA

🏛 1825 📍 CHARLOTTESVILLE, VIRGINIA ✍ THOMAS JEFFERSON 🏛 UNIVERSITY

Thomas Jefferson's university is a model of its kind. Student residences linked by arcades parade up and down an immaculate lawn, at the top of which is a beautiful brick rotunda, effectively a half-size version of the Pantheon in Rome. The university has grown greatly since the completion of the original site in 1826, when Jefferson himself was still hosting college talks, lunches, and dinners at nearby Monticello. The dome of the Rotunda caught fire in 1895 and was rebuilt by the distinguished architect Stanford White, who made significant alterations to Jefferson's interior. The original design was reinstated in time for the 200th anniversary celebration of American independence in 1976.

Classical campus
The Neo-Classical core of the campus forms the lasting image of this august institution.

The industrial world

THE 19TH CENTURY was characterized by industrialization and great leaps forward in transportation and communication. Innovations such as trains, electricity, the telegraph, and, at the century's end, telephones and cars changed Western society completely. For architects, old certainties had to give way to the demands of a re-energized world.

"I am such a locomotive," wrote the English Victorian architect, Augustus Pugin (1812–52), "being always flying about." Pugin, a powerhouse of 19th-century energy, burned himself out and was dead by the age of 40. During a firecracker career, which began at the age of 15 designing Gothic furniture for George IV at Windsor Castle, Pugin built a host of churches in industrial towns across England and Ireland. Pugin worked with a dedicated team of builders, craftsmen, and decorators to achieve a vision of England restored to what he believed to be its full Gothic and Catholic glory of the 14th century. "An assistant, sir?" he barked at a visitor flabbergasted by his prodigious output of designs for monasteries, churches, houses, furniture, books, wallpaper, and every last detail of the new Palace of Westminster, London *(see p.400)*. "Never employ one. I would kill him in a week." The influence of Pugin's Neo-Gothic designs reached as far as Australia and the United States. The reason this evangelizing Victorian architect was able to build so much so quickly—besides his innate drive and furious energy—was the railway.

Locomotion
By the late-19th century, public railroads had spread their iron tentacles across the landscape of an industrialized England.

KEY DATES

1803 Richard Trevithick builds the world's first steam locomotive	**1830** Opening of the Liverpool and Manchester Railway, the first fully steam-operated main line	**1866** First transatlantic telegraph cable laid by Brunel's *The Great Eastern* steamship	**1879** Thomas Edison invents the electric light bulb	***ca.* 1880** Start of massive flow of immigrants into the US from Europe
1800	**1830**	**1860**		**1880**
1829 The Rainhill Trials: George Stephenson's *Rocket* reaches a sensational 52 kph (36 mph)	**1862** Frenchman Louis Pasteur perfects the process of pasteurization to protect food from contamination	**1876** Alexander Graham Bell, a Scot, invents the telephone	**1880** Siemens and Halske invent world's first electric-powered elevator	

THE TRAIN AGE

Not all architects felt as Pugin did. The coming of the railroads and the rapid spread of industry provoked a backlash from sentimentalists and nostalgics. This was forged into the Arts and Crafts Movement, nurtured by the English craftsman and polemicist William Morris (1834–96), which inspired romantic, thoughtful, handmade buildings that did their best to hold the modern world at bay.

The railroads, meanwhile, developed at such an astonishing speed that by the time of Pugin's death, trains had become part of everyday life across Europe and much of the US. By the turn of the century, locomotives were capable of top speeds of 93 mph (150 kmh), with many express trains clocking averages of

50–56 mph (80–90 kmh). Some of these trains were like hotels on wheels, with dining and sleeping cars, barbers, bathrooms, electric light, and attendants galore. Track and signaling had improved by immensely, so that trains rode faster, more smoothly, and more safely than ever before.

The impact of the railways was not limited to making overland travel faster and more comfortable—it also

Telegraph pole and wires
The electric telegraph enabled messages to be sent long distance in Morse code. The first line was set up between Baltimore and Washington in 1844.

1885 First gasoline-driven car, a three-wheeler, produced by Karl Benz, Mannheim, Germany

1886 Invention of aluminum production process, simultaneously, in France and the US

1889 Gustave Eiffel completes his famous tower for the opening of the international Paris Exhibition

1894 Guglielmo Marconi demonstrates the first radio transmission

1900 In Paris, the Otis Elevator Company of New York demonstrates the first escalator

1900

1903 Wright Brothers make world's first powered flight from Kitty Hawke, Ohio

1908 Henry Ford unveils his *Model-T*, a rugged mass-produced automobile for everyman

1914 World War I begins, after the assassination of Archduke Franz Ferdinand

1919 The Bauhaus School of architecture and design is set up in Germany by Walter Gropius

1920

had profound social and economic effects. As the railroad network grew more integrated, previously unthinkable trips became relatively simple by train. In 1869, for example, it became possible to ride right across the US by the "iron road" for the first time. Local time differences gradually vanished as standard railroad time took over—essential for the reliable timetables required to ensure the safe and efficient running of train services.

Not only did trains slash travel times on land, but great steamships also began to quicken sea voyages. The first steamer to regularly cross the Atlantic was *The Great Western* (1838), designed by British engineer Isambard Kingdom Brunel *(see p.387)*, while *The Great Eastern* (1858), also designed by Brunel, laid the first transatlantic telegraph cable in 1866.

With faster transportation and new forms of communication, such as the telegraph and (later) the telephone, the world seemed to be getting smaller. It became increasingly easy for ideas, as well as people, to travel between cities, countries, and even cultures, helping to spread the radical new theories of figures such as Charles Darwin and Karl Marx (1818–83).

IRON WORKHORSES
Being capable of hauling many tons of raw materials, such as coal, timber, and iron ore, long distances from mines and forests to smelting plants and factories, the railroads helped to step up the pace of industrialization. They could also carry manufactured goods to points of distribution. From an architectural perspective, this meant that building materials could be transported readily from one

Steamships on the Suez Canal, Egypt
Opened in 1869, the Suez Canal linked the Mediterranean to the Red Sea, allowing ships to travel between Europe and Asia without circumnavigating Africa.

Otis elevator
In 1854, Elisha Otis (1811–61) demonstrated the first safety passenger elevator, which was steam-powered. Electric elevators were developed in the 1880s.

location to another. Now it became possible to build cheaply in brick in areas where there was no suitable clay for brick-making, or to build relatively cheaply in stone and marble in towns and cities far from the places where these materials were quarried. Many components of the Crystal Palace *(see p.384)*, built for the Great Exhibition of 1851, were transported by train from Birmingham, "Workshop of the World," to London, "The Smoke," where the building was erected in Hyde Park.

Railways gave architects and builders the ability to transport ideas, drawings, and materials wherever they wished, with both positive and negative results. While good architects could now be employed to raise standards in previously neglected towns, there was also a danger of buildings becoming too homogeneous, as testified by the swathes of red brick houses that came to smother Victorian England during the 19th century.

CHARLES DARWIN

The British naturalist Charles Darwin (1809–82) developed the theory of evolution by natural selection, which describes how one species can develop into another as animals adapt to suit their environments. He based his ideas on a study of thousands of plant and animal species from around the world. His book *On the Origin of Species by Means of Natural Selection* (1859) caused not only a revolution in biological science, but also an outcry among Christians because it challenged the creation story in the Bible.

Darwin's compass
Darwin collected his specimens when he was official naturalist on HMS *Beagle* during an around-the-world scientific trip in the 1830s.

THE MACHINE AGE
ca. 1800–1914

The Industrial Revolution broke out in England in the mid-18th century. The application of reliable steam power to productive machinery, the ability to ship goods worldwide, colonies to exploit, and the rise of the enfranchised and industrious middle classes were just some of the many reasons why Britain was quick to industrialize. Conservative architects, however, found themselves wrong-footed.

Industrialism brought misery for the many millions toiling in mechanized sweatshops in cities as yet unable to cope with such sudden, dirty growth. Pollution, disease, and new forms of accident were rife. While the Industrial Revolution also brought many benefits in its wake, these were not always apparent to architects. This was understandable: at the very moment that architects were forming themselves into professional institutes, the Industrial Revolution threatened to mechanize their age-old art and make their craftsmen redundant. To an extent, their fears were well founded.

NEW STRUCTURES, NEW MATERIALS
The earliest industrial structures proved surprisingly beautiful, such as the Iron Bridge *(see p.382)* spanning the Severn River in the English Midlands, built in 1779. Such structures were far removed from the aesthetic path trodden by architects. Many of the first monuments of the Industrial Age were designed and built by engineers. Architects, meanwhile, often choosing to decry what they saw as the uncultivated work of engineers, slugged it out among themselves in an arcane Battle of the Styles that was to rage, more or less, up to World War I. However, the new materials that were revolutionizing engineering, especially steel and reinforced concrete, eventually found their way into architecture, bringing dramatic changes in the way buildings could be constructed and thus opening up new design avenues. Until the Industrial Revolution, the walls of buildings had to carry their own weight. Now they could be reduced to light skins, or what became known in the 20th century as curtain walls. As for prefabrication, Paxton's Crystal Palace *(see p.384)* was the brilliant, if shocking, precursor of buildings yet to come.

◁ COMPLETED IN 1889, THE ELEGANT EIFFEL TOWER, PARIS, WAS DESIGNED BY THE FRENCH ENGINEER AND BRIDGE-BUILDER GUSTAVE EIFFEL. THE 986 FT (300 M) TOWER IS A RUGGED TRACERY OF WROUGHT-IRON GIRDERS.

ELEMENTS

The Industrial Revolution was to rock the world of architectural form and aesthetics, but not immediately. Gothic Revivalists and Neo-Classicists were quite happy to use the new materials and industrial techniques to achieve the effects they wanted. Yet there was no question: a revolution was in the making.

Cast-iron Doric columns

◁ "Curved" glass
The influential design of the Palm House, Kew Gardens, London, by Decimus Burton and Richard Turner, made spectacular use of both cast and wrought iron. The glass follows the smooth curves of the structure with assurance. It was a remarkable feat.

△ Classical cast iron
In the 1820s John Nash, an entrepreneurial Regency architect, specified cast-iron Doric columns in his design for Carlton House Terrace, London, for ease of construction.

▽ Engineering design
In the industrial age, bridges became the province of engineers rather than architects. Isambard Kingdom Brunel combined engineering genius with aspirational design from the past, constructing massive Egyptian-style stone pylons to support the giant iron cables and rods for Clifton Suspension Bridge, England.

◁ Prefabrication
Prefabricated iron-and-glass structures were a marvel of the age. Curving roofs and delicate iron tracery, linked by great expanses of imported plate glass, created translucent exhibition space for Joseph Paxton's Crystal Palace of 1851.

Iron suspension rods

Trains travel 1.5 miles
(2.4 km) across the
Firth of Forth

Immensely strong
riveted tubular
steel trusses

△ Form and function
The vast steel trusses of the
Forth Railway Bridge, Scotland,
designed by Benjamin Baker
and John Fowler, are its
defining feature. Such dramatic
yet honest construction was to
nurture a belief in functionalism
in the coming generation of
architects. The bridge contains
54,000 tons of steel and took
eight years to build.

Huge windows flanked
by opening sashes

Genesis of the skyscraper ▷
Chicago's 14-story Reliance
Building of 1895 was considered
revolutionary. Although the facade
undulates and features Gothic
detailing, this is the prototype of
thousands of tall, steel-framed
20th-century office towers.

△ Iron and glass roofs
Barrel vaulting reminiscent of a
Gothic cathedral was recreated
in iron and glass to create a
spectacular roof at the Galleria
Vittorio Emanuele, in Milan.

△ Design to symbolize function
The versatility of iron created new
design opportunities. The skeletal
frame of the University Museum,
Oxford, evokes the skeletons of the
dinosaurs exhibited there.

△ City attractions
After the Eiffel Tower, every city
wanted an iron landmark. Lisbon
chose the Neo-Gothic Santa Justa
street elevator, for dramatic transportation between street levels.

CLIFTON SUSPENSION BRIDGE

🖳 1863   📍 BRISTOL, SOUTHWEST ENGLAND   ✏️ ISAMBARD KINGDOM BRUNEL   🏛 BRIDGE

This was not the first suspension bridge built in Britain, but it was—and remains—one of the most impressive. It was the first major work by Brunel (1806–59), who was only 24 when he designed it. The bridge was all the more remarkable for having been built against the advice of Thomas Telford (1757–1834), designer in 1815 of the smaller Menai Suspension Bridge, which had been nearly destroyed by crosswinds. The size of Clifton Bridge is impressive: the main span is 702 ft (214 m) long and is suspended 250 ft (76 m) above the Severn Gorge. More memorable still is the sense that this is an engineering project thrillingly transformed into a masterpiece of abstract architecture.

Expensive innovation
Financial difficulties plagued this project, and delayed construction for many years. It was eventually completed four years after Brunel's death.

IRON BRIDGE, COALBROOKDALE

🖳 1779   📍 SHROPSHIRE, ENGLAND   ✏️ ABRAHAM DARBY III & THOMAS PRITCHARD   🏛 BRIDGE

With improvements in iron smelting in the 18th century, iron's potential as a material for engineering and construction naturally increased. Iron was not just stronger and lighter than stone and with a wider range of possible applications, it became progressively cheaper to make. That said, at this stage any uses it might have in architecture were generally considered to be purely utilitarian rather than aesthetic.

Yet what is remarkable about this iron bridge (the world's first) is its obvious, slim elegance; it is a structure that could only have been built in iron. Here, function and form merge seamlessly. The bridge was built by Abraham Darby III (1750–91) and may have been based on a design by the architect Thomas Pritchard. It is a measure of its success that, while it was being built, traffic on the river below it was never disrupted. On the other hand, it highlighted the risks of new technology: it plunged Darby into debt for the rest of his life.

Strength and elegance
The 100 ft (30 m) span of the Iron Bridge is supported on five cast-iron arches, each made in two halves.

THE PALM HOUSE, KEW GARDENS

1848 LONDON, ENGLAND DECIMUS BURTON & RICHARD TURNER GLASSHOUSE

The Palm House at Kew Gardens was a direct descendant of the slightly earlier (and equally large) conservatory at Chatsworth, Derbyshire, built by Joseph Paxton (1801–65), who went on to design the Crystal Palace *(see pp.384–5)*. There are differences between the buildings. Paxton had arranged his glass sheets in sharp ridges and furrows; here, they are applied in even planes to create a single smooth surface. Similarly, though the Palm House echoes the "double vaults" of Chatsworth (in which a shallow vault supported a second smaller one), at Kew these double vaults are confined to a central block from which two single-vault arms, with curved, apselike ends, extend. Yet it is the similarities that count. Both Chatsworth and Kew made triumphantly clear the possibilities of pre-fabrication in iron and glass. A revolutionary style of building, which clearly anticipated mass production, was being created.

The birth of prefabrication
Elegance and utility combine to produce a building that looks fragile but has withstood the test of time.

THE COAL EXCHANGE

1849 LONDON, ENGLAND J. B. BUNNING COMMERCIAL BUILDING

The masonry exterior of the Coal Exchange, since demolished, was built in a respectful Italian Renaissance style of a kind obviously appropriate for polite society. The interior, by contrast, was daringly forward-looking. The building's circular central trading court was almost entirely cast iron. The walls were divided into three stories, each with cast-iron balconies supported on brackets, themselves embellished with more expensive (hence less used) wrought iron. Above them was a glass dome with cast-iron ribs, a direct precursor of that at the slightly later Reading Room of the British Museum.

Elegance and comfort
The central trading court of the exchange, where coal prices were set and shares in production traded, was naturally lit by a 74 ft (22.5 m) high glass dome.

CRYSTAL PALACE

🖼 1851 📍 LONDON, ENGLAND ✎ JOSEPH PAXTON 🏛 PUBLIC BUILDING

CRYSTAL PALACE, ACROSS HYDE PARK

In 1851, Crystal Palace was built in Hyde Park, to house the Great Exhibition. This was a great 1,851 ft (564 m) long, prefabricated structure of glass, iron, and timber. It was the masterpiece of Joseph Paxton (1801–65), who had experimented with the design and construction of lightweight palm and lily houses in

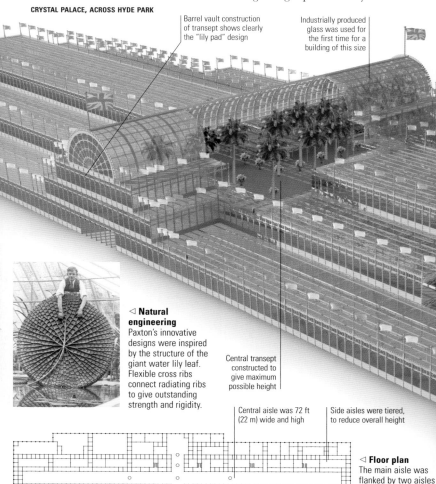

Barrel vault construction of transept shows clearly the "lily pad" design

Industrially produced glass was used for the first time for a building of this size

◁ **Natural engineering**
Paxton's innovative designs were inspired by the structure of the giant water lily leaf. Flexible cross ribs connect radiating ribs to give outstanding strength and rigidity.

Central transept constructed to give maximum possible height

Central aisle was 72 ft (22 m) wide and high

Side aisles were tiered, to reduce overall height

◁ **Floor plan**
The main aisle was flanked by two aisles on either side and broken by an equally wide transept.

the gardens of Chatsworth House, Derbyshire. Paxton made maximum use of plate glass—a recent invention—employing 300,000 sheets rolled for the purpose in France. Iron members were cast near Birmingham, shipped to London by train, and installed within 48 hours, still warm from the foundry. Crystal Palace was the world's first large-scale prefabricated building, foreshadowing a new generation of factories. In 1852, after the Great Exhibition closed, the entire building was moved to Sydenham, in southeast London, but sadly it was destroyed by fire in 1936.

△ **Built as a conservatory**
The roof of the transept was barrel-vaulted, and raised far above the height of the main aisle in order to house a growing tree. This was a last-minute addition to Paxton's original rectilinear design but, visually, a great success.

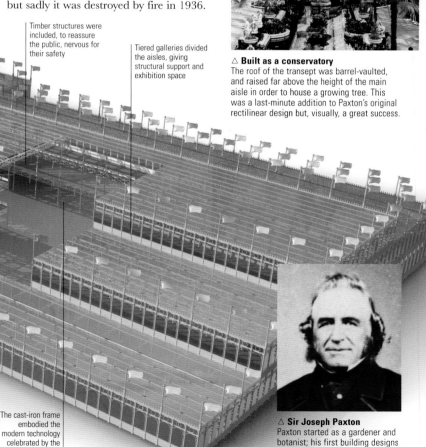

Timber structures were included, to reassure the public, nervous for their safety

Tiered galleries divided the aisles, giving structural support and exhibition space

The cast-iron frame embodied the modern technology celebrated by the exhibition

△ **Sir Joseph Paxton**
Paxton started as a gardener and botanist; his first building designs were for conservatories.

ORIEL CHAMBERS

🏛 1864   📍 LIVERPOOL, ENGLAND
✍ PETER ELLIS   🏛 COMMERCIAL BUILDING

Designed by Peter Ellis (1804–84), a relatively unknown Liverpool architect, Oriel Chambers illustrates how the industrial cities of northern England helped to forge a new architecture for Victorian Britain. In part, this was a straightforward response to new commercial realities, which, inevitably, demanded new kinds of building. But there was a sense, too, of technological novelty being celebrated for its own sake. The frame of Oriel Chambers, for example, is cast iron, while the exterior of the building, dominated by large, projecting oriel windows, makes almost no effort to ape any historical style. Much criticized at the time, Oriel Chambers proved to be one of the most influential buildings of its age.

KING'S CROSS STATION

🏛 1852   📍 LONDON, ENGLAND
✍ LEWIS CUBITT   🏛 TRAIN STATION

King's Cross Station was among the earliest of London's major train stations to be built. As such, it was a building type for which no obvious models or templates existed. Furthermore, although an emphatic statement was clearly required to herald the arrival of the railway age, it was one that had to be married to a purely practical consideration: the need for platforms, preferably under cover. The pragmatic solution of architect Lewis Cubitt (1799–1883) was a vast, almost entirely unadorned, brick-built Italianate structure. Its facade consisted of a central tower between two large arches, which directly echoed the·two glass-and-iron barrel vaults covering the platforms behind them. The result is one of London's most satisfying early Victorian buildings—a pair of triumphal arches pressed into improbable service on behalf of the railways.

GARDNER'S WAREHOUSE

🏛 1856   📍 GLASGOW, SCOTLAND   ✍ JOHN BAIRD I   🏛 COMMERCIAL BUILDING

The new possibilities opened up by iron-and-glass construction in the industrial age were dramatically demonstrated by Gardner's Warehouse. This was not just one of the most technologically advanced buildings in what was rapidly becoming one of the leading industrial centers of the British Empire, but it was also a startlingly elegant example of how purely functional demands, in tandem with new building techniques, could produce structures of genuine merit. At first glance, what is most memorable about Gardner's Warehouse is the exceptional size of the windows and, as a direct consequence, the delicacy of its framework. In an age when

architectural worth was usually equated with ponderous historicism, whether Classical or Gothic, Gardner's Warehouse was busily (and not a little surreptitiously) rewriting the rules. This is not to say that the building entirely forsakes historical precedents. The understated cornice, and the round-headed windows on the second, third, and fourth floors, owe a clear debt to a variety of Italian early Renaissance models. There is similarly no structural reason why the windows should become smaller on each succeeding floor. But these are quibbles. Baird's building was an unmistakable signpost to a new direction in architecture. The Modern was being born.

RAILWAY ARCHITECTURE

Greek temples, Gothic castles, giant greenhouses:
no building was ever too big, bold, or heroic for the
Victorian railway entrepreneurs and their trains.
Railways were the wonder of the age, steaming
their way promiscuously into cities. They
struggled magnificently to find an
architectural style that was distinctly their own.

If Victorian railway architects began with
Greek- and Roman-style public buildings,
it was because they too were building an
empire—of steam and steel—and they
wanted to impress. London's Euston

St. Pancras, London
Built in 1868–77, St.
Pancras was one of the
finest stations of its day.

Arch, a fine Greek
propylaeum, or
pedimented gateway,
marking the
entrance of the
world's first trunk
railway—the
London and
Birmingham (1838)
—testified to the
economic and social
importance of this
revolutionary
new mode of
transportation.

Railway
architecture
continued in this
Classical tradition
into the 20th
century, reaching
its apotheosis with
the designs of New
York's Penn and

**Isambard
Kingdom Brunel**
Perhaps the greatest ever
British engineer, Brunel
(1806–59) built tunnels,
bridges, and viaducts for
the Great Western Railway.
He also designed Bristol
Temple Meads Station.

Grand Central stations. Between the 1830s
and World War I, architectural fashions
came and went. The railways were also
partly responsible for the repetitive design
that sprang up beside their tracks, as they
strove to build cheaply and efficiently to keep
up with the pace of their own development.

Gare de l'Est, Paris
Among the first generation of train stations, the Gare
de l'Est was built between 1847 and 1850 to serve
the line between Paris and Strasbourg.

LES HALLES CENTRALES

⌛ AFTER 1853   📍 PARIS, FRANCE
✍ VICTOR BALTARD   🏛 COMMERCIAL BUILDING

Les Halles, begun in 1853 and added to until as late as the 1930s before being demolished in 1971, were a product of the rebuilding of central Paris by Baron Eugène Georges Haussmann (1809–91). They were the city's principal food markets and, as such, were prime candidates for construction in iron and glass—materials that were not merely functional, but flexible. Their essentially utilitarian character made them ideal for buildings that need have little or no pretension to architectural distinction. In some ways, Les Halles represented a lost opportunity. The original proposal was for an iron and glass vault 300 ft (91 m) wide. This was astonishingly ambitious: much larger than any comparable contemporary structure in England— larger, indeed, than anything built until the end of the century. Nonetheless, what emerged was impressive enough: six individual structures with large glass windows and partly glazed roofs.

LIBRARY OF SAINTE GENEVIÈVE

⌛ 1850   📍 PARIS, FRANCE
✍ HENRI LABROUSTE   🏛 LIBRARY

The Library of Sainte Geneviève marks a key moment in the evolution of iron-framed buildings. It was a major public building with a handsome Renaissance palazzo-style masonry facade and an all-iron frame that was deliberately on view. The length of the Reading Room on the main, upper floor has two high, iron barrel vaults supported in the center by a line of slim cast-iron columns. Unusually, the low-pitched roof is also made of iron.

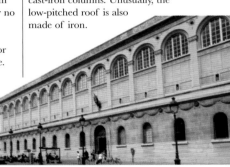

NATIONAL LIBRARY, PARIS

⌛ 1868   📍 PARIS, FRANCE   ✍ HENRI LABROUSTE   🏛 LIBRARY

Labrouste's championship of iron and glass, begun at the Library of Sainte Geneviève in the 1840s, continued in spectacular style in the National Library. Even more than at Sainte Geneviève, Labrouste (1801–75) made no attempt to disguise the building's construction—in fact, he positively reveled in it. Combined with unusually rich levels of delicate decoration, the result is notably successful. The main Reading Room has a series of nine shallow terracotta domes, each with a circular window in the summit to ensure even lighting. They are supported by cast-iron columns, arranged in four rows of three columns each. From these spring the arches supporting the domes, their lower edges picked out in intricate patterns of wrought iron. If the impact of the Reading Room is deliberately grandiose—a utilitarian system of construction used to create maximum visual drama—the Stack Room, by contrast, is deliberately functional, almost factorylike. Here, the stacks are arranged over four floors and top-lit. To allow the light to reach the lower levels, the floors are simple metal grills. Catwalks of similar construction run between the stacks and add to the air of elegant functionality.

Light and air
The spacious elegance of Labrouste's Reading Room reflects the 19th-century expansion of knowledge and the parallel growth in importance of public libraries.

THE EIFFEL TOWER

🖥 1889 📌 PARIS, FRANCE ✍ GUSTAVE EIFFEL & STEPHEN SAUVESTRE 🏛 TOWER

The Eiffel Tower is a triumphantly virile monument to cast-iron construction. Not even by the most generously defined use of the term is it a "building." Instead, it is a pointless, magnificent, and startling statement of the possibilities of late 19th-century engineering, using new technology on a deliberately large scale.

No structure in the world more precisely sums up the aggressive certainties of western Europe's technological lead in the last quarter of the 19th century than the Eiffel Tower. It was built as the centerpiece of the 1889 Universal Exposition in Paris, which was held to mark the 100th anniversary of the start of the French Revolution.

Though the tower was the brainchild of Gustave Eiffel, much of its detailing came from Stephen Sauvestre (1874–1919). It was he who was responsible for the four massive arches linking the base of the tower at its second floor and for the bulb-shaped structure at the summit. The fundamental design was otherwise purely the result of the need to reduce wind resistance: the tower's elegance is precisely the product of

GUSTAVE EIFFEL

Gustave Eiffel (1832–1923) was the pre-eminent engineer of later 19th-century France. He was responsible for a series of revolutionary metal structures across Europe—bridges above all, as well as the Eiffel Tower—and the skeleton of the Statue of Liberty in New York. At the end of his illustrious career, he devoted his time to scientific research in the fields of meteorology, radiotelegraphy, and aerodynamics.

engineering imperatives. Despite predictable objections to this "truly tragic street lamp" in the words of one contemporary, the tower was a staggering success from the start. It was not just a vindication of Eiffel's construction methods—all of the 18,038 separate elements were made in Eiffel's factory on the outskirts of the city and assembled on site—but it became an immediately recognizable symbol of the modern city of Paris.

Vital statistics
The tower is 986 ft (300 m) high, weighs 7,300 tons, and has 2,500,000 rivets and 1,665 steps.

MAISON DU PEUPLE

🕮 1899 📍 BRUSSELS, BELGIUM
✒ VICTOR HORTA 🏛 MEETING HALL

The Maison du Peuple marked a decisive stage in the emergence of a genuinely new architecture based on iron and glass construction. It was built partly as a meeting hall, an auditorium at its heart, and partly as the headquarters of the Socialist Party. The building was ingeniously planned, making spirited use of an awkward site. Even more

importantly, it saw iron and glass pressed into startling service on behalf of Art Nouveau, of which architect Victor Horta (1861–1947) was the leading figure. The result was sinuous and functional by turns and was hugely original. The building was demolished in 1965.

FREYSSINET AIRSHIP HANGARS

🕮 1923 📍 ORLY, PARIS
✒ EUGÈNE FREYSSINET 🏛 AIRPORT

The airship hangars at Orly Airport are a prime example of a pure engineering solution producing a structure of astonishing elegance. The problem facing Eugene Freyssinet (1879–1962) at Orly was to build a durable structure, at the lowest possible cost, to contain airships. As airships are circular, an arched structure, meaning the least wasted space, was clearly desirable. Given that it had to be 574 ft (175 m) long, 299 ft (91 m) wide, and 197 ft (60 m) high, the technical problems were formidable.

Freyssinet's solution was to use reinforced concrete: that is, concrete reinforced by the addition of internal steel rods, so that the compression strength of the concrete was complemented by the tensile strength of the steel. This technique was first introduced, in France, in the early 1890s. What Freyssinet did was to create a series of freestanding parabolic arches linked only by concrete bands containing windows, a solution as practical as it was visually satisfying.

GALLERIA VITTORIO EMANUELE

🕮 1877 📍 MILAN, ITALY ✒ GIUSEPPE MENGONI 🏛 COMMERCIAL BUILDING

Covered arcades with roofs of iron and glass had been built elsewhere in Europe before the Galleria Vittorio Emanuele. None, however, was as large or as lavish. In fact, whatever its superficially utilitarian function as combined shopping center and meeting place, the Galleria was intended as a symbol of the newly unified Italy, specifically of the union between church and state.

As a cross-shaped structure, it echoes the ground plan of a church. As importantly, its two longest arms run north–south, from the Piazza della Scala, site of the (secular) opera house, to the Piazza del Duomo, site of the cathedral. The entrance facing the cathedral is

modeled as a massive triumphal arch, a reference to the country's imperial past.

The architecture within the Galleria looks backward and forward in a similar way: back to the Renaissance and the Baroque

as represented by the conventional masonry walls and giant pilasters; forward to a bold industrial future as represented by the glass-and-iron tunnel-vaulted roof. These tendencies mesh at the crossing of the arms, where an antique form (the octagonal dome) is made in modern materials (glass and iron).

Unifying symbolism
Architecturally conventional but engineeringly daring, the Galleria magnificently symbolized modern Italy.

AEG TURBINE FACTORY

📺 1909 📍 BERLIN, GERMANY 🖊 PETER BEHRENS 🏛 INDUSTRIAL BUILDING

The AEG Turbine Factory, designed by Peter Behrens (1868–1940), was a key precursor of Modernism. It was an entirely new kind of building: a factory that, though wholly functional inside and out, was nonetheless also clearly intended to be read as a work of architecture—in other words, the modern and the utilitarian deliberately made aesthetic. It was achieved by means of simple, bold forms—large windows, with the steel frame of the building clearly shown, the whole under a projecting roof. Only the rustication at the corners can count as ornamentation, though even then as a form of Neo-Classicism at its most schematic.

Architecture in industry
Dignity on the monumental scale of the factory, for a place of work, was quite new.

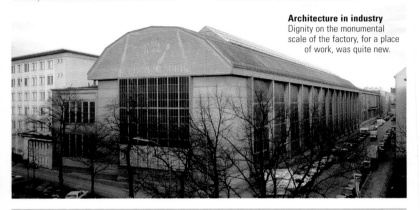

COWSHED, GARKAU FARM

📺 1925 📍 LÜBECK, GERMANY 🖊 HUGO HÄRING 🏛 AGRICULTURAL BUILDING

Hugo Häring (1882–1958) was a pivotal figure in the development of Modernism, a close associate of Mies van der Rohe (1886–1969) in Berlin, and a founder member of The Ring, the most influential association of Modernist architects in Germany in the 1920s.

Yet, for all that, Häring remains a little-known figure. In part, this was because much of his work was theoretical, and he built relatively little. Even the cowshed at Garkau Farm, Lübeck—his most famous building—was intended as part of a larger complex. Häring's starting point was that architecture should be the result of the particular needs of a particular building: that the form of any building should be dictated by its needs, not imposed upon it.

Functional form
The curious shape of Häring's cowshed was the result of extensive research into the needs and traditions of dairy farming.

MARSHALL FIELD MERCHANDISE MART

🗓 1930   📍 CHICAGO, IL   ✎ GRAHAM, ANDERSON, PROBST & WHITE   🏛 COMMERCIAL BUILDING

The Merchandise Mart was the brainchild of James Simpson (president of Marshall Field and Company, 1923–30, and chairman of the Chicago Plan Commission, 1926–35). The purpose was to consolidate Field's wholesale activities, which were scattered around the city in 13 different warehouses. It opened six months into the Great Depression. Not surprisingly, the company went into liquidation.

Today, this mountainous, 25-story building is the world's largest commercial building. At the time of its completion in 1930, it was the largest building of any type in the world, an honor taken by the Pentagon in 1943. The Merchandise Mart now houses trade shows, as it was always meant to, and is the world's largest trade center. It is also a design center and host to dozens of conferences and seminars. The building was restored by its original architects in 1986.

Epic industrial scale
The massive Merchandise Mart has its own Chicago Transit Authority train station and its own zip code.

MONADNOCK BUILDING

🗓 1889–91   📍 CHICAGO, IL   ✎ DANIEL BURNHAM & JOHN ROOT   🏛 COMMERCIAL BUILDING

The Monadnock Building is precisely poised between two architectural eras. In terms of construction, it looks backward. It has been said that this is "the last of the big masonry towers." In other words, though it uses iron in its construction, the building is supported by its load-bearing walls, those on the first floor being 6 ft (2 m) thick.

In most other important respects, this building looks decisively forward. For one thing, it was the largest office block in the world, 197 ft (60 m) and 16 stories high. By any measure, this was an astonishingly bold statement of American confidence. As important, it pioneered an entirely new approach to the decoration of such massive blocks in which all but a lingering sense of historicism was banished. The Monadnock building has a kind of stripped down simplicity, with ornament outlawed, that is seen as a direct precursor of Modernism.

However, this was far from inevitable. The first designs for the building cast it in an improbable Egyptian mode. Only gradually did Burnham (1846–1912) and Root (1850–91) come to see that the impact of the building could be heightened, and given a powerful sense of coherence, by eliminating decoration. Serried bay windows are all that break the building's austere lines.

WAINWRIGHT BUILDING

🖥 1891 📍 ST. LOUIS, MO ✍ LOUIS HENRY SULLIVAN 🏛 COMMERCIAL BUILDING

Sullivan's Wainwright Building is an early pointer toward the development of the skyscraper and Modernism. Sullivan (1856–1924) was an extraordinarily forward-thinking architect, author of a key tenet of Modernism: "Form ever follows function." A crucial point followed: that the exterior of a building should reflect its basic construction, in this case a steel frame.

In fact, Sullivan is not entirely true to this dictum in St. Louis. Only every other bold, brick-clad upright of the exterior marks a steel vertical. Similarly, there is no structural reason why the verticals at the corners should be wider than those elsewhere on the building. Nonetheless, the uniformity of the building's seven principal stories is important. Each window, said Sullivan, was "a cell in a honeycomb." They "must all look alike because they are all alike." That said, he retained a taste for Classical decoration. The bands under the windows have rich terracotta panels; the top floor has even richer panels; and the roof has a strong, projecting cornice.

Function is all
The first floor contained shops, with banks, offices, and services above.

RELIANCE BUILDING

🖥 1894 📍 CHICAGO, IL ✍ DANIEL BURNHAM
& JOHN ROOT 🏛 COMMERCIAL BUILDING

Though only 14 stories high—the first four built in 1890, the remainder in 1894—the Reliance Building is a skyscraper. Every key feature is here, albeit in miniature: a steel frame, clearly expressed on the exterior;

extensive use of concrete; and large windows.

At the time, it was these windows that excited most comment. How could such a large building make such extensive use of glass without fatally weakening the structure?

Other typical Burnham and Root features are the delicate terracotta panels between floors, the projecting bay windows that extend to the full height of the building, and the clearly emphasized cornice.

BRADBURY BUILDING

🖥 1893 📍 LOS ANGELES, CA
✍ GEORGE H. WYMAN 🏛 COMMERCIAL BUILDING

The Bradbury Building is unusual. It was built by an unknown and largely self-taught architect for a mining tycoon. Externally, it is unremarkable—a five-story brick-and-sandstone box in a serviceable Renaissance style. Internally, however, it is quite extraordinary. It is dominated by a central court, lit from above through a large glass roof. At either end are cast-iron staircases. Facing each other on either side of the atrium are two hydraulic glass-cage elevators whose mechanisms are entirely exposed. Wrought iron, glazed bricks, marble, and tiles predominate. The effect is astonishing.

FLATIRON BUILDING

1902   NEW YORK, NY   DANIEL BURNHAM   COMMERCIAL BUILDING

With the Flatiron Building, the skyscraper came of age. Its bombastically overstated decoration is not typical of the genre, but its drama is increased by an unusual triangular shape, the fortuitous result of a cramped location at the meeting of Fifth Avenue and Broadway. The rounded "prow" of the building tapers to less than 6 ft (2 m) wide.

The Flatiron Building, more properly the Fuller Building, was the wonder of the age. "Flatiron" is a nickname, the result of the building's resemblance to an iron, though it has since been given to the area as a whole. This was the tallest office building in the world, 22 stories and 285 ft (87 m) in height, at once adopted as the prime symbol of New York's new-rich sense of energetic destiny. Features of its construction—a steel frame, extensive elevators, and a regular,

Mix of past and future
The limestone wedge is decorated with Greek faces and floral detail.

repeated exterior, with equally strong horizontals and verticals—would all rapidly become the fixed points of skyscraper architecture. Yet Burnham could never entirely free himself from the past. He retained various Renaissance decorative forms, spiced with a certain Gothic quality, even in this, the forerunner of the dramatically different 20th-century skyscrapers.

DANIEL BURNHAM

Burnham (1846–1912) was among the leading figures of the Chicago School. His central role was recognized when he was appointed Chief of Construction for the World's Columbian Exposition in Chicago in 1893. He was closely involved in town plans for Washington D.C., San Francisco, and Chicago itself.

SCHLESINGER-MAYER STORE

🗓 1906 📍 CHICAGO, IL ✎ LOUIS HENRY SULLIVAN 🏛 COMMERCIAL BUILDING

The Schlesinger-Mayer Store, later Carson, Pirie, Scott, and Co., was the last major commission of Louis Henry Sullivan (1856–1924). The building, a department store, was built in three phases. The first

four stories were built in 1899. Between 1903 and 1904, a further 12 stories were added. The building was finished in 1906 by Daniel Burnham *(see opposite)*, though working to Louis Sullivan's original designs.

The building is as complete a statement of Sullivan's approach as any he produced: a characteristic combination of form strictly dictated by function and his taste for opulent decoration. The first two floors, for example, contain richly ornate, slightly Art Nouveau cast-iron decoration. The rest of the building is sheathed in light terracotta. Nonetheless, what dominates are the strong horizontal and vertical accents. These precisely mirror the building's steel structure, entirely uniform throughout other than at the elegantly curved corner, and are framed by wider and stronger verticals. The result is a building that is never less than assured.

Enduring fitness for purpose
The Schlesinger-Mayer Store has been in continuous use as a department store for over a century since it was first built.

FORD ROUGE GLASS PLANT

🗓 FROM 1917 📍 DEARBORN, MI ✎ ALBERT KAHN 🏛 INDUSTRIAL BUILDING

By the late 1920s, Henry Ford's assembly plant at Rouge River, south of Detroit, was the largest manufacturing plant in the world. It was intended to be entirely self-sufficient, with power plants as well as huge assembly halls. At its peak, 120,000 people were employed at Rouge River.

The man principally charged with the construction of the plant was the German-born Albert Kahn (1869–1942), perhaps the most influential and certainly the most productive industrial architect in America. It is estimated that, by 1930, 20 percent of all factory buildings in America were being designed by his firm, Kahn Associates. His straightforward approach, epitomized by the Glass Plant (in full production by 1923), was to find whatever solution worked best in whatever materials worked best. Yet though consistently hailed as a champion of Modernism, he had little time for "those who attempt the novel just for novelty's sake, who disregard fundamentals and indulge in what is queer or eccentric."

Functional Modernism
Factory design was based on the need for efficiency. Vast numbers of cars were assembled at this factory, with high productivity the main objective.

GOTHIC REVIVAL
ca. 1800–1910

The Gothic Revival reached remote corners of the globe. It emerged, after fey and romantic beginnings, as the favored style of the Victorian High Anglican church, and thereafter spread with missionary fervor across the British Empire, Europe, and the United States. A heady reaction to what was feared to be a Godless industrial world, it looked back to the past, even as it looked up to Heaven.

The Gothic Revival began as an English literary movement in the late-18th century, and spread into stage-set design. It also infiltrated architecture, resulting in spindly churches and amusing country villas that were really just over-dressed versions of four-square Georgian buildings. It was only with the fierce polemics of Pugin *(see p.374)*—notably *An Apology for the Revival of Christian Architecture, Contrasts,* and *The True Principles of Pointed or Christian Architecture*—that this dressy style became an earnest architectural pursuit.

GOTHIC STYLE RENEWED
Gothic Revival churches spear the sky in cities as far apart as Melbourne, Shanghai, Bombay, and Seoul. The products of a spirited 19th-century Christian revival, they were designed by architects who felt that Gothicism liberated them from the strictures of Classicism. Gothic was considered free-form, functional, and natural, allowing architects considerable room for maneuver. At a time when England was reaching the height of its global powers, the choice of Gothicism partly reflected a deep-rooted desire for buildings free from foreign influence. The competition to design a new Palace of Westminster *(see p.400)* for London specified that the style should be Gothic or Elizabethan—historical styles romanticized as embodying Englishness. The fact that Gothicism itself originated as a fusion of Western and Middle Eastern styles at the time of the Crusades was conveniently forgotten; it was historical, and thus English. Soon, all things romantically Welsh, Irish, and Scottish were cause for celebration, too. To a zealous young Gothic architect in the mid-1800s, Salisbury Cathedral *(see p.256)* was better than all the villas and churches of Andrea Palladio put together.

◁ SIR CHARLES BARRY'S DESIGN FOR THE PALACE OF WESTMINSTER IS BASED ON THE PERPENDICULAR GOTHIC STYLE, ORIGINALLY POPULAR DURING THE 15TH CENTURY. HE WAS AIDED BY THE GOTHIC ARCHITECT AUGUSTUS PUGIN.

ELEMENTS

Lavishly decorated inside and out, the Gothic Revival created some of the most extreme structures of all, driven by a vigorous and revived Christianity in the 19th century. This flexible style was not just for churches; but whether pressed into service for a Christian building, town hall, or grand hotel, drama was key.

△ **Conical roofs**
Modeled on the turrets of medieval castles, these were a popular device to give the impression of much older roots, as here at Castell Coch, Wales.

△ **Richly colored stained glass**
Often darker than medieval glass, 19th-century stained glass was beautifully made yet tended to block out light.

Tall spires ▷
Lean, spiky towers, such as that of Melbourne's St. Patrick's cathedral, rising above city skylines were one of the style's most unmistakable calling cards.

Eye-catching, needlelike spire

Niches, statue-filled or not, were *de rigueur*

Extravagantly decorated spires ▷
Enriched with crockets, pinnacles, and, in the Albert Memorial, London, gold leaf, Revivalist spires were often highly ornamental.

Prickly pinnacles

Gable adorned with highly elaborate mosaic

▽ **Clock towers**
Based on the precedent of medieval town halls, among the most famous are St. Stephen's Tower, Westminster, by Barry and Pugin and, here, Manchester Town Hall, by Alfred Waterhouse.

Tall spire draws attention from afar

Gables fronting all sides of clock face

Bell tower with Early English lancets

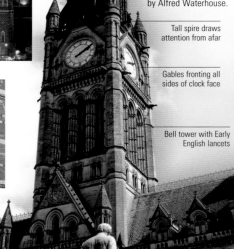

△ **Polychrome brickwork**
New, durable, colored industrial bricks meant that exteriors of secular as well as ecclesiastical buildings could now be as richly decorated as interiors.

FONTHILL ABBEY

🖳 1796 📍 WILTSHIRE, ENGLAND
✍ JAMES WYATT 🏛 RESIDENCE

Fonthill Abbey was built at staggering cost as a residence for the wilfully extravagant William Beckford. It was the first, and most remarkable, example of Gothic architecture as interpreted by the late-18th century desire for Romantic style.

An 278 ft (85 m) octagonal tower rose from its center, enclosing probably the tallest room in the world, 122 ft (37 m) high. Four wings spanned out from here; the north and south wings were each over 400 ft (122 m) long. The tower collapsed in 1807 and again in 1825. Only crumbling ruins remain.

ST. GILES CHURCH, CHEADLE

🖳 1846 📍 STAFFORDSHIRE, ENGLAND
✍ AUGUSTUS PUGIN 🏛 PLACE OF WORSHIP

Augustus Pugin *(see also p.400)*, the most important and brilliant champion of the first phase of the mature Gothic Revival, was a tirelessly industrious and often thrillingly controversial designer. St. Giles Church is Gothic in plan as much as in details and uses local materials in a manner faithful to the style. Its commanding spire has decorated tracery and numerous pinnacles; niches either side of the eastern window contain statues; and there are several different levels of roofs. The inside is lavishly decorated with painted walls and rich stained-glass windows.

STRAWBERRY HILL, TWICKENHAM

🖳 1777 📍 MIDDLESEX, ENGLAND ✍ HORACE WALPOLE 🏛 RESIDENCE

There was no figure more influential in the growing spread of Gothic style in the second half of the 18th century than Horace Walpole (1717–97); nor was any building more important in this initially uncertain revival than Strawberry Hill, Walpole's house outside London.

The Gothic Revival, like Chinoiserie, principally offered an exotic alternative to the august formalities of Palladianism. The result was a fusion of "Rococo" Gothic, occasionally learned, much more often purely decorative, in which charm was always placed first. Its roots are clearly based in the mid-18th century taste for garden follies and sham ruins.

Strawberry Hill includes contributions from a large number of architects, added over several years. It demonstrates a wide range of Gothic elements—towers, turrets, castellations, pinnacles—and is wildly and deliberately asymmetrical.

Inspired unreality
The stage-set elegance of Strawberry Hill dominated Gothic Revival architecture in England for almost half a century.

THE PALACE OF WESTMINSTER

🖥 1860   📍 LONDON, ENGLAND   ⚒ CHARLES BARRY & AUGUSTUS PUGIN   🏛 PUBLIC BUILDING

The destruction of the original Palace of Westminster by fire in 1834 sparked the most furious architectural argument of the 19th century: should the new building be Gothic or Greek? The answer turned out to be both: a building Classical in its planning, Gothic in its detail. The Palace of Westminster is a magnificent hybrid, a turning point in the history of English architecture.

The Palace stands on the north bank of the Thames River, linked to the much older Westminster Hall. The long, riverside facade is dominated by towers. The highest is the Victoria Tower, at 336 ft (102 m). The octagonal Central Tower, above the central lobby, is topped by a spire. The Clock Tower, at the northern end, has four huge clock faces and houses five great bells that chime every quarter-hour. Big Ben, the bell that chimes on the hour, has become a symbol for London itself. Internally, the Palace is a complex of passageways and more than 1,000 rooms over four floors.

CHARLES BARRY AND AUGUSTUS PUGIN

For many years, the question of whether it was Charles Barry (1795–1860) or Augustus Pugin (1812–52) who was responsible for the Palace of Westminster wasted an astonishing amount of academic effort. That it is genuinely a collaboration is obvious. The maverick Pugin could no more have pulled off such a monumental organizational feat than the Classically trained Barry could have devised the building's wealth of decorative Gothic detail.

A fusion of styles
"All Greek, Ssir. Gothic details on a Classic body." Pugin's own comment sums up the improbable appeal of London's best-known and loved public building.

The choice of Charles Barry as architect – a man whose work was fully in the traditions of pure late-Regency Classicism – made sense in terms of his ability to organize such a huge project and his willingness to delegate the detailing to Pugin, an early and irrepressible champion of the Gothic style. If Barry was responsible for the measured calm of the building, its symmetry and stateliness, Pugin was the author of its astoundingly intricate finishing. Inkwells, hat-stands, and stained-glass windows poured from Pugin's pen as easily as the rich styling of the Perpendicular exterior.

KEBLE COLLEGE

🏛 1875 📍 OXFORD, ENGLAND ✍ WILLIAM BUTTERFIELD 🏛 EDUCATIONAL BUILDING

However certain of their triumph over Classicism and of their antiquarian precision, the High Victorian Goths were nonetheless permanently anxious that they were still slaves to a past they could emulate but never surpass. Butterfield (1814–1900) proved them spectacularly wrong. Keble College, muscular and unashamed, is startlingly new. Its starting point may be the championing of Venetian Gothic by writer and critic John Ruskin; its end point is a building of staggeringly assertive originality.

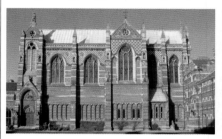

UNIVERSITY MUSEUM, OXFORD

🏛 1859 📍 OXFORD, ENGLAND
✍ BENJAMIN WOODWARD 🏛 MUSEUM

The University Museum is the only important Victorian High Gothic building that directly bears the imprint of John Ruskin, writer and arch-prophet of the Gothic in the 19th century. It is built in the polychromatic Venetian Gothic style that Ruskin did so much to popularize (while warning of its unsuitability for northern climates). The main hall boasts remarkable and forward-looking cast-iron Gothic columns supporting a daring glazed roof. The rich program of sculptured decoration on the exterior, directed by Ruskin, was only partly completed.

CARDIFF CASTLE

🏛 1885 📍 CARDIFF, WALES ✍ WILLIAM BURGES 🏛 FORTIFICATION

In contrast to many Victorian Gothic architects, who anguished endlessly about the propriety of their buildings, William Burges (1827–81) created a series of lavish medieval reconstructions that combined fantasy and elegance in equal measure. His patron was the 3rd Marquess of Bute, reputedly the richest man in Britain, a figure of endless intellectual curiosity and with a passion for the

Middle Ages. Cardiff Castle is the first great monument to their collaboration.

The castle was Norman, but built on Roman foundations. Burges restored the keep and created a series of brilliantly colored and decorated interiors. The result is an eccentric and captivating masterpiece.

The "Palace"
Cardiff Castle reveals Burges's ability to combine strength and formality with maximum drama.

CASTELL COCH

🏛 1891 📍 GLAMORGAN, WALES ✍ WILLIAM BURGES 🏛 FORTIFICATION

"Castell Coch" means Red Castle, a reference to the red sandstone used in its construction. The building stands on the site of a medieval fortress; but whereas Cardiff Castle is a restoration, Castell Coch is an entirely Victorian building in which only fragments of the original have been retained. It is a remarkable example of the shared vision of the Marquess of Bute and architect William Burges for an idealized medieval world.

Despite creating an air of fantasy, both men intended the castle as an accurate reconstruction of a medieval original. It has, therefore, a working drawbridge and portcullis; it also houses a dungeon. The exterior is impressive, with three sturdy circular towers under steep conical roofs, and the interior is a riot of late-Victorian antiquarianism at its most inventive. The vaulted ceiling of the octagonal

drawing room, the most impressive room of all, is thronged with painted birds on a star-filled background. A menagerie of other animals crowds the brilliantly painted walls. In fact, the decorative scheme is esoteric and scholarly, an exotic commentary on life and death devised by Bute and Burges together.

A sense of splendor
The steep wooded hillside on which Castell Coch is built adds to its sense of power.

MANCHESTER TOWN HALL

📅 1877 📍 MANCHESTER, ENGLAND ✍ ALFRED WATERHOUSE 🏛 CIVIC BUILDING

With Scott *(see below)*, Alfred Waterhouse (1830–1905) epitomized the successful Victorian architect, presiding over a vast practice and turning out imposing public buildings— museums, banks, offices, colleges, train stations— in a variety of hugely confident and grandly unapologetic Gothic styles.

Manchester Town Hall was among his first major commissions, a statement of the fitness of Gothic to

express the civic pride of a newly rich and expanding city. It is beautifully detailed inside and out, with a series of opulent halls and an impressive staircase. It is also ingenious. Ever practical, Waterhouse coped with an awkward triangular site by constructing the building around a courtyard to ensure maximum light.

Impressive and varied
Waterhouse gave different facades to each of the building's three sides—this is the rear.

MIDLAND GRAND HOTEL, ST. PANCRAS

📅 1871 📍 LONDON, ENGLAND ✍ GEORGE GILBERT SCOTT 🏛 HOTEL

In the mid-20th century, many people felt that the Midland Grand Hotel at St. Pancras Station, designed by Sir George Gilbert Scott (1811–78), epitomized the vulgarity of Victorian High Gothic. It was often condemned as a building of unsurpassed ugliness. More recent judgments are less harsh; there is no doubt that, like the Palace

Energy and verve
The quintessential "railway hotel" echoes the bustle of the station beyond.

of Westminster *(see p.400)*, this is not just one of the most instantly recognizable buildings in London, but one of the best loved. Its gables, turrets, and tracery, set off by rich red brickwork, have a magnificently unapologetic boldness. Similarly, the great curve of the building, and its consequent asymmetry, generates genuine energy.

Unlike the arch-zealots of the Gothic movement, who hated any deviation from its pure heart, Scott cheerfully regarded the Gothic as a style that could be plundered as he, the architect, thought best.

ROYAL COURTS OF JUSTICE, LONDON

🏛 1882   📍 LONDON, ENGLAND   ✍ GEORGE EDMUND STREET   🏛 CIVIC BUILDING

Few subjects excited the Victorians more than architecture: fierce passions were aroused by the announcement of any major building work. Once chosen as the architect of the Royal Courts of Justice, George Street (1824–81) suffered more than his fair share of public hostility, a contributory cause to his early death. This contentious climate provided the background to the building of the Royal Courts of Justice, the final gasp of Victorian High Gothic architecture. This imposing building draws on 13th-century French sources. It is reminiscent of Chartres Cathedral *(see pp.250–1)*, with hints of a Loire château. Its most notable external feature is its skyline, dominated by steep-pitched roofs, towers, and half-towers. A cloisterlike arcade runs along much of the first floor. Inside, the vast navelike hall proclaims Street's ecclesiastical inspiration.

Meticulous detail
Street was a conscientious architect. Records show that he made more than 3,000 drawings in his designs for the Royal Courts of Justice.

MARISCHAL COLLEGE

🏛 1906   📍 ABERDEEN, SCOTLAND   ✍ ALEXANDER MACKENZIE   🏛 EDUCATIONAL BUILDING

From about 1840, Gothic architecture in Britain was forced to contend with the ruthless demands of self-appointed groups, the best known of which was the Cambridge Camden Society. These groups sought, chiefly for religious reasons, to impose precise rules on the use of the Gothic style. Yet by the end of the century, as this once near-fanatical influence waned, Gothic had become just one of a number of styles available to historically minded architects, and its use became accordingly much freer. Marischal College is a virile exercise in Tudor Gothic, built in white granite. Strongly vertical and deliberately asymmetrical lines are dominated by the 279 ft (85 m) Mitchell Tower, which contrasts dramatically with the length of the principal facade.

Local stone
Marischal College has the distinction of being the world's second-largest granite building.

LIVERPOOL CATHEDRAL

🏛 AFTER 1903 📍 LIVERPOOL, ENGLAND ✍ GILES GILBERT SCOTT 🏛 PLACE OF WORSHIP

Liverpool Cathedral is triumphant evidence that the Gothic style, recast and used with intelligence, could be pressed into service to create an architecture that was fully modern.

Giles Gilbert Scott (1880–1960), grandson of the vastly more assertive Gothic Revivalist George Gilbert Scott, was only 22 when he designed this, the largest Anglican cathedral in Britain. It took 75 years to build and was not finished until after the death of the architect.

This huge cathedral is an extraordinary building, exceptionally sure of itself, at times brilliant in the disposition of its vast, shadowy masses. The exterior is of rich, red sandstone, with concrete used in the roofing above the vaults.

A long gestation
The 331 ft (101 m) tower was completed by Scott in 1932, but he died before the nave was opened.

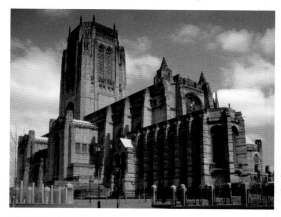

The strong square tower rises above the central crossing. In the interior, there are echoes of Spanish styles of decoration. If it is hard to say whether the building is more impressive internally or externally, there is no doubting its brooding presence. Once seen, it is never likely to be forgotten.

ST. ANDREW, SUNDERLAND

🏛 1907 📍 SUNDERLAND, ENGLAND
✍ E.S. PRIOR 🏛 PLACE OF WORSHIP

At the imaginative church of St. Andrew, in the Sunderland suburb of Roker, E.S. Prior (1852–1932) reworked the style of Durham Cathedral (see pp.240–1) in the dynamic new idiom Scott used for Liverpool Cathedral.

The exterior is unrelieved, undressed stone, rough-hewn and decidedly muscular. This effect is underlined by the hefty tower at the east end, with further angled towers at its corners and only the smallest of windows. Modest moldings provide almost the only concession to decoration. Schematic battlements emphasize the castlelike qualities of the building.

Inside, massive pointed stone arches rise directly from the floor to the apex of the roof, as though a huge stone boat had been upturned. Their bases are pierced, creating tunnel-like aisles. A substantial window, broadly Early English but with forcefully simplified stone tracery, dominates the east end.

GUILDFORD CATHEDRAL

🏛 1961 📍 GUILDFORD, ENGLAND
✍ EDWARD MAUFE 🏛 PLACE OF WORSHIP

Guildford Cathedral was the dying gasp of the Gothic Revival in England. It is municipal Gothic, built entirely of brick to underline its modernity. Its elevated setting is impressive, its execution less so. The three-bay west front has three slender lancet windows over oddly shrunken portals. The crossing is dominated by a square tower, striking from a distance, but close-up the brickwork is unexciting. A valiant effort, Guildford Cathedral only partly succeeds.

VOTIVKIRCHE, VIENNA

📅 1879 📍 VIENNA, AUSTRIA ✎ HEINRICH VON FERSTEL 🏛 PLACE OF WORSHIP

The Gothic Revival was an entirely English affair to begin with: at first, an attempt to exploit its "picturesque" qualities; later, in its High Victorian noon, a more systematic attempt at a properly "national" Christian architecture—an irony perhaps in light of the style's French origins. Given which, it is not surprising that, outside the English-speaking world, it found fewer adherents; indeed, to a large extent it was just one more style to be exploited in the "historicizing" trend of mid-19th century architecture.

Nonetheless, it did spread fitfully through Europe, and Vienna's Votivkirche is an exceptionally accomplished example of 13th-century French Gothic styling, filtered via Cologne Cathedral *(see pp.260–1)*. It was built as a national shrine on the orders of the Emperor Franz Joseph, after he had survived an assassination attempt on exactly this spot.

Its most obvious characteristic is its soaring vertical lines. The slim towers at the western end rise into spires 325 ft (99 m) high. This upward surge is echoed by steeply gabled doors and windows, the flèche (a slender wooden spire) over the crossing, and lacelike flying buttresses. The decorative impact is heightened by intricate diamond patterning on its steep-pitched roofs.

The interior is impressively elegant; if it feels slightly dead, this is probably a consequence of attempts to duplicate styles from the past.

The west front
French High Gothic is recreated with some success.

TRINITY CHURCH, NEW YORK

📅 1846 📍 NEW YORK, NY
✎ RICHARD UPJOHN 🏛 PLACE OF WORSHIP

Trinity Church, designed by British-born Richard Upjohn (1802–78), is the earliest major statement of the Gothic Revival in the US. It is an elegant building that resembles contemporary churches in Britain, with Gothic styling valued for its Christian associations as well as for its "picturesque" qualities. The result is a thinly applied Gothic, as opposed to the earnest and more learned Gothic of the mid-century, but it is attractive. Its slim tower, topped by four elegant turrets, is particularly striking.

ST. JOHN THE DIVINE, NEW YORK

📅 AFTER 1892 📍 NEW YORK, NY
✎ VARIOUS 🏛 PLACE OF WORSHIP

St. John the Divine is a monument to the enduring grip of the Gothic Revival in the US, a massive building begun in 1892 in a boldly Romanesque manner and extensively remodeled after 1911 by Ralph Adams Cram (1863–1942) in a full-blown 13th-century semi-English, semi-French style.

In the first phase of the work, only the choir and the crossing were constructed; a shallow dome, intended to be temporary, was built over the crossing. The second phase, completed in 1918, saw the addition of the French-style chevet east end—a circular apse surrounded by a walkway and seven chapels. From the 1920s, work was begun on the immense nave, and the choir was remodeled to match.

The nave and recast choir were completed in 1941. Sporadic efforts have since been made to complete the building—it still has no transepts nor any of the towers envisaged by Cram—but there is little expectation they will come to fruition.

WOOLWORTH BUILDING

🏛 1913 📍 NEW YORK, NY ✎ CASS GILBERT 🏛 COMMERCIAL BUILDING

New York's Woolworth Building is a curious hybrid, a building whose advanced steel skeleton construction looked aggressively forward, yet which, as if in apology for its modernity, is dressed in Gothic clothing. Originally the idea of F. W. Woolworth himself, for nearly 20 years it was the tallest building in the world, 792 ft (241 m) high, and it boasted the world's most sophisticated system of elevators.

Externally, the Woolworth Building's most memorable feature is the massive central tower, 30 stories high, that surges out of a hardly less massive 29-story base. Its copper-sheathed summit is crowned with an improbable assemblage of towers, turrets, and lanterns.

Cass Gilbert encased the entire exterior in a delicate, cream-colored, lacelike terracotta shell with almost no horizontal elements. The terracotta washes clean in the rain, keeping the building looking fresh and light externally, while skyscraper windows light the interior. The principal entrances are studded with elaborately carved Gothic decoration, which repeats and multiplies as the four stages of the tower rise skyward.

The most striking element of the interior is the lavish lobby arcade. It has a cruciform floor plan and vaulted ceilings, and is sumptuously decorated with Gothic-style marble and bronze around the doorways and elevators. It stands as a monument to American commerce at its most expansive.

CASS GILBERT

Gilbert (1859–1934) had enormous influence over the development of architecture in the US. He designed numerous public buildings and others followed his lead. However, Modernism brought ridicule of the historic overtones of his work. Appreciation of his craftsmanship and visionary style is now returning.

Creating perspective
So that the Gothic detail at the summit can be visible from the ground, it is hugely over-scaled.

NOSTALGIA AND WHIMSY

ca. 1850–1914

A combination of new-found wealth, new ways of building, and nostalgia on the one hand, and the struggle for unity and independence by European nations on the other, led to a spate of fascinating, decadent, and even utterly crazy buildings in the late-19th century. Many were whimsical creations, the stuff of fairytales; others were important nationalistic symbols. All were peerless eye-catchers.

Reaction to industrialism and the Gothic Revival spurred on new architectural styles in the late-19th century. Those houses designed by English Arts and Crafts architects were mainly concerned with stopping the clock and trying to return to a world free of the steam, smoke, and pounding piston-strokes of the all-consuming industrial world. Even when built by the finest craftsmen, they tended, rather contradictorily, to be laced through with the latest domestic technology. In fact they became, much as their architects would have hated, models for the 20th-century suburban housing that eventually sprawled over the very villages and meadows that were so cherished by the Arts and Crafts folk. Elsewhere, a new generation of sentimental nationalistic monuments rising from newly unified European nations, among them Germany and Italy, descended rapidly into kitsch.

FANTASY ARCHITECTURE

Sheer fantasy fueled architectural dreams worldwide—just look at Neuschwanstein *(see p.412)*, the Palácio da Pena *(see p.413)*, the Sagrada Familia *(see p.418)*, and Castle Drogo *(see p.423)*. Some of these works are by truly great architects, notably the Sagrada Familia by Antoni Gaudí and Castle Drogo by Edwin Lutyens. Yet they are still more like playthings than exceptional buildings. Undoubtedly intriguing, and unmissable for tourists, they nevertheless seem self-indulgent and a little crazy. Not that these are necessarily vices in architecture: wealthy clients and visionary architects have always played a crucial role in the story of architecture at its most dramatic. Many of these buildings are also exuberant reactions to years of foreign domination, or political and economic underachievement, and this helps to explain their barely restrained vitality.

◁ WITH ITS MOCK-MEDIEVAL TURRETS AND ITS INTERIORS RANGING FROM BYZANTINE THROUGH ROMANESQUE TO GOTHIC, NEUSCHWANSTEIN WAS BUILT AS A FANTASTICAL RETREAT FOR "MAD" KING LUDWIG II OF BAVARIA.

ELEMENTS

Variety and extravagance were the keys to the architecture of this period. A desire to emulate and outdo the opulence of earlier times combined with some truly innovative designs. The period was characterized by buildings that harked back to the Middle Ages and the Renaissance, yet also forward to the Modern Movement of the 20th century.

Distinctive fairytale turrets

◁ Wedding-cake layers
The desire for opulent display appears to have got the better of many architects and clients in the late 19th century. In terms of its superabundant Baroque decoration, Garnier's Opera House, Paris, is architecture as confectionery.

Detail piled upon detail almost obscures Classical facade

Window tracery based on the design of plant stems

△ Fairytale castles
This was a boom time for the retelling of fairytales. New castles sprang up across Europe, with pinnacles, turrets, and many roofs on different levels. None was so theatrical, however, as this alpine fantasia—King Ludwig II of Bavaria's Neuschwanstein.

△ Free-form windows
Here, Gaudí shapes an organic building, making use of curvilinear forms, treating stone as if it were a malleable material. This is a window from the Casa Batlló, Barcelona, an apartment building.

△ Surreal architectural features
A building might stand in for another artefact altogether: the Grundtvig Church, Copenhagen, designed by Jensen-Klint and completed in 1926, was built to resemble a giant pipe organ.

▽ Overwrought public monuments
The wholly over-the-top Vittorio Emanuele Monument, Rome, was completed in 1911 to commemorate Italy's unification and its first king. Comparison with Bernini's Piazza at St. Peter's *(see p.313)* is revealing.

Quadriga with Winged Spirit of Victory

Bronze statues graced almost every Italian square

Portico over-crowded with sculptural detail

LAHORE STATION

🚂 ca. 1865   📍 LAHORE, PAKISTAN   ✍ WILLIAM BRUNTON   🏛 TRAIN STATION

A red-brick marriage of fairytale Bavarian castle, medieval abbey, Mughal mosque, and mid-19th-century rail technology, Lahore station was built to serve as a fortress as well as a station. William Brunton had been asked to give the station a "defensive character" and to ensure that "a small garrison could secure it against enemy attack." So, the arrow-slits were built as emplacements for Maxim-guns, while the massive train shed—with its Gothic-meets-Mughal arcades—could be sealed in with giant steel shutters. The station still has a headily romantic feel to it, however, even though the forecourt is today dominated by a stone replica of a nuclear missile.

A fusion of styles
The station combined multiple styles and purposes in an age when steam locomotion was opening up the Indian subcontinent.

TURBINE BUILDING, MENIER CHOCOLATE FACTORY

🚂 1872   📍 NOISIEL-SUR-MARNE, FRANCE   ✍ JULES SAULNIER   🏛 INDUSTRIAL BUILDING

The Turbine Building of the Menier chocolate factory is built directly over the Marne River. It is one of the earliest prototypes of an entirely iron-framed building. Its slender iron exo-skeleton (an exposed skeleton)—formed of diagonal, crisscross bracing—provides lateral stability for the inner skeleton behind polychrome brick and ceramic-tiled walls.

The walls are purely infill and have no weight to support other than their own—even so they are given a helping hand by their iron frames. The windows could have been much bigger, but the use of small windows was, as yet, an accepted way of designing among architects who still believed a building had to follow particular forms of propriety, and Classical proportions.

The pretty brickwork and colorful ceramics embedded in the facade are delightful ways of expressing the purpose of a chocolate factory—producing delicious treats. Saulnier (1828–1900) has made the building look like a giant, beautifully wrapped box of fine chocolates.

Hydroelectric power
The powerful turbines were driven by the fast-flowing waters of the Marne River.

NEUSCHWANSTEIN

📺 1886   🏴 BAVARIA, GERMANY   ⚒ EDWARD RIEDEL & GEORG VON DOLLMAN   🏛 PALACE

Against a backdrop of snow-capped mountains, Neuschwanstein rises, dreamlike, over a river gorge in the heart of Bavaria. The castle was designed on a vast scale and at huge expense as a plaything in which King Ludwig II could retreat into a fantasy world of poetry, music, and imagination. By the time of his death, aged just 41 and effectively bankrupt, only one-third of the giant building was complete.

The lavish tapestries, murals, and paintings of the palace express Ludwig's obsession with medieval mythology, especially the story of Lohengrin, the knight who rescues a damsel in distress in a boat pulled by swans. Today, 15 rooms are open to visitors, each a glorious fantasia. The Singers' Hall, based on the minstrel's gallery of Wartburg Castle in Eisenach, Germany, is dedicated to the life of Parsifal, Lohengrin's father, a knight of the Holy Grail. Ludwig's Byzantine-style throne room was inspired by the Hagia Sophia, Constantinople *(see pp.126–7)*, with pillars of imitation porphyry and lapis lazuli, and a vaulted ceiling supported by inlaid stone columns and decorated with stars. Despite its opulence and dreaminess, Neuschwanstein was nevertheless equipped from the outset with hot running water, flushing lavatories, and even a form of central heating.

LUDWIG II

Ludwig II (1845–86) united his kingdom of Bavaria with that of Prussia to form the second German Empire in 1871. Despised by politicians, Ludwig was loved by ordinary people, and preferred the arts to affairs of state (he was patron to German composer Richard Wagner). He drowned in mysterious circumstances.

Fairytale castle
Built of brick faced with limestone, Neuschwanstein was the inspiration for the castle in Walt Disney's film *Sleeping Beauty*.

PALÁCIO DA PENA

1885 SINTRA, PORTUGAL BARON LUDWIG VON ESCHWEGE PALACE

Glorious, colorful, and wildly eccentric, Palácio da Pena is Portugal's answer to Ludwig II's Neuschwanstein. Overlooking the town of Sintra, the palace was built on the site of the ruined Hieronymite Monastery of Nossa Senhora da Pena, for Ferdinand II of Saxe Coburg-Gotha. Fanciful in the extreme, the palace's architectural fabric was inspired by Moorish, Manueline, and Gothic motifs as well the spirit of Bavaria's fairytale castles. The surrounding park is filled with trees and flowers from every corner of the Portuguese empire. The heroic statue on a nearby crag depicts the architect, Baron von Eschwege, in the guise of a medieval knight. Visitors can stroll through interiors virtually unchanged since Queen Amelia left here at the time of World War I.

Mountain marvel
Bright red and yellow, the domed and turreted palace rises from a peak 1,450 ft (450 m) up in the Sierra de Sintra.

THORVALDSEN MUSEUM

1848 COPENHAGEN, DENMARK
 MICHAEL GOTTLIEB BINDESBØLL MUSEUM

Frederick IV of Denmark commissioned this museum to house the work of prolific Danish Neo-Classical sculptor Bertil Thorvaldsen (1770–1844). Sadly, Thorvaldsen died four years before its opening; he is buried in one of its courtyards. The architecture of this rectangular brick building switches gamely from Greek revival on the bright yellow exterior to Pompeiian within the small, barrel-vaulted galleries—numinously lit and floored with dashing mosaics—and then to ancient Egyptian in the courtyards, with their life-sized murals of date palms.

PALAIS DE JUSTICE, BRUSSELS

1883 BRUSSELS, BELGIUM
 JOSEPH POELAERT CIVIC

This terrifying pile, rising from a massive base measuring 590 x 560 ft (180 x 170 m), was for many years the largest building in Europe. Its pompous and heavy-handed design refers principally to ancient Egyptian and Assyrian architecture, but the building is overlaid with myriad other styles—Greek, Roman, Italian Renaissance, and Baroque—piled up in tiers like a wedding cake. The culmination is the dome above the great central hall, which towers 345 ft (105 m) above the sidewalks. The interior has the same heaviness, pierced through with grand vistas and great stairs into the vastness of the central hall, but relatively little space is allocated to the law courts and attendant offices.

Covering 258,000 sq ft (24,000 m²), the Palais de Justice took 20 years to build. Construction required the demolition of Marolles, an entire working-class district of Brussels. The architect, Joseph Poelaert (1817–79), died before building was completed.

RIJKSMUSEUM

🏗 1885   📍 AMSTERDAM, THE NETHERLANDS   ✎ PETRUS CUYPERS   🏛 MUSEUM

Symmetrically planned around two courtyards, this Neo-Gothic-meets-early Renaissance museum is the work of Dutch architect Petrus Cuypers (1827–1921), who made his reputation in building and restoring Catholic churches. Amsterdam's predominantly Calvinist city government objected to his employment, and even more to the gilded facade and elaborate moldings, which they saw as a disgrace to their sober-minded city. (Cuypers got

Renaissance look
Lofty towers and steep roofs give the feel of a French château.

approval for his plan by showing drawings depicting little ornamentation, but he added much more during construction.) Despite this, the museum's architectural character was adopted by many protestant Dutch Neo-Renaissance architects, and Cuypers went on to design the city's central train station. The building has over 150 rooms, including a purpose-built hall for Rembrandt's "The Night Watch."

OPÉRA, PARIS

🏗 1874   📍 PARIS, FRANCE   ✎ CHARLES GARNIER   🏛 OPERA HOUSE

In 1861, Charles Garnier (1825–98), a largely unknown Parisian architect from humble origins and a scholar of the École des Beaux Arts, won Baron Haussmann's competition to design an opera house for central Paris. Garnier's Opéra was intended to represent the cultural diversity of the Second Empire, which it certainly does, and the architect dedicated his life to making his design a reality. Garnier was much criticized for his excessive use of ornament, which included multicolored marbles and intricate statuary. At the time of its completion, one critic described the structure as looking like "an overloaded sideboard." The auditorium itself occupies a surprisingly small part of the building, with much of the space being given over to the huge domed foyer and monumental staircase, which are lavishly gilded, dripping with opulent candelabra, and lined in shining marble. Even so, the plan is rational and well thought out, giving the effect of a great public procession that leads only gradually to the auditorium. The facade is equally elaborate and, perhaps, exactly suited to the operas of the period.

Imperialistic showpiece
The Neo-Baroque style of Garnier's Paris Opéra is monumental, classically based, and opulently expressed.

TOWN HALL, EAST HAM

🗓 1903 📍 LONDON, ENGLAND
✎ CHEERS & SMITH 🏛 CIVIC BUILDING

This handsome Edwardian town hall is part of a distinguished and well-built complex of contemporary civic buildings in east London. The complex also included a technical college, gym and public baths, library, tramsheds, fire station and firemen's cottages, and even its own electricity-generating station. The development was originally set in landscaped gardens and enclosed by a red-brick and terracotta wall that matched the warm materials of the buildings. The Town Hall, designed in an elaborate Edwardian Freestyle, is the great set piece of the ensemble. It culminates in a fine tower, which is both a local landmark and a symbol of how strong and effective these pioneering London boroughs were at a time when it seemed right to lift poorer parts of the city up by their scuffed bootstraps. Proud London plane trees, planted when the Town Hall was built, act as foils to its municipal grandeur.

NEW SCOTLAND YARD

🗓 1890 📍 LONDON, ENGLAND
✎ RICHARD NORMAN SHAW 🏛 CIVIC BUILDING

Based loosely on a Scottish baronial castle, complete with corner turrets capped with turnip-domes, New Scotland Yard was the first foray into civic architecture by Richard Norman Shaw (1831–1912), one of the key British architects of the Victorian age. The beautifully crafted red-brick superstructure, striped with fine stonework, rises from a daunting granite base. The whole building is a well-resolved blend of styles that ended up creating a style very much its own.

TOWN HALL, COPENHAGEN

🗓 1902 📍 COPENHAGEN, DENMARK
✎ MARTIN NYROP 🏛 CIVIC BUILDING

Copenhagen's Town Hall was clearly inspired by Siena's medieval Palazzo Pubblico (see p.267), but it also expresses the rediscovered sense of nationhood and political strength in Denmark at the start of the 20th century. This is most notable in the near 348 ft (106 m) high bell-tower, the castlelike walls, and the sheer massiveness of the structure. The use of handmade red bricks was an allusion to the vernacular styles of traditional Danish farmhouses—the heart and hearth of what was still largely an agricultural country.

P.O. SAVINGS BANK, VIENNA

🗓 ca. 1912 📍 VIENNA, AUSTRIA
✎ OTTO WAGNER 🏛 CIVIC BUILDING

The Imperial Royal Post Office Savings Bank, designed by Austrian architect Otto Wagner (1841–1918), bridges Art Nouveau and early Modernist architecture. It is also a superb example of Viennese architectural craft. The elegant, if severe, facade is clad in granite and marble, but there is extensive use, too, of a material new to architecture— aluminum. This is used for railings, rooftop figurines, door fittings, the freestanding warm vents in the main hall, and the exposed bolts that hold the marble slabs to the exterior walls. The all but sheer curved glass ceiling was originally intended to be suspended from cables, a very high-tech solution for the time. In the event, it is supported by slim steel pillars and slots into flanking walls; it is protected from rain and snow by a secondary flat-paned glass roof above it. The hugely influential Wagner, who had been Professor of the Imperial Academy of Art since 1894, also designed Vienna's new city railway and wrote the much-read book *Moderne Architektur*.

GLASGOW SCHOOL OF ART

🖥 1909   🏴 GLASGOW, SCOTLAND   ✍ CHARLES RENNIE MACKINTOSH   🏛 EDUCATIONAL BUILDING

A building of two formidable halves, the Glasgow (now Mackintosh) School of Art is the masterwork of the Glaswegian architect Charles Rennie Mackintosh (1868–1928). The main building, with its long, stone-fronted facade punctuated by vast studio windows and ancillary windows of different shapes and heights, dates from 1897–99; the imposing west end was completed in 1909. The all but unadorned west facade is dominated by three large oriel windows. These light the intriguing double-height library—a complex frame of dark-stained timber, modeled, in part, on traditional Japanese palace architecture. The library's magnificent exterior walls rise like a granite cliff face from the steeply sloping sidewalks. For a building that was a major influence on young German and Austrian architects, it had little or no lasting impact in Britain.

Aging beauty
After years of weathering, the stone exterior is now a subtle patchwork of rusty colors, laced with fine, tendril-like ironwork and inventive lamps.

MAJOLICA HOUSE

🖥 1899   🏴 VIENNA, AUSTRIA   ✍ OTTO WAGNER   🏛 RESIDENCES

The Majolica House—one of a pair of six-story Viennese apartment blocks with stores on the first and second floors—is named after the colorful majolica tiles used by Otto Wagner to clad its otherwise austere facade. Vivid fuchsia, white, and green flowers, on porous ceramic glazed with bright metallic oxides, writhe up, through, and between wrought-iron balconies decorated with sunflower motifs. The decoration gets richer as the building climbs higher above the sidewalk to reach an elaborately carved projecting cornice. The finished design was quite shocking to many Viennese and was even described as "hideous beyond measure." Wagner was only able to get away with such a flamboyant gesture because he owned the buildings.

The Majolica House marked Wagner's transition from an architect whose major influence was historical, to a proto-Modernist. The building shows the influence of his bright and aesthetically wilful students and young colleagues, notably Joseph Maria Olbrich and Josef Plecnik *(see Post Office Savings Bank, p.415; Steinhof Church, p.420).*

Stay-bright tiles
The majolica tiles have proved so hard-wearing and weatherproof that, with periodic cleaning, the building still looks remarkably new.

PALAIS STOCLET

🖥 1911   📍 BRUSSELS, BELGIUM   ✍ JOSEF HOFFMANN   🏛 RESIDENCE

Born in Moravia (now part of the Czech Republic), Josef Hoffmann (1870–1956) moved to Vienna to study at the Imperial Academy of Art under Otto Wagner *(see opposite)*. He later founded the Vienna Secession, an all-embracing arts movement, with fellow architects and designers, including Koloman Moser and Joseph Maria Olbrich. Hoffmann's Wiener Werkstätte, a workshop that produced "artistic" furniture for Secessionist houses, was his other major achievement. His finest piece of architecture was the Palais Stoclet. Heavily influenced by Charles Rennie Mackintosh, the three-story house is clad in dazzling white marble framed by geometric bronze moldings, some picked out with gold leaf. Hoffmann involved the entire Wiener Werkstätte team in the project and also commissioned the celebrated Viennese painter Gustav Klimt to design two murals, "Expectation" and "Fulfilment," for the dining room. Decorated with black and white marble, rare wood, and gold-embossed leather furniture, enriched with silver table decor and silverware designed by Hoffmann, and graced by Klimt's white-gold artworks, the dining room secured the reputation of the Stoclet house: here was a truly complete and up-to-the-minute architectural *Gesamtkunstwerk*, or unified work of art.

Stepped tower
Palais Stoclet—all white cubes, straight lines, and rectangles—culminates in a slim, stepped tower that anticipates the styling of an Art Deco cinema.

HÔTEL TASSEL

🖥 1893   📍 BRUSSELS, BELGIUM   ✍ VICTOR HORTA   🏛 RESIDENCE

The first completed Art Nouveau building was built by Victor Horta (1861–1947) for his friend, Émile Tassel, in Brussels, and caused a sensation when it was completed. The exterior of the house is unremarkable except for a double-height oriel bay window. In fact, it is almost indistinguishable from its more modest neighbors, while the street it stands in is dominated by a dull 1960s office block. Inside, however, it positively writhes with metal tendrils, and the sensational hall —all oranges, browns, and pale greens—is like some super-exotic palm house, with columns turning into surreal iron stalks as they creep up from their capitals and a curving staircase that appears to have been draped across the room and is defined by a sinuous iron support and tendril-like floral ornamentation. Banisters, wallpapers, and mosaics here are all restlessly alive; straight lines appear to have been banished, and the light, filtered through oddly colored stained glass, is very strange indeed. The overall effect is almost hallucinogenic. The house was, of course, designed to be sensational and sensual, for this was the beginning of the Aesthetic Movement—of Art for Art's Sake, absinthe, *The Yellow Book*, cheroots, Oscar Wilde, Aubrey Beardsley, and the Ballet Russe.

PARK GÜELL

🏆 1914   📍 BARCELONA, SPAIN
✎ ANTONI GAUDÍ   🏛 CIVIC PARK

Overlooking central Barcelona, this beautiful park was originally planned as a housing development in the style of an English Garden City. Work on the project ceased at the start of World War I; what remains is a whimsical urban playground, with just three houses, designed by Catalan architect Antoni Gaudí. The park's focus is a grand, serpentine terrace on top of what was intended to be a partly covered market, its cavelike roof supported by 100 Doric columns. The bench along the terrace perimeter has a mosaic of broken factory-reject tiles.

CASA MILÁ

🏆 1910   📍 BARCELONA, SPAIN
✎ ANTONI GAUDÍ   🏛 RESIDENCES

Gaudí built two apartment buildings in Barcelona, the brightly colored and dragon-like Casa Batlló and the Casa Milá. The latter, known locally as *la Pedrera* (the quarry), is famous for its gray stone, lack of straight lines, surrealist roofline, and organically planned apartments clustered around two ciruclar courtyards. The facade is a rippling wall of stone, but the stone is only cosmetic—it is supported by a steel frame and, in places, by brick and concrete pillars. The roof has hundreds of stretched parabolic brick arches, bizarre chimneys, highly sculpted stairway exits, and mosaic-clad ventilation shafts; it is all very dream-like. Gaudí hoped that residents would deck the facade in roof boxes so that, over time, the building would resemble a kind of urban geological outcrop rather than conventional architecture.

SAGRADA FAMILIA

🏆 AFTER 1881   📍 BARCELONA, SPAIN
✎ ANTONI GAUDÍ   🏛 PLACE OF WORSHIP

Rising up from the streets of Barcelona like a natural, slightly surreal outgrowth, the church of the Sagrada Familia—the Expiatory Temple of the Holy Family—still evokes the architectural spirit of the great European cathedrals.

DETAIL FROM THE NATIVITY FACADE

Commissioned in Neo-Gothic style by the Spiritual Association of the Devotees of St. Joseph, only part of the crypt was complete when Antoni Gaudí took over the design in 1883. Gaudí finished the crypt, and then his own design blossomed like a hundred exotic flowers: the church was to be as close to nature as possible. The nave was to be ringed around by an ambulatory (walkway) to keep the noise of the city at bay. Three giant facades represented the themes of Christ's Nativity, his Passion and Death, and his Resurrection. Each facade would be characterized by four 350 ft (107 m) high towers decorated with mosaic and glass and ringing to the sound of tubular bells hanging down through their hollow cores. Above these would rise the great nave, made without the need for flying buttresses, capped by a further six towers.

By the time of Gaudí's death in 1926, only the crypt, apse, and Nativity facade had been completed. Unfortunately, a fire destroyed most of his drawings in 1936, and, while work continues today, architects have had to guess at what Gaudí intended.

ANTONI GAUDÍ

Antoni Gaudí i Cornet (1852–1926) was born in Reus, Catalonia. In Barcelona, he fell in with rich textile merchant Eusebio Güell and with aristocratic Catholics, who together encouraged him to develop a new style for Barcelona, *Modernismo*, that would express Catalonia's independent spirit. For a time he lived in one of Parc Güell's gnomish houses and later in the crypt of Sagrada Familia. He was run over by a tram in 1926 and died, taken for a tramp, among the city's poor. He may yet be made a saint.

Unfinished business
Still incomplete, Sagrada
Família is one of the
most extraordinary
buildings of all time.

HELSINKI RAILWAY STATION

🚆 1914   📍 HELSINKI, FINLAND   ✍ ELIEL SAARINEN   🏛 RAILWAY STATION

A competition to redesign Helsinki's central station was won by Eliel Saarinen (1873–1950) in 1904. The result is one of the world's most civilized downtown train stations, with an interior as calm and beautiful as a Lutheran cathedral. Emil Wikström's huge statues, which flank the entrance, are the only full-blooded form of decoration used by Saarinen on this functional yet romantic building, which is constructed of granite blocks over a concrete frame. The classical entrance arch is influenced by the Viennese Secessionists, but otherwise the design is very much Saarinen's own—the expression of an aesthetic of national romanticism that had been growing in Finland as the country headed toward independence from Russia. The station concourse is flanked by a grand ticket office on one side and an equally impressive restaurant on the other.

Saarinen moved to the US in 1923, where he designed the Cranbrook Academy of Art in Michigan, becoming its president in 1932; among his students were the brilliant designers Charles and Ray Eames.

Station approach
The facade of the station is dominated by its entrance arch, copper-clad clock-tower, and stylized statues bearing globelike lanterns.

VICTOR EMMANUEL MONUMENT

🚆 1911   📍 ROME, ITALY   ✍ GIUSEPPE SACCONI   🏛 CIVIC BUILDING

This bombastic white marble edifice, known locally as "The Typewriter," was built on the slopes of the Capitol Hill to commemorate Italy's unification. Conceived by Giuseppe Sacconi (1854–1905) as a kind of acropolis in Rome, it features a huge equestrian statue of Victor Emmanuel II at the top of a flight of steps leading to the Altar of the Nation. The surrounding arcade, 50 ft (15 m) high and curved, is adorned by two bronze chariots, each driven by a Winged Victory.

STEINHOF CHURCH

🚆 1907   📍 VIENNA, AUSTRIA   ✍ OTTO WAGNER   🏛 PLACE OF WORSHIP

Otto Wagner's Steinhof Church in Vienna rises in solemn and dignified fashion above the psychiatric hospital that Wagner also designed. For all its essential severity, it has a wealth of rich and coolly sensual decoration. The brick nave is sheathed in white Carrara marble, shot through with stylized *Jugendstil* (Art Nouveau) ornamentation. The half-spherical, copper-tiled dome was once gilded, as were the iron windows; even the bolts used to fasten the marble panels were coated in copper. Internally, large expanses of white wall exude a formal simplicity, yet, punctuated by marble and golden ornaments, they are far from stark. The design combines functional details, such as rounded pew edges to prevent injury to the patients, with a soaring, airy dome and a glittering mosaic glass window intended to lift the spirits.

METRO STATIONS, PARIS

🚇 1906 📍 PARIS, FRANCE ✍ HECTOR GUIMARD 🏛 UNDERGROUND RAILWAY STATIONS

Between 1898 and 1905, French architect Hector Guimard (1867–1942) designed a series of delightful Art Nouveau entrances for the stations of the new Paris Metro. They ranged from simple open staircases illuminated by electric lights, to covered stairways with delicate iron-framed canopies and glass panels, and even complete pavilions. The integration of structure, materials, typography, and

art owes much to the work of Belgian architect Victor Horta. Even so, they were not universally liked, being dubbed "galvanized zinc ichthyosaurus skeletons" by one critic. Sadly, they went the way of dinosaurs, and by 1978, when Guimard's Paris Metro work was listed, only two of the original entrances were still in place.

Art Nouveau ironwork
The entrances were based on a modular design that utilized iron, bronze, and glass components.

SACRÉ COEUR

🚇 1914 📍 PARIS, FRANCE ✍ PAUL ABADIE 🏛 PLACE OF WORSHIP

The chalk-white Basilica of the Sacred Heart (Sacré Coeur) sits high above central Paris on the top of Montmartre. Commissioned by the state in 1875 and designed by Paul Abadie (1812–84) in an unconvincing Romano-Byzantine style, it dominates many views of the city, and even more postcards. The basilica was difficult to build: 83 concrete columns had to be driven into the hillside to support it; as a result, it is often said that it is the church

that holds up the hill, not the hill the church. The exterior is dominated by three domes—two lesser and one major—which are stretched into ovoids. The bell tower is 260 ft (80 m) tall and houses a mighty 19-ton bell that can, sometimes, be heard above the angry traffic roaring below.

Hilltop facade
The facade, with its triple portico, boasts bronze equestrian statues of St. Joan of Arc and St. Louis, with Christ standing above.

GRUNDTVIG'S CHURCH

🏛 1940   📍 COPENHAGEN, DENMARK   ✏ P. V. JENSEN-KLINT   🏛 PLACE OF WORSHIP

This hugely powerful yet slightly frightening yellow-brick church was designed to resemble a giant organ, even though it takes its strictly architectural cues from the stepped gable facades of traditional Danish medieval churches. Involving the work of three generations of architects from the same family, the church is a memorial to the popular theologian and hymn writer N. F. S. Grundtvig.

Of cathedral-like proportions and constructed of around six million handmade bricks, Grundtvig's Church took many years to complete. The architect, P. V. Jensen-Klint, died in 1930, before the church's completion. He was succeeded by his son, Kaare Klint, who also designed many of the furnishings, including the wooden chairs that line the vertiginous nave. The building houses two magnificent organs: the second of these, installed over the main entrance in 1965, was designed by Kaare's son Esben. The interior of the church, measuring 249 ft (76 m) wide and 115 ft (35 m) high, is daunting in its scale. The Gothic arches, free of all decoration, soar relentlessly with music from the organs and voices from the choir. The two pulpits are simply extensions of the brick structure; the only part of the building that is not brick is the limestone font. The church, which stands in the suburb of Bispebjerg, forms the heart of a low-rise residential development also designed by Jensen-Klint.

P. V. JENSEN-KLINT

Danish architect P. V. Jensen-Klint (1853–1930) aimed to recover "the scarlet thread of tradition that binds generation to generation." Viewing Classicism as an unhealthy break with the past, he sought to embody the spirit of Danish folk styles in his largely Gothic and Baroque designs. These display a simplicity and strength, and an integrity of craftsmanship and materials. His enthusiasm for medieval Danish brick architecture is clearly expressed in Grundtvig's Church.

Church marriage
With its tall, narrow windows, small entrances, and gabled facades, Grundtvig's Church marries historical forms with functional simplicity.

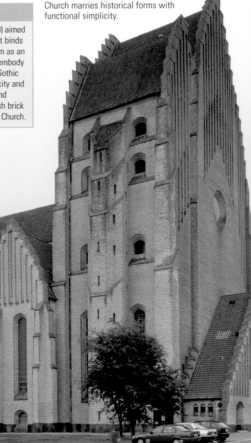

DEANERY GARDEN

1901 | SONNING, BERKSHIRE, ENGLAND | SIR EDWIN LUTYENS | RESIDENCE

Deanery Garden is an idyllic, asymmetric, and yet highly disciplined brick-and-timber English country house inspired by the Arts and Crafts movement. It was designed by Edwin Lutyens *(see p.455)* for Edward Hudson, the founder of *Country Life* magazine, which championed the architect's work. The garden that girdles the house was planned by Lutyens's long-time collaborator, Gertrude Jekyll (1843–1932). Together, they created a new country house aesthetic for the emerging rich upper middle classes that has yet to lose its hold on the imagination. Lutyens's houses are so convincing partly because he worked from an early age in a local building supplier's yard, and partly because he was schooled by such rigorous yet inventive Victorian architects as Ernest George, Harold Peto, Norman Shaw, and Philip Webb. The brilliance of Deanery Garden is that it shows how age-old building traditions, modern free-form house plans, and a sense of timelessness could be fused together in an original, compelling architecture.

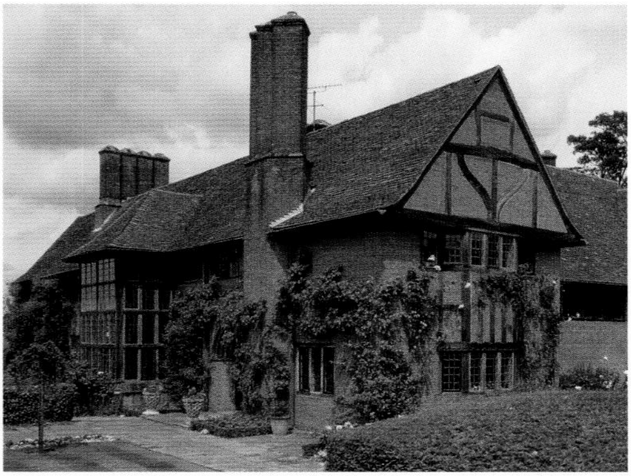

Romantic idyll
Constructed from local materials and beautifully crafted, this deep-eaved house is a play on the romantic idea of an English yeoman's farmhouse.

CASTLE DROGO

1930 | DREWSTEIGNTON, DEVON, ENGLAND | SIR EDWIN LUTYENS | RESIDENCE

One of the last English castles to be built, Castle Drogo is dramatically situated above the Teign Gorge, commanding panoramic views of Dartmoor. Designed for millionaire Julius Drewe by Edwin Lutyens, this house has the grand scale and rugged appearance of a medieval castle, yet inside it is perfectly comfortable and homely. The sloping walls are punctuated by vast transomed, mullioned windows, while the entrance is through a gateway complete with working portcullis. The interior is a thoughtful composition of vaulted staircases, huge windows, grand arches, and changing floor levels. The drawing room, lit on three sides, is especially fine; the top-lit kitchens are magnificent.

House of granite
The granite walls, entirely free of gutters and drainpipes, are sloped to increase the perceived height of what is, in any case, a very tall building.

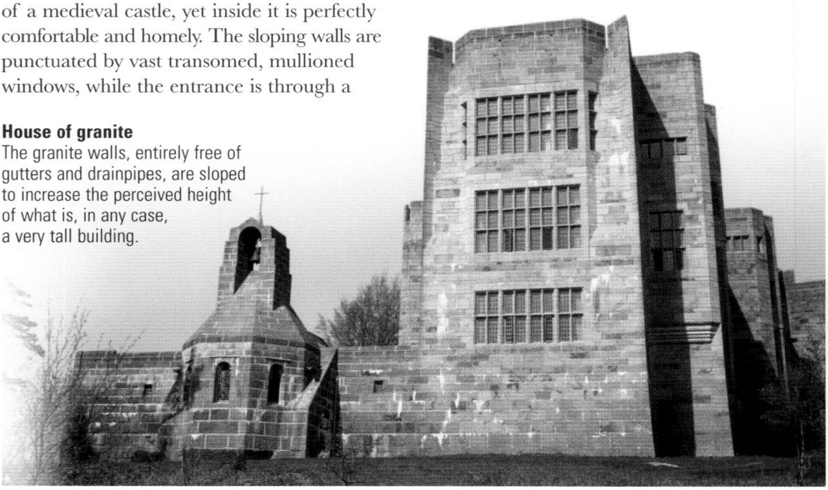

The modern world

I N THE 20TH CENTURY, technological development went into overdrive. The world of 1900, even at its most advanced, was a place of steam, silent movies, and tentative experiments in flight. Yet within 100 years it had become a realm of satellites and space exploration, mass car ownership, computers, and instant communication.

Despite many life-enhancing inventions and life-saving medical developments, this was the bloodiest and most aggressive century in our history. The world was twice engulfed by global conflict, and dictators such as Adolf Hitler, Joseph Stalin, Mao Zedong, and Pol Pot presided over the murder of millions. And yet, out of all this death and suffering came radical new architecture, along with new approaches to music, philosophy,

Wright brothers' *Flyer*
As important as it was, the first powered flight by the Wright brothers in 1903 was so brief it could have taken place inside a Boeing 747 Jumbo jet.

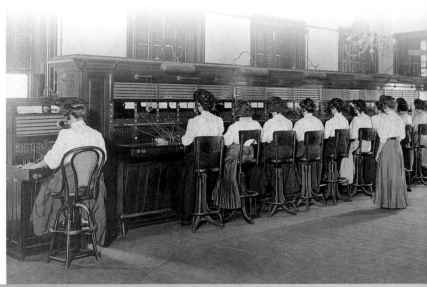

KEY DATES

1917 The Russian Revolution sees the installation of the world's first Communist government under Lenin

1923 Le Corbusier publishes *Vers une Architecture*, the blueprint for avant-garde Modernism

1928 The Milam Building, San Antonio, Texas, is the world's first air-conditioned office building

1933 Adolf Hitler sworn in as German Chancellor after the Nazi Party is voted into power

1900

1925

1919 Treaty of Versailles: Germany humiliated by Allies; the seeds of World War II are sown

1925 The word's first motel, The Motel Inn, opens in San Luis Obispo, California

1929 The Wall Street Crash; the New York Stock Exchange melts down, triggering the Great Depression

1939 Germany invades Poland, triggering the start of World War II

literature, physics, and ways of living. The mud, squalor, carnage, and waste of life synonymous with World War I made many architects to rethink their position. In reaction to this early-20th-century "Dark Age," they created an architecture of sun, light, air, and sanitation. They devised a clean-cut white architecture, Modernism, drawing its inspiration from ocean liners, as if suggesting that humankind should sail off on a collective cruise away from the political and economic regimes that had led to bloody trench warfare.

Telephone exchange, Philadelphia, 1915
The telephone made speaking to people long distances away—previously only contactable by letter or telegraph—a commonplace event.

Le Corbusier *(see pp.445, 472)*, the most prominent Modernist, included many images of ships in his seminal treatise *Vers une Architecture* (1923). Fittingly, the fourth meeting of the Congrès Internationaux d'Architecture Moderne, a think tank for this new generation of architects and urban planners, was held in 1933 on board a white ocean liner. Ever since, it has been common to give apartment buildings, sanatoria, and hotels the

SOUND AND VISION

Communications and entertainment media developed rapidly in the early 20th century. In 1906, the first public radio transmission was made in the US, and in 1936 regular TV broadcasts began in the UK. The movies were well established by this time, having moved from silent films to "talkies" by 1927, and, in the early 1930s, color pictures. The record industry had also taken off, bringing popular music to the masses. By the end of the century, the Internet had made movies, news, music, TV, and radio shows all accessible from a computer keyboard.

His Master's Voice (HMV)
This record label became one of the world's best-known trademarks, and it is still in use today.

"HIS MASTER'S VOICE"

Buzz Aldrin on the moon
In 1969, astronauts from the Apollo 11 spacecraft walked on the moon's surface for the first time, illustrating just how far technology had come in less than 70 years since the Wright brother's first flight.

bracing, balconied look of great passenger ships.

AIR-RAID DESTRUCTION

Sadly, the peace settlement of World War I sowed the seed of future conflict. Just as the world was clawing its way out of the Great Depression of the 1930s, it was again plunged into war. One of the features that made World War II so devastating was the tactic of aerial bombing, with the express

aim of destroying the centers of cities, making architecture a specific target rather than an accidental casualty.

In 1942, Britain's RAF fire-bombed Lubeck and Rostock, two handsome Hanseatic cities on the north coast of Germany, killing hundreds of people and making thousands homeless. The Luftwaffe retaliated with the "Baedeker Raids," aimed at destroying England's architectural heritage, and thus its morale. Picking targets from the three-star-rated buildings listed in the famous Baedeker travel guides, the German bombers did their best to erase the cultural legacy of places such as Bath, Exeter, and Canterbury. These tit-for-tat raids culminated in the incineration, by the RAF and the USAF, of the beautiful medieval and Baroque city of Dresden, Saxony, in 1945.

The same year, two USAF B-29 Superfortress bombers used a new type of weapon against the Japanese cities of Hiroshima and Nagasaki—the atomic bomb. The results were horrific. Now humankind could vaporize entire cities in an instant.

POST-WAR ARCHITECTURE

The notion of human progress had been mocked and challenged by Auschwitz, and the post-war world, overshadowed by the Cold-War threat of nuclear Armageddon, was a much-changed place. Architecture had to readjust to the new reality. To meet the reconstruction needs, architects designed buildings that could be mass-produced. These system-built, prefabricated homes, hospitals, schools, and

Transportation
In the post-war years, urban planning and architecture had to adapt to the seemingly limitless growth in car traffic. Towns and cities became increasingly oriented toward the car.

universities all too often proved to be failures, both practically and socially.

More inspiring was the creation of a new style of free-form architecture, originated in Germany by architects and engineers wishing to express the ideals of freedom, democracy, and civility. This project was later boosted by the development of new materials and the computer, allowing architects to shake off convention and produce such provocative yet popular designs as the Sydney Opera House *(see p.484)* and Bilbao's Guggenheim *(see p.491)*.

As the 21st century began, war raged on. The US-led invasion of Iraq in 2003 put the ancient monuments described in the early pages of this book *(see pp.47–50)*, just as striking as those above, at risk of destruction.

COMPUTERS AND ARCHITECTURE

The most important recent development in architecture is computer-aided design (CAD). This software makes it relatively easy to generate graphics whose mathematics—scale, proportions, dimensions, curvatures, and so on—would have made it near impossible to draw by hand. In addition, CAD can calculate the nature of the internal structure required to support a building's surface design. It is also possible to link CAD-using computers to factories, giving the architect more control over the manufacturing process.

Models and visualization
CAD enables architects and their clients to see virtual models of their buildings in situ.

MODERNISM
ca. 1910–40

Modernism took very different turns in Europe and the US, before flying across the world in a tide of concrete, steel, and glass. In Europe, it was largely the product of those who wanted to change the world—lock, stock, and barrel vault. Driven by the underlying philosophy of the Bauhaus design school in Germany *(see p.441)*, the Modernists' concrete designs were intended to be revolutionary, presaging a brave new socialist world.

Many of the first truly Modern houses were playthings for the artistic wealthy, and the public had difficulty taking Modernism's radical approach seriously. Modernism was cleverly satirized as early as 1928 by the English novelist Evelyn Waugh. In *Decline and Fall*, a young aristocrat, Margot Beste-Chetwynde, demolishes her ancestral English pile in favor of a Le Corbusier-style *machine à habiter*. The architect is Otto Silenus, whose only claim to fame is a design for an unbuilt bubble-gum factory published in an obscure journal. Silenus's ambition, he says, is to remove the human element from architecture (he questions the need for staircases). This gives us an idea of how Modern design must have seemed to many contemporary observers. The more Modernist architects claimed that their work was not a style but a purely rational form of design, the more people wanted to disbelieve them.

MODERNISM IN THE UNITED STATES
The opening of the International Style exhibition at New York's Museum of Modern Art in 1932 was a seminal moment for Modernism in the US. There had been Modern architecture before this, especially in California, where architects including Rudolph Schindler (1887–1953) and Richard Neutra (1892–1970) from Vienna had settled to escape World War I. However, the New York exhibition focused attention on the genre, and opened the eyes of the wider American audience. Soon, Modernism was being taken up by big business, as well as by fashionable patrons. In retrospect, it seems highly ironic that an approach to architecture initially wrapped up in concerns for shaping a fairer, more humane world for the masses eventually became a symbol for the might of corporate America and, ultimately, for global capitalism.

◁ THE BAUHAUS BUILDING AT DESSAU, GERMANY, WAS DESIGNED BY WALTER GROPIUS AND BUILT IN 1925–26. BAUHAUS DESIGN HAD A MAJOR IMPACT ON ART AND ARCHITECTURE TRENDS IN WESTERN EUROPE AND THE US.

ELEMENTS

The Modernist dream was one of a smoothly functioning, machine-driven Utopia. It never happened, although much of the best Modernist architecture is a highly optimistic part-realization of that dream, making use of the latest materials and sometimes stretching them into something truly radical. Sunlight was welcomed with open walls.

△ **Pilotis**
Le Corbusier restated the idea of the Renaissance *piano nobile*, raising the first floors, or living rooms, of his early white modern villas up on slim, undecorated versions of Classical columns. He called these "pilotis." This example is from the Villa Savoye, Poissy, France, completed in 1929.

△ **Reinforced concrete ramps**
The orthogonal geometry of much zealous early Modernist architecture was, at times, subverted beautifully. This is the smoothly spiraling ramp of the Penguin Pool at London Zoo, designed by Berthold Lubetkin and Ove Arup.

◁ **Glass-brick walls**
The French architect Pierre Chareau designed the Maison de Verre, Paris, with walls made of the latest glass bricks, a homage to new building technology and to the notion of maximizing sunlight at all costs.

Concrete brises-soleil ▷
Conscious that the new architecture was in danger of creating buildings that were too hot for comfort in summer, Le Corbusier devised these concrete *brises-soleil*, or "sun-breaks."

▽ **Horizontal windows**
The German Pavilion, Barcelona, by Mies van der Rohe, demonstrates an idealistic use of sheer planes of concrete, glass, steel, and marble.

Simple use of rich materials highlights their quality

The Pavilion was influenced by Classical and Japanese design

ROBIE HOUSE

🪦 1910 📍 CHICAGO, IL ✍ FRANK LLOYD WRIGHT 🏛 RESIDENCE

This low-lying house, built for the bicycle and motorcycle manufacturer Frederick C. Robie, marked a revolution in domestic architecture. Rooms are arranged on an open plan. Deep eaves prevent the midday sun reaching the south-facing living and dining room; the eaves also seem to stretch, in spirit, wide out to the yard and beyond. This sense of horizontality is exaggerated by long, shallow Roman bricks that help give the house its streamlined appearance.

ROCKEFELLER CENTER

🪦 1940 📍 NEW YORK, NY ✍ RAYMOND HOOD & OTHERS 🏛 COMMERCIAL BUILDING

The Rockefeller Center is an enormous commercial development in mid-town Manhattan, famous for the beautifully sculpted, giant RCA Tower, the Radio City Music Hall, and the world's most famous outdoor public ice-skating rink.

Expensively and imaginatively finished, the complex serves as a civic building as well as a commercial center. New Yorkers can walk right through its dramatically lit first-floor mall, stop off in its cafés, watch movies, and skate in its famous sunken plaza. A cluster of towers, some not added until the 1970s, surrounds the RCA Tower.

Construction began in 1929, with extraordinary optimism. John D. Rockefeller had intended to build an opera house here, but the Great Crash changed his mind. The RCA building—designed by Raymond Hood (1881–1934) and now known as the GE Building—is 70 stories and 850 ft (259 m) high; it is clad in a distinctive mix of granite, Indiana limestone, and aluminum.

JOHNSON WAX ADMINISTRATION BUILDING

🪦 1939 📍 RACINE, WI ✍ FRANK LLOYD WRIGHT 🏛 COMMERCIAL BUILDING

The Great Workroom at the heart of the Johnson Wax building is like something from a 1930s science fiction illustration. There are no windows from which to look out; light filters in from clerestory windows set high around the massive room—lined not with glass but with translucent Pyrex tubes.

To compound the futuristic effect, the lofty ceiling is held up by a forest of slender, tapering lilypad columns. These have a diameter of just 9 in (23 cm) as they meet the floor. Initially, building inspectors thought that these columns would be unable to meet the statutory load of 12 tons before collapsing; in a test for their benefit, Wright (1867–1959) proved that his novel columns could shoulder 60 tons before breaking.

Wright reinvented not just the modern office at Racine, but modern architecture itself. This is a truly groundbreaking work. From the outside, the streamlined offices are clad in red bricks and are overshadowed by Wright's 14-story Research Tower, added between 1944 and 1951.

Lasting modernity
Wright designed new typing chairs, and red, streamlined steel tables for the Modernist office; 21st-century furnishings are equally at home.

FALLINGWATER

⚰ 1939   📍 BEAR RUN, PA   ✐ FRANK LLOYD WRIGHT   🏛 RESIDENCE

FALLINGWATER EXTERIOR

This was the finest house designed by Frank Lloyd Wright (1867–1959), built over a waterfall hidden deep in wooded countryside between 1936 and 1939. The house is actually dug right into the rocks over which the water falls, and an outcrop appears from the floor in the living room. The main rooms and balconies are cantilevered away from the center to give a seemingly gravity-defying effect. The reinforced concrete house has been expensive to

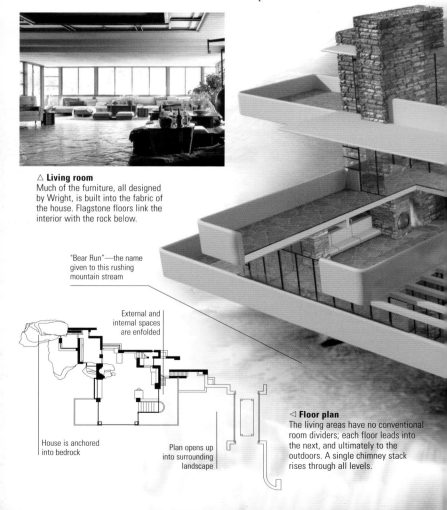

△ **Living room**
Much of the furniture, all designed by Wright, is built into the fabric of the house. Flagstone floors link the interior with the rock below.

"Bear Run"—the name given to this rushing mountain stream

External and internal spaces are enfolded

House is anchored into bedrock

Plan opens up into surrounding landscape

◁ **Floor plan**
The living areas have no conventional room dividers; each floor leads into the next, and ultimately to the outdoors. A single chimney stack rises through all levels.

maintain and, indeed, has been in danger of serious structural failure. Its beauty and location, are, however, enough to keep it in safe hands for posterity. Fallingwater is a house in which inside and outside flow seamlessly from one to the other. This is the house as streamlined design. For all its faults, it proves that an ultramodern house can enhance rather than reduce a glorious natural landscape.

△ **Exterior balcony**
Even though the design of Wright's Fallingwater is ultramodern, its plan and structure are rooted in the nature of its woodland site.

Tops of parapet walls were rounded off by hand

House is massively counterweighted at the rear to support the layers

Layered slabs of local sandstone form the vertical structure

Layers take the form of vast poured-concrete "trays"

EMPIRE STATE BUILDING

🏛 1931   📍 NEW YORK, NY   ✍ SHREVE, LAMB & HARMON   🏛 COMMERCIAL BUILDING

Soaring nearly one third of a mile (½ a kilometer) into the Manhattan sky, the Empire State Building offers visitors breathtaking views of up to 80 miles (130 km) from its observatories. For over 40 years this was the world's tallest building, but its beginnings were far from auspicious—while it rose, Wall Street crashed and the US plunged into the Great Depression.

CENTRAL LOBBY

As a result of New York zoning laws at the time of this iconic skyscraper's construction, tall structures had to be stepped back to allow light to reach the ground and to keep the shadows they cast to a minimum. The result was a spate of fine stepped buildings that called to mind the ziggurats of Mesopotamia and the great medieval cathedrals of Europe. The Empire State Building was the greatest of these temples of commerce, rising 1,250 ft (381 m) above Fifth Avenue. The spire was intended as a mooring mast for airships, but fierce updrafts made this too dangerous. In 1951, a broadcasting antenna was added, topping 1,455 ft (443.5 m). The building is strong: in July 1945, a B-25 bomber crashed into the 79th and 80th floors; 14 people died and the tower swayed, but the fire was put out within 40 minutes and the building got back to business.

Known as the "Empty State Building" in the 1930s because it was hard to rent, the skyscraper came into its own in World War II, when it was filled with government offices. Today it thrives both as a commercial building and as a national historic monument.

Empire State statistics
The Empire State Building has 103 floors, 73 elevators, and 6,500 windows and weighs 330,000 tons. It remains a much-loved landmark.

SHREVE, LAMB & HARMON

Established in 1929, Shreve, Lamb, and Harmon's daunting first commission was the Empire State Building. Richmond H. Shreve (1877–1946) was lead designer. His client, John Jacob Raskob, had asked, "How high can you make it so it won't fall down?" The trio saw the building through to completion in a year and 45 days, $9m under budget. They built many more skyscrapers, but none as accomplished as this.

CHRYSLER BUILDING

🏛 1930 📍 NEW YORK, NY ✍ WILLIAM VAN ALEN 🏛 COMMERCIAL BUILDING

Art Deco, a decorative design movement emerging from the Paris Exhibition of 1925, was expressed with greatest vigor in the magnificent skyscrapers of New York built soon after. The most elegant of these was the Chrysler Building, designed by William Van Alen (1883–1954). From the tip of its spire, 1,047 ft (319 m) above the Manhattan sidewalks, down to its Croesus-rich marble and chrome-steel lobby, it epitomizes the stylishness and happily decadent opulence of Art Deco. Walter P. Chrysler, the car magnate, had wanted the tallest building in the world, and he got it—albeit briefly, since a year later the Empire State Building took the title and held it until 1974. The building is clad in silvery stone decorated with stylized Chrysler hub and radiator caps. The eye-catching stainless steel spire seems to unfold from the top of the tower like an immense concertina.

Spire construction
The seven-story spire was assembled inside the building, then hoisted into position through the roof opening before being anchored in place.

HOOVER DAM

🏛 1935 📍 NEAR LAS VEGAS, NEVADA ✍ GORDON KAUFMANN 🏛 DAM

When it was completed in 1935, the Hoover Dam was instantly acclaimed as the Eighth Wonder of the World. It was the first single structure to contain more masonry than the Great Pyramid at Giza. It provided water, reliably, to 25 million thirsty Americans, and had a generating capacity of 2.8 million kW. Although awesome, it was also a superb

work of art and architecture. The original engineering design was made over in a restrained Art Deco style by the British-born architect Gordon Kaufmann, who had made his name with the design of the Santa Anita racetrack and luxurious Spanish-Colonial-style houses in California. Kaufmann streamlined the form of the dam and its outbuildings, resolving them into an utterly convincing cinematic whole. He employed designers and artists to endow the mighty structure with much the same kind of detail as went into Raymond Hood's Rockefeller Center (see p.433).

Modern wonder
Nearly 727 ft (222 m) high and spanning 1,244 ft (379 m), the dam took 25,000 workers more than five years to build.

Manhattan skyline
From the start of the industrial age, skyscrapers have formed the distinctive New York City skyline. The Art-Deco Chrysler Building, with its elegant, silver-colored, layered spire, remains unique; all proclaim mercantile wealth.

FAGUS FACTORY

📐 1911   📍 ALFELD-AN-DER-LEINE, GERMANY   ✍ WALTER GROPIUS & ADOLF MEYER   🏛 INDUSTRIAL BUILDING

The young German architects Walter Gropius *(see opposite)* and Adolf Meyer (1881–1929) made their mark in 1911 with the radical Fagus shoe-last factory for Karl Benscheidt, funded by American United Shoe Machinery Corporation (USM). The building needed to express the company's break from centuries of tradition. Gropius and Meyer responded with a crisp, modern design fronted by a steel-and-glass "curtain" wall. The structural frame of the building was set well back from the facade, so that the steel-and-glass facade hung just like a curtain, a form of sleek design soon to be copied worldwide. The elegant,

functional design of the Fagus Factory was influenced by USM's highly glazed factory at Beverly, Massachusetts, designed by English-born engineer Ernest L. Ransome (1852–1917). Ransome's *Reinforced Concrete Buildings* (1912) was to have a huge impact on Modernism in Europe.

See-through style
The glazing continued around the corners of the building, making it as transparent as logic, practicality, and building technology allowed.

STEINER HOUSE

📐 1910   📍 VIENNA, AUSTRIA   ✍ ADOLF LOOS   🏛 RESIDENCE

Designed by Czech architect Adolf Loos (1870–1933) for the painter Lilly Steiner and her husband, this is a house with a split personality. For many years, the three-story, white concrete-and-glass rear aspect was cited as a model of how a rational modern house ought to look; however, the front aspect is very different indeed. The local planning

authority would only allow Steiner a one-story house with a mansard roof in this suburban setting. To get around the spatial limitations of this, Loos swept the mansard roof up very high and right over, to the extent that it reached a height of three stories at the rear of the house. Since the rear aspect is the one normally shown in

architecture books, many students and historians who come looking for the house assume that it has either been demolished or completely rebuilt. The house was built in the same year that Loos, a fierce polemicist, published his influential book, *Architektur*, and two years after his essay, "Ornament and Crime," in which he linked decoration with decadent, even criminal behavior.

Different aspects
The straight-laced rear aspect is much at odds with the squat facade at the front, with its high, curving mansard roof.

BAUHAUS

🏛 1926   📍 DESSAU, GERMANY   ✒ WALTER GROPIUS   🏛 EDUCATIONAL BUILDING

The German Bauhaus design school, founded in 1919 by Walter Gropius in Weimar, sought to encourage the production of functional, yet artistic objects for mass society, rather than individual items for the rich. It moved to Dessau in 1925, where Gropius designed the famous campus that is synonymous with Bauhaus ideas. The campus is now a World Heritage Site.

INTERIOR, MASTER'S HOUSE

Curiously, the school did not offer classes in architecture until 1927, even though the definitive Bauhaus building *(see also pp.430–1)*, the school itself, had been completed by then. Built largely of reinforced concrete with brick infill and distinctive square glazing bars, and set out in the shape of a propeller, this factorylike structure included lecture rooms, studios, offices, dining rooms, an assembly room, and accommodation for students and staff. The building was

abandoned in 1932, when the Bauhaus moved to Berlin under the direction of Ludwig Mies van der Rohe *(see p.443)*, but he closed it the following year, since it displeased the Nazis. Most of the school's teaching staff and graduates left Germany to spread the Modernist gospel worldwide. The Dessau campus survived World War II and several different incarnations, and is now a design school once again, under the auspices of the Bauhaus Dessau Foundation.

Master's house
The estate of houses for the Bauhaus masters and director was planned and erected at the same time as the main Bauhaus building.

WALTER GROPIUS

Berlin-born Gropius (1883–1969) worked for Peter Behrens, before setting up practice with Adolf Meyer in 1910. He founded the Bauhaus in 1919, but moved to England in 1933 when the Nazis came to power. Gropius emigrated to the US in 1937, becoming a Professor of Architecture at Harvard. He designed the US Embassy in Athens (1960), Baghdad University (1960), and New York's Pan Am Building (1963).

SCHRÖDER HOUSE

1924   UTRECHT, THE NETHERLANDS
GERRIT THOMAS RIETVELD   RESIDENCE

The Schröder House is much influenced by the Dutch painter Piet Mondrian, who was, with Gerrit Rietveld (1888–1964), a founder of the art movement De Stijl. Rooted in functionalism, De Stijl insisted on straight lines, planes of primary color, and a total absence of surface decoration. The Schröder House is the most complete realization of the movement's architectural ideas. The result is an intriguing house that looks as much like a piece of furniture as it does a building. Behind those Mondrian facades, the walls of the upper-floor rooms can be slid in and out of place to make either one large or several smaller rooms. Much of the essential furniture is built in, and the house as a whole is a fine piece of traditional craftsmanship. This is not surprising: Rietveld trained as a jeweler and cabinet-maker before turning to architecture. This gem is his only important building.

VAN NELLE FACTORY

1930   ROTTERDAM, THE NETHERLANDS
JOHANNES ANDREAS BRINKMANN   FACTORY

This factory on the banks of the Schie River was designed as a packaging plant for coffee, tea, and tobacco. Conveyor belts straddling the main access road delivered raw materials to the factory floors. The factory's steel and glass facades were curtain walls, while the curving reception building seemed to embrace visitors' cars. The cafeteria sat on top of the building, like the bridge of a ship. This was a truly Modernist factory, and the finest work of its young architect Johannes Brinkmann (1902–49). Now converted into offices, conference rooms, and exhibition halls, the building is a World Heritage Site.

KIEFHOEK HOUSING

1927   ROTTERDAM, THE NETHERLANDS
J. J. P. OUD   RESIDENCES

Functional, clean-cut, low-lying, and precise, this street of early Modernist social housing is both graceful and matter of fact. The houses were designed by J. J. P. Oud (1890–1963), a De Stijl-influenced socialist architect who was Municipal Housing Architect of Rotterdam at the time. Modern in style, the Kiefhoek houses were built in a traditional manner using bricks and timber studwork. The Kiefhoek houses featured in the New York International Style exhibition of 1932, alongside truly radical works by Le Corbusier and Mies van der Rohe. Oud went on to form his own practice in 1933, away from housing and town planning.

HILVERSUM TOWN HALL

1931   HILVERSUM, THE NETHERLANDS
WILLEM MARINUS DUDOK   CIVIC BUILDING

This superb brick town hall rises from landscaped gardens on the outskirts of Hilversum, a Dutch new town built along the lines of an English garden city. The building's lines may be severe, but its interior is wonderful—spacious, light-filled, and beautifully crafted. Architect Willem Dudok (1884–1974) was trained as an engineer at the Royal Military Academy, Breda, and his first buildings were forts and barracks. The slightly militaristic feel of Hilversum Town Hall suggests that his army background had a major influence on his later career in civic architecture. Although clearly modern and with more than a passing resemblance to a power station, the building's central courtyard and lofty tower recall the planning and appearance of medieval town halls *(see Palazzo Pubblico, p.267)*. Appointed Director of Public Works at Hilversum in 1915, Dudok devoted nearly 40 years to the design and planning of the new town.

GERMAN PAVILION, BARCELONA

🏛 1929 📍 BARCELONA, SPAIN ✍ LUDWIG MIES VAN DER ROHE 🏛 PUBLIC BUILDING

Ludwig Mies van der Rohe (1886–1969), famous for his dictum "Less is More," tried to create contemplative, neutral spaces through an architecture based on material honesty and structural integrity. The pavilion he designed *(see also p.432)* for the Barcelona Expo of 1929—one of the 20th century's most beautiful buildings—was proof that the new architecture emerging out of the Bauhaus *(see p.441)* and elsewhere in Germany was far from puritanical. Built of marble, onyx, travertine, steel, and glass and hinting at ancient Japanese tradition, the pavilion connected architecture to landscape and served as a quiet space for reflection in what was a busy fairground. Sitting on Mies's elegant Barcelona chairs, visitors could enjoy views across the city while watching changing patterns of light reflected from an integral pool play across the gleaming walls. This was the model for the gridlike, purist, yet rich designs that later became Mies's trademark.

Although demolished in 1930, it had made such a profound impact that a replica was erected in its place in 1981–86. Mies emigrated to the US in 1937, where he designed such seminal works as the Seagram Building, New York *(see p.475)*. He remained a potent force in architecture well after his death in 1969.

Pavilion exhibit
The pavilion was remarkable in that there was nothing on show inside its open-plan interior during the exhibition; it was an exhibit in itself.

TUGENDHAT HOUSE

🏛 1930 📍 BRNO, CZECH REPUBLIC ✍ LUDWIG MIES VAN DER ROHE 🏛 RESIDENCE

The two-story Tugendhat House, which sits on a hillside in Brno, in what is now the Czech Republic, was essentially a reworking of Mies's German Pavilion. The plan is similar, as are the rich materials. The living and dining areas, measuring 80 x 40 ft (24 x 12 m) and stretching across the width of the first floor, are walled with a sweeping plane of glass. Two of the individual panes slide down into the ground like car windows. Inside, the palette of materials employed in the living spaces is beautifully resolved. Screens of onyx and ebony are set in play with a white linoleum floor covered with a white wool rug. The black curtains are fashioned from raw silk and white velvet. Most of the new Bauhaus-inspired houses at this time were a little on the austere side; Mies took a cue from those built by Adolf Loos *(see p.440)* in Vienna, which made great use of the costliest and most luxurious materials. From now on, Mies's brand of rigorous, yet opulent Modernism was to have an increasing appeal to the haute bourgeoisie.

Open spaces, open vistas
The floor-to-ceiling glass walls and open-plan interior generate a sense of freedom and openness by merging indoor and outdoor spaces.

VILLA SAVOYE

🏛 1929   📍 POISSY, PARIS   ✍ LE CORBUSIER   🏛 RESIDENCE

The radical design of Villa Savoye, a freestanding dwelling in suburban Paris, has long been cited as the exemplar of what Le Corbusier meant by the house being a "machine for living," a dictum that first appeared in his influential polemic *Vers une Architecture*, published in 1923. Villa Savoye was a vehicle for many of Le Corbusier's ideas, not just on architecture, but also on how people should live in the 20th century.

Le Corbusier set up practice with his cousin Pierre Jeanneret (1896–1967) in 1922 at 35 rue de Sèvres, Paris. In 1925, he designed Le Pavillon de L'Esprit Nouveau at the Paris Exhibition—a white prefabricated cubist house garnished with paintings by Braque and Picasso, and with a tree growing up through the center. The Parisian avant-garde loved it, and commissions for his revolutionary "machines for living" were soon pouring in.

Villa Savoye is the most notable example of these houses. The first floor is really little more than an elaborate garage, while the

open-plan second floor, which is lit by an almost continuous band of horizontal strip windows, is reached by a spiral staircase and a processional ramp. The principal rooms open out onto a roof garden, or courtyard; with the infinite sky above framed by the

Basic structure
The Villa Savoye is a hollow, lightweight concrete box, with its principal floor raised on slender columns, or "piloti," as Le Corbusier called them.

LE CORBUSIER

Swiss-born Charles-Edouard Jeanneret (1887–1965) trained as an engraver before learning architecture under Peter Behrens in Berlin and Auguste Perret in Paris. He changed his name to Le Corbusier—a play on the word "raven" (he looked like one) and his mother's maiden name—before devoting himself to architecture. From 1922 onward, he made his name designing a string of pure white Modernist villas for the newly artistic rich in Paris. *(See also p.473.)*

ROOFTOP COURTYARD OF THE VILLA SAVOYE

white concrete walls, there is an exhilarating feeling of freedom, openness, and healthy living. Although in theory an ultra-modern design, Villa Savoye is also an ingenious reworking of the ideal villas created by Palladio some four hundred years earlier in Italy *(see p.288)*.

Villa Savoye is at once rational, romantic, and idealistic—a kind of architectural kick-back against the darkness, devastation, and despair of World War I and the economic depression that followed. The house fell into disrepair during World War II, but has since been painstakingly restored.

PAVILLON SUISSE

🏛 1932 📍 PARIS, FRANCE
✎ LE CORBUSIER 🏛 UNIVERSITY

Monastic in spirit, this dormitory for Swiss students at Paris's Cité Universitaire is a steel-framed construction faced with concrete panels. The building is raised up on muscular concrete piloti, leaving it almost completely open on the first floor. The tightly planned student rooms are stacked up symmetrically on four floors, while the communal rooms and entrance lobby are housed in the concave-walled tower that adjoins the student block. The hostel shows Le Corbusier breaking away from straight lines and beginning to explore a more solid, monumental architecture, very much in contrast with that of his white villas.

VILLA STEIN

🏛 1927 📍 GARCHES, PARIS, FRANCE
✎ LE CORBUSIER 🏛 RESIDENCE

Although Le Corbusier spoke passionately about creating mass-produced, machine-made houses for the working classes, in reality he designed houses as art objects for the rich. Villa Stein was commissioned by Michael Stein (brother of writer Gertrude Stein), his wife Sarah, and Gabrielle de Monzie, Minister of Culture. A hollowed-out cube partly supported by piloti, it comprised two main floors, each with a garden. It also had sculptured stairs, suspended entrance canopies, and long, uninterrupted ribbon windows. Tellingly, it also had servants' quarters. It survives, but has been divided into apartments.

PAIMIO SANATORIUM

🛏 1933 📍 PAIMIO, NEAR TURKU, FINLAND
✎ ALVAR AALTO 🏛 PUBLIC BUILDING

The tuberculosis sanatorium at Paimio rises like a white ocean liner above the surrounding forests. It represents an extraordinary achievement by the young Alvar Aalto (1898–1976), reconciling Modernism and nature in a large, complex building designed to serve a wide public in urgent need of health care.

The sanatorium building comprises a number of crisply modeled wings, with each block angled to make optimum use of sunshine. The top floor of the elegant ward block opens into a long, well-protected balcony with views over the terraced gardens, and on through the forests beyond.

VILLA MAIREA

🛏 1939 📍 NOORMARKKU, FINLAND
✎ ALVAR AALTO 🏛 RESIDENCE

Designed for the industrialist Harry Gullichsen and his wife, Maire, the Villa Mairea marked a turning point in Modernism, favoring a return to nature, to the idea of architecture becoming organic, emotional, and warm. The house makes much use of warm wood, brick, and tiles; it includes subtle references to age-old farmhouse architecture and timeless ways of living. There are clear connections to the surrounding forest inside the house, notably in the poles flanking the main stair, and in the many columns, some bound in rattan, others faced with timber slats, supporting the generously proportioned rooms.

DE LA WARR PAVILION

🛏 1935 📍 BEXHILL, SUSSEX, ENGLAND ✎ ERICH MENDELSOHN & SERGE CHERMAYEFF 🏛 PUBLIC BUILDING

Set by the sea in front of cliffs of grim Edwardian apartment blocks, this pavilion was commissioned, through a competition, from the émigré German architect Erich Mendelsohn (1887–1953) and the Russian Serge Chermayeff (1900–96). At its opening, by the Duke and Duchess of York (who later became King George VI and Queen Elizabeth), the Mayor of Bexhill described it as "part of a great national movement… giving that relaxation, that pleasure, that culture, which hitherto the gloom and dreariness of British resorts have driven our fellow countrymen to seek in foreign lands." The building was exotic. It was the first major welded steel-framed building in

Britain and the country's first public building built in the Modernist style. Professor Charles Reilly, former Professor of Architecture at Liverpool University, wrote: "the straight-forward spaciousness of the interiors and the great spiral stairs gracefully mounting in their glass cylinders are things we have all dreamed about but none of us have done on their scale or with their sureness of touch."

Bringing in fresh ideas
Two immigrant architects, Chermayeff also a decorator and ballroom dancer, were chosen to enliven Bexhill as a British seaside resort.

HIGHPOINT, LONDON

🛏 1935 📍 LONDON, ENGLAND ✍ BERTHOLD LUBETKIN 🏛 RESIDENCE

Highpoint was commissioned by Sigmund Gestetner, the office equipment magnate, as a block of ideal high-rise apartments for company workers. Today, it is a much-sought-after block of expensive flats in Highgate, standing high above London in extensive grounds. The crisp, white, inventive design was by the Georgian émigré architect Berthold Lubetkin (1901–90), best known until then for his sensational penguin pool at London Zoo and for his avant-garde studio, Tecton. With more than a little help from Ove Arup (1896–1988)—the Danish engineer also recently settled in London—Lubetkin rose to the challenge at Highpoint.

Highpoint is a white double-cruciform, seven-story block housing 64 centrally heated

apartments reached by elevators rising from a high-ceilinged entrance lobby. There was originally a tea room here. The apartments were arranged so that the living rooms caught the sun in the day, while bedrooms were in the shade.

Socialist ideals
Lubetkin had recently traveled to Russia to see how workers' housing was built there.

MINISTRY OF EDUCATION & HEALTH

🛏 1943 📍 RIO DE JANEIRO, BRAZIL
✍ OSCAR NIEMEYER 🏛 GOVERNMENT BUILDING

A relentless series of concrete *brises-soleil* (sun screens) gives this 15-story office block a powerful, sculpted quality. At the base of the tower, and at right angles to it, is a low-lying block with a landscaped roof, housing an amphitheatre and exhibition halls. The concrete tower is clad in a veneer of pink-grey granite, while the block at its base is finished in custom-made blue and white tiles, with a tile mural by Candido Portinari.

SÃO FRANCISCO CHURCH, BRAZIL

🛏 1943 📍 PAMPULHA, BRAZIL
✍ OSCAR NIEMEYER 🏛 PLACE OF WORSHIP

A glorious sequence of wave-like concrete parabolas, the church of São Francisco at the resort of Pampulha is a happy marriage of the skills of Oscar Niemeyer (b.1907) and engineer Joaquim Cardozo. Two great concrete vaults wrap over the nave and choir of the church, while the campanile and entrance porch are freestanding. Light penetrates the vaults through vertical louvres at the entrance and above the altar. Overlying the concrete walls is a lively wash of white, blue, and brown mosaics. The controversial design provoked a great deal of animosity among conservative Catholics.

LINGOTTO FIAT FACTORY

🖥 1923 📍 LINGOTTO, TURIN, ITALY ✍ GIACOMO MATTE-TRUCCO 🏛 INDUSTRIAL BUILDING

Proclaimed at the time as "the first-built manifestation of Futurism" (an iconoclastic art movement obsessed with speed), Fiat's Lingotto factory was never intended to be an artwork, or even particularly a great work of architecture. Yet with its heroic scale, relentless lines, and race-track speeding around its roof, it caught and even defined the spirit of the age for many young artists and architects in Italy.

A truly outstanding example of early reinforced concrete industrial architecture, the factory was designed not by an architect, but by the engineer Giacomo Matte-Trucco. Built between 1915 and 1923, it consisted of two parallel five-story production blocks. These were linked by service towers containing staircases and bathrooms. When completed, the factory housed Europe's longest production line.

Matte-Trucco's design was, by any standards, a brilliant solution to the question of how best to organize cohesive production

FACTORY INTERIOR, SHOWING HELICAL RAMP

in a self-contained structure. Raw materials entered on the first floor and, through a series of production lines, cars emerged on the top floor, and then out onto the roof for testing on a 1½ mile (2.4 km) long test track. The rooftop track rightly caught the public imagination, and it must have been a thrilling sight and sound in its heyday. Internal helical ramps climbing around the building not only allowed cars to be taken up and down from the roof, but also gave executives the luxury of driving through the factory to check progress on production.

GIACOMO MATTE-TRUCCO

An Italian naval architect and engineer, Giacomo Matte-Trucco (1869–1934) is known primarily for a single major building—the Lingotto Fiat factory. He was not, as he has often been described, a Futurist architect, but an engineer responding to a brief from Fiat's founder, Giovanni Agnelli, for a factory to rival Ford's US factories, which were based on scientific management and mass production. Despite himself, Matte-Trucco became a hero among early Modernists.

All good things come to an end, and the factory closed in 1982. Although cars are no longer made there, it has found a new lease of life. Since the late 1980s, it has been the subject of a massive remodeling carried out under the direction of the Genoese architect Renzo Piano. The former factory is home to offices, art galleries, cafes, restaurants, performance spaces, a hotel, a dental school, student residences, a conference center, and, appropriately, the Turin Polytechnic faculty of automotive engineering. A podlike art gallery, sponsored by the Fiat Agnelli family, sits on top of the rooftop track.

Rooftop racing
The test track, set 70 ft (21.3 m) above ground, was banked to stop cars from flying off the edge.

AIRCRAFT HANGARS, ORVIETO

🗓 1942　📍 ORVIETO, UMBRIA, CENTRAL ITALY
✎ PIER LUIGI NERVI　🏛 INDUSTRIAL BUILDINGS

Between 1935 and 1942, Italian engineer Pier Luigi Nervi (1891–1979) designed a series of concrete aircraft hangars for the Italian air force. The first, which set the structure and look of all that followed, was built at Orvieto in 1938. It consisted of long, pointed barrel vaults formed by a grid of light, crisscrossing ribs rising from complex triangulated edge-beams. The ribs were prefabricated from reinforced concrete. Creating a distinctive diamond lattice, these were both unusually strong and very beautiful. When retreating German forces tried to destroy the hangars in 1944, most of the rib joints remained intact—proof of their strength.

CASA DEL FASCIO

🗓 1935　📍 COMO, NORTHERN ITALY
✎ GIUSEPPE TERRAGNI　🏛 CIVIC BUILDING

This magnificent building in front of Como Cathedral is the work of the Italian Fascist architect Giuseppe Terragni (1904–43). Built as the headquarters of the local Fascist Party, it was renamed Casa del Popolo after the war and has since served a number of municipal roles, including as a Caribinieri station and a tax office. Looking like a giant Rubik's Cube, the building is a serious game of architectural logic. Planned around a concrete grid, the marble-clad facades hint at the internal layout. Only here and there is the severe grid broken open, as it is on the top floor, to suggest that the building is not a solid block. Inside, cantilevered stairways and offices are arranged around a great covered courtyard.

TRADITIONALISM
ca. 1900–40

Bauhaus Modernism was not the only way forward for new architecture in the 20th century—far from it. Across the world, many architects not only continued to work in local and historical traditions, but also learned to reinvent them with verve and élan. Others worked in ways that defy categorizing, and some, given free rein and working for overambitious clients, went completely over the top.

A revived monumental Neo-Classicism, or Traditionalism, flourished in the 20th century's great democracies, as well as in its most brutal dictatorships. The much-missed Pennsylvania Station *(see p.453)* in New York City was the ancient Roman Baths of Caracalla *(see p.115)* reworked to sensational effect, while Albert Speer's design for a vast Grosse Halle as the centerpiece of a post-war Nazi Berlin was on such a heartless scale it would have been truly overwhelming. Some architects, however, managed to satisfactorily blend modern concerns and functions with the sensibilities and forms of much older architecture. The modern Classicism of Charles Holden's designs *(see pp.457–8)* was exemplary. Equally, the ways in which Edwin Lutyens married traditional Indian design with English Classicism *(see p.455)* led to romantic yet practical buildings that changed ownership

quite happily as the British Empire gave way to Indian independence. There are buildings, too, like those of the Art-Deco years, that, while modern, were playful and far removed from the intellectual strictures of Bauhaus Modernism. And then there are those buildings that are simply one-offs, such as the Orthodox Cathedral, Asmara *(see p.464)* and the Einstein Tower, Potsdam *(see p.461)*.

FALSE HISTORY

There was, from 1920s onward, an attempt to tell the story of 20th-century architecture as if it were one smooth progression from the Arts and Crafts Movement, through the Bauhaus, to an all-encompassing, style-free, functional Modernism. As the following pages make clear, this was always an intellectual conceit, and deceit. The story of architecture has always been rich, complex, and often contradictory.

◁ THE OLYMPIC STADIUM, BERLIN, WAS BUILT IN 1935–36 TO PLANS BY THE ARCHITECT WERNER MARCH. IT IS TYPICAL OF THE MONUMENTALIST ARCHITECTURE THAT CHARACTERIZED NAZI GERMANY.

ELEMENTS

Traditionalism in the 20th century took many forms. There were many architects who were not anti-progress *per se* but were against what, to them, would have seemed a wilful rejection of precedent by the self-conscious young Modernists. They were also very much in favor of the use of the best materials and the finest craftsmanship.

◁ **Roman arcades**
Rome's "Square Colosseum" is an example of ancient Roman architecture reinvented for a political regime that was both forward- and backward-looking.

Traditional tower form is much enlarged

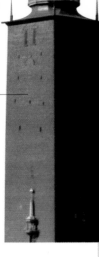

The medieval tower updated ▷
Traditionalists proved it was possible to stretch old designs; Stockholm City Hall evokes one of the great medieval town halls, although it is clearly built to 20th-century scale and ambition.

▽ **Complex play on history**
One of Stalin's ambitious "Seven Sisters," the Ministry of Commerce in Moscow, echoes, in part, the design of the Municipal Building, New York, and the Moorish tower of Seville Cathedral.

◁ **Hindu-Mughal style**
A stepped rooftop based on hybrid Hindu-Mughal precedent is used here in a wing of the Viceroy's Palace, New Delhi, designed by Edwin Lutyens—a marriage between English Edwardian Classicism and Indian design.

Moorish and medieval silhouette

Brick drum

Ribbing enhances vertical emphasis

△ **Primary forms**
Blocky, elemental forms underlie the design of many great traditional buildings, such as the drum—both circle-within-a-square and cylinder—crowning Stockholm City Library, a triumph of Nordic Classicism designed by Erik Gunnar Asplund.

PENNSYLVANIA STATION

🚊 1910 📍 NEW YORK, NY ✍ McKIM, MEADE & WHITE 🏛 TRAIN STATION

"Any city gets what it admires, will pay for, and, ultimately, deserves," thundered a New York Times editorial in 1963. At the time, the demolition of Pennsylvania Station, on New York's Eighth Avenue, was widely considered to be a great act of vandalism. It led to the rise of an effective conservation lobby in New York, and to the listing of many important buildings.

Pennsylvania Station had been truly spectacular—a train station fronted by long, Roman, Doric temple fronts and with a

concourse modeled on the Baths of Caracalla *(see p.115)*; the effect was remarkable. The trains arrived and departed from an equally magnificent train shed.

From 1966, the site was used for a grim commercial development that now, in turn, is making way for a brand-new station by Skidmore, Owings & Merrill *(see p.476)*.

Roman-style grandeur
The colonnade made a splendid welcome point and covered walkway for travelers. High windows over the concourse brought maximum light to the interior.

LINCOLN MEMORIAL

🚊 1922 📍 WASHINGTON, D.C.
🏛 HENRY BACON 🏛 MONUMENT

A vast and noble Doric temple raised in honor of president Abraham Lincoln, the memorial is supported by 36 columns, one for each of the 36 states of the Union at the time of Lincoln's assassination in 1865. The giant, seated statue in white Georgia marble is by Daniel Chester French. The first plans for a memorial date back to 1867, but it took 44 years before architect Henry Bacon (1866–1924) was commissioned.

The Lincoln Memorial was Bacon's last project. It blends stone from various states: white Colorado marble for the exterior, limestone from Indiana for the interior walls, pink Tennessee marble for the floor, and Alabama marble for the ceiling.

SAN SIMEON

🚊 1939 📍 SAN SIMEON, CA
✍ JULIA MORGAN 🏛 RESIDENCE

San Simeon, also known as Hearst Castle, is the home of William Randolph Hearst, the publishing mogul. It takes the form of a 165-room Moorish castle, inspired by the Alhambra *(see p.204)*, the church towers at Ronda, and southern Spanish hill towns. Built of concrete, it covers a vast area of gardens, terraces, pools, and walkways on a hillside that overlooks the Pacific Ocean.

The interiors are beautifully crafted, while the gardens are articulated by colonnades, pergolas, and carefully positioned works of art, including a Greco-Roman temple facade facing the Neptune Pool *(above)*.

MEIJI SHRINE

👤 1920   📍 TOKYO, JAPAN   ✎ UNKNOWN   🏛 PLACE OF WORSHIP

A spiritual haven amid the hustle and bustle of city life, this Shinto shrine in the heart of Tokyo was originally built by 100,000 volunteers in honor of Emperor Meiji and his wife, Shoken. The Meiji Shrine—the largest Shinto shrine in Tokyo—was destroyed during World War II but was reconstructed in 1958.

TORII (ENTRANCE GATE)

Set in a forestlike park of 120,000 trees transplanted here from all over Japan, the Meiji Shrine takes its inspiration from a style of shrine architecture that dates back to the 8th century. Utterly simple in design—and all the more special for it—the Meiji Shrine is constructed of unpainted timber. Color is used sparingly, with white and green predominating (the green comes from the copper detailing). Decoration is limited to the square lanterns that hang from the deep eaves of the shrine and the chrysanthemum crests of the Japanese royal family.

Worshipers and visitors approach the shrine through the thickly wooded, well-manicured park, past custom-made street lamps in the guise of little temples on poles, pebble paths, and wooden barrels of saké

donated to the Shinto monks by local businesses. They then pass under two torii (traditional gateways), the second of which is the largest wooden torii in Japan. Reaching two templelike pavilions, they drink water from one and wash their hands at the other. Next they stop at one of the trees to hang wooden prayer tablets, and finally they arrive at the shrine itself, with its richly decorated doors and great upturned roofs. Here, they throw money at the altar and clap to awaken the gods.

Traditional reconstruction
Unlike other historic buildings reconstructed in and around Tokyo in the 1950s, the Meiji Shrine made use of the correct traditional building materials—in this case mostly cypress wood and copper, as can be seen in this picture of the Inner Shrine.

EMPEROR MEIJI

Born in 1852, Emperor Meiji ("enlightened ruler") presided over Japan's transformation from an isolated feudal society into a modern industrialized nation. He moved the court from Kyoto to Tokyo, introduced compulsory education, adopted western clothes, and saw his country win wars against China (1894–95) and Russia (1904–05) largely as a result of superior technology. By the time of his death in 1912, Japan had become a major world power.

VICEROY'S HOUSE

🏆 1930 📍 NEW DELHI, INDIA ✍ SIR EDWIN LUTYENS 🏛 RESIDENCE

When the capital of the British Raj moved from Calcutta to New Delhi in 1912, work commenced on the Viceroy's House. Built on grand scale, this masterpiece of Anglo-Indian design was the work of English architect Edwin Lutyens. The building, which still commands New Delhi with absolute architectural assurance from Raisina Hill, is now Rashtrapati Bawan—the President's House.

The focus of the Viceroy's House is its great dome, fashioned out of magnificent pink and cream sandstone, and surely one of the finest and most original domes in all the world. Based on the design of the Great Stupa at Sanchi *(see p.144)*, it performs the same magic in the dry heat of New Delhi as the dome of St. Paul's Cathedral *(see p.326)* does in the damp chill of London.

Lutyens's genius was to plan a grand, Beaux-Arts style imperial palace that, while drawing on Neo-Classical principles, also incorporated aspects of India's rich architectural tradition. Such is the brilliance of his design that the Indian elements, such as chattris (roof pavilions) and chujjas (broadly projecting cornices), blend seamlessly with those from Europe and the Classical tradition. The result is a true fusion of very different design traditions, each enhancing the others.

SIR EDWIN LUTYENS

Edwin Lutyens (1869–1944), a pupil of Arts and Crafts architect Ernest George, designed a variety of beautifully crafted houses *(see p.423)* before establishing himself as a grand classicist in the inventive spirit of Wren. Instrumental in the layout and construction of New Delhi, Lutyens left a legacy of many solemn, heroic, and often daunting buildings.

EDWIN LUTYENS

The house is centrally planned, with a great flight of broad steps leading up to a colonnaded entrance and then to the Durbar Hall under the dome. Beyond and on either side are the impressive state rooms, and a loggia leading into the exquisite Mughal Garden. The four wings of the house were originally the Viceroy's offices and living quarters, and accommodation for guests.

Design fusion
The Viceroy's House is a fusion of Classical, European, and Indian design styles.

ST. MARTIN'S GARRISON CHURCH, NEW DELHI

📺 1930 📍 NEW DELHI, INDIA ✍ ARTHUR GORDON SHOOSMITH 🏛 PLACE OF WORSHIP

Home today to a school for local children and a congregation of the Church of India, St. Martin's was originally built as a church for the Indian Army. It definitely has the air of a fortress about it, with its massive brick walls, muscular tower, and little in the way of decoration. However, it is also a work of art of the very highest order, sprung from the mind of Arthur Gordon Shoosmith (1888–1974), an

assistant of Edwin Lutyens *(see p.455)*. Looking from the outside like a single block of stone, it has a generous, lofty, haunting interior, with daylight filtering through only a few high windows, to keep out the fierce light and cruel heat of the Delhi summer. The nave vaults are supported by a massive reinforced concrete skeleton. This gradually fell apart over some 60 years of neglect but was restored in the 1990s, as was the roof.

ELAN VALLEY DAMS

📺 1904 📍 ELAN VALLEY, RHAYDER, MID-WALES ✍ CITY OF BIRMINGHAM ENGINEERS DEPARTMENT 🏛 DAMS

Nothing quite prepares first-time visitors to the dams of the Elan Valley in mid-Wales. Opened in 1904, these impressive works of architecture were built to supply water to the city of Birmingham, 73 miles (118 km) away. The towers on top of the dams might well be mistaken for works by the English Baroque masters Nicholas Hawksmoor and John Vanbrugh *(see pp.328 and 329)*; indeed, the buildings of the Elan Valley are often fondly referred to as "Birmingham Baroque." Faced with massive rusticated granite blocks, the finest works here are the Pen y Garreg dam

and the Garreg Ddu viaduct, and the copper-domed Foel tower that controls the flow of water—up to 66 million gallons (300 million liters) per day. The dams are particularly wonderful after heavy rain, when water pours in great cavalry charges down their sides or over their tops. A second phase of dam construction, in the nearby Claerwen valley, was completed in 1956.

Pen y Garreg dam
Locally quarried rock was only suitable for use inside the dams. The hand-chiseled granite stones that face the dams were transported from south Wales.

SENATE HOUSE, UNIVERSITY OF LONDON

1937   LONDON, ENGLAND   CHARLES HOLDEN   UNIVERSITY

Founded in 1836, the University of London lacked an architectural focus until Senate House, with its mighty Portland stone tower, opened a century later. Originally, Charles Holden (1875–1960) had been asked to design a far more ambitious scheme here in Georgian Bloomsbury, with two heroic towers and 17 courtyards. Yet what he did manage to build was grand enough: a range of essentially Greco-Roman buildings stripped of most external detail but given great presence by their powerfully molded blocks of masonry. There is no steel frame behind the stones; Holden believed he was building here for at least 500 years, so only traditional masonry was appropriate. Inside is a sequence of fine rooms, including the superb Library, most of them a celebration of crafted oak, marble, bronze, and even stained glass.

Senate House tower
The Portland stone tower rises steadily into the sky from a base of sea-gray Cornish granite.

RIBA BUILDING, LONDON

1934   LONDON, ENGLAND
GREY WORNUM   INSTITUTIONAL BUILDING

Punctuating Georgian terraces and discreet 1920s apartment blocks, the headquarters of the Royal Institute of British Architects (RIBA) looks very much out of context. Resembling a giant tombstone, this solemn, handsome building is a feast of 1930s architectural craft, displaying fine relief carving, lettering, and etched glass. Materials throughout are robust, while details such as lamps, door handles, and handrails are a delight.

55 BROADWAY, LONDON

1929   LONDON, ENGLAND
CHARLES HOLDEN   COMMERCIAL BUILDING

Charles Holden, a teetotal, non-smoking, vegetarian Quaker, met his ideal client in the quietly charismatic figure of Frank Pick (1878–1941), a non-smoking, teetotal Congregationalist. In 1933, Pick became Chief Executive of the London Passenger Transport Board, a public corporation well known for championing new art, engineering, and architecture. In the late 1920s, he chose Holden to design the new headquarters of London Underground overlooking St. James's Park. Pick wanted light, and Holden made sure there was plenty of it in his zigguratlike, steel-framed, stone-clad office tower. Arranged on a cruciform plan, with a 175 ft (53 m) high clock tower over the crossing, 55 Broadway was the tallest office building in London at the time of its completion. Straddling the platforms of St. James's Park station, the building steps up from a low-lying base to the wings of offices above. Although radical in plan, 55 Broadway drew attention mostly for the controversial sculptures around its base by, among others, Henry Moore, Eric Gill, and Jacob Epstein.

ARNOS GROVE UNDERGROUND STATION

🚇 1932 📍 LONDON, ENGLAND ✍ CHARLES HOLDEN 🏛 UNDERGROUND RAILWAY STATION

In the early 1920s, Charles Holden began to design new London Underground stations for Frank Pick, such as 55 Broadway *(see p.457)*, but it was only in the 1930s that he really got into his stride with a series of brick-and-concrete stations on the Piccadilly Line. Holden had accompanied Pick on an architectural tour of Germany, Scandinavia, and the Netherlands and had been especially impressed by the work of Willem Dudok in Hilversum *(see p.442)* and Gunnar Asplund in Stockholm. The best of Holden's new stations was Arnos Grove, north London—a particularly fine meeting of ancient Roman and modern Dutch design and English craftsmanship. It has a high, generously glazed rotunda, capped with a pronounced

concrete cornice that rises above the station building. Here, Holden makes a brilliant play with a palette of traditional and modern materials, from reinforced concrete to brick and bronze. It was a superb achievement to have created an uncompromisingly functional building that, nevertheless, harked back to older, even timeless traditions in architecture.

Holden's trademarks
Holden's stations for London Underground were characterized by sweeping curves, exposed brickwork, concrete, and geometric detailing.

CITY HALL, NORWICH

🚇 1938 📍 NORWICH, NORFOLK, ENGLAND
✍ C. H. JAMES & S. R. PIERCE 🏛 CIVIC BUILDING

This fine Scandinavian-influenced city hall, with its handsome 184 ft (56 m) clock tower, is set on a podium above Norwich's market square, and reached up steps guarded by fierce bronze lions. City Hall is an excellent example of a design form that was developing healthily in 1930s England as a reaction to the white-cube Modernism of the Bauhaus. Its strength, as evidenced by this clean-cut yet well detailed and highly crafted building, is that it connected tradition with modernity, both formally and in terms of structure.

CITY HALL, STOCKHOLM

🚇 1923 📍 STOCKHOLM, SWEDEN
✍ RAGNAR OSTBERG 🏛 CIVIC

Stockholm's City Hall—at once medieval, modern, and gloriously romantic—has a wonderful, dragonlike exterior. Inside, it is a thing of endless delights: the Blue Hall (which is not blue), with its 10,000-pipe organ; the Council Chamber, with its roof modeled on a Viking longship; and the Golden Hall, its walls lined with over 18 million glass and gold mosaic pieces. These and other fairy-tale rooms face a huge colonnaded courtyard around which the entire building is gathered. Outside or in, the craftsmanship is breathtaking.

NOTRE DAME DU RAINCY

🖥 1923 📍 LE RAINCY, NEAR PARIS ✍ AUGUSTE PERRET 🏛 PLACE OF WORSHIP

Standing in the town of Le Raincy, some 8 miles (13 km) northeast of Paris, Notre Dame du Raincy is a deeply strange, flawed, but nevertheless special building. Designed by Auguste Perret (1874–1954), it was built as a war memorial and constructed entirely of exposed reinforced concrete. In fact, this was the first time that raw concrete had been used in such a context; although concrete was much in use by 1823, a building like this would normally have been clad in stone or marble for reasons of propriety and civility, if nothing else. As it happened, a lack of such cladding meant that, by the 1980s, the exposed structure of the church was in poor shape. The rolling program of repairs has involved gradual replacement of the deteriorating concrete, leaving the original design but little of the original material.

Inside, the walls are seen to be all window, with the structure of the church taking the form of high concrete vaults curving to meet slender concrete columns that taper as they rise. The effect of so much light and of such a lightweight structure has prompted many observers to feel that they are standing in the spiritual and architectural heir to the last of the truly great medieval Gothic churches, such as St. George's Chapel, Windsor, or the chapel of King's College, Cambridge *(see p.257)*. The church's tower is certainly medieval in inspiration.

KARL MARX HOF

🖥 1930 📍 VIENNA, AUSTRIA ✍ KARL EHN 🏛 RESIDENCES

Karl Marx Hof was built when "Red Vienna" was under socialist control in the late 1920s and Karl Ehn (1884–1957) was city architect. The plan was to house up to 5,000 people in 1,382 tightly planned apartments, served by a daycare center, library, laundry, doctor's office, and other services and a huge communal garden. In fact, housing occupies just 18.5 percent of the site available to Ehn; the rest was not needed, since the dream had been realized. Between 1923 and 1934, the City of Vienna built 64,000 new apartments, housing a tenth of the population. In 1934, during the Austrian Civil War, Karl Marx Hof was bombarded by the Austrian Army and paramilitary forces sympathetic to the Nazis. It lost its name soon after. It was assaulted again by the Red Army at the end of World War II. Restored between 1989 and 1992, it proudly bears its original name today.

World's longest apartment block
A tram stops four times between one end of Karl Marx Hof and the other: at 3,610 ft (1,100 m), this is the longest single residential building in the world.

STUTTGART STATION

1928 **STUTTGART, GERMANY** **PAUL BONATZ** **RAILWAY STATION**

Paul Bonatz (1877–1956) completed his plan for Stuttgart station in 1913, but construction was delayed until after World War I. The design, said Bonatz, was "purified through the gravity of war;" he moved it away from national romantic bombast toward a sober, soldierly style that appears to herald the work of Adolf Hitler's architects Albert Speer and Werner March *(see p.462)*. Bonatz himself was not a Nazi, and he left Germany for Turkey in 1940. New metro and international stations, built by German architects Ingenhoven und Partner and engineer Frei Otto *(see also p.483)*, will be added by 2013.

Spartan and rugged
The Neo-Romanesque station is both noble and fine. Its rough limestone-faced walls and tower are like those of some mighty 11th-century castle.

CHILEHAUS, HAMBURG

1924 **HAMBURG, GERMANY** **FRITZ HÖGER** **COMMERCIAL BUILDING**

A stunning, 10-story, shiplike building, Chilehaus was designed by Fritz Höger (1877–1949) for the Hamburg shipowner Henry Sloman, who had made his fortune in the potassium nitrate trade with Chile. Every photographer's favorite view of the building is the east corner, which rises like the prow of a ship over the intersection of Hamburg's Burchardstrasse and Pumpenstrasse. Despite other nautical references —railings, porthole-like windows, balconies, and a figurehead like a statue of a condor (borrowed from the Chilean coat-of-arms)—local people originally likened the building to a flatiron. Höger had trained initially as a craftsman before turning to architecture, and this background shows clearly in every last detail of this enduring building, which has become one of the most popular sights in Hamburg.

Reinterpreting tradition
Approximately 4.8 million bricks were used to realize the Chilehaus, in an inspired reinterpretation of the type of traditional brick building found in the old Hanseatic cities of the Baltic coast.

EINSTEIN TOWER

🎓 1921   📍 POTSDAM, GERMANY   ✎ ERICH MENDELSOHN   🏛 LABORATORY

During his time as a German artillery officer during World War I, Erich Mendelsohn made many sketches of futuristic buildings; these ideas were later expressed in the curious design of this observatory and laboratory built for the physicist Albert Einstein and his team of researchers. The smooth, curving white building appears to be made of modeling clay, yet it is actually built of brick and concrete. The building

Constantly in use
The building includes dormitories as well as workrooms; researchers were expected to work around the clock, following the sun.

had no precedent, although it did look a little like illustrations of the children's nursery rhyme about the old lady who lived in a shoe. Mendelsohn himself claimed that the design of this Expressionist tour de force was based on musical theories and those of Einstein. This is impossible to prove, yet what we do know is that the architect created an appropriately radical building for one of the most innovative of all scientists. This national monument is still very much in use by the Potsdam Astrophysical Institute.

CENTENNIAL HALL, BRESLAU

🎓 1913   📍 WROCLAW, LOWER SILESIA, POLAND   ✎ MAX BERG   🏛 CIVIC BUILDING

This sensational domed public hall was built in what was then Breslau (now Wroclaw) to celebrate the centenary of the Battle of Nations (1813), when Napoleon's army was defeated by the combined might of Prussia, Austria, Russia, and Sweden. The reinforced concrete design is a triumph of contemporary structural engineering by Willi Gehler (1876–1953), working in close collaboration with the city architect Max Berg (1870–1947). It takes the form of a dome 203 ft (62 m) in diameter riding high on 32 concrete ribs above a huge

square auditorium for 10,000 people. The dome rests on the four corners of the square and reminds one of the domes by the Islamic architect Sinan *(see p.207)*. The surrounding walls, punctuated by generous windows, are stepped up in tiers, so that the breathtaking domed space inside comes as a real surprise. Built in less than two years, the speed of construction was made possible by automated machinery. Breslau was almost completely destroyed in World War II, but Centennial Hall survives; it is now the People's Hall.

OLYMPIC STADIUM, BERLIN

1936   BERLIN, GERMANY   WERNER MARCH   SPORTS ARENA

Still very much in use today and renovated in time for the 2006 FIFA World Cup, the Olympic Stadium in Berlin had been the architectural star, 70 years before, of Leni Riefenstahl's famous Nazi documentary film *Olympiad*—an idealization of the 1936 Berlin Olympics Games. The steel-framed structure, designed by Werner March (1894–1976), was clad in stone on the orders of Adolf Hitler after construction had been completed. It was not that Hitler was against modern steel-framed architecture, but he believed that, while appropriate for industrial and military buildings, it was wholly unsuitable for civic monuments. March, who had been commissioned to design the building before the Nazis came to power, had intended the building to be altogether more modern in appearance. Nevertheless, the 110,000-seat stadium was certainly an impressive site, and remains so today. Hitler's hopes that it would be the venue where his "Aryan" *übermensch* (supermen) athletes would prove their sporting superiority were dashed by African-American athlete Jesse Owens, who won four gold medals here in 1936.

Clarity and symmetry
The clear structure and strict symmetry is typical of the architecture of the Nazi era.

AIR FORCE MINISTRY, BERLIN

1936   BERLIN, GERMANY   ERNST SAGEBIEL   GOVERNMENT BUILDING

Ernst Sagebiel (1892–1970) designed the magnificent Berlin Tempelhof airport, as well as this bare classical office building on the corner of Wilhelmstrasse and Leipzigstrasse. This was Hermann Goering's headquarters for what was, for a few short years, the most devastating air force in the world. The building was appropriately martial in spirit, and vast; for a time it was Europe's largest office building. Escaping destruction, it became the first home of the communist government of the German Democratic Republic. Today, it is the headquarters of the German Finance Ministry.

REICH CHANCELLERY

1938   BERLIN, GERMANY   ALBERT SPEER   GOVERNMENT BUILDING

The severe, stripped Classical chancellery building designed by Albert Speer (1905–81) for Adolf Hitler, although crafted from solid stone, was pure theater. No more than a single room deep, the idea of the building was to create an exhausting, and, by default, pretentious walk from the main entrance on Wilhelmstrasse to Hitler's 4,306 sq ft (400 m²) office. Designed and built in a great hurry, the chancellery made use of rich materials drawn from across the Third Reich and of a workforce of 4,000 craftsmen and laborers. The building was badly damaged during the siege of Berlin in 1945.

SANTA MARIA NOVELLA STATION

🕮 1936 📌 FLORENCE, ITALY ✍ GIOVANNI MICHELUCCI 🏛 RAILWAY STATION

Commissioned in 1932, Santa Maria Novella station was designed by a team of architects under the leadership of Giovanni Michelucci (1891–1991). It was built during the Fascist years of Mussolini, who promised buildings and cities as fine as anything produced by Ancient Rome. Unlike Hitler, Mussolini was not set on Neo-Classical architecture and welcomed Michelucci's "rationalism." The stone-clad interior relies on its fine proportions, the fall of light and shadow, and its sheer usefulness to win the day for an architectural style that was neither modern nor Classical. An underground annex, with a spectacular glass roof by Norman Foster and the engineers Arup, is due for completion in 2008.

Station interior
Low-ceilinged and clad in local stone, the determinedly horizontal building is a design of great power, sharply defined focus, and welcome practicality.

MILAN CENTRAL STATION

🕮 1931 📌 MILAN, ITALY ✍ ULISSE STACCHINI 🏛 RAILWAY STATION

A monster of a station, Milan Central is fronted by a vast concourse, 656 ft (200 m) long and 236 ft (72 m) high. Its 24 platforms are sheltered by gigantic steel canopies that stretch for 1,119 ft (341 m). The 1906 contest for the reconstruction of the original station was won by Arrigo Cantoni, but his design was eventually discarded as being too tame. A second competition, in 1912, proclaimed Ulisse Stacchini (1871–1947) the winner. World War I delayed construction, and the station was only finally completed nine years into Mussolini s regime. Stacchini revised his plans during World War II, blending ideas taken from Futurist architect Antonio Sant Elia with those drawn from the baths of Ancient Rome. The result was a heroic and purposeful building that, behind its encrusted, clifflike facade, is remarkably free of gratuitous decoration, although there are plenty of mosaics, ceramics, stained glass, and bas-relief sculptures to marvel at.

Beauty of a beast
Truly enormous and somewhat stylistically clumsy, Milan Central is nevertheless a fine railway terminus in the tradition of New York's Grand Central Station.

MARIAM ORTHODOX CATHEDRAL, ASMARA

🎖 1938 📍 ASMARA, ERITREA ✍ EDUARDO CAVAGNARI 🏛 PLACE OF WORSHIP

Dedicated to St. Mary, Asmara's Orthodox Cathedral stands on the top of a hill in an extensive compound reached through imposing gate towers. It commands views across the Eritrean capital, a city built mostly in the 1930s by Italian imperialists on a mission to spread out from here across East Africa. It is a design of great power and of striking and unusual beauty. The mosaiced entrance to the main church is flanked by a pair of freestanding red stone towers employing distinctive "monkey head" construction. Each of these is topped with a severe white geometric belfry, which is itself capped with a roof shaped like a *tukul*, the traditional hut of the East African highlands.

In 1920, the original Coptic church on this site was replaced with a new church planned by an architect named Gallo; this, in turn, was rebuilt in the late 1930s to the current design by Eduardo Cavagnari. His genius was to successfully marry two utterly

Entrance mosaic
Above the doors, with their frames of red ceramic tesserae, there is an impressive mosaic, divided into seven vertical panels, by the Italian painter Nenne Sanguineti Poggi, dating from the 1950s.

unrelated traditions: 1930s Italian Rationalism and East African highlands vernacular. The result is magical. The nave is a modern take on an ancient arcaded basilica, bustling with painted saints and devout worshipers.

CINEMA IMPERO, ASMARA

🎖 1937 📍 ASMARA, ERITREA ✍ MARIO MESSINA 🏛 CINEMA

With its noble imperial-red facade, the exterior of the Cinema Impero is a brilliant play on ancient Roman design and insignia; this is clearly a building on parade. It is one of the finest buildings on Harnet Avenue, the city of Asmara's main street. The fully restored lobby is equally impressive.

Originally, the Impero was to have been part of a much bigger entertainment complex, complete with two art galleries, a bowling alley, and a cocktail bar. This was one of the city's nine movie theaters; two others, equally special, are The Capitol, with its sliding roof, and the Roma, looking like a centurion on parade. The remarkable thing is the way in which each of Asmara's 1930s buildings was a part of an integrated and well-executed city plan. While a movie theater was for entertainment, there was no reason why it could not also be a noble civic building that would add to the overall luster of the city. In Asmara, Art Deco and Italian Rationalist design work together to give the city its unique character.

Long-term landmark
With its clean, geometric lines and porthole windows, the cinema's soaring facade has been a landmark of downtown Asmara for 70 years.

THE RALEIGH HOTEL, MIAMI BEACH

🖵 1940 📍 MIAMI BEACH, FLORIDA, USA ✍ LAWRENCE MURRAY DIXON 🏛 HOTEL

In 1928, Lawrence Murray Dixon (1901–49) moved to Miami Beach from New York, where he had worked for the architects Schultze and Weaver. He set up his own prolific practice in 1931 and began working at a staggering pace. During the 1930s and 1940s he designed 38 hotels, 87 apartment buildings, 220 homes, two housing developments, and 33 stores. Dixon is credited with the design of some of the most popular hotels in Miami Beach. These include The Victor Hotel (1937), The Raleigh Hotel (1940), The Marlin (1939), The Tides Hotel (1936), The Senator (1939), and The Ritz Plaza Hotel (1940).

Dixon's style was sophisticated. His was not a case of transferring fashionable Art Deco cinema facades to high-rise hotels, but of shaping buildings whose form and function were neatly resolved through plays of sensuous curves. The eight-floor Raleigh on Collins Avenue was one of the first resort-style hotels on Miami Beach. This fine civil hotel boasts a lagoon pool encircled by straw-roofed beach huts.

Style with substance
Restored in the 1990s, the Raleigh Hotel proves that, in the right hands, Art Deco could be more than just a showy style.

EL DORADO APARTMENT BUILDING, NEW YORK

🖵 1931 📍 NEW YORK, NY ✍ EMERY ROTH 🏛 RESIDENCES

A cinematic, 28-story Art Deco apartment block rocketing up into the Manhattan sky, the El Dorado building was the fourth and largest of a sequence designed by Emery Roth (1871–1948) along Central Park West. The building is planned around a U-shaped courtyard, to let as much daylight as possible into the 1,300 rooms of the 186 apartments. It is fronted by a pair of sensational towers, lit red at night, and based loosely on the Giralda tower of Seville Cathedral (see p.268), which, in turn, would inspire Stalin's Seven Sisters buildings in Moscow.

Roth himself, an orphan, came from Czechoslovakia to Chicago at the age of 13. He made his way up as a draftsman, working for the dynamic firm Burnham and Root in the 1890s, before moving to New York. The El Dorado's futuristic sculptural detailing, as well as its geometric ornament and patterns and its contrasting materials and textures, make it one of New York's finest Art Deco structures. The towers are terminated by ornamented setbacks with abstract geometric spires that have been described, in suitably cinematic terms, as "Flash Gordon finials."

CARS AND FREEWAYS

The German autobahns engineered by Fritz Todt (1891–1942) were the successors to the famous Roman roads that once crisscrossed Europe and north Africa. From now on, the car would travel further and faster than ever before in its brief history, encouraging the development of new forms of architecture, while threatening the very existence of older ones.

There had been fast roads before, but Fritz Todt's car-only roads were the finest of their age. With their Portland-cement concrete carriageways and subtle curvatures, they were designed for maximum speeds of 99 mph (160 kmh) on the straight and 93 mph (150 kmh) on banked curves. These fine-looking roads became aesthetic and engineering laws unto themselves, winning approval by keeping cars away from old towns and villages. Impressed by the autobahns, President Dwight D. Eisenhower pushed through legislation in 1956 to create 43,500 miles (70,000 km) of Interstate Highways across the United States, a huge 30-year project.

Before long, these fast roads were sprouting new types of building with their own distinct architectural style, from service stations to

Autobahns
Germany's autobahn network was the world's first truly modern road system, enabling fast, direct travel between major centers of population and industry.

entire shopping and business complexes. They also encouraged urban sprawl, demolishing anything that lay in their path—whatever its age. Meanwhile, the car itself led to the growth of new forms of urban and domestic architecture, from parking ramps to houses that increasingly served their four-wheeled, rather than two-legged, residents.

Spaghetti Junction
While the new roads took simple, direct routes across the countryside, their junctions with other roads were often complex affairs, as is seen here at "Spaghetti Junction" on Britain's M6 near Birmingham.

MOSCOW STATE UNIVERSITY

🖳 1953 📭 MOSCOW, RUSSIA ✍ LEV VLADIMIROVICH RUDNEV 🏛 UNIVERSITY

Moscow University's wedding-cake tower was one of Stalin's "Seven Sisters" buildings designed to compete with the skyscrapers of Manhattan. The 36-story tower rises 787 ft (240 m) on massively broad shoulders to a delicate spire, crowned with a viewing platform under a 12-ton Red Star. The tower, which stands before a terrace with statues of students gazing confidently into the Soviet future, is flanked by four vast wings of dorm rooms, lecture halls, libraries, offices, and canteens. Designed by Lev Rudnev (1885–1956), the complex is said to have 20 miles (33 km) of hallways and 5,000 rooms. The building was largely built by prisoners, including many German POWs held captive until the mid-1950s.

Initially a fan of Romanesque design, Rudnev moved on to Neo-Classicism and, finally, to the powerful, eclectic style forever associated with Stalin.

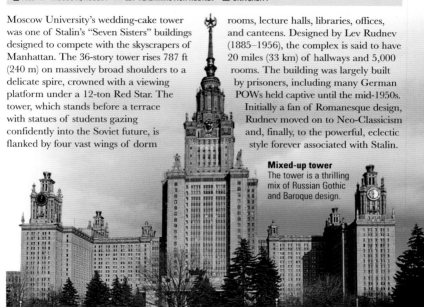

Mixed-up tower
The tower is a thrilling mix of Russian Gothic and Baroque design.

MOSCOW METRO

🖳 1935 📭 MOSCOW, RUSSIA ✍ VARIOUS 🏛 UNDERGROUND RAILWAY STATIONS

Constructed deep under Moscow and lavishly decorated with marble, mosaics, sculpture, and even chandeliers, these "people's palaces," built on the orders of Stalin from the mid-1930s onward, were a sumptuous display of the latest Soviet architecture, design, and decorative art married to heroic engineering. Much of the hard graft was done using forced labor.

The first line—the Sokolnicheskaya, with 13 stations—opened in May 1935. The marble walls of Kropotinskaya station, designed to serve the proposed, and monstrous, Palace of the Soviets, were removed from the Cathedral of Christ the Savior, which Stalin demolished so that he could build the palace in its place. Marble benches from the same 19th-century Byzantine-style cathedral can be found along the platforms of Novokusnetskaya station. Ploschad Revolutsii Station is peopled with 76 statues of heroic Soviet soldiers, workers, and collective-farm laborers. Mayakovskaya Station, perhaps the best of all, boasts glistening chrome columns and soaring vaults adorned with mosaic panels depicting "A Day in the Land of Soviets." Commuters revel in the sight of muscular Soviet workers rising with the dawn, toiling happily in fields and factories, and then returning to their beds as the sun sets. Komsomolskaya, dedicated to the army, is like a Byzantine cathedral. Extraordinary.

Arbatskaya metro station
This is the ornate, cavernous interior of Arbatskaya station. The entrance building at ground level is designed in the shape of a Soviet Red Star.

THE CONTEMPORARY WORLD

ca. 1945 ONWARD

For a brief while, it had seemed as if nearly every other building in the world was going to be a lesser version of a Mies van der Rohe office tower or a Le Corbusier apartment building. Reactions to mainstream Modernism, however, were rife as early as the 1950s, led by one of its mentors and giants—Le Corbusier himself. By the end of the 20th century, modern architecture had become a kaleidoscope of styles.

Something was astir. The clear-cut certainties of prewar Modernism were now anything but. From Le Corbusier's magical church at Ronchamp *(see p.473)* onward, Modern architecture burst its neat, geometric banks, fueled by new ways of thinking about art, theology, history, and sense of place. History was no longer, as Henry Ford had declared, "bunk," but a treasure trove to be explored. From the late 1960s, however, would-be witty architects, starting in the US, but not exclusively so, began designing in a cut-and-paste style labeled "Post-Modernism." One of its champions was Robert Venturi, whose *Complexity and Contradiction in Modern Architecture* (1964) became the Po-Mo bible. Venturi's "Less is a Bore" was a play on Mies van der Rohe's famous dictum "Less is More." He wanted architecture to be inclusive, populist, and playful. This was fine in the hands of clever architects funded by indulgent clients, but when a wave of tiresome, jokey buildings inundated cities from Los Angeles to Shanghai in the 1980s, Post-Modernism itself began to bore.

THE CAD REVOLUTION

Far more interesting was the coming together of new forms of architecture with computer-aided design, or CAD *(see p.429).* When young engineer Peter Rice was asked to make the daring, wavelike roofs of Sydney Opera House possible *(see p.484),* he used a slide-rule and calculus tables to sail architecture into uncharted waters. But within just a few years, computers were allowing architects to design striking, even crazy, buildings knowing that they would stand up when built, even if they looked on screen as though they were falling over. By the 1990s, CAD software had replaced the drawing board and T-square in most parts of the world.

◁ LONDON LANDMARK: NORMAN FOSTER'S PICKLE-SHAPED TOWER FOR SWISS RE INSURANCE IN THE CITY OF LONDON IS BASED ON AN EXPOSED AND GLEAMING DIAGONAL STEEL GRID.

ELEMENTS

After World War II, what had seemed to be the rational certainties of the Modern Movement exploded into a myriad fresh approaches to architectural design. New technologies and materials encouraged change, yet equally so, perhaps, did new social and political ideals.

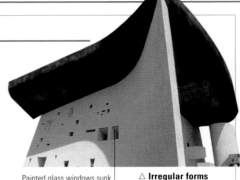

Painted glass windows sunk into curving, shiplike walls

△ **Irregular forms**
With his hugely influential design of the pilgrimage chapel at Ronchamp, France, Le Corbusier showed how art and emotion, as well as function, could be the generator of significant and powerful forms.

△ **Zigzag windows**
Contemporary architects took design in radical new directions, such as these highly stylized windows at the Jewish Museum, Berlin, by Daniel Libeskind—sharp incisions shaped like bolts of lightning.

△ **Tent-style roofs**
The lightweight, tensile-structure fabric roofs of the stadium designed for the 1972 Munich Olympic Games by the pioneer of lightweight construction, Frei Otto, were to be copied and reinterpreted around the world.

△ **External elevators**
A fashion for expressing the inside workings of buildings in their exterior architecture was established by Richard Rogers and Renzo Piano. This is an elevator at the Lloyd's of London building by Rogers.

△ **Communications equipment**
Skyscrapers make useful communications towers. Here, the antennae on top of the John Hancock Tower, Chicago, have been stylized—to look, perhaps, a little too much like missiles.

▽ **Architecture as sculpture**
Oscar Niemeyer's concrete and glass Brasilia Cathedral, 1970, is about as close to pure sculpture as architecture gets. Lauded worldwide, it showed how concrete design could be popular.

Design based on the image of the Crown of Thorns

Dramatic celebration of concrete

Concealed entrance

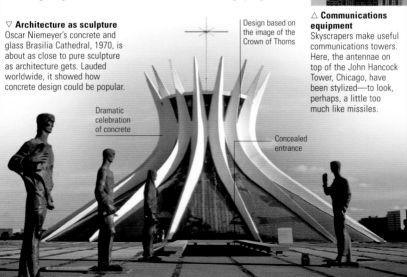

FARNSWORTH HOUSE

⌨ 1951   📍 PLANO, IL
✍ LUDWIG MIES VAN DER ROHE   🏛 RESIDENCE

This elegant International-style house was commissioned as a weekend, riverbank retreat for Dr. Edith Farnsworth. A steel frame supports two concrete planes—floor and ceiling—with sheets of glass between. The steelwork is welded, sandblasted, primed, and painted, so that it appears utterly smooth. Floor-to-ceiling panes of glass create a sense of the house floating in its natural surroundings. Inside, a central core contains fireplace, kitchen, and bathroom with neatly concealed plumbing.

CASE STUDY HOUSE NO. 21

⌨ 1958   📍 LOS ANGELES, CA
✍ PIERRE KOENIG   🏛 RESIDENCE

Pierre Koenig (1925–2004) built his first steel-and-glass house while he was a student at the University of Southern California. When John Entenza, editor of *Arts and Architecture* magazine, was looking for young, innovative architects to design equally innovative homes for his Case Study Houses program, Koenig was therefore a natural choice.

Case Study House No. 21 is a beautifully resolved, modern home that combines a Zen-like Japanese garden with the flow of the interior of the single-story house. Water flows over the roof and walls, keeping it cool in the long Los Angeles summers, while breezes pass beneath its floating floors. The cooling effect is so efficient that there has never been any need to install air conditioning. The house is also "cool" in the other sense of the word: it promises relaxed, easy living and has been a set in a number of Hollywood films. Koenig completed the restoration of the house before he died.

CASE STUDY HOUSE NO. 22

⌨ 1960   📍 LOS ANGELES, USA
✍ PIERRE KOENIG   🏛 RESIDENCE

Hanging over a steep crag above Los Angeles, Case Study House No. 22 has been celebrated in films, books, magazines, and advertisements, yet was never caught so well as in a famous photograph by Julius Schulman of stylish people lounging in the sensational living room as night descends over the city. British architect Norman Foster (b.1935) wrote of it: "There, hovering almost weightlessly above the bright lights of Los Angeles, spread out like a carpet below, is an elegant, light, economical and transparent enclosure whose apparent simplicity belies the rigorous process of investigation that made it possible. If I had to choose one snapshot, one architectural moment, of which I would like to have been the author, this is surely it. As both image and artefact, Case Study House 22 has long been a touchstone for contemporary architects."

Koenig continued to experiment with steel-framed houses, all of which seem to adapt well to their environments.

EAMES HOUSE

⌨ 1949   📍 LOS ANGELES, CA
✍ CHARLES EAMES   🏛 RESIDENCE

Charles Eames (1907–78) divided a two-story industrial shed into a house and studio— No. 8 in the Case Study Houses program *(see above)*—for himself and his wife, with bedrooms on a mezzanine. The steel skeleton has transparent and translucent industrial panels slotted between, and is finished in varied materials and colors. A splendid, full-height living room at the south end takes up eight of the total 17 bays of the house.

CHANDIGARH

🖵 1962 📍 EAST PUNJAB, INDIA ✍ LE CORBUSIER 🏛 CITY

When India and Pakistan were partitioned in August 1947, the Punjab was split in two. West Punjab, in Pakistan, retained the old capital, Lahore, but East Punjab, in India, needed a new capital. The site chosen was a gently sloping plain, not quite in the shadow of the Himalayan foothills, dotted with 24 villages. The city that rose here, named Chandigarh after one of the villages, was utterly unexpected.

The city's original planner, New York architect Albert Mayer, withdrew after his assistant, Matthew Nowicki, died in August 1950. By the end of the year, Le Corbusier had been appointed their successor, working with Swiss architect Pierre Jeanneret and the English pair Max Fry and Jane Drew. The new architecture was astonishing. Le Corbusier took the lead with three powerfully sculpted monuments for the Capitol complex: the High Court (1956), the Secretariat (1962), and the Assembly (1962). In the latter, we see architecture as sculpture, seemingly free-form, yet highly disciplined. Behind the Assembly's upwardly curving portico lies the great

circular hall, lit and cooled by a strangely haunting hyperbolic concrete shell that, cut at its top at an oblique angle, gives the building such eye-catching impact. Sadly, the relentless concrete homes built for the inhabitants of Chandigarh lack both art and practicality and stand in utter contrast to the magnificent solemnity of Le Corbusier's downtown.

LE CORBUSIER

After World War II, Le Corbusier *(see also p.444)* adopted a darkly romantic architecture, often characterized by raw concrete. He designed some of the most deeply spiritual and intellectually stimulating buildings of the 1950s, notably the monastery of La Tourette and the chapel at Ronchamp. His work in India was sublime, if controversial. He lived modestly in later life, especially after his experiences in India and the death of his wife, Yvonne Gallis, in 1957.

The Assembly, Chandigarh
Both mythical and modern, Chandigarh's Assembly building, with its troughlike portico, retains its power to shock more than 50 years after its completion.

NOTRE DAME-DU-HAUT

🖳 1955 📌 RONCHAMP, EASTERN FRANCE ✍ LE CORBUSIER 🏛 PLACE OF WORSHIP

Le Corbusier's hilltop chapel at Ronchamp replaced a 19th-century church destroyed in World War II. The lightweight concrete roofshell soars above deep, whitewashed masonry walls, and above a curving nave lit by irregularly spaced windows with glass painted by the architect. The roof is raised 4 in (10 cm) above the walls on columns running up through them, with the gap between filled with clear glass. The result is a halo of light around the numinous nave. The nave is crowned with three towers, each painted a different rich color inside. The acoustics are astonishing: the human voice sounds otherworldly inside; outside, the east wall is curved to reflect the voices of priests celebrating Mass at the outdoor altar. Rich in symbolism, inlaid with echoes of Picasso, and a hymn as much to nature as to the Virgin Mary, it proved that Europe's contemporary architects could create settings for worship that were equal to, if very different from, those of the Gothic masters.

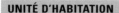

Spiritual high
Le Corbusier's arresting chapel at Ronchamp took his postwar work to new heights.

UNITÉ D'HABITATION

🖳 1952 📌 MARSEILLES, FRANCE
✍ LE CORBUSIER 🏛 RESIDENCES

Le Corbusier's Unité d'Habitation was a daring experiment in low-cost housing. The 12-story concrete building contains 337 apartments arranged in 23 different configurations, and is more complex than its raw exterior suggests. Stacked like wine bottles in a rack, the apartments step up over the hallways running through the building, so that they stretch across the entire depth of the block. On the roof is a playground with a swimming pool. One floor is for shops, and there is even a hotel. The building is raised off the ground on heroic "piloti."

MAISONS JAOUL

🖳 1956 📌 NEUILLY-SUR-SEINE, PARIS, FRANCE
✍ LE CORBUSIER 🏛 RESIDENCES

These two houses in the Parisian suburb of Neuilly-sur-Seine mark a radical departure from the pure white villas that Le Corbusier built some 30 years earlier. By now, he had entered a darkly poetic phase of his life and art, and was shaping a rugged architecture built from raw and even brutal materials. Inevitably, this caused much the same sort of controversy among his fans as Bob Dylan did when, a decade on from Maisons Jaoul, he swapped his acoustic guitar for an electric one.

Cavelike, snug, and carefully lit under barrel-vaulted roofs, Maisons Jaoul are, in fact, delightful houses by any standards. The walls are of load-bearing brick supporting concrete-covered, brick-faced vaults. This is the beginning of the "Brutalist" aesthetic in which raw materials were set off vigorously against one another, a style that could be disastrous in the hands of a lesser architect but was realized here with a sense of the sublime by Le Corbusier.

JESPERSEN OFFICE, COPENHAGEN

🏆 1955   📖 COPENHAGEN, DENMARK   ✎ ARNE JACOBSEN   🏛 COMMERCIAL BUILDING

The Jespersen Office is disciplined, focused, and thoroughly detailed in design, and built with handcrafted skill. The result is something very special: the language of an overtly modern architecture fused to age-old craft skills. Arne Jacobsen (1902–71) was trained, as Danish architects continue to be, as a craftsman as well as an architect. By 1927, he was designing family houses, furniture, and cutlery. He set up his own design practice in 1930 and always refused to limit himself to architecture. Many of his classic designs continue to sell well. Like the Jespersen Office, they are pure-spirited, easy to live with, and beautifully made. His model 3107 chair of 1955 has sold over 5 million copies (this was the chair in Lewis Morley's 1963 photograph of English call-girl Christine Keeler), and his cutlery featured in Stanley Kubrick's seminal film *2001: A Space Odyssey*. The interior of the Jespersen building is typically light, and finished with the kind of quality that you always hope to find in 1950s offices, yet so rarely do this side of the Seagram Building.

PIRELLI TOWER

🏆 1956   📖 MILAN, ITALY   ✎ GIO PONTI   🏛 COMMERCIAL BUILDING

On April 18th, 2002, 68-year-old Luigi Gino Fasulo flew his light aircraft into the 26th floor of the 417 ft (127 m) high Pirelli Tower. For a horrible moment, it seemed as if September 11 had been repeated. No one knows what happened—pilot error, probably —but it brought the world's attention to Milan's tallest building, designed by architect Gio Ponti (1891–1979) and engineer Pier Luigi Nervi (1891–1979). Ponti, who founded *Domus* magazine in 1928, was also an industrial designer, and a decorator too, working with some of the most avant-garde talents of the time. "Love architecture," Ponti said, "be it ancient or modern… for its fantastic, adventurous, and solemn creations… for the abstract, allusive, and figurative forms that enchant our spirit and enrapture our thoughts." True to his word, Ponti loved all styles, and was good at them, too. Here, he was at his most thrilling with the 32-story, pencil-thin tower that rises from the site of the original Pirelli tire factory. Today, it serves as the offices of the Lombardy regional government.

Tapered for distinction
The Pirelli Tower's tapering corners set it apart from the many rectangular, slablike office blocks of the day.

SEAGRAM BUILDING

🖳 1958 🏛 NEW YORK, NY ✍ LUDWIG MIES VAN DER ROHE 🏛 COMMERCIAL BUILDING

Mies waited 35 years before he finally got to build his ideal steel-and-glass tower—the Seagram Building. Set back 90 ft (27 m) from Park Avenue in a stepped, granite-paved plaza with two rectangular pools, this building vaults 38 stories into the New York sky. Mies's first designs, dating from 1919, were far more free-flowing than this super-cool, super-refined, Schinkelesque design—a Prussian temple inspired by ancient Greek precedent, but stripped of all exterior decoration. Complete with double-height travertine lobby, swish elevators, bronze mullions, bronze spandrels, dark amber-tinted glass, and a grand restaurant designed by Philip Johnson (see p.488), the Seagram Building is an experience to be treasured. With this wonderful example of self-confident, bespoke design, Mies created one of the truly great buildings of 20th-century America.

Flattered by imitation
Imposing and superbly crafted, the Seagram Building has been often imitated, but never matched.

LEVER HOUSE

🖳 1952 🏛 NEW YORK, NY ✍ SKIDMORE, OWINGS & MERRILL 🏛 COMMERCIAL BUILDING

In many ways the epitome of the modern office block, Lever House's sleek steel-and-glass curtain-walled design has been widely copied throughout the world. Commissioned by Lever Brothers, the US soap and detergent manufacturer, it was the work of Skidmore, Owings & Merrill (SOM; see p.476). Their chief designer, Gordon Bunshaft (1909–90), modeled the building on the earlier work of Le Corbusier and Mies van der Rohe (who had yet to build the Seagram Building). Designated a landmark building in 1992, Lever House was renovated by SOM in 1998.

Garden tower
The narrow, 20-story tower rises from a horizontal slab, which in turn is supported on Le Corbusier-style "piloti." This lower block frames a garden courtyard and is topped with a roof garden.

AIR FORCE ACADEMY, COLORADO SPRINGS

🏆 1962   📍 COLORADO SPRINGS, COLORADO   ✍ SKIDMORE, OWINGS & MERRILL   🏛 MILITARY BUILDING

The US Air Force Academy is justly proud of its architecture. Its own brochure states that the Academy's "sleek modern architecture, monumental scale, and dramatic setting combine to create a stunning national monument. Its gleaming aluminum, steel, and glass buildings are… a living embodiment of the modernity of flying." They are quite right.

CHAPEL BY WALTER NETSCH

Founded in the first decade of the Cold War, the Academy buildings symbolized the perceived importance of US air power in the ideological battle against the Soviet Union. This proud display of what has become known as Mid-Century Modern styling is at once low-lying, sleek, cool, and quietly heroic. Construction began in 1954, (the first class graduated in 1959), and the 28 sq mile (73 km²) campus was largely completed in 1962 with the dedication of the striking chapel designed by Walter Netsch (b.1920). The interior of the multifaith chapel is just as sensational as its skyward-thrusting exterior, lit as it is by shafts of bright light that pierce their way through the rich colors of the stained glass filling the gaps between the bays of the vertiginous nave. A national landmark and a thriving school, the Air Force Academy, despite its remote location, attracts a million visitors each year. The original buildings seem just as crisp and modern today as they did when the Academy opened in 1958.

SKIDMORE, OWINGS & MERRILL

Skidmore, Owings & Merrill (SOM), founded in 1936, helped popularize the International style in the US, marrying American "get-up-and-go" zest with ambitious modern design. Their best-known early work is Lever House *(see p.475)*. Today, SOM is at work on the Freedom Tower on the site of New York's ill-fated World Trade Center.

Academy chapel
The chapel has been described as being like "a phalanx of fighters" standing on their tails ready to take off.

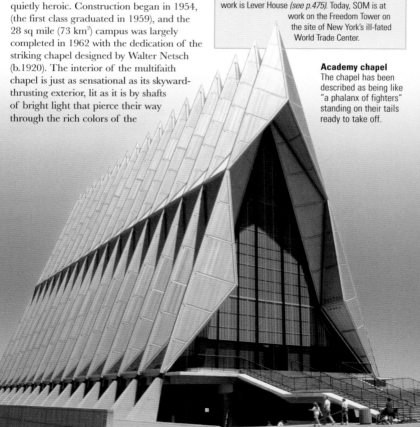

TWA TERMINAL, JOHN F. KENNEDY AIRPORT

🖵 1962   🏳 NEW YORK, NEW YORK   ✍ EERO SAARINEN   🏛 AIRPORT

Eero Saarinen's outlandish air terminal for TWA at New York's Idlewild (now John F. Kennedy) Airport was sculpted as an abstract symbol of flight. Unlike most air terminals, which seemed intent on depressing passengers, Saarinen's not only raised the spirits, but also showed that concrete structures could be truly delightful.

Saarinen himself described this intriguing building as one "in which the architecture itself would express the drama and excitement of travel…the shapes deliberately chosen in order to emphasize an upward-soaring quality of line." Many architects, in the thrall of chaste Modernism, were shocked by this swooping concrete cavern. Yet, unlike the childish "iconic" buildings of the early 2000s, Saarinen's was a thing of real invention, daring, and mastery. So ahead of its time as to make the aircraft serving it seem old-fashioned, it proved that a building could be

TERMINAL APPROACH

low-lying and still evoke the spirit of flight. Light filtered in from windows and slits all over the structure, so that passengers had a sense of the outside and sky. The terminal, as crucial in the history of American transportation design as New York's Grand Central station, was long closed for renovation. Surrounded by controversy in case Saarinen's work was spoiled or diluted, the terminal reopened in 2005.

EERO SAARINEN

Eero Saarinen (1910–61) was born in Kirkkonummi, Finland. He studied sculpture in Paris and architecture at Yale, after which he joined his father's practice. His buildings were as much sculpture as architecture. He moved freely, though, between sleek corporate Modernism, as in the General Motors Technical Center near Detroit (see p.478), and free-flowing expressionism, as in the TWA terminal building and the Gateway Arch, St. Louis, Mississippi.

Terminal interior

Every last detail was custom-designed, from stairs, bars, departure boards, and ticket counters to chairs, signs, and phone booths, all coming together to form an utterly convincing whole.

CROWN HALL, CHICAGO

⏳ 1956   📍 CHICAGO, IL
🏛 LUDWIG MIES VAN DER ROHE   🏛 UNIVERSITY

An open-planned pavilion, the Crown Hall, on the campus of the Illinois Institute of Technology, is a fine display of Mies van der Rohe's ability to cover a great deal of space with minimal structure, while still shaping a formal building with Classical associations. The overhanging roof is held up by just eight I-beams. Inside, the space can be divided by screens. Stairs lead down to a basement used for workshops, bathrooms, mechanical services, and offices. Of Crown Hall, Mies wrote, "It has a scientific character, but it is not scientific…. It is conservative, as it is based on the eternal laws of architecture: Order, Space, Proportion."

GM TECHNICAL CENTER

⏳ 1955   📍 WARREN, MI
🏛 EERO SAARINEN   🏛 INDUSTRIAL

Described as an "industrial Versailles," the General Motors Technical Center is a sleek research development of three-story buildings gathered around a lake, from which rises a sci-fi-style water tower. The gaps between the wall cladding panels are made airtight with neoprene gaskets, as used in aircraft windows. The windows, which do not open, are set flush with the walls and tinted green to absorb heat and light; air-conditioning is installed all but invisibly in false ceilings. The GM Technical Center was later a huge influence on the "High-Tech" designs of British architects such as Norman Foster and Richard Rogers.

GUGGENHEIM MUSEUM, NEW YORK

⏳ 1959   📍 NEW YORK, NY
🏛 FRANK LLOYD WRIGHT   🏛 ART GALLERY

"Entering into the spirit of this interior, you will discover the best possible atmosphere in which to show fine paintings…". So wrote Frank Lloyd Wright of this famous gallery on Fifth Avenue. Did he really think it a great idea to stand at an angle on a spiral ramp to look at paintings? We will never know!

Whatever the Guggenheim's shortcomings, it remains a glorious, slightly crazy building that pushes concrete technology to new limits. In essence, it is a circular ramp that climbs

Architectural exhibitionism
Few exhibitions can live up to the art of Wright, and probably more people visit the Guggenheim to see the building itself—utterly out of step with anything else in New York—than the artworks on display.

DOME OVER CENTRAL WELL

up and around a concrete well, like the inside of a shell, and it is capped with a flat-ribbed glass dome. It is hard to tire of the experience of walking into this challenging, playful space. Wright, who spent 16 years on the design, had intended that visitors would take an elevator to the top floor and walk down the ramp. The gallery, however, starts its exhibitions on the first floor, so visitors have to climb up the ramp.

A 10-story, limestone-clad tower, designed by the architects Gwathmey, Siegel, and Associates, was added to the Guggenheim in 1992. This provides flat walls for paintings and allows visitors to stand up straight. Would Wright have been impressed? Probably not. As he said, modest to the end, his goal was to "make the building and the painting an uninterrupted, beautiful symphony such as never existed in the World of Art before." Or after.

FRANK LLOYD WRIGHT

Frank Lloyd Wright (1867–1959) was born in Richland, Wisconsin. He studied engineering, worked for the architect Louis Sullivan in Chicago, designed his first house in 1887, married well, and created Oak Park, a suburb of "prairie-style" homes. From 1900 he began "streamlining" his designs, taking mistresses, and becoming flamboyant. After a series of scandals and misfortunes in mid-life, he became a great star, although his later buildings descended into kitsch.

BRYNMAWR RUBBER FACTORY

🏛 1951   📍 BRYNMAWR, EBBW VALE, SOUTH WALES
🖉 ARCHITECTS' CO-PARTNERSHIP   🏛 INDUSTRIAL BUILDING

This rubber factory provided much-needed employment for the Ebbw Vale area in the postwar years. It was designed by a team of idealistic young architects and the Danish-British engineer Ove Arup (1895–1988). The building was stunning: generous floors, light-filled canteens, and heroic murals roofed over with a sensational series of low, lightweight, concrete domes. The contemporary English critic Reyner Banham said that it had "one of the most impressive interiors in Britain since St. Paul's." It was compared favorably with the best work of Le Corbusier and Alvar Aalto. The first postwar building to be listed in Britain, it has sadly since been demolished.

ST. BRIDE'S CHURCH, EAST KILBRIDE

🏛 1964   📍 LANARKSHIRE, SCOTLAND
🖉 GILLESPIE, KIDD & COIA   🏛 PLACE OF WORSHIP

With its chimneylike tower and apparently windowless expanses of brickwork, St. Bride's Catholic church resembles a power station when seen from afar, but as you get closer, it reveals itself to be a church with a profoundly spiritual atmosphere. The haunting interior is imaginatively lit by six hidden clerestory windows. It evokes Le Corbusier's monastery church at La Tourette, outside Lyon, but the brickwork is warmer than the monastery's concrete. Gillespie, Kidd, and Coia produced a number of forceful designs for the Roman Catholic Church, including the abandoned St Peter's Seminary at Cardross (1966), which was also inspired by Le Corbusier's later work.

ENGINEERING BUILDING, LEICESTER UNIVERSITY

🏛 1963   📍 LEICESTER, ENGLAND   🖉 SIR JAMES STIRLING & JAMES GOWAN   🏛 UNIVERSITY

With its bright-orange tower rising over Leicester University's rather demure campus, the new Engineering Building caused shock waves throughout British architecture. Through this building, James Stirling (1926–92) and James Gowan (b.1923) proved that it was possible to break away from rectilinear Modernism while staying loyal to the roots of Modernist architecture. The associations the building made were intriguing and, at the time, controversial. Where else in Britain, this side of Berthold Lubetkin's Finsbury Health Centre in London,

had anyone seen a building so powerfully influenced by Soviet Constructivism? When else had a building so far from the sea seemed as if it might be better placed beside a dock serving ships rather than science? The Glaswegian-born, Liverpool-educated Stirling was a largely intuitive designer who believed that architecture was above all an art form, at a time when beauty was a dirty word among his British peers. Stirling's was a questioning, ever-shifting art, and he designed in many styles. Here, with fellow Glaswegian Gowan, he produced perhaps his finest work.

Learning factory
The slim, factorylike tower of Leicester University's Engineering Building rises from a low-lying block top-lit by rooflights set at an angle.

NATIONAL THEATRE, LONDON

🖥 1976 🏙 LONDON, ENGLAND ◿ SIR DENYS LASDUN 🏛 THEATRE

After years of lobbying, construction of a National Theater in London began in 1967 and was completed a decade later. The result was a concrete mountain, stepped up like a low-lying ziggurat, on the South Bank of the Thames. The challenging design, by Denys Lasdun (1914–2001), was a complex of interlocking sections containing three

Dramatic viewpoints
The three auditoria are wrapped around with terraced bars that open out onto balconies offering suitably theatrical views of central London.

auditoria: the Olivier, with an open stage inspired by the ancient Greek amphitheater at Epidaurus; the Lyttelton, with a proscenium stage; and the Cottesloe, a black-box theater for experimental productions. The building, although a successful theater and a popular meeting place, was not universally liked. The Prince of Wales described it as "a clever way of building a nuclear power station in the middle of London without anyone objecting." The building's one truly poor aspect is from behind, where it fails to link with the street.

SAINSBURY CENTRE FOR VISUAL ARTS

🖥 1978 🏙 NORWICH, NORFOLK, ENGLAND ◿ LORD NORMAN FOSTER 🏛 UNIVERSITY

Designed like an ultramodern and ultra-refined aircraft hangar, the Sainsbury Centre was one of the first of a sequence of high-quality "High-Tech" designs from the dynamic office of Norman Foster (b.1935). A public art gallery and a teaching department of the University of East Anglia, the gleaming silver edifice stands near student accommodation designed in the guise of stepped concrete pyramids by Denys Lasdun. The end walls of the Sainsbury Centre are almost entirely glazed, revealing the building's finely wrought prefabricated skeleton. The great open-plan interior, with mezzanine levels, is beautifully lit, both naturally and artificially. It is also clutter-free, since all services are contained within the sandwich construction walls.

Post-construction changes
The Sainsbury Centre has now been partly re-clad with white panels. The building was extended underground with the Crescent Wing of 1991.

CONGRESS BUILDING, BRASILIA

🏛 1960   📍 CENTRAL BRAZIL   ✎ OSCAR NIEMEYER   🏛 GOVERNMENT BUILDING

A new capital city—Brasilia—had been written into the Brazilian constitution, but it remained little more than a dream for many generations. The dream finally became reality in 1956, when president Juscelino Kubitschek commissioned planner Lúcio Costa (1902–98) and architect Oscar Niemeyer to design and build its center from a scrub landscape at 3,300 ft (1,005 m) in just five years… and they did.

At the center of this astonishing city is Niemeyer's Congress Building. Dramatic and simple, this is the building, along with Niemeyer's "crown of thorns" cathedral *(see p.470)*, that every visitor to Brasilia recalls. The low, horizontal, slablike structure on which the rest of the building appears to be constructed is topped with a large saucer-dome (the roof of the Senate) and an inverted saucer-dome (the roof of the Chamber of Deputies). A twin-towered administration block, linked by a glazed bridge, rises between the two domes. Most of the "slab" is devoted to lobbies, offices, restaurants, and the like. The Congress Building faces a long, narrow central park. It was once possible to walk up

the ramps from the park to the terrace on top of the horizontal block and stand between the twin towers and the strange domes (the idea being that the people of Brasilia would feel that parliament was their own). A military coup in 1964 put paid to that idea. For the next few years, the terrace became an army gun emplacement. Since the restoration of democracy in Brazil, security issues have put this striking building largely out of bounds.

OSCAR NIEMEYER

Rio de Janeiro-born Oscar Niemeyer (b.1907), brought an unprecedented degree of sensuality to Modernist architecture. Inspired, he claims, by views over the ocean from his studio, by mountainous backdrops, and by the female form, his most famous buildings —including the wavelike chapel at Pampulha (1943), Brasilia Cathedral (1970), and the Museum of Contemporary Art, Niterói (1996)—might be described as Baroque.

Work of art
As a work of breathtaking sculpture, Brasilia's Congress Building has few rivals.

NATIONAL GYMNASIUMS, TOKYO

🏊 1964   📍 TOKYO, JAPAN   ✍ KENZO TANGE   🏛 SPORTS ARENA

Japanese architect Kenzo Tange (1913–2005) designed two National Gymnasiums for the 1964 Tokyo Olympics. The larger consists of two semicircles, slightly displaced in relation to one another, with their ends elongated into points, or prows. Over this is a great sweeping roof held up by two reinforced concrete pillars and a web of steel cables. The smaller building, which is linked to its larger cousin by an immense promenade, is also circular. Once again, the skin that roofs the building is suspended from a concrete mast.

Taut and exciting, the buildings have all the pent-up energy of sprinters on the starting blocks. Tange began his career, influenced by Le Corbusier, with the design of the Hiroshima Peace Pavilion in 1949. He was very much the author of a new-look Japan, viewing tradition as a useful catalyst for inventive design, but something that should not be detectable in the end result.

Stylish but strong
The roofs of the gymnasiums, the smaller of which is shown here, were designed to withstand hurricane-force winds, as well as to impress.

OLYMPIC STADIUM, MUNICH

🏊 1972   📍 MUNICH, GERMANY   ✍ GÜNTHER BEHNISCH & FREI OTTO   🏛 SPORTS ARENA

The roof of this revolutionary building, by Germany's Günther Behnisch (b.1922) and Frei Otto (b.1925), was produced using computer-aided design and rigorous mathematics to determine its structure and flowing shape. The result of years of research by Otto, it was made of a PVC-coated polyester suspended on hangers, which in turn were supported by cables held in tension from steel masts. Although the 1972 Games were overshadowed by the murder of Israeli athletes by Arab terrorists, the stadium represented a very different Germany from that of 1936, when the Olympic Games were held in Werner March's Berlin Stadium *(see p.462)* to demonstrate the racial superiority of German "Aryans." Between then, Behnisch, a wartime U-Boat commander, and

Otto, a former Luftwaffe fighter pilot, were responsible for a joyous, democratic architecture that was as light and free-form as Nazi architecture had been heavy and regimented. The 80,000-seat Olympic Stadium was home to the Bayern Munich soccer club until 2005, when the team moved to a new, purpose-built stadium designed by Herzog and de Meuron. The Olympic Stadium has now been turned into a giant movie theater and performance venue. It remains a much loved building.

Flowing roof
The tentlike PVC-and-polyester roof covered the Olympic Hall and swimming pool, as well as the main athletics stadium.

SYDNEY OPERA HOUSE

⌨ 1973   📍 SYDNEY, AUSTRALIA   ✍ JØRN UTZON   🏛 THEATER

SYDNEY OPERA HOUSE FROM THE AIR

World-famous for its sensational roofs, Sydney Opera House was designed, from 1957, by the Danish architect Jørn Utzon (b.1918) and engineered by Peter Rice of Ove Arup. Set bravely on Bennelong Point, a peninsula jutting into Sydney Harbor, the building is pretty much all roofs, rising from a rather mundane base. Utzon resigned in 1966 after political rows and huge cost overruns, and the building beneath the sail-like roofs was completed without his magic touch. He was brought back to remodel parts of it at the beginning of the 21st century, and the Utzon Room, to his

Monumental steps at rear look over forecourt

High-tension steel visible through glazing

Auditoria sit side by side

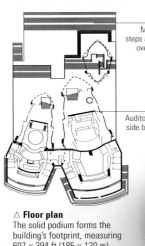

△ **Floor plan**
The solid podium forms the building's footprint, measuring 607 × 394 ft (185 × 120 m).

▽ **Opera House interior**
The concert hall *(see below)* holds an audience of 2,679; the opera theater seats 1,507. Over 2 million people in total attend events here each year.

Podium is faced with stone

Solid podium houses small performance and exhibition areas, plus services

design, was opened in 2004. The daring roof is made up of 2,194 remarkably thin pre-cast concrete sections, held in place by 217 miles (350 km) of tensioned steel cables. The building contains 1,000 rooms and is home to 3,000 events each year. The first performance, in 1973, was of Prokofiev's *War and Peace*, which might have described the actual and the ideal relationship between architect and client.

△ **Exterior detail**
Some 67,006 sq ft (6,225 m²) of glass complement the steel-and-concrete construction.

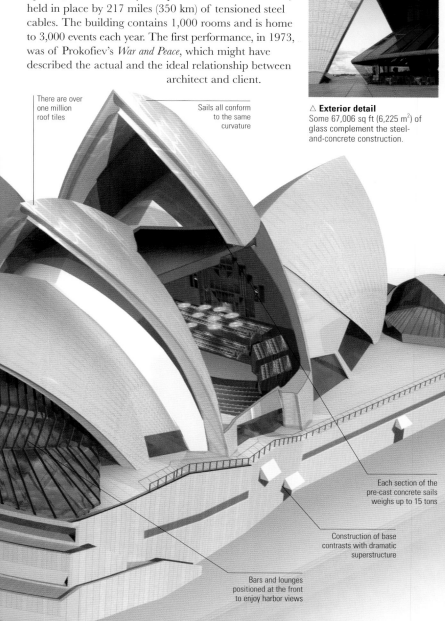

There are over one million roof tiles

Sails all conform to the same curvature

Each section of the pre-cast concrete sails weighs up to 15 tons

Construction of base contrasts with dramatic superstructure

Bars and lounges positioned at the front to enjoy harbor views

POMPIDOU CENTER

🏛 1977   📍 PARIS, FRANCE   ✍ RENZO PIANO, RICHARD ROGERS & PETER RICE   🏛 ART GALLERY

The winning entry in the 1971 competition to design the Centre Georges Pompidou art complex, on the site of Les Halles market in central Paris, was by a team made up of British architect Richard Rogers (b.1933), Italian architect Renzo Piano (b.1937), and Irish structural engineer Peter Rice. Famously, the team posted their radical entry at the very last moment.

POMPIDOU PIPEWORK

French President Georges Pompidou came to power in 1969 to put a lid on the political upheaval that a year earlier had very nearly caused a second French Revolution, but the outlandish winning design for the new art complex sparked an architectural revolution in its own right. The open-plan floors of the multistory building were supported by an iron-and-steel exoskeleton, while all services were hung on the outside of the building, including escalators in glass tubes zigzagging up the building's principal facade. This inside-out approach to design and construction gave rise to the ugly term "Bowellism," as well as to many cartoons depicting Richard Rogers—who continued the approach for some years—

with his guts spilling over his clothes. Satire aside, the Pompidou Center was an ingenious design that caught the imagination of a generation of architects, engineers, and artists who were looking for a new break in architecture after years of being restrained by straight lines and concrete boxes. Interestingly, the music commissioned for the opening of the center was by Iannis Xenakis, master of "concrete music" and a former assistant of Le Corbusier. The Pompidou Center was renovated and remodeled by Renzo Piano in time for the Millennium celebrations in 2000.

PETER RICE

Peter Rice (1935–92) was a brilliant engineer and mathematician who made several key late-20th-century buildings possible, notably the Pompidou Center, the Sydney Opera House, and the De Menil Gallery, Houston, Texas. From Rice onward, radical architects increasingly worked with imaginative engineers to determine just how far a structure could be pushed before the form became overstretched and redundant.

Pompidou contents

The massive red, white, and blue building houses a museum of modern art, a reference library, a center for industrial design, and a laboratory for music and research into acoustics.

LES ESPACES D'ABRAXAS

🖵 1982   📍 MARNE-LA-VALLÉE, PARIS, FRANCE
✍ TALLER DE ARQUITECTURA   🏛 RESIDENCES

Son of a Catalan builder, architect Ricardo Bofill (b.1939) established his own radical studio, Taller de Arquitectura, in a former cement works on the edge of Barcelona in the late 1960s. Anything was permissible, as evidenced by the design of this complex of apartments in one of the new Parisian suburbs. The apartments were grouped behind giant prefabricated concrete facades decorated with Neo-Classical detailing. The blocks were certainly dramatic and a change from the slablike and soulless apartment blocks of the 1960s and 70s; yet, despite their Classical pretensions, the Bofill blocks —largely the work of Peter Hodgkinson (b.1940), an English architect—contained apartments little different from those of their unloved predecessors. The experiment was continued at Montpellier in France, where some Classical detailing was worked into the interiors of the apartments.

GRAND PYRAMID, LOUVRE

🖵 1989   📍 PARIS, FRANCE
✍ IEOH MING PEI   🏛 MUSEUM

It seems astonishing that this entrance pavilion by Ieoh Ming Pei (b.1917) at the heart of the Louvre was once a source of great controversy, perceived by some to ruin the museum's architectural integrity. Today, it is hard to imagine the museum without it. Made of reflective glass over a steel frame and balanced, as a composition, by two smaller pyramids, it leads down to a vast entrance lobby and a slightly later shopping mall.

ORIENTE STATION, LISBON

🖵 1998   📍 LISBON, PORTUGAL   ✍ SANTIAGO CALATRAVA   🏛 RAILWAY STATION

Built to serve visitors to Expo 98, Lisbon's Oriente Station, designed by Spanish architect Santiago Calatrava *(see p.489)* is now a key interchange for travelers on intercity and local trains, metro lines, and buses. The raised platforms, which give fine views over Parque das Nações, the Expo site, are sheltered by a

Station entrance
Calatrava's Gothic-inspired Oriente Station features innovative steel-frame truss assembly. Seen here are the entrance awning and roof over the rail platforms.

roof made up of numerous glass-and-steel pyramids; this is supported by rows of slender, branching steel pillars that resemble palms or giant lilies. The cavernous first floor ticket hall, with its elevators, hanging bridges, and connecting tunnels, is over-arched by vast ribs of concrete. Entering from the Parque des Nações side, travelers pass under a winglike awning of steel and glass. On the other side, the gently curving canopies over the bus bays perhaps allude to waves on the nearby sea.

AT&T BUILDING

🖼 1984 📍 NEW YORK, NY ✍ PHILIP JOHNSON 🏛 COMMERCIAL BUILDING

Hugely controversial when completed, this 648 ft (197 m) high Manhattan skyscraper was designed by American architect Philip Johnson (1906–2005) for the American Telephone and Telegraph Company. The apotheosis of Post-Modern architecture, this camp and corny building is simply a conventional office tower dressed up in pink granite and Classical costume. It resembles some giant early-18th-century wardrobe, complete with a split pediment. The enormous domed lobby is a feast of marble and gilded kitsch. The AT&T (now Sony) Building was, perhaps, the building that Philip Johnson had wanted to build above all others. Johnson had begun his

architectural career as founder, funder, and first director of New York's Museum of Modern Art. In 1932, with the historian Henry-Russell Hitchcock, he co-curated the famous show "The International Style," which introduced New York to the Modern Movement. For Johnson, a clever, witty man, architecture was merely a game. He flitted from style to style during a long and powerful career as a cultural power-broker in New York—from Modernist to Historicist, then Post-Modernist, Deconstructivist, and so on.

Post-Modern kitsch
With its unusual split pediment and pink exterior, the AT&T is one of the most memorable skyscrapers in New York.

LLOYDS BUILDING

🖼 1986 📍 LONDON, ENGLAND ✍ RICHARD ROGERS 🏛 COMMERCIAL BUILDING

When it opened in the mid-1980s, at the height of the "greed is good" culture of the City of London and Wall Street, the Lloyds Building was likened to an oil refinery. Within a decade, however, it had become one of London's most popular architectural sights. A terrific mass of pipes, ducts, cranes, external elevators, bathroom pods, and steel braces, lit blue at night, it is a thrilling spectacle.

The entire exposed structure wraps around a gigantic atrium in the heart of the building, at the bottom of which deals are made. From here, exposed escalators climb up to serve offices on upper floors. Theoretically, the clip-together format of the building means that it could be extended upward and outward, although this has not happened to date, nor is it realistically ever likely to.

Shape of things to come
Like a set from Ridley Scott's film *Blade Runner*, the futuristic Lloyds Building represents British "High-Tech" design at its imaginative best.

LYON SATOLAS STATION

🚄 1994 📍 LYON, FRANCE ✍ SANTIAGO CALATRAVA 🏛 RAILWAY STATION

Shaped like a giant bird with raised wings, this powerfully sculpted train station brings passengers to and from Lyon St. Exupéry airport. Highly dramatic, it was an act of confirmation by the French state railway, boasting its formidable 186 mph (300 kmh) TGV trains, that travel by modern train could be far more glamorous than flights on crowded jets.

INTERIOR VIEW

Lyon Satolas station rises some 130 ft (40 m) above the parking ramps surrounding it. The structure is in the form of two high, vaulting 394 ft (120 m) concrete arches, with steel arches below them, that tilt toward one another, creating a sharply defined spine. This is used as a lightwell over a 1,476 ft (450 m) tunnel-like passageway that gives access to the platforms below. The arches come down to the ground, together, as a pointed beak. On either side of the arches, steel wings project out, supported by steel struts. These are designed to act as sun screens, as well as to create the sculptural

Winged station
Dynamic and full of energy, Calatrava's station design for Lyon airport, which straddles an existing TGV track, perfectly embodies the idea of flight and a sense of lightness.

effect desired by the architect. In fact, Calatrava has always maintained that the building represents an eye rather than a bird.

Inside, the height of the arches equals a lofty concourse. The main hall is 426 ft (130 m) long, 328 ft (100 m) wide, and 128 ft (39 m) high. It boasts spaces and structures as dramatic in their own way as Eero Saarinen's expressive TWA terminal at John F. Kennedy Airport *(see p.477)*. However, because the station is served by relatively few trains, it feels too empty for its own good—more a museum of spectacular architecture and engineering than a fully working train station. On the other hand, the provision of space here is truly luxurious, far removed from the overcrowded feel in many airports.

SANTIAGO CALATRAVA

Santiago Calatrava was born in Valencia in 1951, where he trained as an architect before studying engineering in Zurich. He set up his own design practice in 1981. Since then, his work has included sculpture, furniture, bridges, stations, airports, and museums. His most ambitious work is Valencia's City of Science, a gathering of vast, bonelike galleries, a bit like bleached dinosaur skeletons, on the edge of the city.

GREEN BUILDINGS

The 1968 Apollo 8 images of the Earth gleaming like a jewel in deep space made the planet's fragility and beauty all too apparent, and galvanized the environmental movement into action. By the late 1980s, "green" issues were mainstream. Everyone could do their bit to help "save the planet." For architects, this meant making buildings as energy-efficient as possible.

Early efforts at green architecture in the 1960s, much influenced by the work of Frank Lloyd Wright, were uncoordinated and too self-regarding. Since then, architects such as Renzo Piano, Norman Foster, and Ralph Erskine have proved that civil and commercial buildings can be both green and ultramodern, using as little fuel as possible, minimizing carbon emissions, and optimizing water use.

It is not just grand architecture that needs "greening." With the realization that global warming is now a reality rather than a distant threat, there is an increasing pressure for domestic buildings to be more environmentally friendly. There have been many quirky, individual green homes, but the real need is for an attractive, economical green architecture that can be adapted to large housing projects. One pilot scheme is BedZED, on the outskirts of

BedZED housing
The Beddington Zero Energy Development uses only renewable energy generated on site. Rain is captured and domestic water recycled to reduce mains usage.

London, designed by Bill Dunster (b.1959). Like a 21st-century English garden city, this complex of 100 homes plus workspaces is the first attempt in the UK to achieve a near "carbon-neutral" lifestyle. Since buildings generate a large proportion of carbon dioxide emissions (as high as 30 percent in the USA), green will be the color that shapes how architecture looks, functions, and is used in the decades to come.

The London Ark
Ralph Erskine's Ark is one of Europe's most energy-efficient buildings.

GUGGENHEIM MUSEUM, BILBAO

🏛 1997　📍 BILBAO, SPAIN　✍ FRANK GEHRY　🏛 ART GALLERY

The "Bilbao Effect" was a cliché of politicians worldwide charged with encouraging the design of sensational buildings to attract visitors and rejuvenate ailing cities. The highly photogenic Guggenheim Museum, designed by the Canadian-born Californian architect Frank Gehry (b.1929) and sited in Bilbao's downtown docklands, did indeed attract a great influx of cultural tourists to the Basque capital; whether or not it single-handedly transformed the local economy is a moot point. It hardly matters, since the Guggenheim is architecture as outlandish sculpture and glorious entertainment. Some curators complain that the galleries are hard to work with, yet most people come to see the building and not the shows. High-spirited and fun, it should bring a smile to anyone's face.

Dockside galleries
Clad in sheets of titanium, the galleries sweep and swoop over the docks like a flight of crazy gulls.

TATE MODERN

🏛 2000　📍 LONDON, ENGLAND
✍ HERZOG & DE MEURON　🏛 ART GALLERY

Sitting opposite St. Paul's Cathedral and linked to it by a pedestrian bridge over the Thames designed by Norman Foster, Tate Modern is the popular remodeling of what was formerly Bankside Power Station into a gigantic modern art gallery. The original building was designed by Giles Gilbert Scott (1880–1960), architect of Liverpool's Gothic Anglican cathedral and also Battersea Power Station, westward along the Thames. Jacques Herzog (b.1950) and Pierre de Meuron (b.1950), two energetic Swiss architects, were charged with transforming Bankside from a temple of power into a cathedral for art. Their solution was simple, powerful, and effective: industrial-sized floors, mezzanines with rough-hewn timber boards, giant cafes—everything on a titanic scale. A downtown location, controversial art, and bravura architecture all add up to make Tate Modern phenomenally popular. The downside is that it can sometimes seem like an overcrowded shopping mall or airport terminal.

JEWISH MUSEUM, BERLIN

🏛 1999　📍 BERLIN, GERMANY
✍ DANIEL LIBESKIND　🏛 MUSEUM

This memorial to the Berlin Jews murdered by the Nazis is famous for having a series of empty rooms to represent the loss of a people. Its zinc-clad exterior is slashed through by windows at unexpected angles. It has no obvious entrance: the museum can only be reached by stairs leading down from the Baroque building alongside. Visitors descend into a realm of corridors at oblique angles that lead into a cold steel tower, then into a garden set at crazy angles, and up through a maze of galleries, all empty. The building carries its message brilliantly.

Bilbao's Guggenheim Museum
A mathematically complex combination of right-angled limestone blocks and titanium-covered curves creates a startlingly beautiful museum building. Glass curtain walls provide transparency but also protect exhibits from radiation.